# JOHN AUBREY AND THE REALM OF LEARNING

Frontispiece.
John Aubrey by William Faithorne (1666). Aubrey intended to have this portrait engraved for his unpublished *Monumenta Britannica*. Ashmolean Museum, Oxford

# JOHN AUBREY
## AND THE
## REALM OF LEARNING

Michael Hunter

'. . . One that's studious too, whose boundlesse mind
Scarce within Learneings compasse is confind'

George Ent 'To his honoured
Freind John Awbrey Esquire.'

Duckworth

First published in 1975 by
Gerald Duckworth & Company Limited
The Old Piano Factory, 43 Gloucester Crescent, London N.W.1.

ISBN 0 7156 0818 5

Printed in Great Britain by
Ebenezer Baylis and Son Limited
The Trinity Press, Worcester, and London

The quotation on the title-
page is taken from British
Library MS Stowe 182, 33v

# PREFACE

As Aubrey's prefaces were often rather autobiographical, I feel bound to begin this book by briefly explaining how I came to write it, as well as acknowledging the help I have had in doing so. I came across *Brief Lives* as a schoolboy, but my scholarly concern with Aubrey grew out of an undergraduate interest in the history of antiquarian thought, kindly encouraged by Glyn Daniel, which bore fruit in two articles in *Antiquity* on 'The Royal Society and the origins of British archaeology'. Since 1971, when they were published, I have been making a more general study of the intellectual history of seventeenth-century England, particularly the scientific movement, and this book is centred on Aubrey's relationship to that. Hugh Trevor-Roper and Charles Webster have been my constant valued advisers during this time, and I am also grateful to Keith Thomas, whose invitation to read a paper on Aubrey at his seminar on 'Problems of Early Modern History' in January 1972 helped to crystallise the ideas about Aubrey as a scientist that I have developed in Chapter II.

I have done most of the work for this book while a Research Fellow of Worcester College, Oxford, and I am greatly indebted to the Provost and Fellows for electing me to their number. John Buchanan-Brown and Anthony Turner have generously joined me in many discussions of Aubrey and his work, which must at times have seemed to them almost interminable. They also read and commented on the typescript draft of the book, and so did the following: David Bebbington, Iain Brown, James Campbell, Randall Caudill, Sheridan Gilley, Robin Robbins, Lindsay Sharp and Kevin Sharpe. I am grateful to all these friends, whose stimulating comments have helped to form my theories and check my less guarded speculations, though they are themselves aware of their disagreement with a few of my statements and conclusions. Sandra Raphael also read the book in both typescript and proof, and she has very kindly made the index. I have acknowledged the help of other individuals and institutions who have answered my inquiries or allowed me to reproduce material in their custody in the course of the book.

Above all, I am indebted to Aubrey himself, who has brought the research for this book to life, as he enlivens the book itself. Echoing the words he used of his 'Perambulation of Surrey' in 1673, I can safely say that 'I have taken a great deale of payns, but with great delight'.[1]

Throughout this book I have used italics to denote whole works by Aubrey, whether published or not, and inverted commas for parts of works (including pieces that at one time had an independent existence but were subsequently incorporated in larger works).

For all editorial insertions into quotations from manuscripts I have used angled brackets (i.e. $\langle \, , \rangle$): all square, as well as round, brackets are Aubrey's own.

All manuscripts or printed books which I have referred to in the notes with Ashmole, Aubrey, Tanner or Wood class-marks are in the Bodleian Library.

Oxford, July 1974                                                    M.C.W.H.

---

[1] A-W, 16 Sept. 1673, F 39, 223.

# CONTENTS

# ILLUSTRATIONS

All illustrations are reproduced from originals in the Bodleian Library, Oxford, by kind permission of the Curators, unless otherwise stated.

*Frontispiece*: John Aubrey by William Faithorne (1666). Aubrey intended to have this portrait engraved for his unpublished *Monumenta Britannica* (cf. T.G.c.24, 17). Reproduced by kind permission of the Visitors of the Ashmolean Museum, Oxford

*Between pages 152 and 153*

10. Osney Abbey, engraved by Wenceslaus Hollar for Dodsworth's and Dugdale's *Monasticon Anglicanum* from a drawing provided by Aubrey (*Monasticon Anglicanum*, volume 11 (London, 1661), facing page 136)

11. Aubrey's plan of Avebury, from his *Monumenta Britannica* (T.G.c.24, 39v–40)

12. Old Sarum 'by Imagination', from Aubrey's *Monumenta Britannica* (T.G.c.24, 201)

13. A page of Aubrey's 'Chronologica Graphica', showing his facsimiles of the old scripts that he studied (T.G.c.25, 189v)

*Between pages 184 and 185*

14. A page of Aubrey's 'Chronologia Architectonica' (T.G.c.25, 156)

15. Aubrey's map of Ancient Wessex, from his *Monumenta Britannica* (T.G.c.24, 250v–1)

16. The east front of the Old Ashmolean Museum, Oxford, engraved by Michael Burghers, 1685. Reproduced by kind permission of the Curator of the Museum of the History of Science, Oxford

17. The inscription in the Old Ashmolean commemorating Aubrey's and other bequests

The lower part of the inscription was restored in the 1920s (cf. *Oxford University Gazette*, no. 1766 (1925), 473), possibly incorrectly, since the transcript of the inscription in John Britton's *Memoir of John Aubrey* (London, 1845, p. 83) has the additional words 'et physica' after 'antiquaria' in the description of Aubrey; these do not, however, appear in the transcript in *Biographia Britannica* (London, 1747, 1, 233n.).

# ABBREVIATIONS

| | |
|---|---|
| A–L | John Aubrey to Edward Lhwyd |
| A–T | John Aubrey to Thomas Tanner |
| A–W | John Aubrey to Anthony Wood |
| *Analecta* | *Analecta Ro⟨berti⟩ Plot*, transcribed by Thomas Hearne, Bodleian MS Hearne's Diaries 158–9. See 'A Note on *Analecta*' |
| A. 1814 | Edward Lhwyd's Correspondence, A–D, Bodleian MS Ashmole 1814 |
| A. 1829 | *Reliquae Lhwydianae*, volume X, Bodleian MS Ashmole 1829 |
| *B.L.* | Andrew Clark *ed.*, *'Brief Lives', chiefly of Contemporaries, set down by John Aubrey, between the Years 1669 & 1696*, two volumes (Oxford, 1898) |
| Bacon, *Works* | J. Spedding, R. L. Ellis and D. N. Heath *eds.*, *The Works of Francis Bacon*, fourteen volumes (London, 1857–74) |
| B. 14 | Letters of Aubrey and others to Wood and Charlett, Bodleian MS Ballard 14 |
| Birch, *History* | Thomas Birch, *The History of the Royal Society of London*, four volumes (London, 1756–7) |
| Boyle, *Works* | Thomas Birch *ed.*, *The Works of the Honourable Robert Boyle*, six volumes (new edition, London, 1772) |
| F 39 | Letters to Wood, A, Bodleian MS Wood F 39 |
| *Gentilisme* | John Aubrey, *Remaines of Gentilisme and Judaisme* in John Buchanan-Brown *ed.*, *Three Prose Works* (Fontwell, Sussex, 1972), 127 f. |
| Hobbes, *Works* | Sir William Molesworth *ed.*, *The English Works of Thomas Hobbes of Malmesbury*, eleven volumes (London, 1839–45) |

| | |
|---|---|
| Hooke, *Diary* | H. W. Robinson and W. Adams *eds.*, *The Diary of Robert Hooke, 1672–1680* (London, 1935) |
| Hooke, *Works* | Richard Waller *ed.*, *The Posthumous Works of Robert Hooke* (London, 1705) |
| MS A 1 | John Aubrey, *The Naturall Historie of Wiltshire*, part I, Bodleian MS Aubrey 1 |
| MS A 2 | John Aubrey, *The Naturall Historie of Wiltshire*, part II, Bodleian MS Aubrey 2 |
| MS A 3 | John Aubrey, *An Essay towards the Description of the North Division of Wiltshire*, Bodleian MS Aubrey 3 |
| MS A 4 | John Aubrey, *A Perambulation of Surrey*, Bodleian MS Aubrey 4 |
| MS A 5 | John Aubrey, *An Interpretation of Villare Anglicanum*, Bodleian MS Aubrey 5 |
| MS A 10 | John Aubrey, *An Idea of Education of Young Gentlemen* and *Idea Filioli seu Educatio Pueri*, Bodleian MS Aubrey 10 |
| MS A 11 | (John Aubrey), *An Extract or Summary of the Lemmata of Stone-heng restored to the Danes, by Walter Charlton*, Bodleian MS Aubrey 11 |
| MS A 12 | Letters to Aubrey, A-N, Bodleian MS Aubrey 12 |
| MS A 13 | Letters to Aubrey, P-Y, Bodleian MS Aubrey 13 |
| MS A 17 | John Aubrey, *Designatio de Easton-Piers in Com⟨itatu⟩ Wilts*, Bodleian MS Aubrey 17 |
| MS A 21 | John Aubrey, *⟨The⟩ Countrey Revell, or The Revell at Aldford*, and miscellaneous papers, mainly in Aubrey's hand, Bodleian MS Aubrey 21 |
| MS A 23 | John Aubrey, *Collectio Gentiturarum*, Bodleian MS Aubrey 23 |
| MS A 24 | *Zecorbeni, sive Claviculæ Salmonis Libri IV*, transcribed by Aubrey, with his additions, Bodleian MS Aubrey 24 |

MS A 26            John Aubrey, *Faber Fortunæ*, Bodleian MS
                   Aubrey 26

*Miscellanies*     John Aubrey, *Miscellanies, upon the Following
                   Subjects* . . . (second edition, London, 1721)

Plot, *Plinius*    Robert Plot, *Plinius Anglicus sive Angliae His-
                   toria naturalis ac Artium*, Society of Anti-
                   quaries MS 85

Plot, *Oxfordshire*   Robert Plot, *The Natural History of Oxford-shire*
                   (Oxford, 1677)

R.S. MS 92         B. G. Cramer's transcript of John Aubrey's
                   *Naturall Historie of Wiltshire*, Royal Society
                   MS 92 (shelved at XI.2.21)

Ray, *Letters*     W. Derham *ed.*, *Philosophical Letters Between the
                   late Learned Mr. Ray And several of his
                   Ingenious Correspondents* (London, 1718)

Sprat, *History*   J. I. Cope and H. W. Jones *ed.*, Thomas Sprat,
                   *History of the Royal Society* (1667) (St.
                   Louis, 1959)

T.G.c.24           John Aubrey, *Monumenta Britannica or A Mis-
                   cellanie of British Antiquities*, volume I, Bod-
                   leian MS Top. Gen.c.24

T.G.c.25           John Aubrey, *Monumenta Britannica or A Mis-
                   cellanie of British Antiquities*, volume II,
                   Bodleian MS Top. Gen.c.25

T.25               Letters to Tanner and others, Bodleian MS
                   Tanner 25

T.456a             Letters of Dugdale, Wood, Aubrey, etc., Bod-
                   leian MS Tanner 456a

*T.P.W.*           John Buchanan-Brown *ed.*, John Aubrey, *Three
                   Prose Works* (Fontwell, Sussex, 1972)

# INTRODUCTION

This is a study of John Aubrey's writings and their background, an attempt to understand and evaluate the intellectual activity of a prolific scholar whose contribution to learning has been almost entirely ignored. As the amiable and slightly eccentric author of *Brief Lives*, Aubrey is now well known. But his reputation as a biographer has almost eclipsed his wider achievement as a writer, and few are aware either of the sheer range of his works, or of the originality of some of the most notable of them.

Perhaps most striking are three studies of antiquities which alone would ensure Aubrey an important place in the evolution of English historical writing. His *Monumenta Britannica* is the first English book that can be called 'archaeological' in the modern sense. His *Remaines of Gentilisme and Judaisme* was the first substantial English collection of folk-lore. His *Interpretation of Villare Anglicanum* was the first English book to be entirely devoted to the elucidation of place-names. These were highly novel departures from the orthodox antiquarian traditions of his day, though he also participated in these, producing *An Essay towards the Description of the North Division of Wiltshire*, or *Wiltshire Antiquities*, as I have called it,[1] and a topographical description of Surrey, *A Perambulation of Surrey*.

But Aubrey was a scientist as well as an antiquary, and two of his most substantial works were scientific—his *Adversaria Physica* and his *Naturall Historie of Wiltshire*, which, though basically descriptive of the natural phenomena of his native county, also contains theoretical and descriptive material of more general interest. Related to these are a number of more minor works: *Miscellanies*, a collection of papers on occult phenomena, *Faber Fortunæ*, a brief tract listing schemes for making Aubrey's fortune, *Collectio Geniturarum*, an astrological work, and some notes on magic. Though the relationship between these and his science may not seem immediately obvious, it is in fact crucial, and it makes a consideration of Aubrey's activity as a scientist particularly revealing.

Even this is not the limit of his intellectual activity, however, for,

---

[1] This is a title that Aubrey sometimes uses for it himself. On its cover, the work is also called *Hypomnemata Antiquaria*, ⟨Liber⟩ A. On the lost Liber B, see below, p. 91, and 'Aubrey's Lost Works'.

like other contemporaries, Aubrey ranged widely through many fields of knowledge. He wrote a treatise on education, *An Idea of Education of Young Gentlemen*. He produced a tract on religion, *Hypothesis Ethicorum & Scala Religionis*. He tried his hand at a comedy, *The Countrey Revell*, and wrote a few other minor literary pieces. He drew up a broadsheet expounding *Elements of Architecture*; and he was an amateur artist, as is shown best by his *Designatio de Easton-Piers in Com⟨itatu⟩ Wilts*, a collection of water-colours of his ancestral home and its surroundings, some of which are reproduced here.

Few of Aubrey's works are well known and few are even fully printed. Only one was published in his lifetime, *Miscellanies*, which appeared in 1696. Many of the others have been published more or less adequately since his death, but one of the most important, *Monumenta Britannica*, still remains almost entirely in manuscript.[1] A few works are lost, including his *Hypothesis Ethicorum* and his *Adversaria Physica*: but the latter can luckily be reconstructed from some early notes on it that have recently been rediscovered.[2]

All this perhaps makes it less surprising that there has hitherto been no adequate study of Aubrey's writings. The fullest account of them yet in print is an appendix to Anthony Powell's *John Aubrey and his Friends*.[3] But a twenty-page appendix to a three-hundred-page book scarcely does justice to the work of a scholar who devoted his entire life to his writings, and I hope that this book may do something to redress the balance in favour of Aubrey's intellectual rather than social activities. It is, however, intended to complement and in no way to replace Mr Powell's book, and I have been as cursory in treating Aubrey's life as Powell was in assessing his ideas. Though there is naturally some overlap between the two books, I think the reader will be surprised how small it is, and for biographical information he should turn to Powell's excellent and easily available volume.

Past readers of *John Aubrey and his Friends* may, however, have

---

[1] See 'A Note on Manuscript and Printed Texts of Aubrey's Works'.

[2] See 'A Note on *Analecta*' and 'Aubrey's Lost Works'.

[3] New edition, London, 1963. There are two unpublished theses on Aubrey: Patricia Owen, 'A Revaluation of the Writings of John Aubrey with particular reference to his contributions to the theory and practice of biography' (Oxford B. Litt., 1954) and N. P. Barker, 'John Aubrey's *Brief Lives*: A Strange Rare Way of Conserving a Corps' (Minnesota Ph.D., 1966). See also John Buchanan-Brown's Introduction to his edition of *Three Prose Works*.

been puzzled by Aubrey's active membership of the Royal Society and his close association with so many of the most prominent scientists of his time. They may have wondered what these were likely to have in common with an antiquary whose interests were, in Powell's phrase, 'on the whole, in the past rather than in the future'.[1] I hope that my account of Aubrey's vigorous intellectual life will show how enthusiastically and actively he was involved with the scientific movement, and I hope too that I have succeeded in vindicating him as a serious intellectual, many of whose interests and views were respected by the most advanced scientific thinkers of his age.

Among Aubrey's closest friends were William Harvey, Thomas Hobbes, Robert Hooke, John Pell, William Petty, Seth Ward and Christopher Wren; his acquaintance included Robert Boyle, Edmond Halley, Martin Lister, John Locke, Marcello Malpighi, Nicholas Mercator, Isaac Newton, John Ray and Thomas Willis; and among his intellectual idols were Francis Bacon and René Descartes. This list of names is representative of many facets of the new philosophy of the seventeenth century; it includes many of the chief protagonists of the scientific movement, which continued and developed the traditions of experiment and precise observation of natural phenomena pioneered in earlier investigations like the anatomical studies of Vesalius, the magnetical experiments of William Gilbert and the astronomy of Tycho Brahe, Kepler and Galileo.[2] Harvey's epoch-making discovery of the circulation of the blood; Boyle's famous experiments designed to vindicate the corpuscular approach to matter; Hooke's well-known *Micrographia* and his original studies of subjects ranging from astronomy to geology; Ray's painstaking botanical observations and classification: these were the characteristic products of an age which prized 'ocular inspection' of '*Nature* her selfe' above all.[3]

For Aubrey and his friends, this approach was especially associated with the Royal Society, founded in 1660. That 'famous Academy of our philosophicall scepticks that beleive nothing not

---

[1] *John Aubrey and his Friends*, 106.

[2] For general accounts, see A. R. Hall, *The Scientific Revolution, 1500–1800* (second edition, London, 1962) and *From Galileo to Newton, 1630–1720* (London, 1963). I have deliberately given my summary of some prominent themes in the scientific movement an English bias, since Aubrey's view of the movement was primarily English.

[3] Harvey, *Anatomical Exercitations* (London, 1653), a5, a6v.

tryed'[1] stressed above all the ideals of co-operation and careful induction advocated by Bacon, who hoped thus to produce 'such a natural history as may serve for a foundation to build philosophy upon'.[2] In fact the empiricism which Bacon championed had earlier roots,[3] and not all who practised it were in any sense his disciples— Harvey, for instance, worked out his advocacy of precise observation within the framework of an Aristotelianism purged of the accretions of the schoolmen.[4] But these scientists, whatever their intellectual affiliations, agreed in advocating induction, attacking the sterile scholasticism which they considered had obstructed the advancement of knowledge in the Middle Ages and the sixteenth century, full of 'fruitless and obstreperous Verbosity', whose science had been limited to a worthless discussion of Aristotle's 'onely defects and animosities', 'all of them much fitter to beget *Eternal* Controversies, than to administer any satisfaction to a reasonable Understanding'.[5]

In the view of the new scientists, such unproductive activities should be replaced by 'real' knowledge, concerned with things instead of words, where action would be valued instead of verbal polemic. In all the scientific manifestos of this period there is a constant stress on 'The Usefulnesse of Experimental Naturall Philosophy' (to quote the title of a work by Boyle), partly because of the intrinsic value of more accurate knowledge and partly because investigations could produce immediate practical benefits. Few thinkers made the modern distinction of 'science' and 'technology', and the Royal Society was as dedicated to the latter as to the former in its early years.[6] The ideal of improvement—of finding out things 'new, true and useful'[7]—was frequently emphasised by the protagonists of the new science, and even if the ultimate benefit

---

[1] John Hoskyns—Aubrey, 12/22 July 1661, MS A 12, 190. In some ways, the Royal Society's importance may have been more symbolic than real: cf., for example, Q. Skinner, 'Hobbes and the nature of the early Royal Society', *Historical Journal* XII (1969), 217f.

[2] *Instauratio Magna*, Bacon, *Works*, IV, 28.

[3] On his sixteenth-century precursors, see W. P. D. Wightman, *Science in a Renaissance Society* (London, 1972).

[4] Harvey, *Anatomical Exercitations*, preface.

[5] *Philosophical Transactions* II (1666), 411–12.

[6] Sir George Clark, *Science and Social Welfare in the Age of Newton* (second edition, Oxford, 1949).

[7] Birch, *History*, I, 391.

resulting from technological investigations of the period was small,[1] this is less significant than the propagandists' stress on them. Similar motives underlay attempts to devise a universal language, which flourished in the intellectual circles in which Aubrey moved in the Restoration period. It was hoped that such schemes would both ease communication and provide a newly clear and logical classification of knowledge, and, though they succumbed to technical difficulties, they are symptomatic of the total reforming urge of this hopeful new age.[2]

This hope for the improvement both of knowledge and of the condition of human life underlay the increasing influence of ideas of progress, which challenged earlier views that all things, including human, tended naturally to decay, and the consequent adulation of the authority of the past. A whole literature arose asserting the superiority of the 'Moderns' over the 'Ancients', citing the discoveries and inventions of the last century and a half, so that novelty became a virtue instead of the disadvantage that it had been in the authoritarian culture of the Middle Ages and the Renaissance.[3]

The implications of the challenge to authority were wide. The Reformation had shaken certainties, raising problems as to the proper criteria of truth, and a tradition of scepticism continued throughout the sixteenth and seventeenth centuries, reinforced by discoveries like those of Copernicus, which seemed to throw the whole order of the world in doubt.[4] Its most significant results were the philosophies that Descartes and Hobbes produced in reaction to it. In their efforts to reduce all natural effects to the simple interaction of matter and motion, they provided a basis for a new interpretation of the universe to replace the outmoded views of Aristotle, with his complicated theories of elements and qualities. Their views, and the ancient atomist ideas revived by Pierre Gassendi, won a growing popularity in the seventeenth century.[5] They appealed not least because they could be quantified, and no feature of the seventeenth century is more striking than its near obsession with mathematics as the basis of real and demonstrable

---

[1] P. Mathias, 'Who unbound Prometheus? Science and technical change, 1600–1800' in *Science and Society, 1600–1900* (Cambridge, 1972), 54 f.
[2] Cf. V. Salmon, *The Works of Francis Lodwick* (London, 1972).
[3] Cf. R. F. Jones, *Ancients and Moderns* (second edition, St. Louis, 1961).
[4] R. H. Popkin, *The History of Scepticism from Erasmus to Descartes* (Assen, 1960).
[5] R. H. Kargon, *Atomism in England from Hariot to Newton* (Oxford, 1966).

truth and with mathematical logic as the means of attaining it. Boyle's experiments were vital for applying corpuscular theories based on assumptions of this mechanist kind, and it was Newton's great achievement to reduce to mathematical laws the dynamic relations between the heavenly bodies.

The implications of the new philosophy were in fact wider still, as Hobbes showed. He compared ratiocination with addition and subtraction, hoping that politics could be as scientific as geometry,[1] and just as mechanism replaced occult qualities to explain how the world worked, so his uncompromising rationalism shifted the basis of human relationships from transcendental norms to the need for self-preservation, from duties to rights. Hobbes was only the most articulate spokesman of a wider tradition,[2] and even the most orthodox thinkers of his age appealed increasingly to reason, not least, in England after the Restoration, in reaction to the fanaticism that was seen as the cause of the Civil War. Such an appeal paved the way for the apologetics of Locke and, later, for Deism, where so much in religion was reasonable that Revelation almost lost all significance,[3] and in this climate of opinion even ostensibly orthodox thinkers like the Cambridge Platonists could unwittingly secularise morality, by arguing that it depended on absolute reasonable norms beyond the will of God.[4] Meanwhile in political thought utilitarian reasoning became increasingly common as the century progressed,[5] while there were equally symptomatic attempts to achieve objectivity in public policy through quantification, an approach epitomised by the writings of Sir William Petty.[6]

But there were two sides in the dispute of ancients and moderns, and the new science was never without opponents, whose reactionary arguments were numerous. Hobbes' system was widely attacked for its atheistic connotations, its implied negation of free-will.[7] Some attacked all studies of natural phenomena because they diverted men from the proper study of God's Revelation, even

---

[1] *De Corpore*, Epistle Dedicatory and chapter I, Hobbes, *Works*, I, vii f.

[2] Q. Skinner, 'The ideological context of Hobbes's political thought', *Historical Journal* IX (1966), 286 f.

[3] G. R. Cragg, *From Puritanism to the Age of Reason* (Cambridge, 1950).

[4] J. Passmore, *Ralph Cudworth: An Interpretation* (Cambridge, 1951), esp. 83-4.

[5] J. A. W. Gunn, *Politics and the Public Interest in the Seventeenth Century* (London, 1969). Cf. W. H. Greenleaf, *Order, Empiricism and Politics* (London, 1964).

[6] W. Letwin, *The Origins of Scientific Economics* (London, 1963).

[7] S. I. Mintz, *The Hunting of Leviathan* (Cambridge, 1962).

going to the extreme of seeing the new science as a popish plot to
lure Protestants away from the defence of their church against
Rome.[1] Others opposed the over-vociferous adulation of the moderns
by the less restrained of their champions, pointing out the value of
traditional studies, if only as a basis for the new learning,[2] while the
most sophisticated, like Meric Casaubon, pointed out the limitations
of the concepts of usefulness to which the scientists so often appealed.[3] Perhaps the commonest reactions merely reflected the
innate conservatism of those who distrusted the new discoveries
primarily because they were new, for even at the end of the century
the appeal to established authority, though declining, remained
strong, and rationalism was often subordinated to it in political and
other argument.[4]

In fact, the quarrel between old and new made the contrast
between reactionaries and innovators seem clearer than it really
was. Even Hobbes was not fully consistent in his empirical stress
on self-interest, and his philosophy contains contradictory elements
which show how far he shared with his opponents preconceptions
which they ignored in their eagerness to attack his more subversive
ideas.[5] Moreover the new scientists were in general deeply religious
men—like Boyle, 'The Christian Virtuoso', as he entitled one of his
books—and they advocated the study of nature as a kind of natural
theology, revealing the glory of God in his creation. Indeed, it has
been argued that the Idea of Progress grew up as a secular counterpart to millenarianism, a belief in an upward movement towards
enlightenment in natural philosophy paralleling mystical revelation
as a sign of the coming of the end of the world.[6]

[1] E.g. 'Another Letter to Sir *J.B.*' in Thomas Barlow, *The Genuine Remains* (London,
1693), 157 f.
[2] Cf., for instance, R. Bohun to John Evelyn in Christ Church, Oxford, Evelyn
Collection, Correspondence no. 301 (I cite this and all Evelyn MSS mentioned hereafter
by kind permission of the Trustees of the Will of the late J. H. C. Evelyn). On the
virtues of scholasticism see W. T. Costello, *The Scholastic Curriculum at Early Seventeenth-century Cambridge* (Cambridge, Mass., 1958).
[3] *A Letter of Meric Casaubon D.D. &c. to Peter du Moulin D.D.* (Cambridge, 1669).
Cf. R. H. Syfret, 'Some early critics of the Royal Society', *Notes and Records of the
Royal Society* VIII (1950), 20 f.
[4] Arguments from custom were still given a higher place than those from reason in
the propaganda of the Exclusion Crisis: cf. B. Behrens, 'The Whig theory of the
constitution in the reign of Charles II', *Cambridge Historical Journal* VII (1941), esp. 67.
[5] M. Oakeshott, 'The moral life in the writings of Thomas Hobbes' in *Rationalism in
Politics* (London, 1962), esp. 284 f. Cf. K. Thomas, 'The social origins of Hobbes's
political thought' in K. C. Brown *ed.*, *Hobbes Studies* (Oxford, 1965), 185 f.
[6] E. L. Tuveson, *Millennium and Utopia* (Berkeley and Los Angeles, 1949).

The scientists were also less eager to dismiss authority than their opponents implied. Not only were they prepared to accept Aristotle as a useful text so long as his disciples avoided 'The Vanity of Dogmatizing' (the title of one of Joseph Glanvill's virulent tracts in defence of the Royal Society); they were as anxious for alternative ancient sources as their opponents. Perhaps the most striking instance of this is the *scholium* that Newton devoted in his *Principia* to proving that his theory of gravity had been known to the ancients,[1] but others can easily be cited. A book that proved that King Solomon knew of the circulation of the blood was reviewed in the *Philosophical Transactions* of the Royal Society, for instance,[2] and Hooke considered Ovid's views on the early history of the world as well as the evidence of fossils in his palaeontological writings, for he saw him as heir to 'the most ancient and most knowing Philosophers among the *Ægyptians* and *Greeks*'.[3]

Nor is there a straightforward contrast between mechanist moderns and mystical ancients. The sixteenth century had seen not only a growing stress on empiricism but also the new popularity of occult views of the universe, stimulated by the revival of neo-Platonic ideas by authors like Marsilio Ficino and the rediscovery of the writings of Hermes Trismegistus, believed by most Renaissance scholars to have been a primeval and therefore oracular Egyptian sage.[4] The universe postulated by these authors was full of astrological influences, occult sympathies and antipathies, magical signatures and effluvia, which could be exploited to gain control of nature, and these fitted readily with alchemical ideas of essences and specific properties which were becoming increasingly common under the influence of writers like the Swiss iatrochemist Paracelsus.[5] Recent scholarship has attached great significance to such irrational ideologies in the creation of the modern scientific attitude, pointing out how Hermeticism made man a magus, who controlled rather than observed natural effects, concerned with investigating the particular rather than speculating about universals; they thus

---

[1] J. E. MacGuire and P. M. Rattansi, 'Newton and the "Pipes of Pan",' *Notes and Records of the Royal Society*, XXI (1966), 108 f.

[2] *Philosophical Transactions* I (1666), 254. The book in question was John Smith's *King Solomon's Pourtraiture of Old Age* (1666).

[3] Hooke, *Works*, 379. Cf. below, p. 222.

[4] D. P. Walker, *Spiritual and Demonic Magic from Ficino to Campanella* (London, 1958); F. A. Yates, *Giordano Bruno and the Hermetic Tradition* (London, 1964).

[5] W. Pagel, *Paracelsus* (Basel, 1958); A. G. Debus, *The English Paracelsians* (London, 1965).

opened the way for the empirical and practical tradition of the seventeenth century,[1] and special attention has been given to the importance of the magical tradition for Bacon.[2]

The relationship between occult and empirical ideas remained complex in the seventeenth century. Thus it has been shown that the controversy over the role of scientific teaching in the universities between John Webster and Seth Ward in the 1650s was more complicated than earlier writers on the scientific movement realised. For Ward was not a reactionary holding out against the 'modern' empiricism advocated by Webster, but a moderate mechanist objecting to Webster's muddled combination of Baconianism with the 'mystical ideal reasons' of the Paracelsian tradition.[3] Non-mechanist views of the workings of the world remained common in the mid-seventeenth century, partly in reaction to atheistic materialism, partly as an element in the muddled legacy of explanatory theories applied by scientists to natural phenomena in this interim period when Aristotle's world-view had been questioned but no new synthesis had yet replaced it. Joseph Glanvill, the vociferous defender of the useful empiricism of the early Royal Society, was typical with his belief in an *anima mundi* and his defence of spirits, and many scientists of the period held eclectic cosmologies which owed something to neo-Platonic notions, something to Paracelsian ideas, often as reinterpreted by seventeenth-century thinkers like J. B. van Helmont, and something to views derived from Descartes and other mechanists.[4]

Aubrey's scientific ideas, which I have examined in detail in Chapter II, belong to this setting, and he was typical in deriving scientific and magical theories and explanations from all sorts of old and new sources. Indeed, in a manner characteristic of his Baconian age, his attitude was independent and empirical; on these,

[1] F. A. Yates, 'The Hermetic tradition in Renaissance science', in C. S. Singleton *ed., Art, Science, and History in the Renaissance* (Baltimore, 1967), 255 f.

[2] P. Rossi, *Francis Bacon: from Magic to Science* (English translation, London, 1968).

[3] A. G. Debus, *Science and Education in the Seventeenth Century* (London, 1970). Contrast the Ancient-Modern stance assumed by Jones, *Ancients and Moderns*, esp. 108–9.

[4] P. M. Rattansi, 'The intellectual origins of the Royal Society', *Notes and Records of the Royal Society* XXIII (1968), 129 f., and 'The social interpretation of science in the seventeenth century' in P. Mathias *ed., Science and Society, 1600–1900* (Cambridge, 1972), 1 f.; C. Webster, 'Henry Power's experimental philosophy', *Ambix* XIV (1967), 150 f.; R. Colie, *Light and Enlightenment* (Cambridge, 1957), ch. VII, 'Cudworth and the Vitalist controversy'.

as on philosophical and antiquarian topics, he ranged widely and
eclectically in search of information on themes that interested him,
considering not the intellectual origins of the theories he espoused
but their usefulness and truth. Though some of his ideas were
similar to van Helmont's, he showed no interest in certain Helmontian theories that were commonly discussed in the scientific circles
in which he moved,[1] and though he occasionally quoted van Helmont, at least some of his knowledge of him was at second-hand.[2]
Similarly, his only reference to Ficino came through a quotation
from Bacon, his chief mentor on such topics,[3] and his general non-
chalance about the origins of his ideas is shown by his attribution
to Bacon of views that Bacon ascribed to Paracelsus and others.[4]
Moreover though his views were generally close to Bacon's, they
were not dominated by his: he sometimes disagreed with him and
he dabbled in occult activities that Bacon rejected.[5]

Aubrey's more arcane studies illustrate the dangers of seeking
a pervasive 'great tradition' among seventeenth-century occultists.[6]
Though he was curious about angelic communication, like John
Dee, the famous Elizabethan neo-Platonist, his concern with it
was far less sophisticated than that of either Dee[7] or of Aubrey's
friend Elias Ashmole, who rescued Dee's papers and tried to
copy his practices.[8] Aubrey entirely lacked Dee's interest in mystical
numerology and is certainly no candidate for any 'Dee-tradition' of
super-celestial mathematicians.[9] He never dabbled in the alchemy
that fascinated Ashmole—indeed, his views on this subject seem
all to come second-hand from others,[10] as did at least some of his

---

[1] For example, the view that water was the ultimate element: cf. C. Webster, 'Water
as the ultimate principle of Nature: the background to Boyle's Sceptical Chymist',
*Ambix* XIII (1966), 96 f.

[2] Though he quoted him as if at first hand in MS A 10, 11, his citation concerning the
efficacy of the touch of a dead man's hand in *Analecta*, 217x, was 'from Dr Ridgely &
Van Helmont'.

[3] Aubrey's disagreement with the views of Ficino in *Analecta*, 211, is an almost exact
quotation from Bacon, *Works*, V, 307, whence the next sentence also comes.

[4] See below, p. 125, n. 3.       [5] See below, pp. 97, n. 3, 124.

[6] Implications of this kind concerning Aubrey's period in F. A. Yates, *The Rosicrucian
Enlightenment* (London, 1972), seem to me highly contentious.

[7] Cf. P. J. French, *John Dee: The World of an Elizabethan Magus* (London, 1972).

[8] Cf. C. H. Josten, *Elias Ashmole* (Oxford, 1966), esp. 184 f.

[9] See below, p. 47, n. 7.

[10] Particularly Meredith Lloyd, who is quoted on such topics in, e.g., *B.L.* I, 243, II,
201–2 (and on Dee in ibid., I, 212).

knowledge of foreign books on the occult[1]—and he had none of the fascination with the arcana of Hermeticism shown by some of his friends.[2] On the other hand, as a collector of occult phenomena and magical remedies from all kinds of informants Aubrey had something to offer Ashmole, who was glad to make notes of charms, spells and sympathetic cures from Aubrey's collections.[3]

In many ways, Aubrey's occult ideas are most interesting for their overlap with his natural history, with the resulting implications of this for the science of his age. In examining his ideas on these subjects in Chapter II I have therefore concentrated on seeing how they operated as a system and in considering why he and some of his scientist friends believed what they did, while others denounced the same views as fallacious. I have arbitrarily but necessarily limited my treatment of this topic largely to the Aubrey manuscripts, but they illustrate well the complications of views on such subjects at the time. For if the mixed and rather capacious systems of explanation that most scientists then employed made occult theories and magical activities like Aubrey's seem not unreasonable,[4] the fact remains that irrational world-views like Aubrey's were under mounting attack. Though vitalist cosmologies remained common, they were increasingly 'rational' rather than occult.[5] Magic was no longer as respectable in Aubrey's day as it had been in Dee's, and the contrast between Aubrey and those of his friends who questioned his beliefs shows why.

Some of the contrasts between these scientists and Aubrey were connected with intellectual personality and preconceptions; but questions of method are also vital, for Aubrey was essentially

---

[1] For example, Dr Luke Ridgeley, the medical friend who told Aubrey about van Helmont (see above, p. 22, n. 2) also told him about a book by Colerus that Aubrey cited on the value of dreams (see below, p. 105), which Aubrey had certainly not read for himself since it was in High Dutch and ' 'Tis pity it is not translated' (MS A 10, 117), and about a recipe for invisibility from another book in High Dutch by 'Johannes de Florentiâ [a Rosy-crusian]' (*Gentilisme*, 253). On Aubrey and the Rosicrucians, see below, p. 139, n. 9.

[2] E.g. Andrew Paschall in the letters cited below, p. 141. n. 9.

[3] British Library MS Sloane 3846, 114v–115v, comprises Ashmole's notes from 'Mr Aubry's Collection of dreames, phantasmes, Instincts &c:'. Cf. below, p. 103, n. 5, and, on the range of Aubrey's sources on the occult, p. 105, n. 7.

[4] For some interesting comments on the mid-century tendency to accept everything and then to try to explain it, see H. W. Jones, 'Sir Christopher Wren and Natural Philosophy', *Notes and Records of the Royal Society* XIII (1958), 21, and B. J. Dobbs, 'Studies in the Natural Philosophy of Sir Kenelm Digby', *Ambix* XVIII (1971), 1 f.

[5] Cf. P. C. Ritterbusch, *Overtures to Biology* (New Haven, 1964).

uncritical in his scientific views, whereas science was becoming an increasingly critical discipline. The most fruitful experiments of the early Royal Society were concerned with testing and quantifying phenomena, with rigorous proof and with exact weighing and measuring. Aubrey, on the other hand, never carried out more than the most rudimentary experiments,[1] and he rarely attempted to test or quantify anything. He was no more illogical than his sixteenth-century magician predecessors, but the empiricism which had only rarely threatened their beliefs had made many abandon them by Aubrey's time. Whatever the importance of irrational ideas to the early growth of the scientific movement, by the end of the seventeenth century its rationalising tendencies were making their survival increasingly difficult.

The limitation of Aubrey and his like was, therefore primarily one of method. But the perplexing case of Newton, who combined epoch-making quantification in physics with secret mysticism in alchemy,[2] should warn one against drawing too easy conclusions about this complex period, and even Aubrey illustrates this: for though his science was entirely uncritical, the best of his antiquarian work reached an inductive excellence worthy of the most accomplished of his scientific peers, though the quality of his antiquarian deductions was uneven.

This inconsistency of method raises a problem which I have considered in Chapter III, where, after describing Aubrey's historical writings, I have tried to evaluate the influence of his scientific studies on his interest in the past. This involves a wider consideration of the impact of the scientific movement on historiography, which seems to me to have been dealt with rather inadequately up to now, largely because it has always been assumed that this influence would have been manifest mainly in improved method. Such views stem from the tendency of historians to use the word 'scientific' with the implication that the natural sciences have a discrete methodology not found in other disciplines, a position into the philosophical difficulties of which I cannot enter here. I have taken 'science' to mean what Aubrey's contemporaries would have called 'Natural Philosophy'—the study of natural and mechanical phenomena—thus referring to areas of study rather than to

---

[1] He did do 'experiments', as he called them, on the medicinal virtues of springs. Cf. MS A 1, 40, etc. See also below, pp. 42-3.

[2] Cf. F. E. Manuel, *A Portrait of Isaac Newton* (Cambridge, Mass., 1968).

method, which naturally varied according to the individual ability of scientists. It therefore seems to me that it is primarily in interests rather than techniques that the influence of the scientific movement on historiography should be sought.

Though it has been argued that the sixteenth and seventeenth centuries saw a 'Historical Revolution' paralleling the scientific,[1] such claims are in danger of truism, of illustrating no more than the increasing commonness of critical attitudes towards all areas of human activity in the Reformation period.[2] Certainly, the sixteenth century was a great historical age,[3] and the origins of a modern critical approach to the past have been not unreasonably attributed to the influence of philological and legal studies on historiography in sixteenth-century France. This brought with it a new awareness of anachronism and of the possibility of reconstructing different past conditions of society from vestigial evidence, with, as its most notable result, the more careful study of linguistic usage which led to the discovery of feudalism.[4] The new critical historiography extended from France to England in the seventeenth century, where it can be seen in the activity of scholars like Sir Henry Spelman, John Selden, Sir William Dugdale and Robert Brady, compiling collections of documents, searching records and laws for evidence, questioning, interpreting and validating.[5] The methods of such scholars were impeccable, and they can be compared in the vaguest terms with the activity of their scientific contemporaries in intensifying the inductive method, in classifying and collecting. But to postulate any direct scientific influence is highly dubious, for there is no proof of it, and scholars had been capable of such methods of analysis long before the scientific movement.

Besides, this newly sophisticated approach to textual evidence is what might have been expected in the text-based Renaissance, whereas the scientific movement was in many ways a reaction against a literary culture, advocating the study of nature instead of

[1] F. S. Fussner, *The Historical Revolution* (London, 1962).

[2] Cf., for example, the growth of reforming ideas chronicled in A. B. Ferguson, *The Articulate Citizen and the English Renaissance* (Durham, N. C., 1965).

[3] P. Burke, *The Renaissance Sense of the Past* (London, 1969); F. J. Levy, *Tudor Historical Thought* (San Marino, 1967).

[4] D. R. Kelley, *Foundations of Modern Historical Scholarship. Language, Law and History in the French Renaissance* (New York, 1970).

[5] J. G. A. Pococke, *The Ancient Constitution and the Feudal Law* (Cambridge, 1957); D. C. Douglas, *English Scholars, 1660–1730* (second edition, London, 1951).

books, preferring things to the words that had preoccupied their
predecessors. The change in approach to the past that this change in
priorities could bring is illustrated, it seems to me, by a detailed
consideration of the antiquarian activity of Aubrey. For, as I have
shown in Chapter III, his studies of natural phenomena certainly
affected his interest in the past: he took more interest in field antiquities than antiquaries had previously, and in studying them he
showed an 'archaeological' rather than an historical attitude, seeking
conclusions about the past through considering such material
remains as stone-circles and architecture in their own right, in contrast to those predecessors who had preferred written sources.[1]
Aubrey's concern with improvement also made him lay an increased
stress on technological change in the past, which was linked to his
hopes for progress in the future, in contrast to earlier antiquaries
preoccupied with ideas of decay, who were interested in change
largely so as to reflect on the natural tendency of all things to
mutability.[2]

In Chapter III I have briefly indicated how the natural historical
studies of others had an effect on their study of the past similar to
Aubrey's, giving them an increased concern with tangible and visual
rather than textual evidence. Such an approach to the past naturally
did not completely supersede a text-based approach, just as it was
not entirely unprecedented.[3] But there was a definite change of
emphasis, which can certainly be attributed to the influence of the
new science. In terms of method, however, the influence of the new
philosophy is much more dubious, for the method of Aubrey and
others whose natural history made them archaeologists fluctuated
widely. The quality of their interpretations was equally varied, and
it is to Aubrey's characteristically vivid imagination rather than to
any external factors that we owe the best of his historical writing,
his vivid reconstruction of the way of life of past ages. This was the
fruit of the personal gifts of an inspired historian, reminiscent of the
imaginative and original approach to the past of Sir Walter Scott
over a century later,[4] and, as I have shown in Chapter III, it also

[1] Cf. M. C. W. Hunter, 'The Royal Society and the origins of British archaeology',
*Antiquity* LXV (1971), 113 f. and 187 f.

[2] Cf., for example, W. Camden, *Remaines, concerning Britaine* (second edition,
London, 1614), 237.

[3] Cf. Hunter, art. cit.

[4] H. R. Trevor-Roper, *The Romantic Movement and the Study of History* (London,
1969).

has something in common with Aubrey's brilliant miniatures of his contemporaries in *Brief Lives*, the work on which his reputation as an author justly rests.

CHAPTER ONE

# The Life of a Scholar

Though Aubrey's life is as well known and has been as well written as any in the seventeenth century, it can be briefly summarised, for its notable events were few. Born in 1626 at Easton Pierse in the parish of Kington St. Michael in North Wiltshire, 'that place (of my birth and birth-right) which I so much love',[1] Aubrey was sent to school locally and at Blandford in Dorset. In 1642 he went up to Oxford, 'my dearly beloved Oxford',[2] 'our English Athens',[3] but his studies were interrupted by the Civil War and the illness of his father, and his subsequent training at the Middle Temple was more superficial still.[4] In the 1650s and 1660s he lived as a country gentleman in Wiltshire—'Johannes Aubrey de Easton-Piers in Agro Wilton⟨ensi⟩ Arm⟨iger⟩ Regalis Societatis Socius', as he proudly styled himself[5]—and he emulated his most cultured contemporaries in the mansion that he planned to build at Easton.[6] But law-suits and a disastrous courtship reduced him to poverty, and from the early 1670s his life-style changed. He 'absconded as a banishd man'[7] and was reduced, in the sour words of Anthony Wood, that rather peevish Oxford antiquary who was closely associated with Aubrey for nearly half his life, to 'a very sorry condition, and at length made shift to rub out by hanging on Edmund Wyld esq. living in Blomesbury neare London, on James ⟨Bertie⟩ earle of

---

[1] A-W, 13 Dec. 1673, F 39, 243.     [2] A-W, 14 July 1681, F 39, 360v.

[3] A-W, 15 July 1689, F 39, 390.

[4] He was only there 'off and on' (*B.L.* i, 38), and 'my father's sicknesse, and businesse, never permitted me to make any settlement to my studie' (ibid., i, 46).

[5] This is from a design for his tombstone, dating from within a few years of his death, MS A 5, 122; but the sentiment is a memory of his early prosperity.

[6] Drawings of this survive in MS A 17. Unlike Anthony Powell (*John Aubrey and his Friends*, 28 and plate facing 136), however, I do not believe that these schemes were ever implemented: John Britton, who was brought up locally, remembered an old house at Easton Pierse demolished since *c*.1780 which he thought was the original one in which Aubrey was born (cf. his *Memoir of John Aubrey* (London, 1845), 25–6), and I think that the new house and gardens delineated in MS A 17 were only planned (though possibly quite seriously: cf., e.g., the carefully drawn 'Profil' at 19v) and never carried out, perhaps because Aubrey could never afford it; other drawings in the volume (e.g., that on f. 18) are entirely imaginary.

[7] *B.L.* i, 40.

29

Abendon, whose first wife was related to him, and on Sir John
Aubrey, his kinsman, living somtimes in Glamorganshire, and
somtimes at Borstall neare Brill in Bucks'.[1]

Aubrey never held any public office, nor took any employment
for more than a few weeks. When he wrote his own biography, 'to
be interposed as a sheet of wast paper only in the binding of a
booke',[2] he devoted most space to his intellectual development—
his education, his writings and his role in encouraging and recording the endeavours of others. It was for his shortcomings in the
'advancement of learning' that he apologised, and it was for his
contribution towards it that he wished to be remembered. For
Aubrey devoted his entire career to scholarship, to collecting information and compiling learned works. By the end of his life he
could boast '20 Diatribes (bigger or lesser)'[3] on a whole range of
subjects, and, as John Ray observed in 1691, 'I find by the Titles
of your manuscript works you were pleased to communicate that
you are not idle'.[4]

Apart from his scholarly activity, Aubrey's life was a succession
of impediments to it. His worldly transactions, as he often sadly
noted, were almost invariably disastrous. 'The trueth is,' he con-
fided to Anthony Wood, 'I was never made to manage an estate, &
was predestinated to be cosind & cheated.'[5] His father left him
debts, and money troubles and law-suits dogged him all his life.
'I can safely say,' he told Thomas Tanner, a young antiquary whom
he befriended in his later years, 'that since I was 22, I never was
master of six weekes entire, for study, being involved & perplexed
in law-suites & domestick differences: and shall find no rest till
in the grave.'[6] Even in 1665 he complained to Robert Boyle that 'I
have long been so perplexed with the unpleasant affairs of this
earthen world, that I cannot mind so much as I would the intellectual one,'[7] and his first letter to Anthony Wood bewailed his 'Fate
to be plagued with a suite in Lawe'.[8] Not only did such matters
take time; his misfortunes also depressed him. 'A man's spirit
rises and falls with his fortune: makes me lethargique', he sadly
noted,[9] and to illustrate the point he copied out a design from

---

[1] Wood, *Life and Times* (*ed.* A. Clark), II (Oxford, 1892), 117.   [2] *B.L.* I, 34.
[3] A-W, 3 Aug. 1689, Wood F 40, 372.
[4] Ray-Aubrey, 17 Aug. 1691, MS A 13, 173.   [5] A-W, 27 Oct. 1691, F 39, 435.
[6] A-T, 6 April 1693, T. 25, 30. Cf. *B.L.* I, 42.
[7] Aubrey-Boyle, 15 March 1665, Boyle, *Works*, VI, 544.
[8] A-W, 8 Jan. 1667/8, B. 14, 80.   [9] *B.L.* I, 42.

George Withers' *Collection of Emblemes*, showing a man trying to rise with a pair of wings attached to his right arm but held down by a stone chained to his left. Withers explained this with

'My *Wit* got *Wings*, and, high had flowne;
But, *Povertie* did keepe mee downe'

and Aubrey added under his copy of the picture 'The Application is obvious'.[1]

Though he claimed that he had 'never quiett, nor anything of happinesse till divested of all, 1670, 1671',[2] his new situation had hardly fewer problems. When he went into hiding to avoid his creditors he enjoyed himself greatly, but complained of the difficulties of making scholarly enquiries for fear of arrest.[3] In 1674 he was at once 'solliciting some Right that I have in Wales, and looking after some preferment at Court'.[4] Even the hospitality that he received from his friends and patrons had its disadvantages. He frequently apologised to Anthony Wood because his affairs were delayed by drinking till one or two with the hospitable Edmund Wyld,[5] because 'Mr Wyld is now having me abroad with him to be merry',[6] or because 'my late walkings & sitting-up with my old deare friend, puts these matters much out of order'.[7] On another occasion he apologised that 'I am so much taken-up by my Patron's, (besides my Lethargiquenesse) that I cannot be so intent as I would, on this Designe, which I am most *zealous* for';[8] there were times when he would have stayed at Oxford but 'my Lord would not be denyed, but would have me with him & so to London';[9] and business could only be done at Christmas 1680 after 'the Menced pies & good ale & wine are perspired'.[10] In the 1680s law-suits were as urgent as ever. 'I have been so weekely perplext, and plagued with letters from my brother; and with running up & downe, to Lawyers,

[1] In MS A 5, 124v, Aubrey draws the design and gives a reference to Withers, but does not actually quote the verse, which is here given from *A Collection of Emblemes* (London, 1635), 176 (Book 3, no. 42).
[2] *B,L.* 1, 41.
[3] E.g. A-W, 27 Oct. 1671, 6 July 1672, 29 Nov. 1673; F 39, 142, 178, 238 ('I dare not *by day* goe to him for it').
[4] A-W, 12 Jan. 1674/5, F 39, 288.
[5] E.g. A-W, 9 April 1679, F 39, 316; 19 March 1680/1, B. 14, 129v.
[6] A-W, 7 Nov. 1674, B. 14, 113v.    [7] A-W, Easter Monday 1691, F 39, 421v.
[8] A-W, 30 Dec. 1679, F 39, 334 (this was of the project for a life of Hobbes; see below, pp. 78–9).
[9] A-T, 13 Oct. 1694, T. 25, 240.    [10] A-W, 13 Jan. 1680/1, F 39, 351v.

and Proctors, that I have had no time to thinke my owne thoughts: or doe any thing for you, or my naturall Hist⟨orie⟩,' he told Wood,[1] and his letters from his brother in Wiltshire in these years refer to 'the dayly damage wee both sustaine, & the many dangers that atends us'.[2]

But Aubrey's plans for altering his condition were almost entirely unreal. He recorded offers of employment or preferment from numerous friends and acquaintances—Robert Hooke, who gave Aubrey hospitality at Gresham College in the 1670s and 1680s;[3] Sir Christopher Wren, 'one of the necessariest Friends I have to preserve me';[4] Sir William Petty, a 'singular friend' of Aubrey,[5] who much admired 'the great Elevation of his Understanding which like a Meteor moves above the Sphare of other Mortalls';[6] Sir Robert Moray, an enthusiastic scientist and 'a Courtier, that would doe Courtesies for Friend-ship-sake';[7] James Bertie, Earl of Abingdon, a Lord Chief Justice who was one of Aubrey's valued patrons;[8] and others.[9] He would have valued preferment if only because 'I should have dispensed the profit, ad Majorem Dei gloriam: and have been usefull & gratefull and benefactive to my ingeniose friends'.[10] But only Wren's scheme for having Aubrey employed by the publisher and King's cosmographer John Ogilby came to anything, and that ended disastrously.[11]

He considered joining a Jesuit religious house, where, he thought, they studied 'what they have a mind too: musick. Heraldry. chymistry &c:'.[12] But nothing came of this extraordinary idea, or of his friends' suggestion that he should take Anglican orders and settle

---

[1] A-W, 5 Feb. 1686/7, B. 14, 141.
[2] William Aubrey-John Aubrey, St James's Eve 1688, MS A 12, 185.
[3] A-W, 28 July 1674, B. 14, 105.
[4] A-W, 9 Dec. 1673, F 39, 241v. Cf. A-W, 12 Aug. 1672, F 39, 181.   [5] *B.L.* I, 43.
[6] A-W, 23 June 1675, F 39, 275. On sig. C4v of Ashmole D 60 (4), a copy of Lilly's almanac for 1675, Aubrey marked 5 February and wrote 'The 5th Sir W⟨illiam⟩ P⟨etty⟩ voluntary told me he was contriving ⟨replaced by 'had contrived'⟩ Preferment for me.— Privy-councell—Deo Gracias': cf. Aubrey-Petty, 17 July 1675, in which he thanks Petty for his care 'to so unlucky and unfortunate a thing as your humble servant'. (I am indebted to Mr Lindsay Sharp of The Queen's College, Oxford, for showing me a copy of this unpublished letter among the Petty papers at Bowood, Bound Volume VI, no. 21.)
[7] T.G.c.24, 78v. Cf. *B.L.* II, 82.   [8] A-W, 21 June 1681, F 39, 354v.
[9] Including Sir Leoline Jenkins (*B.L.* I, 44) and George Johnson (A-W, 26 Jan. 1683/4, B. 14, 137, and MS A 23, 38v).
[10] A-W, 26 Jan. 1683/4, B. 14, 137.
[11] See Powell, *John Aubrey and his Friends*, 149 f.
[12] A-W, 27 Oct. 1671, F 39, 141.

down as a parish priest.[1] 'Lord how should I looke in a Cassoque', Aubrey exclaimed,[2] and 'fough the Cassock stinkes',[3] and though he might have become 'an honest poore old Bachelor parson' of the kind that he exempted from his usual anti-clerical sentiment,[4] this was never very likely. Another possibility was emigration to the colonies: at different times, Aubrey considered settling in Maryland,[5] Carolina,[6] Jamaica,[7] Tobago[8] or New York, which he thought 'a delicious Country'.[9] His patron, the Earl of Thanet, at whose Kentish home Aubrey often stayed in the 1670s, tried to persuade him of the superior merits of the Bermudas, where, he claimed, the inhabitants enjoyed 'soe sweete an Ayre, soe perfect a health, and all thinges soe usefull and delightfull to the life of man' that it seemed irresistible;[10] indeed by attracting selected friends he hoped to make it 'a more renowned place for learning than ould Athens ever was'.[11] 'But cui bono?' Aubrey asked of his plans for Maryland, 'to whose good?';[12] he was discouraged by those of his friends who preferred his company at home;[13] and none of these schemes materialised.

Instead, Aubrey continued his normal style of life, travelling around England and Wales and mixing in cosmopolitan circles in London where he could gather and exchange information on the wide range of subjects that interested him. Even when considering emigrating to Carolina he wanted first to 'take a turne about Eng⟨land⟩ & Wales'[14] and his researches could never have been pursued on a desert island or in a monastery, where he would have become 'in time for want of ingeniose converse ... like an old Pole in an orchard grown o'er with moss: as I have known some

---

[1] A-W, 23 Feb. 1673/4, F 39, 255v; 29 Aug. 1676, B. 14, 119. Cf. Charles Snell-Aubrey, 12 Aug. 1676, MS A 23, 116-17.

[2] A-W, 23 Feb. 1673/4, F 39, 255v.   [3] A-W, 9 April 1674, B. 14, 98.

[4] A-W, 23 Feb. 1673/4, F 39, 255v. On the whole he thought, 'Amongst the Clergy, Humility & Charity very rare': see also below, p. 56, and cf. A-W, 2 Jan. 1685/6, F 39, 377, where Aubrey points out that Pell was so poor that his burial was still not paid for, 'to the shame of the Ecclesiasticks', or Aubrey-Anthony Henley, 27 Feb. 1693/4, MS A 10, 2: 'if the Nobless have a mind to have their Children be putt in the Clergies pockets, much good may do 'em'.

[5] A-W, 27 Oct. 1671, F 39, 141v.   [6] A-W, 19 Aug. 1672, F 49, 183.

[7] A-W, 9 April 1674, B. 14, 98.   [8] Cf. Petty-Aubrey, 22 Aug. 1685, MS A 13, 103.

[9] Thanet-Aubrey, 19 April 1675, MS A 13, 213. Evidently Wyld was thinking of buying land there.

[10] Id., 7 June 1675, ibid., 220.   [11] Id., 19 April 1675, ibid., 213v.

[12] A-W, 17 Nov. 1670, F 39, 128v.

[13] Cf. Hoskyns-Aubrey, 8 Nov. 1671, 21 Aug. 1672; MS A 12, 198, 204.

[14] A-W, 19 Aug. 1672, F 39, 183.

3

Countrey Parsons: who were sharp men in the University, come downe to the understanding of a Thrasher'.[1] His Jesuit scheme was partly a blind to put off his creditors,[2] and his aspiration to the 'happy life that the innocent poore Hermits doe enjoy'[3] partly a conceit. He was himself half aware of the contradiction between this and the evident relish with which he recalled rumours he had heard among 'Parl⟨iament⟩ men & courtiers, persons of great intelligence' at 'our R⟨oyal⟩ Soc⟨iety⟩ club' (though worried about some information he had divulged, 'my head being fuller of good wine then prudence'). For 'though no mortall loves Solitude, contemplation, & an innocent life &c: more then I, yet the tricks that are discoursed at our Clubbes, are not agreable to that old pious Tho⟨mas⟩ á Kempis-way'.[4]

Aubrey could never have lived without his friends. 'I have a great mind to make my selfe once more happy in your so good, so ingeniose, innocent, and friendly conversation', he told Anthony Wood;[5] 'I long to see you for one whole day, with the longing of a woman',[6] and 'I can not expresse what a wonderfull refreshing 'tis to my soule to spend a weeke at Oxon, among so many good & ingeniose acquaintance'.[7] He meant as much to them: 'I cannot thinck my selfe compleately happy without Mr John Aubry's company,' wrote Stafford Tyndale, a Wiltshire friend, in 1659,[8] and more than ordinary warmth was reflected in the plea of Sir John Stawell, one of Aubrey's 'Amici', that he should join him on the Salisbury coach: 'Let mee beg your favour in graunting this earnest request. I will not admit a deniall. let no slovenly, paltry, pittifull excuse been invented. wee shall bee truely merry in this progresse'.[9] One catches constant glimpses of Aubrey drinking with his friends, 'very [ingeniously] merry',[10] perhaps telling the stories which he recorded in his *Brief Lives*, which are often almost conversational in their presentation. 'I fancy my selfe all along discourseing with you,' he told Wood when he sent them to him,[11] and he interspersed them with 'Well . . .'[12] and colloquial sentences

[1] MS A 10, 144v.    [2] Cf. A-W, 27 Oct. 1671, F 39, 141; 7 Dec. 1671, B. 14, 89.
[3] A-W, St Peter's Day 1689, F 39, 386.    [4] A-W, 26 June 1679, F 39, 328.
[5] A-W, 14 April 1673, F 39, 202.    [6] A-W, 1 April 1672, B. 14, 92.
[7] A-W, 22 Oct. 1681, T. 456a, 27.
[8] Tyndale-Aubrey, 28 July/7 Aug. 1659, MS A 13, 230.
[9] Stawell-Aubrey, 8 Dec. (no year), ibid., 191. Cf. *B.L.* 1, 44.
[10] Aubrey-William Holder, 2 Jan. 1693/4, British Library MS Sloane 1388, 149.
[11] A-W, 15 June 1680, *B.L.* I, 11.    [12] E.g. *B.L.* I, 291, II, 58, 76, 287.

like 'I'le tell you a story of our old friend'.[1]

Something of the quality of Aubrey's conversation, trenchant, whimsical, mocking, can occasionally be caught from his writings. When he was preparing a posthumous tribute to Hobbes in 1679, he considered inserting an attack on John Fell, Dean of Christ Church and Bishop of Oxford, who had censored Wood's *History and Antiquities of the University of Oxford*, and he outlined what he hoped to say in a letter to Wood: 'Rumpatur quisquis rumpit eor-⟨um⟩ Individiâ ⟨let everyone who breaks be broken by their envy⟩. Could a man have imagined that such a Ghostlike-ghostly father, so continuall & assiduous in the prayers of the Ch⟨urch⟩ of Eng⟨land⟩ that made *Almighty & most mercifull Father* ⟨in pseudo black-letter⟩, nauseous to his Lodgers, [viz. 6 times a day]. That upheld the *Arke* in the late times, that adeo pomposam sanctitatis speciem geririt ⟨wore a countenance so pompous in its sanctity⟩, I say could one have thought that this great Practiser of Piety, & walking Common-prayer-booke, could have made such a breach in the Moralls & Justice? & to have such a pruritus ⟨lasciviousness⟩, (or what worse shall I call it) in the Tyranny of the Presse, & in scratching-out authors due prayses, & expunging & interposing? that have made the Universitys worse thought of then ever they were before? who can pardon such a dry bone? a stalking, consecrated engine of Hypocrisy &c. ———— tell me if I rayle well. How much should goe in?'[2] Clearly Aubrey was a great character, and he was doubtless very good company, not least because he enjoyed it so much himself—

> 'Hey ho! it is nought but mirth,
> That keepes the body from the earth'

he reflected, as he looked forward to sconcing Wood at Oxford.[3]

But there was more to his friendship than merriment. John Lydall, an Oxford friend of Aubrey's undergraduate days, found him 'so truly sincere & ingenious a freind'[4] and Thomas Flatman, poet, painter and another acquaintance, praised his 'Ingenuity & candor'.[5] After his death, the astrologer John Gadbury mourned him for 'he

[1] *B.L.* II, 264.

[2] A-W, St. John the Evangelist's Day 1679, F 39, 327. There is a slightly different version of this on a leaf in MS A 21, 76, marked 'TH: vitam'.

[3] A-W, 21 June 1681, F 39, 355.

[4] Lydall-Aubrey, 18 Sept. 1649, MS A 12, 304.

[5] Flatman-Aubrey, 6 Sept. 1679, ibid., 116.

was a Learned, Honest Gentleman; And a true Friend: Whose
Loss I really mourn, as having had a more than XXX years Acquaintance with him. A time sufficient to experience any man's
Integrity'.[1] Aubrey had been 'much tumbled up and downe' in
the world,[2] and, with his great gift of friendship, he had an extraordinary range of more or less intimate contacts, from Wiltshire
neighbours and scholarly acquaintances to the greatest of his age.
In his role as antiquarian scholar, he waited on King Charles II
and the Duke of York in 1663;[3] he found William Sancroft, Archbishop of Canterbury in the 1680s, 'extraordinarily kind to me';[4]
and he claimed on occasion to have influence with such eminent
figures as Lady Cavendish, daughter of the Earl of Ormond, Lord
Lieutenant of Ireland, and Sir Leoline Jenkins, Secretary of State
in the early 1680s.[5] For his life of Hobbes, he was promised verses
by Charles Sackville, Earl of Dorset, John Wilmot, Earl of Rochester,
Dryden, Waller and others,[6] and in 1693/4, with characteristic
confidence, he hoped for help in promoting his educational theories
from the Earl of Leicester, the Marquis of Worcester, Lord Ashley,
and perhaps also Viscount Weymouth and the Earl of Pembroke,
one of his patrons.[7] The detail of Aubrey's life consists mainly of
his friendships and acquaintances, and Anthony Powell's *John
Aubrey and his Friends* describes this almost Proustian succession
of personalities and situations, interweaving with the whole of the
life of late seventeenth-century England.

Apart from this, the narrative of Aubrey's career is merely a
record of his travels, to the London courts and among his estates
while he owned them, to his various friends after his absconding,
and occasionally abroad. He valued his travels not least for the
information that he collected on them. While in Ireland in 1661 he
carefully examined ancient Irish gospel books at Trinity College,
Dublin;[8] he 'saw the manner of living of the Natives, scorning
industry and luxury, contenting themselves only with things
necessary';[9] and he was able to insert his observations on various

[1] Gadbury-Tanner, 29 Oct. 1698, Tanner 22, 126.
[2] A-W, 15 June 1680, *B.L.* I, 10.        [3] See below, pp. 158-9.
[4] A-W, 21 June 1681, F 39, 354.
[5] A-W, 20 Dec. 1681, St John the Evangelist's Day 1681; B. 14, 134, 135.
[6] A-W, 21 Feb. 1679/80 and 27 March 1680; B. 14, 127, 131.
[7] Aubrey-Henley, 27 Feb. 1693/4, MS A 10, 2.
[8] MS A 5, 19b, and T.G.c.24, 73v.
[9] Aubrey-Hobbes, 30 Aug. 1661, inserted in a grangerised copy of C. R. Weld's
*History of the Royal Society* (London, 1848) now in the Executive Secretary's office at

topics in his copy of the *Interrogatory Relating more particularly to the Husbandry and Naturall History of Ireland* appended to Samuel Hartlib's *Legacie*.[1] In France in 1664, he noted the features of the people and the colour of the kine in Picardy;[2] he observed the similarity to an old Roman road of the French king's highway from Paris to Orleans;[3] he mentions an altar on an old oak near Orleans and a man who claimed to have been bitten by a werewolf whom he saw in the hospital there;[4] and he measured the French inch from a carpenter's rule at Tours.[5] His most important single English excursion was the 'Perambulation of Surrey' which he undertook in 1673 for John Ogilby's 'Geographical and Historical Description' of England and Wales, doubtless welcoming an opportunity to satisfy both his impecuniosity and his inquisitiveness.[6] But his more general studies of natural history and antiquities owed much to his frequent travels in England and Wales throughout his life, from London, Kent and Sussex to Somerset, Yorkshire, Essex, Herefordshire and Glamorgan. Such widespread journeys he valued just as he valued his travels among his estates in Wiltshire before he lost them, which gave him 'more opportunities than most men, to make Remarques in this Countrey & particularly on Salisbury-plaines'.[7]

### Aubrey and the Scientific Movement

It had, indeed, been Aubrey's habit to 'make Remarques' since his earliest years. 'Admiration the first step to knowledge & Arts, next Inquisition, hence Traditio Lampadis, which we call Learning,' he observed, when writing about the education of children, and he

---

the Royal Society, Vol. II, following page 246. I am indebted to John Buchanan-Brown for informing me of the whereabouts of this letter, formerly known only through the transcription in *European Magazine* XXXIV (1798), 307, and John Britton, *Memoir of John Aubrey*, 37–8.

[1] Ashmole 1621, 12–13 is Aubrey's copy of the second edition of Hartlib's *Legacie: or an Enlargement of the Discourse of Husbandry used in Brabant & Flaunders* (London 1652), which has appended the *Interrogatory*, with notes by Aubrey in pencil and ink. The *Legacie* is inscribed on its title-page 'Jo⟨hn⟩ Aubrey 165...' (damaged).

[2] MS A 4, 54v.    [3] T.G.c.25, 94v.    [4] *Gentilisme*, 197, 227.

[5] T.G.c.25, 224. Aubrey planned a trip to Italy in the 1650s, which is referred to in letters from Hartlib (8 March 1652/3, MS A 12, 155) and Potter (24 March 1652/3, MS A 13, 145), but it proved abortive (cf. *B.L.* I, 39, 300).

[6] Cf. Powell, *John Aubrey and his Friends*, 149 f.    [7] T.G.c.24, 138.

believed it possible to tell even at an early age whether a child would be ingenious 'by his Curiosity, or non-curiositie'.[1] In the case of the young Aubrey, there could be no doubt about this. 'I was from my Childhood affected with the view of things rare; which is the beginning of Philosophy,' he explained in the preface to his *Naturall Historie of Wiltshire*,[2] and his description of his early intellectual development stresses his interest in the visual and tangible, the technological and the old. His earliest memories already show the vivid feeling for atmosphere and texture that were always to remain with him and even to make him consider his vocation as an artist: 'poore & meane objects did displease my phancy, e.g. as old Kingtons rough wall & poore howse, smell of yarne; Darke shades under the Oakes. ∧ ∧ ∧ . gable ends at Kington or &c: è contra prospects & seræne skye pleased me. and the Kite & clowdes ... Yatton schoole, fancied painting but concealed it: & could have drawne had he been putt to it. Observd the varnishing of the gilt fillet of his grammar by a drop of ... q⟨uaere⟩ turpentine or Lin⟨seed⟩ oile. Transparent pebble at ⟨cross⟩ way. & every remarkeable thing. eager after the prints'.[3]

Such vivid recollections characterise all of Aubrey's writings. His concise observation of the appearance of his subjects does much to recreate personality in his *Brief Lives*: 'he is of middle stature, strong sett, high coloured, a head of sorrell haire, a severe and sound judgment: a good fellowe,' he wrote of Samuel Butler, author of *Hudibras*,[4] or of John Tombes, the divine, 'but a little man, neat limbed, a little quick searching eie, sad, gray'.[5] In describing complexion, Aubrey was conscious of using 'the Painters phrase',[6] and he often felt that such remarks were 'better expressed with a pencill, than a penne'.[7] His observations of nature were similar. Stones he might describe as 'of an oriental horse flesh-colour',[8] and he tried in his writings to grasp the texture of the views which he constantly admired on his travels and would have used to illustrate his *Naturall Historie of Wiltshire*, if not to form a 'glorious Volumne' of their own.[9] He compared their 'most pleasant variegated ver-

---

[1] MS A 10, 163v. 'Traditio Lampadis', 'the handing on of the torch', echoes Lucretius, *De Rerum Natura*, II, 79. I am indebted to Jeremy Black for help in elucidating this and other classical allusions.

[2] MS A 1, 6.　　[3] MS A 10, 163v, 165v. The omission before 'q⟨uaere⟩' is Aubrey's.

[4] *B.L.* I, 136.　　[5] *B.L.* II, 260.　　[6] MS A 1, 23.　　[7] Ibid., 22v.　　[8] Ibid., 60.

[9] MS A 2, 177v. 175 f. is 'My Wish, an Appendix' of views he would have had drawn. Cf MS A 3, 3.

dure' with 'the workes in Irish-stitch',[1] and he noted how, in the view over the Weald from St Martha's Chapel at Chilworth in Surrey, 'the Elmes at the villages & hedges and the meadowes being of different *greens* looke like tufted velvet'.[2]

The illustrations in this book show Aubrey's ability as an artist. He considered that 'if ever I had been good for anything, 'twould have been a painter, I could fancy a thing so strongly and had so cleare an idaea of it'.[3] In his autobiography he elaborated on his earliest artistic efforts, despite the lack of encouragement he encountered. When he was eight years old, he 'fell then to drawing, beginning first with plaine outlines, e.g. in draughts of curtaines. Then at 9 (crossed herein by father and schoolmaster), to colours, having no body to instruct me; copied pictures in the parlour in a table booke'.[4] Evidence of his later artistic development is limited to a single reference to Jacob de Valke, 'who taught me to paint'.[5] But Aubrey collected pictures,[6] and when he later considered the *desiderata* of education, he urged that boys be taught to copy the diagrams when reading Anatomy, 'which will wonderfully fix them in their memories',[7] and to 'proceed so far, as to be able to draw Prospects, or Engines &c. and to expresse their owne Inventions of them';[8] he also wanted them to be surrounded by depictions of 'fine florid Landscapes' 'to highten and enliven their Fancies'.[9]

In the 'eremeticall solitude' of Easton Pierse, the young Aubrey 'was very curious; his greatest delight to be continually with the artificers that came there (e.g. joyners, carpenters, coupers, masons), and understood their trades'.[10] 'I was wont (I remember) much to lament with my selfe that I lived not in a city, e.g. Bristol, where I might have accesse to watchmakers, locksmiths, etc.'[11] His 'inventive and philosophicall' temperament also showed 'a strong and early impulse to antiquitie'.[12] 'When a boy, he did ever love to converse

---

[1] *B.L.* I, 79.  [2] MS A 4, 129.  [3] *B.L.* I, 43.  [4] *B.L.* I, 36.

[5] *B.L.* I, 152. This was probably Gerard Valck, a Dutch engraver employed by Loggan.

[6] Cf. Hoskyns-Aubrey, 16 April 1661, 13/23 July 1664, 2 March 1664/5; MS A 12, 189, 195, 196; Tyndale-Aubrey, 21 Aug. 1661, MS A 13, 231.

[7] MS A 10, 41v.  [8] Ibid., 40a.  [9] Ibid., 125.  [10] *B.L.* I, 35.

[11] *B.L.* I, 36. Though such memories are very like Petty's (ibid., II, 140), this doubtless only illustrates 'the consimility of their dispositions' (ibid., II, 283). It should, however, be pointed out that none of the autobiographical notes quoted here date from earlier than the 1660s, and though I have used them, since they are almost the only evidence for Aubrey's early intellectual development, they are occasionally mutually contradictory, as over the source of the copy of Bacon that he had as a boy (below, p. 41, n. 3).

[12] *B.L.* I, 36-7.

with old men, as living histories';[1] he was horrified at the way that 'the MSS flew-about like butterflies';[2] and 'I was alwayes enquiring of my grandfather of the old time, the rood-loft, etc., ceremonies, of the priory, etc.'.[3] He later recalled, too, his debt to Theophilus Wodenote, a scholarly priest living locally at that time, who 'answered me my questions of antiq⟨uities⟩ etc.' and showed him a book of old proverbs.[4] No external stimulus was needed to make Aubrey an antiquary: 'I was inclin'd by my *Genius* from my Childhood to the Love of Antiquities,' he explained,[5] and he prosecuted such studies indefatigably all his life.

His own account of his education shows an early fascination with 'things', natural and technological, combined with a certain disdain for traditional book-learning. 'Nature is the best Guide, & the best Paterne: 'tis better to copie nature than Bookes: as the best Painters imitate nature, not copies,' he claimed,[6] and he quoted several scientist friends, Hobbes, Petty, Wren and Hooke, all of whom told him that if they had read as much as other men, they would have known no more.[7] It is symptomatic that in later life Aubrey recalled that he found a flint of liver colour when he was learning to read,[8] and that as a schoolboy he had been interested in water stained blue by marl in ditches,[9] although he claimed that his 'not very much care for grammar' was due to the fact that although he had 'apprehension enough', 'my memorie not tenacious'.[10] 'I my selfe learn't by the Examples in, not by the Rules, of the Grammar,' he recalled;[11] he noted that although his 'witt was alwaies working', it was 'not adroict for verse';[12] and though he read various Latin authors during his adolescence, it was English translations like Sandys' *Ovid* and Holland's *Livy* that he found the most 'wonderfull helpe to my phansie'.[13]

At Oxford he was still ill at ease with the traditional academic system. He remembered gratefully the kindness of Ralph Bathurst, a Fellow of his college, Trinity, and a life-long friend, who let him turn over and peruse his 'excellent Collection of well chosen Bookes: of all kinds of Learning', which 'made me first in love with Bookes'.[14]

---

[1] *B.L.*, I, 43.    [2] MS A 2, 18v.    [3] *B.L.* I, 36.    [4] *B.L.* II, 307.    [5] T.G.c.24, 23.
[6] MS A 10, 95.    [7] Ibid., 96b.    [8] MS A I, 79.    [9] Ibid., 9.    [10] *B.L.* I, 36.
[11] MS A 10, 168.    [12] *B.L.* I, 37.    [13] *B.L.* I, 36. Cf. MS A 5, 91.

[14] MS A 10, 97. Aubrey echoes his view of the 'good' fellows like Bathurst in his autobiography: 'was much made of by the fellowes; had their learned conversation, lookt on bookes, musique' (*B.L.* I, 38: cf. ibid., I, 37 'Lookt through Logique and some Ethiques'). Books that Aubrey bought while at Oxford in the 1640s include mathe-

1. One of Aubrey's drawings of Easton Pierse, from his *Designatio de Easton-Piers*

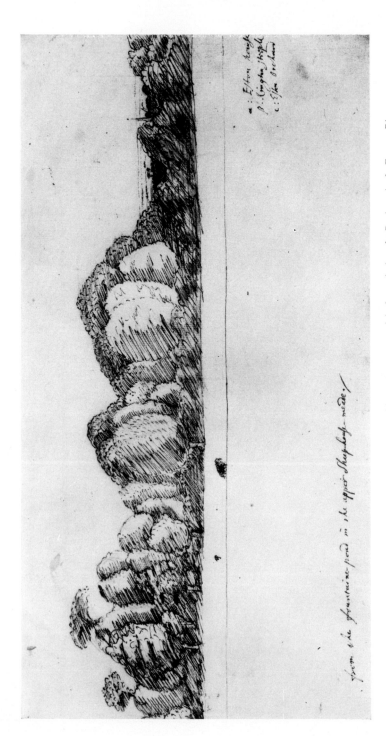

2. View 'from the fountaine-pond in the upper Sheep-house-meade', from Aubrey's *Designatio de Easton-Piers*

3. View of Easton Pierse, from Aubrey's *Designatio de Easton-Piers*

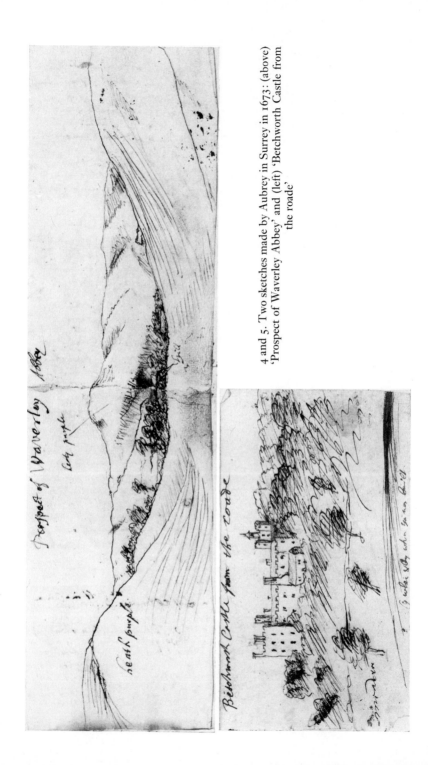

4 and 5. Two sketches made by Aubrey in Surrey in 1673: (above) 'Prospect of Waverley Abbey' and (left) 'Betchworth Castle from the roade'

In general, the 'currish fellowes' refused to provide such facilities, and they were, moreover, 'generally ignorant in Arithmetique and Geometrie'.[1] They read the young men logic 'and then exercised them to dispute on dry Logicall Questions, which nauseate the young Gentlemen, & make 'em loath it'; so that they ended 'with the learning (if any at all) of a Benedictine Monke; with some Scholastique Canting'.[2] It is scarcely surprising that Aubrey early felt the appeal of the new philosophy of Francis Bacon, whose *Essays* had 'first opened my understanding as to moralls',[3] and when he wrote a history of seventeenth-century learning, it was Bacon's influence that he placed first in importance.

Learning in the century from Erasmus' time to his own boyhood had been, Aubrey considered, 'Pædantry, i.e. criticall learning, Mathematics & experimentall philosophy was not known: and Morall Philosophy understood not as by men, but boyes. The conversation and habitts of those times viz. Q⟨ueen⟩ Eliz⟨abeth⟩ & K⟨ing⟩ James accordingly stiffe & starch't as their bands & square beards. Their stile pedantique, stuff't with Latin, & Greeke sentences, like their Clothes, which was sattin doublet cutt, under that another colourd taffata cutt, under that a 3d taffata.[4] Gravity was then taken for Wisdome; a steddy gate, a well sett falling ruffe, a spade beard & gold girdle, gave a venerable estimate in those dayes. 'Tis true, (and we must with thanks acknowledge it) that in those dayes were very learned men in their kinds; & that they were the πρόδομοι,[5] they made the rough waies smooth and removed the rubbish; but yet that was but a sad, & slavish labour; they understood not mankind aright; and though then it was the fashion vehemently to fall upon the church of Rome, yet these

---

matical works by Recorde (Worcester College, Oxford, E x 5) and Euclid (Worcester College MS 5.4), astronomical ones by Michaelis (Worcester College E x 9) and Blaeu (Worcester College E x 2), and poems by Beaumont (Ashmole 1663), Corbet (Ashmole E 15) and Denham (*Cooper's Hill*: Ashmole 1672(7) ).

[1] MS A 10, 97, 143.   [2] Ibid., 143.

[3] *B.L.* I, 36. He here claims that he met the *Essays* accidentally among his mother's books, but at ibid., II, 307 he claims that he was advised to read them by Wodenote.

[4] Aubrey identifies the source of his imagery by quoting this couplet from Butler's *Hudibras*, Part I, Canto I, in the margin:   'Twas English cutt on Greek and Latin
Like Fustian heretofore on Sattin'.

[5] Sic: Aubrey means πρόδρομοι, 'fore-runners'. Aubrey's Greek was always rather shaky, and even in his Latin he often used curious forms, suggesting some lack of mastery of the language: it is hardly surprising that he had to find someone to translate his life of Hobbes into Latin (cf. below, p. 78).

men were as superstitious, but did not know it. *Things* were not
then studied. My Lord Bacon first led that dance.' 'The searching
into Naturall knowledge began but since or about the death of
King Charles the first,' he considered; previously ' 'twas held a
strange presumption for ⟨any⟩ man to attempt improvement of any
knowledge whatsoever, even of Husbandry it selfe; they thought
it not fitt to be wiser then their fathers & not good manners to be
wiser then their neighbours; and a sin to search into the wayes of
nature wheras Solomon saies tradidit mundum Disputationibus
Rerum', 'he gave up the world to investigate things'.[1]

He dated this change to 'about the yeare 1649', because 'Experimentall Philosophy was then first cultivated by a Club in Oxon',[2]
and his own active involvement with the scientific movement went
back to this very dawn. Trinity, his college, numbered amateurs of
science among its Fellows, some of whom were associated with
William Harvey, with whom Aubrey later became intimate.[3] One
of them, John Lydall, kept Aubrey informed about developments
in science there and elsewhere in the university after he had gone
down.[4] They ranged from the chemical experiments of Thomas
Willis[5] to the investigations of Petty and Wren, apart from 'some
other inventions & experiments wee have made in Natural philosophy
which would bee too tædious to relate'.[6] The letters also show that
even after retiring to Wiltshire Aubrey continued to develop the
scientific studies that he must have begun at Oxford. Like the
scientists there, he was interested in astronomy, navigation and
applied mathematics, in *aurum fulminans* and in investigating the
nature of combustion, and in trying out the experiments published
by the Jesuit scientist, Athanasius Kircher.[7] Aubrey clearly carried

[1] MS A 3, 18v. In his edition of the *Wiltshire Antiquities* (Devizes, 1862), Jackson
unfortunately fails to print more than short extracts from these additions to Aubrey's
preface (one marginal addition is dated 'now about 1680'; the original preface was
dated 1670 (MS A 3, 11av) ).

[2] MS A 1, 5. On the background to this view, cf. C. Webster, 'The origins of the
Royal Society', *History of Science* VI (1967), 106 f.

[3] On Aubrey's friendship with Harvey, see *B.L.* I, 295 f. and Sir Geoffrey Keynes,
*Harvey Through John Aubrey's Eyes* (Harveian oration, London, 1958). The prescription
quoted by Keynes on p. 10 is in the Bodleian library, MS A 21, 107. MS A 13, 277v
and MS A 21, 112 also concern Harvey's medical advice to Aubrey.

[4] Cf. R. G. Frank, jr., 'John Aubrey, F.R.S., John Lydall, and science at Commonwealth Oxford', *Notes and Records of the Royal Society* XXVII (1973), 193 f., which prints
extracts from Lydall's letters.

[5] Lydall-Aubrey, 23 Jan. 1648/9, MS A 12, 294.

[6] Id., 27 May 1651, ibid., 308.

[7] On these and other interests and their background, cf. Frank, art. cit.

out experiments at home, for he requested chemicals for them from Lydall,[1] who desired him 'to write what new discovery or experiment you shall chance to make or meet with in your studys'.[2]

Aubrey continued to prosecute scientific studies in the 1650s. In 1650 he participated in the pioneering experiments on blood transfusion made at the nearby village of Kilmington by Francis Potter, rector of the parish and an amateur scientist,[3] whose mechanical inventions and scientific speculations never ceased to fascinate Aubrey, from the time he first met him at Oxford in 1649. 'I never was with him but I learn't, and always tooke notes,' he later recalled,[4] and frequent citations of Potter's views and experiments in his *Naturall Historie of Wiltshire* and *Adversaria Physica* bear witness to his admiration for Potter's scientific work.[5] Throughout the 1650s Aubrey carried on a well-informed correspondence with Potter on such subjects as anatomy,[6] logarithms[7] and mathematical instruments;[8] they also discussed the works of scientists like Sir Kenelm Digby, the Royalist natural philosopher,[9] and John Wilkins,[10] 'the principall reviver of experimentall philosophy' in Interregnum Oxford, when he was Warden of Wadham College.[11]

Books that Aubrey owned and annotated at this time suggest some interest in medical matters, notably a copy of Sanctorius Sanctorius' *Ars de Statica Medicina*, which he obtained in 1653,[12] and a copy of Willis's extremely influential *De Fermentatione* which he acquired in 1658, evidently as soon as it was published,[13] though he

[1] Cf. id., 23 Jan. 1648/9, 20 Feb. 1648/9, 5 April 1649; ibid., 294, 296, 302.

[2] Id., 18 Sept. 1649, ibid., 304.

[3] Cf. C. Webster, 'The origins of blood transfusion: a reassessment', *Medical History* XV (1971), 387 f.

[4] *B.L.* II, 165.

[5] Cf. below, p. 98. It is symptomatic that among the objects that Aubrey gave to the Ashmolean at the end of his life were a pair of dividing compasses, a quadrant and an agate haft that clouded over in a strange manner that he had had from Potter (cf. A-L, 21 April 1691, MS A 5, 2, and 19 March 1695/6, A. 1829, 13). On the agate haft, which Aubrey showed to Harvey, cf. Potter-Aubrey, 8 Nov. 1655 and 8 May 1656; MS A 13, 150, 152.

[6] Potter's letters to Aubrey are in MS A 13, 141 f. and *B.L.* II, 166 f. Aubrey's to Potter do not survive, but his active interest in anatomy is shown by the fact that he sent Potter a surgeon's lancet (*B.L.* II, 166). Cf. Potter-Aubrey, 17 Nov. 1652, MS A 13, 144, which speaks of an experiment mentioned by Aubrey.

[7] Potter-Aubrey, 29 April 1654, 29 Nov. 1654; MS A 13, 148, 149.

[8] Id., 23 May 1653, 29 Nov. 1654, 8 May 1656; ibid., 146, 149, 152.

[9] Id., 3 Oct. 1653, ibid., 147.  [10] Id., 10 April 1651, ibid., 141-2.

[11] *B.L.* II, 301.  [12] Now Wood 850.

[13] Now Ashmole D 65. Aubrey inscribed his copy 1658, though the publication date on the title-page is 1659.

had 'much commended' it in 1656, presumably after seeing it in manuscript.[1] His notes indicate his interest in fevers and their cures (partly for autobiographical reasons) and in the life-giving properties of substances and environments, preoccupations that evidently owed something to the interests of the Oxford scientists of the Interregnum, and perhaps also something to the influence of the scientific views of Bacon.[2]

In 1652 Aubrey met Samuel Hartlib, the social and religious reformer, whose concerns ranged from eschatology to the improvement of agriculture, technology and education.[3] Hartlib found Aubrey 'a very witty man and a mighty favourer and promoter of all Ingenious and Verulamian designes',[4] and Aubrey was evidently fascinated by Hartlib's practical scientific programme which could be seen as the successor to Bacon's, although he showed no enthusiasm for Hartlib's chiliasm. A surviving letter from Hartlib to Aubrey apparently covers the ground they had in common: he mentioned his 'Office of Address' scheme; he told Aubrey about a piece by Bacon never yet in print; and he 'very heartily' joined him in 'all your wishes prayers and endeavours for the advancement of science truly so called'.[5] It is through Hartlib that we know that Aubrey was about to write a biography of Bacon in 1655—'I wish he may do it to the life,' he told a correspondent[6]—and it was presumably for this that Aubrey made lengthy notes about Bacon's house at Gorhambury in 1656.[7] Indeed, Bacon's importance for Aubrey is symbolised by the fact that this visit provided the model for the decoration of the rooms of the educational establishment

---

[1] Hartlib, *Ephemerides*, 1656. I am indebted to Dr Charles Webster for transcriptions of this and other references to Aubrey in the Hartlib MSS in Sheffield University Library, which are quoted here with the kind permission of their owner, Lord Delamere. They are printed in G. H. Turnbull, 'Samuel Hartlib's acquaintance with John Aubrey', *Notes and Queries* CXCV (1950), 31 f.

[2] On Aubrey's indebtedness to Bacon and others, see below, pp. 97–8. In general the surviving hints of Aubrey's interests at this time show much overlap with his later interests, examined in Chapter II, but they are somewhat biased towards the interests of his friends, particularly in medicine.

[3] Cf. C. Webster, *Samuel Hartlib and the Advancement of Learning* (Cambridge, 1970).

[4] *Ephemerides*, 1652.

[5] Hartlib-Aubrey, 8 March 1652/3, MS A 12, 155. It also mentions Aubrey's promise of information on Potter.

[6] Hartlib-Worthington, 12 Dec. 1655 and 10 March 1655/6, in J. Crossley *ed.*, *The Diary and Correspondence of Dr John Worthington*, I (Chetham Society, 1847), 68–9, 82. Cf. *Ephemerides*, 1655.

[7] *B.L.* I, 78f.

that he projected after the Restoration, in which Bacon's influence is constantly apparent.[1]

The Royal Society was founded in 1660. It 'haz been a Ferment to the Inventive heads of the world,' wrote Aubrey: 'by this way, Knowledge will make a greater shoote in 10 yeares then it did before in an hundred'.[2] He was elected a member early in 1663,[3] and throughout the rest of his life he attended its meetings, often contributing to their discussions on a wide range of scientific topics, from astronomy to medicinal waters.[4] Like other active members, Aubrey carried out administrative tasks like auditing accounts[5] and supervising the election of officers;[6] he was also a member of the Georgical committee,[7] and in 1674 he was engaged in cataloguing the Society's Repository.[8] Such was his prominence in the Society that he considered standing as secretary after Henry Oldenburg's death in 1677;[9] and though nothing came of this, early in 1678 he was in a position to send John Ray a letter 'conteining a proposition concerning the Secretaryship of the Royall Society'.[10]

Aubrey's central position in the scientific circles of his time is also illustrated by his residence for several years at Gresham College with Robert Hooke, curator of experiments to the Royal Society

---

[1] MS A 10, 125. Cf. the fact that Bacon's prayers were to be used (ibid., 128–9) and all his works were to be in the library (ibid., 105).

[2] MS A 3, 18v.

[3] He was proposed as candidate by Walter Charleton (an 'old & faithfull friend' of Aubrey: A-W, 27 Jan. 1671/2, F 39, 163) on 24 Dec. 1662, was elected on 7 Jan. 1662/3 and was admitted on 21 Jan. (Birch, *History*, I, 166, 172, 179).

[4] See below, p. 96.

[5] Birch, *History*, I, 329, 336 (1663), II, 123, 130 (1666), III, 325 (1676); Copy Journal Books of the Royal Society, VII, 149 (1688), VIII, 83 (1691) (I am indebted to John Buchanan-Brown for transcripts of the entries relating to Aubrey in these).

[6] 'Scrutator for Elections': Birch, *History*, IV, 337 (1684); cf. III, 442 (1678) when he inspected the proceedings of the secretaries, and also Hooke, *Diary*, 331 (30 Nov. 1677).

[7] Birch, *History*, I, 407 (1664).

[8] Ibid., III, 159 (1674) mentions that Aubrey was requested to assist with various tasks, including cataloguing the collections. Cf. A-W, 31 March 1674, F 39, 261v, where he claims to be writing the catalogue of the repository 'according to that incomparable Method of Dr Wilkins Philos⟨ophical⟩ Grammar, which will hardly be finished by the beginning of May'. The method referred to was presumably the scheme of classification worked out as a basis for the universal language; according to Sprat (*History*, 251), Hooke had already begun cataloguing the repository in this way. In his letter to Petty of 17 July 1675 (see above, p. 32, n. 6) Aubrey implied that he had completed the catalogue except for making a fair copy.

[9] Hooke, *Diary*, 311 (9 Sept. 1677): 'Aubery will stand for Secretary'.

[10] Ray-Aubrey, 3 March 1677/8, MS A 13, 169. Hooke, *Diary*, 319 (10 Oct. 1677) contains this puzzling reference: 'Aubery undertook for correspondence which the J. Hoskins's caballd against'.

and one of the most fertile and original scientific thinkers of his day.[1] Aubrey is frequently mentioned in Hooke's diary, often as a member of coffee-house discussion groups; and though these may sometimes have been rather unintellectual affairs, where they 'laught . . . heartily'[2] as they helped themselves to claret,[3] on other occasions they were as seriously scientific as meetings of the Royal Society—indeed on some occasions they formed a 'select clubb' within it.[4] The diary shows Aubrey joining Hooke in observing eclipses,[5] in proving 'the Resistance of air to be in duplicate to the velocity or rather in a musicall proportion',[6] and in discoursing about Newton's new hypothesis in 1675.[7]

It is also striking how many scientists Aubrey could number among his 'honourd and obligeing' friends,[8] though his acquaintance was wide among all classes of society. *Brief Lives* and other works show that he was more or less closely associated with all the prominent English scientists of his age, and his closest friends in the Restoration period included six of the most eminent of them. Apart from Hooke, Aubrey's 'Amici' included Hobbes, Petty and Seth Ward, Bishop of Salisbury, an eminent mathematician and patron of science. He was also very closely associated with John Pell, the famous mathematician, whom he often cited on mathematical and other subjects, and with Sir Christopher Wren, who, among his other interests, shared Aubrey's enthusiasm for natural history and antiquities.[9] Though he lacked some of their interests and

---

[1] See Margaret 'Espinasse, *Robert Hooke* (London, 1956), 118–20.

[2] A–W, 9 April 1679, F 39, 316: this was over a piece called *The Hue and Cry* that Wood sent Aubrey.

[3] Compare 24 April 1677, when they missed a comet, but the assembled company drank two bottles of claret (Hooke, *Diary*, 287).

[4] Hooke-Aubrey, 24 Aug. 1675, MS A 12, 186.

[5] Hooke, *Diary*, 235 (1 June 1676), 381 (18 Oct. 1678).

[6] Ibid., 106 (6 June 1674).

[7] Ibid., 200 (11 Dec. 1675). This was evidently Newton's theory of colours: cf. F. E. Manuel, *A Portrait of Isaac Newton*, 142.

[8] T.G.c.25, 47. This was of Sir Thomas Browne.

[9] On the 'Amici', see Powell, *John Aubrey and his Friends*, 248 f. I have invidiously singled out the most famous: but one might also include William Holder, author of *Elements of Speech*, and Wyld, Hoskyns and Long all had amateur scientific interests, while Potter and Lydall have been mentioned above. My addition of Pell and Wren to the list of Aubrey's intimate friends is based on my impression from the Aubrey MSS: the first four contemporaries whose lives Aubrey wrote when he began his book of lives in 1679/80 were Petty, Wren, Hooke and Pell (see below, p. 80) and he cites Hobbes, Petty, Wren and Hooke as a kind of survey of informed opinion in his *Idea* (e.g. MS A 10, 96b).

developed others that they did not share, Aubrey's respect for the views of these eminent friends is clear, and he frequently quoted them, both on specific points, and also to bolster his own opinion on general issues with what was a genuine consensus of the most advanced scientific opinion of his day.

The new science appealed to Aubrey for its clarity and usefulness. He admired Hobbes for his 'great felicity in well defining';[1] he advocated the study of 'Mr Hobbes way of thinking. also Mr Pells, & des Cartes', and he urged that boys should get used 'to thinke & contemplate, the not doeing wherof hath made the witt stand, & hindred the progresse of knowledge till lately'.[2] He was especially fascinated by mathematics: 'Arithmetique, & Geometrie,' he explained, 'are the Keys, that open unto us all Mathematicall and Philosophicall Knowledge: and by consequence (and indeed) all other Knowledge, sc. by teaching us to reason aright, and carefully, not to conclude hastily and not to make a false steppe'.[3] He cited Bacon as well as Hobbes in support of this view,[4] and 'the Algebraicall method of Monsieur Des Cartes' could even, he hoped, be used to solve law-cases.[5] His faith in the potentialities of mathematics was immense: 'Staticks, Musique, Fencing, Architecture, Bitts of Bridles, &c are all reducible to the Lawes of Geometrie,' he noted. 'Nay ⟨Peter⟩ Gunning Bishop of Ely, proved by Geometrie that there was a Deitie'.[6]

Aubrey's interest in mathematics as an aid to clear thought was characteristic of his century, and he showed no interest in the more old-fashioned and occult concern with mystical numerology of sixteenth-century thinkers.[7] This is further illustrated by his views on music and its relationship with mathematics. He believed that 'there are left undiscovered to us yet (no doubt) very curious, and usefull things that may be elicited from Harmonicall Proportions:

---

[1] Aubrey-Locke, Shrove Tuesday 1672/3, printed in Maurice Cranston, *John Locke: a biography* (London, 1957), 152.

[2] MS A 10, 169v.    [3] Ibid., 8.    [4] Ibid., 169v.

[5] Ibid., 75. He was hoping to insert 'Solutions of some easie Lawe-cases' by this method into his *Idea*, but the friend who was to provide them died.

[6] MS A 10, 41.

[7] Though John Buchanan-Brown has suggested that the section in Aubrey's *Miscellanies* on day fatality should be seen in the tradition of Dee's mathematics (*Notes and Records of the Royal Society* XXVIII (1974), 185), the connection is very tenuous, and it is in any case significant that this section is mainly composed of the work of others.

fitt for the learned to make search of',[1] and he even quoted Gilbert
Ironside, Bishop of Bristol, that the best way to convert the savage
Americans would be 'to winne them & mollifie theire minds with
Musick'.[2] But on the only occasion on which he went beyond such
vague speculations, his interest was not in the occult link between
number and musical harmony postulated by the neo-Platonists,
but in the attempts to reduce musical sounds to mathematical
terms associated with thinkers like the French natural philosopher
Martin Mersenne:[3] among Aubrey's manuscripts is a transcript he
made in 1672–3 of a tract entitled *Musica* by Nicholas Mercator, a
German expert on chronometry and mathematics who was prominent in the early Royal Society, which gave a theoretical account of
concord and harmony in mathematical terms.[4]

The life-long importance of mathematics for Aubrey is symbolised by the series of 'Lives of our English Mathematical Writers'
that he compiled in 1690, using material that he had been collecting
for some years.[5] Though he regretted his own lack of an early
mathematical training,[6] he later mended this, and there is evidence
from the 1650s onwards of his discussion of mathematical problems
in correspondence and conversation with learned friends like
Lancelot Morehouse and Edward Davenant, both of them divines
with mathematical interests who lived near Aubrey's Wiltshire
home.[7] He spent many hours solving problems of geometry and
algebra, 'on horse back, and ⟨in⟩ the house of office'[8] or at greater
length—as in October 1672, when, bad weather keeping him
indoors, he was glad to 'divertise my selfe very pleasantly with
Algebra'.[9] A tangible witness to his activity survives in the library
of Worcester College, Oxford, to the forerunner of which, Gloucester
Hall, he gave forty printed books, most of them mathematical,[10]
and three manuscript volumes that he had filled between the 1650s

---

[1] MS A 10, 119.     [2] *Analecta*, 219x.

[3] Cf. A. C. Crombie, 'Mathematics, music and medical science', in *XIIe Congres
International d'Histoire des Sciences (Paris, 1968)*, Actes, I (B) (1971), 295 f.

[4] MS Aubrey 25.     [5] See below, p. 81.

[6] MS A 10, 28v: 'My Ignorance, and want of a good early mathematicall Education
makes me (perhaps) write this *Idea* more feelingly, than a more learned man would have
donne.'

[7] Cf. Davenant-Aubrey, 14 June 1661(?), MS A 12, 94; Morehouse-Aubrey, 15 Oct.
1670, ibid., 340; and some notes by Aubrey on MS A 13, 232v. The Worcester College
MSS illustrates his discussions by notes like '1st. March 1660. Probleme, from Dr.
Davenant' (MS 4.9; unpaginated).

[8] *B.L.* I, 42.     [9] A-W, 22 Oct. 1672, F 39, 190.     [10] See 'Aubrey's Library.'

and 1680s with arithmetical and algebraic calculations, and with treatises, cribs and hints that he had had from more expert mathematicians like John Collins, Edward Davenant, Nicholas Mercator, Sir Jonas Moore, John Pell and Sir Christopher Wren[1]—for Aubrey was modest about his mathematics, and claimed to be a pupil rather than an original thinker.

These manuscripts show some interest in pure mathematics, in solving problems as an intellectual exercise: pages and pages are devoted to finding square roots and mean proportionals, or to elementary algebraic problems like 'What number is that whose $\frac{1}{4}$ being multiplied by 5, and to the product if you adde 9, the summe will be 90',[2] while Aubrey's transcriptions of the works of his learned friends indicate concern about theoretical topics. But he quoted the sixteenth-century pedagogue Roger Ascham about the dangers of too much mathematics[3]—and he himself knew of the case of one Mr Austin, a pupil of the great mathematician William Oughtred, 'a most ingeniose man', who 'became mad by studying Algebra, laughed, & dyed'.[4] 'Mathematics applied,' he felt, on the other hand, 'according to Sir William Petty's method, does worke a contrary effect: it makes men most adroict & fitt for Businesse: it makes them to reason a-right, & to become Prudent: to be good Lawyers, & Soldiers: and 'tis cleare that ἀγηομετροί can never be so accomplisht of either kind'.[5]

Much of Aubrey's own mathematics was more or less explicitly practical. He wanted John Pell to 'Pelliare Oughtredismos', to write a commentary on William Oughtred's *Clavis Mathematicæ* (1631), an algebraic work that Aubrey used,[6] 'which would be of

---

[1] MS 4.9: 'Mr Nich⟨olas⟩ Mercator's Lessons to me, which are a good Commentary on Mr Oughtred's Clavis Mathem⟨aticæ⟩', Jonas Moore, *An Introduction to the Art of Species* (extracted from Barrow's *Euclide's Elements* (London, 1660) ) and material by Gunton, Collins, etc; MS 5.4: *Elementorum Euclidis Libri Tredecim* (London, 1620), Mercator, *Hypothesis Astronomica Nova* (London, 1664), Collins, *Doctrine of Decimal Arithmetick* (London, 1665), material by Pell, Mercator, Gunton, etc. and mathematical calculations by Aubrey; MS 5.5: Aubrey's transcription of Davenant, *Algebra Literalis*, with other mathematical notes, including material by Moore, Pell, Wren and Collins. Mathematical notes by Aubrey are also bound in Worcester College E π 1, John Kersey, *Elements of Algebra* (London, 1673) and there are a few MS notes by him in other printed books that he gave to the library.

[2] Esp. MS 5.4 (unpaginated); this quotation comes from the section entitled 'Algebra Literalis'.

[3] MS A 10, 41b.     [4] MS A 4, 104.

[5] MS A 10, 41b. For Petty's method, cf. his *Discourse of Duplicate Proportion* (1674). By ἀγηομετροί Aubrey means ἀγεωμέτρητοι.

[6] Cf. *B.L.* 1, 42 and Worcester College MS 4.9.

good use'[1] and he thought Edward Davenant's treatment of cyclical progression was 'of admirable use especially in Astronomie'.[2] Among the works he copied was 'A Discourse to prove that all Æquations may be solved by Tables' by John Collins;[3] another concerned compound interest and annuities;[4] and in his mathematical notes he devoted much space to calculating rates of commission and interest and to the reduction of one unit of measurement to another.[5] He was also interested in mathematical instruments, not least for surveying, from the 1650s until just before his death,[6] and he actually used them in his fieldwork, mapping the stone-circle at Avebury with a plane table and drawing it to a half-inch scale.[7]

This interest in clear and useful knowledge, combined with an almost paranoiac hatred of the useless obfuscation of traditional learning, forms the theme of Aubrey's *Idea of Education of Young Gentlemen*. Though it has much in common with other progressive schemes of the time for making education more pleasant and more useful,[8] and, like many of them, was never implemented, Aubrey valued this work above all his others.[9] He wrote it in its present form in the 1680s—its title-page is dated 1683/4[10]—but many of its ideas are already present in an earlier sketch dated 1669,[11] and

---

[1] MS 5.5, flyleaf.  [2] Ibid., 61v.

[3] Loosely inserted between ff. 73 and 74 of MS 5.5.

[4] 'Twelve problems' invented by Adam Martindale and submitted to the Royal Society by John Collins, transcribed on the leaves bound at the front of E π 1.

[5] MS 5.4, passim.

[6] Cf. above, p. 43. On the list of instruments in Aubrey's *Idea* (MS A 10, 109) and its context, see A. J. Turner, 'Mathematical instruments and the education of gentlemen', *Annals of Science* xxx (1973), 51 f. On Aubrey's later interest, note especially Lhwyd-Aubrey, 9 Jan. 1693/4, MS A 12, 251, which shows that he wanted a copy of Potter's quadrant made.

[7] Plate 11; cf. T.G.c.24, 25, 39v.

[8] For a useful survey of such ideas, cf. F. Watson, *The Beginning of the Teaching of Modern Subjects in England* (London, 1909).

[9] A-W, 22 Dec. 1688, MS A 12, 2v.

[10] MS A 10, 5. There are two short articles on Aubrey's *Idea*: W. J. Battersby, 'John Aubrey's "Idea of Education" ', *British Journal of Educational Studies* VII (1958), 50 f., and J. E. Stephens, 'John Aubrey's Idea of Education of Young Gentlemen', *Journal of Educational Administration and History* I (1968), 1 f. (much of it identical with the introduction to his *Aubrey on Education* (London, 1972)).

[11] *Idea Filioli seu Educatio Pueri*, now MS A 10, 162 f. This small paper-book was evidently formerly in Ashmole 1840 and was placed in MS A 10 in the last century. It is clearly dated 1669 (though some of the additions may be later), and it is less radical than the final version: it still assumes that after a private education up to the age of twelve the boys will be sent to Westminster (MS A 10, 168v), and it therefore devotes relatively more space to the boys' early education. J. E. Stephens, in his *Aubrey on*

several reflect attitudes that Aubrey had held longer still. 'A Method, very plaine, and practicable',[1] its detail extended even from the location and lay-out of the six schools that Aubrey planned throughout England and Wales to the character and salary of their 'Informators' and the precise content of each school library. He also outlined courses in all subjects he considered essential to adolescent education, from mathematics, grammar and logic, to rhetoric, ethics and law.

He was anxious that later generations should not suffer his own and his friends' harsh experiences as schoolboys, a motive underlying many of the more humane educational schemes of the period.[2] 'I very well remember, that excessive whipping when I was a little child, did make a convulsive pain in my tender braine, which doubtless did doe me a great deale of hurt,' he wrote,[3] frequently attacking old-fashioned schools for 'their tyrannicall beating, & disperiting of children, which many tender ingeniose children doe never recover again.'[4] The common method of teaching grammar was 'so long, tædious and præposterous, that it breakes the spirits of the fine tender ingeniose youths, and causes 'em perfectly to hate learning: and they are not to be blamed for it'.[5]

In his school such insensitive pedagogy was to be abandoned, and indeed one of his principal aims was to turn out well-balanced people. ' 'Tis a very ill thing to cross children: it makes them ill-natured: therefore let them not be crosst in things indifferent';[6] he would forbid whipping,[7] and 'youth should be indulged as to all lawfull Pleasures'.[8] The masters were to be understanding[9] and learning was to be made more humane and imaginative. ' 'Tis good to shew children all manner of rare Sights,' he thought, for 'they see Colours with other Eies, and heare Sounds with other Eares: all their Senses are more nice & subtile'.[10] Their curriculum was to make it easy 'to find to what kind of Learning their Genius's doe lead 'em',[11] and 'they must be enticed on by pleasure, & delight'.[12]

---

*Education*, interpolates sections of this earlier work at intervals into the main text of the *Idea*, though he gives no indication that he has done so. He is quite mistaken in calling it 'Aubrey's additions', as he does in the caption to his frontispiece, reproduced from MS A 10, 164.

[1] MS A 10, 145.

[2] Cf., for instance, Roger Ascham's *Scholemaster*, which Aubrey quotes several times in the *Idea*: e.g. MS A 10, 22, 25, 91, 152v.

[3] MS A 10, 89.  [4] Ibid., 7.  [5] loc. cit.  [6] Ibid., 89.  [7] Ibid., 137.

[8] Ibid., 118.  [9] Ibid., 11.  [10] Ibid., 118.  [11] Ibid., 96b.  [12] Ibid., 29a.

He would have them learn multiplication by making a table for
themselves by addition, explaining, 'This method is so easy, &
naturall that the childs tender understanding can comprehend it:
& 'tis a pleasure to him to see the demonstration of it: whereas
when he learnes it meerly by rote, he takes it upon Trust only, &
sees not the reason of it, & besides it will make a stronger impression on his tender memorie'.[1] Similarly, composition could be
taught by cutting up orations into sentences and having the boys
rearrange them,[2] and 'Greeke will insensibly steale upon them' by
studying Euclid in the original after first reading it in English.[3]

Needless to say, arithmetic and geometry, 'demonstrative,
delightfull, and usefull',[4] were to be the basis of teaching, and in
every section of the curriculum he advocated clarity through the
mathematically-based, analytic approach of Hobbes, Pell and
Descartes, from whose *Discourse on Method* he transcribed several
passages.[5] He thought extemporary epigrams mere 'Jot's and
quibbles', whereas 'the solving of a Mathematicall Probleme is
worth an hundred Epigrames',[6] and he quoted Hobbes that 'Distinctions are but Cobling': 'Let men *Define* well, and there will be no
need of Distinctions'.[7] Geometry was to be used to teach boys in
drawing to reduce objects to their basic shapes of cubes, circles and
triangles,[8] and in logic he recommended Pell's 'ratiocination by
Syllogisms', quoting him that 'let the Question be but well-stated,
and it will worke of it selfe'.[9] In law, he suggested that the boys
should use Descartes' method to criticise the reports of the great
Jacobean legist Sir Edward Coke, adding 'I doubt not, but there
would be discovered severall paralogisms',[10] and he was eager for
legal reform both here and elsewhere. He quoted John Selden, a
more radical lawyer of the early seventeenth century, that 'the
Reports alone, teach not a man Lawe',[11] arguing that the student's
approach should be analytical, not 'per fac simile',[12] and he proudly
claimed that he had suggested Hobbes' *Dialogue of the Common
Laws* to him: 'now every one will doe him the Right to acknowledge
he is rare for definitions & the Lawyers building on old fashiond
maximes (some right some wrong) must needs fall into severall

---

[1] Ibid., 29.      [2] Ibid., 23.      [3] Ibid., 38.      [4] Ibid., 29.      [5] Ibid., 52–3.
[6] Ibid., 96a.      [7] Ibid., 50.      [8] Ibid., 40a.
[9] Ibid., 51, 54v. There are notes by Aubrey on Pell's method of ratiocination in
Worcester College MS 5.5.
[10] MS A 10, 69.      [11] Ibid., 68.      [12] Ibid., 69–70.

paralogismes; upon this consideration I was earnest with him to consider these things'.[1]

But clarity was only a means to an end, and that was the acquisition of learning useful to the young men in later life. In each subject, Aubrey quickly moved from theoretical strictures to practical application. Mathematics would be handy for surveying, for measuring timber, for calculating household accounts and unmasking the dishonesty of bailiffs.[2] 'Mathematicall Prudence', to which he devoted a chapter,[3] was entirely concerned with rents, leases and other details of estate management, for after the age of twenty-five he expected this to take up most of the young men's time: 'Qui habet terras, habet guerras', 'he who has lands has wars'.[4] The *Idea* is full of warnings of the need for such practical knowledge, warnings that often seem poignantly autobiographical. Ethics, reading and philosophy led Aubrey on to discuss 'Mundane Prudence',[5] intended to prevent his pupils from being naively vulnerable in later life, and even card-playing and chess were justified because they could give them 'a foresight in the world'.[6]

Other recommendations were more practical still: Aubrey wanted the young men to travel in England and abroad to study husbandry,[7] and he justified chemistry as useful for making medicines,[8] while dancing 'makes them have a good Gate'.[9] He would even encourage boys to 'practise Drawing, Painting, Turning, Grinding of Glasses for Telescopes, Watchmaking &c: To which I will adde the *Tinneman*'s Trade, which is easily learn'd, & requires not above 3, or 4 Tooles: the use whereof is, that those that have Mechanicall heads will be able to make the Modells of their owne Ideas, and Inventions themselves'.[10] 'Knowledge is a sort of Riches, wherof there can be no Diription,' he explained, and by such means he hoped to make them 'Fabri suae fortunae', 'forgers of their own destiny', like 'that noble & ingeniose Knight', his 'ever honored Friend', Sir William Petty.[11]

Aubrey's *Idea* owes much to the anti-traditionalist and practical educational theories championed by Hartlib in the Interregnum,[12] though he had read widely among educational theorists of the

---

[1] A-W, 3 Feb. 1672/3, F 39, 196v. He gave Hobbes Bacon's *Maxims of the Law* 'in order to it'.
[2] MS A 10, 34, 38.    [3] Ibid., 35af.    [4] Ibid., 139.    [5] Ibid., 81f.
[6] Ibid., 121.    [7] Ibid., 79. f. and 117.    [8] Ibid., 144. Cf. 120.    [9] Ibid., 121.
[10] Ibid., 120.    [11] Ibid., 143.
[12] Cf. C. Webster, *Samuel Hartlib and the Advancement of Learning*.

previous century and his own.[1] Hartlib had given him a copy of his *True and Readie Way to Learne the Latine Tongue* in 1654,[2] and Aubrey used this in the *Idea*, as well as the similar writings of J. A. Comenius, the great Czech educationalist,[3] and such members of Hartlib's circle as John Dury,[4] Ezerel Tonge,[5] Petty[6] and Milton, from whose *Of Education* he made several pages of notes.[7] Pell, whose influence on the work was crucial,[8] had also been associated with Hartlib. The *Idea* lacked Hartlib's radical social ideals, however, for Aubrey intended to educate young aristocrats, 'the Pillars and Ornaments' of Government, 'the Atlases that beare-up the weight of it',[9] to qualify them 'for Lawyers, Ambassadors, Commanders by Land or Sea, Architects, Sollicitors, Chymists, Surveyors, &c:'.[10] In his view 'Youths of this Qualitie, ought to be brought-up among their Equalls': 'A Cobblers sonne may have a good Witt, and may perchance be a good man; but he would not

[1] Aubrey mentions a very large number of educational works in the *Idea*, particularly 'The Librarie' (MS A 10, 98af.). His citations in his *Idea Filioli seu Educatio Pueri* perhaps give some idea of the works he admired at a formative stage in his educational writing: he cited the educational theories of Charron (ibid., 162), Dury (165, 167), Keckerman (164v), Montaigne (167) and others; he hoped to annex the 'Admonitions' of Cordier and Vives (164v: cf. M. Cordier, *Principia Latine Loquendi, Scribendique* (London, 1575), A5v-A8: Aubrey's copy, with his own pencil markings, Ashmole A 39); and he recommended the textbooks of Comenius (164v, 165, 167), Cordier (164v, 167, 167v), Dugrès (167v), etc. He knew of Cowley's *Proposition* (145), but he makes no reference to such earlier academy schemes as Gerbier's and Kynaston's. J. E. Stephens, *Aubrey on Education*, 160, draws attention to Aubrey's relative neglect of physical education in comparison with earlier academy proposals: but in MS A 10, 150, Aubrey makes it clear that he considered 'robust exercise's' like the quasi-martial pursuits advocated by Milton 'better and more *timely* learnt at the Academies, the Camp, or Artillery-ground'. His scheme also lacks provision for the teaching of foreign languages, unlike, e.g., Gerbier's *Interpreter of the Academie* (London, 1648); he thought the young men could learn them during their subsequent travels (MS A 10, 45).
[2] This is bound with other educational tracts in MS Aubrey 22: Aubrey's marginal markings show how he read them and digested their anti-traditional sentiments. He quotes the *True and Readie Way* in MS A 10, 21.
[3] Esp. MS A 10, 90, 92; and see note 1, above.
[4] See note 1, above.
[5] MS Aubrey 22 contains tracts by him on grammar and punctuation, and Chapter 3 of the *Idea* comprises his 'Introduction to the Latin tongue'.
[6] MS Aubrey 22(8) is a copy of his *Advice of Mr W. P. to Mr Samuel Hartlib* (London, 1648), quoted in MS A 10, 39, 120.
[7] Esp. MS A 10, 147 f.
[8] Many recommendations of books, and other facts and theories, in the *Idea* are cited by Aubrey as Pell's, whose influence on Aubrey's educational thought was evidently great. It is possible that Aubrey's title was deliberately copied from Pell's *Idea of Mathematics*, of which Aubrey sent a copy to Boyle in 1665—Aubrey-Boyle, 15 March 1665, Boyle, *Works*, VI, 544.
[9] MS A 10, 7.    [10] Ibid., 144.

be proper for a friend to a person of Honour'.[1] The *Idea* even lacked some of the most radical of educational views of the Restoration: Aubrey would not have entirely abandoned the study of Latin or the practice of declamation, unlike some theorists he quoted.[2]

Even so the *Idea* was too radical for some. Aubrey's friend, Andrew Paschall, rector of Chedzoy in Somerset, wondered 'whether it may not be most advisable to make no Mention of Schools and Universities, and particularly of their Defects; they are a Sort of Men that are very sensible and tender'.[3] Aubrey was aware that the *Idea* would be unpopular with the Universities.[4] 'The Clergy & Pædants will never endure it. I should irritare crabrones ⟨stir up a hornet's nest⟩, to publish it,' he told John Evelyn, the diarist,[5] and John Ray assured him that it would give offence to many.[6]

But Aubrey was used to being considered one of the intellectual *avant garde* of his day. He was proud to be a friend of William Harvey, who told him that he fell in practice because of conservative distrust after his great discovery.[7] He was a member of the 'Rota', the republican group organised by James Harrington, author of *Oceana*, in the Interregnum.[8] He was honoured to be a Fellow of the Royal Society, even when it was unpopular among conservatives—just as he was glad to be a natural philosopher although 'credit there was none; for it getts the contempt of a mans Neighbours'.[9] Above all, he gloried in the intimate friendship of Thomas Hobbes, despite the 'Hunting of Leviathan' which meant that Aubrey's correspondents wrote to him asking him to get them copies of Hobbes' works before they were burnt by the public hangman.[10] He considered his 'Life of Mr Thomas Hobbes of

[1] Ibid., 10.

[2] Newton of Ross had abandoned Latin (ibid., 8) and 'Sir W. Petty saies, that twenty men are enough to doe all the Latin-businesse of England' (96a). But Aubrey disagreed (loc. cit.), as he did (113) with Hooke, who 'sayeth, that Declayming is of no use but only in the Universities' (112v); Wren agreed with Aubrey (loc. cit.).

[3] Paschall-Aubrey, 25 Aug. 1684, printed in Rawlinson's edition of Aubrey's *Surrey* (London, 1718–19), I, xv.

[4] A-W, 22 Dec. 1688, MS A 12, 2v.

[5] Aubrey-Evelyn, 15 May 1692, bound in Bodleian Thorn-Drury e.11, a copy of the 1890 edition of Aubrey's *Miscellanies*. Ray used the same phrase in the letter cited in the next note, so Aubrey was presumably echoing him.

[6] Ray-Aubrey, n.d., MS A 13, 180.    [7] *B.L.* I, 300.    [8] Cf. *B.L.* I, 289 f.

[9] MS A 1, 6.

[10] Hoskyns-Aubrey, 12/22 July 1661, MS A 12, 190. Cf. S. I. Mintz, *The Hunting of Leviathan*.

Malmesbury' one of his most important works, though aware that 'the University Doctors would not like it'.[1] He wanted to give his copy of the 'so formidable' *Leviathan*[2]—'which I much value'[3]—to New Inn Hall at Oxford,[4] although Anthony Wood attacked this gesture: 'Do you think that that is a book for young students to study in? No, rather to make them Hobbists, & confound them.'[5]

Aubrey's radicalism is reflected in his religious views, for these were rationalist and anti-traditional, not unlike Hobbes', to whom they doubtless owed something.[6] He distrusted religious controversy—'I shall be well enough contented to let the Fathers be thumbed by the Divines,' he told Wood.[7] In his view, 'your Genevists &c: are as superstitious as the Romans', and he regretted that 'we have amongst us now so much Saving faithe, that justice & charity, are out of fashion'.[8] He quoted Harrington 'that if we endeavour to goe an inch above Vertue, we doe fall an ell below it. This, as to the Enthusiasts & Phanatiques',[9] and he had no sympathy for the Puritans, calling the Interregnum 'the hypocriticall times'.[10] Quoting Robert Sanderson, Bishop of Lincoln, that 'what ever does tend to the quieting of the mind & contemplation, tends to Devotion', he added, 'quod N.B. contrary to the Presbyterians & Fanaticks'.[11] He likewise criticised 'that super-zeale in the Canon Lawe' which made the Catholics refuse to let alone Protestants buried at Limerick during the Civil War on the characteristic ground that it was 'too inhumane'.[12] And in his virulent anti-clericalism, he agreed with Dryden that 'in all Religions Priest-craft is the same',[13] dismissing the priesthood with: 'I wonder how they doe, to pick out such dunces'.[14]

He expounded his ethical and religious views in the sections on these topics in the *Idea of Education*; though he wrote a complete book on this subject, *Hypothesis Ethicorum & Scala Religionis*,

---

[1] A-T, 1 June 1693, T. 25, 49v.
[2] *B.L.* I, 334. Aubrey in fact wrote 'so formidable and ...', but never inserted a second adjective.
[3] A-W, St Anne's Day 1682, F 39, 368v.   [4] A-W, 4 Feb. 1690/1, F 39, 414.
[5] Wood-Aubrey, 15 Sept. 1694, T. 456a, 48.
[6] He also quoted Lord Herbert of Cherbury in this context (MS A 10, 45).
[7] A-W, 14 May 1673, F 39, 206v.   [8] A-W, 17 Nov. 1670, F 39, 128v.
[9] MS A 10, 45.   [10] *B.L.* II, 77.   [11] *Gentilisme*, 158.   [12] *B.L.* II, 294.
[13] *Gentilisme*, 220.
[14] A-W, 22 May 1680, F 39, 340: this was in connection with unsuitable bequests by churchmen. Cf. above, p. 33, n. 4.

'The Foundation of Ethics and the Ladder of Religion',[1] or *Religio Naturalis*, as he called it on another occasion,[2] this is unfortunately lost. His attitude was typical of the eirenic and sceptical traditions of the time, attempting to strip down to essentials, to make as much as possible reasonable. He quoted Cicero's *De Natura Deorum* that 'Religio est Justitia nostra adversus Deum', 'Religion is our due return to God'.[3] The first rule that children in his school would be taught was 'Doe as you would be donne to';[4] in Aubrey's opinion, 'This little Rule is the Basis of Right Reason & Justice, and consequently all other vertues', and it may not be coincidental that it echoes Hobbes' summary of the Laws of Nature in *Leviathan*.[5] To this Aubrey would add 'a Rationall Catechisme', of which he cited examples, including Sir William Petty's,[6] and he thought that 'our Saviours Sermon on the Mount is, as it were the Quintessence of all distilled in an Alembic'.[7]

He also advocated a sort of natural theology, considering it 'a profound part of Religion to glorifie GOD in his Workes',[8] and alluding to this view by texts on the title-page of his *Naturall Historie of Wiltshire*.[9] He had evidently taken a similar line when, during the Interregnum, he had been involved in a quarrel between the brothers Francis and Hannibal Potter, who lived together at Kilmington Rectory while Hannibal was deprived of his Presidency of Trinity College, Oxford. Hannibal had disapproved of Francis' scientific pursuits because he thought it more important to devote time to the pursuit of Divine truth, and he quoted the Fathers about the dangers of neglecting 'the prime obiect of all knowledge'.[10] Aubrey, like Francis, had entirely disagreed, and he evidently cited Bacon in support of investigations of natural phenomena, dismissing those who distrusted them on religious grounds.[11] Yet Aubrey,

---

[1] It is described thus in the list of Aubrey's works that he drew up for Lhwyd in 1692 (MS A 5, 123v). It was a quarto.

[2] It appears thus in the list of his MSS deposited with Hooke in 1690 (T.G.c.24, 13v); the full title is *Religio Naturalis, or a Scale of the decay of the Christian Religion, with a prospect or foresight where it will settle*. Cf. also below, pp. 217, 220.

[3] MS A 10, 127. He changed 'Deos' to 'Deum'.    [4] Ibid., 132.

[5] *Leviathan*, ch. XVII, Hobbes, *Works*, III, 153. It also, of course, echoes *Matthew*, VII. 12.

[6] MS A 10, 132. Cf. *The Petty Papers* (ed. the Marquis of Lansdowne, London, 1927), I, 129–30.

[7] MS A 10, 45.    [8] MS A 1, 5.    [9] Ibid., 12.

[10] H. Potter-Aubrey, 26 May 1653, MS A 13, 162.

[11] Cf. id., 3 Aug. 1653, ibid., 163. There also appear to have been personal tensions between the brothers: cf. F. Potter-Aubrey, 23 May 1653, ibid., 146.

like others at the time who argued similarly, was no nascent Deist. His schoolboys were to 'make a kind of Theologie of their own, out of their Observations' not only 'of GOD's wonderful Workes' but also 'of his miraculous preservation of some persons; of their owne particular deliverances from Dangers',[1] and they were to study not only a 'Rationall Catechisme' but also 'God's Judgements upon Oppressors' to see how 'Perjury, & sacrilege goes not unpunished in this Life'.[2] His tolerant, rational but fideistic creed was perhaps closest to Sir Thomas Browne's in *Religio Medici*, the book 'which first opened my understanding', as Aubrey wrote in his auto-biography,[3] but Hobbes and others had religious views of a similarly 'fideist-sceptical' kind.[4]

Aubrey was more radical in his views on the geological history of the world, which was much discussed at this time[5] and which is significant in this connection because of its dangerous overlap with biblical authority. The most famous work on the subject was Thomas Burnet's *Sacred Theory of the Earth* (1681, et seq.), which sought to reconcile a mechanistic account of the formation of the earth with the narrative of the creation and Noah's flood in *Genesis*. But though Aubrey considered the work 'ingeniose'[6] and read through it carefully,[7] his own ideas were more heterodox. In a chapter entitled 'An Hypothesis of the Terraquious Globe' in his *Naturall Historie of Wiltshire*,[8] he gave a brief summary of the theory, advanced by Robert Hooke in a lecture to the Royal Society, that the present surface of the earth was formed by a series of earthquakes during its early history, and could not have been caused by the flood alone. He also considered that the world would 'goe out like a Comet',[9] and he quoted Pliny on the manner in which the increasingly 'ardent heat of the elementarie fire' was

---

[1] MS A 10, 115.

[2] Ibid., 133. He cited Plutarch's *De sera numinis vindicta* in this connection.

[3] *B.L.* I, 37.

[4] J. G. A. Pocock, 'Time, history and eschatology in the thought of Thomas Hobbes' in *Politics, Language and Time* (London, 1972), 192. Cf. W. B. Glover, 'God and Thomas Hobbes' in K. C. Brown *ed., Hobbes Studies*, 141 f. Others include Petty, as is revealed by the sections on religion in *The Petty Papers*, I, 116f.

[5] See F. C. Haber, *The Age of the World, Moses to Darwin* (Baltimore, 1959), ch. 11, and M. J. S. Rudwick, *The Meaning of Fossils* (London, 1972), ch. 11.

[6] MS A 1, 101.

[7] Aubrey's copy of the 1684 edition of the first part of Burnet's *Sacred Theory*, now Ashmole G 26, has many marginal markings.

[8] MS A 1, 87 f. See also below, pp. 222–3.   [9] MS A 1, 101.

already preparing for this by consuming 'that plentifull humour and moisture of naturall seed, that engendereth all things'.[1]

Geological views like these were offensive to John Ray and others, as Ray assured Aubrey when he read the *Naturall Historie of Wiltshire*, for many found it difficult to accept any theory which challenged 'the truth of the Letter of the Scripture'.[2] Aubrey, like others who proposed mechanistic theories of the origin of the world, did not intend to be atheistic—he had no doubt that 'when Providence destines the Ends, it orders the Means'.[3] But he admitted that 'it (indeed) does interfere with the 1 chap⟨ter⟩ of Genesis',[4] resolving the difficulty by quoting Paul's Epistle to Timothy that the scriptures were intended 'to make thee wise unto Salvation', adding, 'the Apostle doth not say, to teach naturall Philosophie'.[5] In this separation of the proper realms of faith and reason Aubrey was among the most advanced thinkers of his age. He was unusually radical even among these, however, in his view that 'the world is much older, than is commonly supposed', which he thought could be proved by stratigraphy;[6] for most contemporaries believed that biblical chronology gave an accurate estimate of the age of the world.[7] It is therefore not surprising that he cited the French divine, Richard Simon, who shocked contemporaries by illustrating the unreliability of the text of Holy Writ, to support his view that the Bible need not give a reliable account of the early history of the world.[8] It is also understandable that in his later years he was associated with John Toland, the Deist, whose works so much alarmed the orthodox, though Toland's *Christianity Not Mysterious* was published only in the year Aubrey died, and the extent of his knowledge of Toland's views is uncertain.[9]

---

[1] On the back fly-leaf of the first volume of a Latin edition of Pliny's *Natural History* that he owned, Ashmole D 19, Aubrey wrote 'Decay of the World. 421. lib VII: see the English transla⟨tion⟩', and on the inside of the back cover he copied the English translation of the passage (which is also marked on page 421 of this volume) from Holland's translation, presumably intending to incorporate it into one of his works.

[2] Ray-Aubrey, 27 Oct. 1691, MS A 1, 13.      [3] *Miscellanies*, 118.

[4] MS A 13, 174 (a note by Aubrey on the back of a letter from Ray of 22 Sept. 1691).

[5] MS A 1, 102.      [6] MS A 1, 100.      [7] Rudwick, *The Meaning of Fossils*, 68 f.

[8] MS A 1, 102. Though Aubrey quoted his view that the Church might be right while the Bible was wrong, I think that this was only with the implication that something could be anti-biblical without being irreligious. On Simon's views and their context, see L. I. Bredvold, *The Intellectual Milieu of John Dryden* (Michigan, 1956), 98 f.

[9] He borrowed the *Remaines of Gentilisme* in 1694 (A-L, 10 Oct. 1694, A. 1814, 117), and T.G.c.25, 5v shows that Aubrey sought his advice on what to omit from the

On these and similar subjects Aubrey always showed at least a superficial familiarity with the most up-to-date thought. He considered the treatise *Of the Law of Nature and Nations* (1672) by the great German legist Samuel von Puffendorf 'the best that ever was writt, or (perhaps) will ever be',[1] and it may be significant that William Fanshawe thought Aubrey a good person to ask how to get a copy of 'Puffendorfs booke of Naturall Religion'.[2] He recommended the works of Hobbes to Locke,[3] pronounced Locke's *Essay concerning Humane Understanding* the 'best Booke that ever was writt by *one* man' and hoped that Puffendorf would hear of it.[4] In 1693 he told Anthony Wood that he had 'read over Mr Locks book',[5] presumably either the *Essay* or *Some Thoughts concerning Education*, which had just been published, and he evidently talked to Robert Hooke about 'Locks book' at this time too.[6] In 1675 he had discussed Newton's theories with Hooke,[7] and in his *Idea of Education* he declared that the *Principia* was 'the greatest highth of Knowledge that humane nature has yet arrived to'.[8]

Equally characteristic was Aubrey's interest in the universal language schemes of this period; indeed in his *Idea* he coupled this with his religious views—'I would have them learn the Real Character and the Real Religion'.[9] Even in the 1650s Aubrey had been interested in projects for 'a common-language to bee written in ordinary characters' and 'a common or universal character',[10] and he had a related curiosity about shorthand.[11] He admired John

---

*Monumenta Britannica* (for which he provided information about Irish stone-circles: T.G.c.24, 78).

[1] MS A 10, 70. This echoes Locke, who thought the book 'the best book of that kind' (P. Laslett *ed.*, *Two Treatises of Government* (Cambridge, 1960), 74).

[2] Fanshawe-Aubrey, 7 Aug. 1691, MS A 12, 115. Aubrey quotes Fanshawe in *Gentilisme*, 133, but I know nothing else about him. The book was presumably *The Whole Duty of Man According to the Law of Nature*, of which an English translation was published in 1691.

[3] Aubrey-Locke, Shrove Tuesday 1672/3, M. Cranston, *John Locke*, 151–2.

[4] Aubrey-Locke, Shrove Tuesday 1693/4, Bodleian MS Locke c. 3, 62. Aubrey quoted this as Richard Blackbourne's view but made it clear that 'I am of his opinion'.

[5] A-W, 21 Oct. 1693, Wood F 51, 6.

[6] Hooke's *Diary*, Part II, 29 June 1693 (printed by R. T. Gunther in *Early Science in Oxford*, x ('The Life and Work of Robert Hooke', IV), 254): 'J. Auber about Locks book'.

[7] See above, p. 46.     [8] MS A 10, 56b.     [9] Ibid., 133.

[10] Hartlib, *Ephemerides*, 1653, 1652 (respectively). These were ideas of Francis Potter's.

[11] MS Aubrey 32 is a copy of Jeremiah Rich's shorthand New Testament, bought by Aubrey in 1669; Aubrey wrote out 'The Alphabet' in shorthand on one of the back fly-leaves.

Wilkins' *Essay Towards a Real Character, And a Philosophical Language* (1668), the classic exposition of such attempts, which Wilkins hoped, even if they failed to introduce a universal language that would be useful to merchants, divines and scientists, at least might begin a classification of things and notions which could 'prove the shortest and plainest way for the attainment of real Knowledge, that hath been yet offered to the World'.[1] Aubrey thought Wilkins' method 'incomparable',[2] and in the 1670s he was involved in attempts to 'compleat' the *Essay* made by a group of scholars, Hooke, Ray, Andrew Paschall, Francis Lodwick, a London merchant, and Thomas Pigott, a young Fellow of Wadham College, Oxford.[3] They hoped to improve both Wilkins' classification and his character, if not to develop the scheme towards the analysis of transcendental or general notions and thus make 'ratiocinations & demonstrations cleare & short and strong', as advocated by Seth Ward.[4] Aubrey's fascination with the project was typical of his eagerness to achieve clarity: concerning the reduction of notions to characters, he felt that these 'should proceed in the same method that notions doe of which they are the Signes. e.g. the Ch⟨aracter⟩ of Substance, ought to be the first & so secundum Log⟨icam⟩ ⟨secondly, logic⟩ & Transcendents'. He added that 'Some beleeve the best employment for the R⟨eal⟩ ch⟨aracter⟩ would be a short and clear nomenclator of plants', for 'men cannot agree of names, & names are hard to remember',[5] and he was similarly interested in a man who 'hathe reduced the Common-Law into a Method by Dr Wilkins's way'.[6] In the *Idea* he valued the character in connection with elementary language teaching[7] and as a way of eliminating ambiguity in philosophical terminology,[8] apart from its use as a means of communication in its own right: 'The Real Character will never grow in Fashion till taught to Boies'.[9]

---

[1] Wilkins, *An Essay*... (London, 1668), blv.

[2] A-W, 31 March 1674, F 39, 261v.    [3] *B.L.* II, 302.

[4] Paschall-Hooke, 21 Feb. 1679/80, Royal Society Early Letters P 57. Cf. V. Salmon, 'John Wilkins' *Essay* (1668): Critics and continuators', *Historiographica Linguistica* I, 2 (1974). I am indebted to Mrs Salmon for showing me a copy of this article before it was published.

[5] These notes in Aubrey's hand, beginning 'p⟨ro⟩ Mr Paschal', are on the back of a letter from Pigott to Aubrey of 23 Feb. 1677/8, MS A 13, 111: they are evidently a draft of a letter to Paschall.

[6] MS A 10, 68v. It was done by Christopher Merret's son. Cf. Aubrey-Ray, 9 July 1678, Ray, *Letters*, 145.

[7] MS A 10, 27. Cf. 21v.    [8] Ibid., 47, 49, 50.    [9] Ibid., 94. Cf. 25.

But though Aubrey clearly understood what was involved in the language schemes, and though Thomas Pigott considered Hooke and Aubrey 'the chiefest patrons of this design, the most competent judges'[1] and Paschall referred to Aubrey's theories,[2] little is known of his views on the subject, and he was certainly less expert at it than others.[3] Aubrey's particular role was that of postman among these language planners in the 1670s and 1680s, for which, as a personal friend of Paschall who moved in scientific circles in London, he was well qualified. They remarked on his enthusiasm for this role at the time: 'For the Character I am very glad your zeale for it continues, & your designes extend themselves so farre,' wrote Paschall.[4] Aubrey preserved a long series of letters on the subject from Paschall,[5] which he evidently showed to others who were interested, passing on to Paschall the objections made to his ideas by Hooke, Lodwick, Pigott and Ward. It was through Aubrey that Lodwick forwarded linguistic material to Paschall,[6] that Paschall consulted Ray,[7] and that Pigott began his own correspondence with Paschall, for which he was incapable of thanking Aubrey enough.[8] Aubrey's activity in connection with the project also included an attempt to get Wilkins' *Essay* translated into French,[9] and he pre-

---

[1] Pigott-Aubrey, 24 March 1677/8, MS A 13, 107.

[2] Paschall-Aubrey, 16 May 1676, T.G.c.25, 82: 'I am not sorry to heare that Mr. Hooke doth not dislike your fancy about the character'.

[3] He had to send a letter in the character that he received from Pigott to Paschall for translation because he and Hooke were 'not at leisure enough, and not readie in it', though Lodwick could have done it (MS A 13, 135; n.d.). It was a letter of introduction, which suggests that Pigott thought that Aubrey would be able to read it easily. Similarly, when Aubrey wanted a secret concerning an agricultural improvement translated into the Universal Language, he had to get Lodwick to do it (MS A 2, 97v). But Aubrey was not alone in the difficulties he had in translating: Paschall's letters sometimes show uncertainty about translation (e.g. Paschall-Aubrey, 11 June 1678, MS A 13, 31), and Hooke, though 'not readie', was well informed about the theories involved (cf., e.g., Hooke-Paschall, 10 March 1679/80, Royal Society Early Letters H 3 61 and Salmon, art. cit.).

[4] Paschall-Aubrey, 13 Aug. 1677, MS A 13, 23.     [5] Ibid., 2 f.

[6] Lodwick-Aubrey, 29 Sept. 1676, MS A 12, 264.

[7] Aubrey-Ray, 9 July 1678, Ray, *Letters*, 144–5, and Ray's letters to Aubrey in MS A 13, 169v f.

[8] Pigott-Aubrey, 24 March 1677, MS A 13, 107. Aubrey evidently also consulted George Dalgarno, author of *Ars Signorum* (1661) in this connection; in MS A 23, 47b is this note: 'q⟨uaere⟩ Mr Dulgarno within Bocardo—de Reall char⟨acter⟩.'

[9] Aubrey-Ray, 7 May 1678, Ray, *Letters*, 144. Aubrey would also liked to have had William Holder's 'ingeniose' *Elements of Speech* translated into French (A-W, 9 July 1678, T. 456a, 20v): he sent it to Anthony Lucas at Liège hoping that he (or someone else) might do it.

served Paschall's scheme for the character among his papers when Paschall had given it up in disillusion.[1]

## The Advancement of Learning

Aubrey positively prided himself on playing this role of co-ordinator in the intellectual circles in which he moved. When he asked himself in his autobiography 'Quid digni feci, hîc process⟨isse⟩ viam', 'what have I done of value, in following the course of life here?', his reply was '*Cos*, a wheatstone, *exors ipse secandi* ⟨though himself unable to cut⟩, e.g. universall character which was neglected and quite forgott and had sunk had not I engaged in the worke' and 'caused to revive by engaging 6 or 7'.[2] His Latin allusion was to Horace's *Ars Poetica*, which he quoted at greater length when telling Wood how he had suggested Hobbes' *Dialogue of the Common Laws* to him:

> '. . . Fungor vice cotis, acutum
> Reddere quae ferrum valet exors ipsa secandi'

'I perform the function of a whetstone, which can make the iron sharp though itself unable to cut.'[3]

It was for such a co-operative and truly Baconian contribution to the advancement of learning that Samuel Hartlib was impressed by Aubrey in the 1650s. The references to Aubrey in Hartlib's *Ephemerides* concern not Aubrey's own ideas and discoveries, but those of his friends, Thomas Willis, Edward Davenant, Lancelot Morehouse and Francis Potter, 'whom he knows intimatly and written several Letters unto him to oblige him to communication and publishing of all his Experiments and Inventions, but could never prevaile'.[4] Aubrey told Hartlib about inventions by Potter that ranged from a watch without wheels to double writing, from a new pair of compasses to a threshing machine.[5] As a member of

---

[1] MS A 13, 56–7.
[2] *B.L.* I, 39, 43. Aubrey perhaps overemphasises his personal role: cf. Salmon, art. cit. Clark's interpolation of 'my' before 'universall character' and 'that' before 'which was neglected' on p. 39, and his footnote suggesting that Aubrey was speaking in general rather than specific terms, are wholly unnecessary.
[3] A-W, 3 Feb. 1672/3, F 39, 197.
[4] *Ephemerides*, 1652. I take it that Hartlib's 'Wood-house' is an error for Morehouse.
[5] Ibid., 1652–3.

the Royal Society Aubrey was equally active in communicating ideas and observations among scientists. In 1663 Potter was delighted to help the Society through Aubrey;[1] Aubrey often read out at meetings letters about natural things from his country correspondents;[2] and in 1666 he persuaded the deputy-governor of Chepstow to observe the tides there for the Society.[3] 'There is no member of the R⟨oyal⟩ S⟨ociety⟩ more unworthy than I am, but I will avow there is none that has more zeale for them', Aubrey assured Sir William Petty,[4] and the Society evidently saw his value: in 1673/4 Aubrey told Wood that the Society 'have been pleased to lay their Commands upon me to keepe a Correspondence with my numerous company of ingeniose Virtuosi in severall Counties ... for things *naturall* or *artificiall* or any thing remarqueble in phylosophy, or mathem⟨atics⟩'.[5]

Aubrey's wide acquaintance and valuable connections doubtless made him a particularly suitable organiser for such a task, but his chief motive in helping the Society in this way was a simple feeling that information should be recorded and not lost to scholarship and posterity. For similar reasons he gave books to the Society's library and specimens to its museum,[6] and he was constantly concerned that the manuscripts of the learned should be preserved, for ' 'tis great pity the paines of so great an Artist should be lost'.[7] Even in the 1650s he had been labouring to obtain 'the remainder of all Verulam's Ms.',[8] and he appears in the minutes of the Royal Society on more than one occasion telling the members about mathematical and scientific manuscripts of famous scholars which the Society ought to keep in its repository or publish.[9] Moreover

---

[1] Cf. Potter-Aubrey, 22 Feb. 1662/3, Royal Society Early Letters P 39, and Birch, *History*, I, 206 (concerning Potter's cart with legs instead of wheels); also, Potter-Aubrey, 17 May 1664, MS A 13, 157–9, and Birch, *History*, II, 224, 226 (his watch worked by air), and *T.P.W.*, 359–60 (where Potter's work on blood transfusion is also mentioned: cf. Birch, *History*, II, 361 (1669) ).

[2] Birch, *History*, III, 280 (1675–6), IV, 41 (1680), 81, 89 (1681), 220 (1683). Copy Journal Books of the Society, VII, 251 (1690), VIII, 94 (1692).

[3] Birch, *History*, II, 121, 127.

[4] Aubrey-Petty, 17 July 1675 (see above, p. 32, n. 6).

[5] A-W, Jan. 1673/4, F 39, 253v. Nothing more is heard of this.

[6] See N. Grew, *Musæum Regalis Societatis* (London, 1681), 331, 380–2, and 'Aubrey's Library'.

[7] MS A 2, 72v. This was of Wren's survey of Salisbury cathedral.

[8] Hartlib, *Ephemerides*, 1652. He was hoping to get them from Lady Mitton.

[9] Birch, *History*, III, 316 (1676) (concerning papers of Foster; cf. Paschall-Aubrey, 7 April 1676, MS A 13, 8); IV, 223, 296 (1684) (papers of Thomas Merry: cf. A-W, 26 Jan. 1683/4. B. 14, 137). Cf. Birch, *History*, IV, 245 (1683/4), where Aubrey was in-

when he found the archival standards of the Royal Society disappointing, he deposited letters with the Oxford Philosophical
Society instead, which were 'worthy the keeping of so learned and
carefull a Societie: I dare not trust them with ours, we are so careles'.[1]

His letters to Wood and his *Brief Lives* show an equal concern
for the papers of celebrities like the poet George Herbert,[2] the
Elizabethan scientist John Dee,[3] or the antiquaries William Camden[4]
and Daniel King,[5] and in one of his books he preserved a paper of
Seth Ward's on the Common Law, noting 'I found this paper
[which is his owne hand-writing], amongst his scatterd papers, which
I rescued from being used by the Cooke, since his death; which was
destinated with many other good papers & letters, to be put under
Pies'.[6] 'The good huswives had sacrificed them,' he complained of
some papers he had sought,[7] and he was always horrified by stories
of manuscripts used to wrap herrings,[8] sold 'by weight to the past-
board makers for wast paper',[9] used 'to stopp gunnes'[10] or sacrificed
to 'the tayler's sheeres'.[11]

His attitude towards books was similar: 'Oh Anth⟨ony⟩,' he
exclaimed, 'what worke doe the Executors and widowes make with
Librarys which were so dearly beloved by their late Masters! and
Oh that men would be but more publique spirited and make their
handes their Executors, and their Eies their Overseers'.[12] He considered that books were more use to scholars in public than in
private libraries,[13] and he hoped, for instance, that the choice collection of pamphlets made by Sir John Berkenhead, the Royalist
Civil War pamphleteer, could go to one, perhaps in Oxford.[14] The
only surviving letter to Aubrey from Newton concerns the possible

---

volved in having a copy made of some of Vernon's papers in the possession of Sir
William Estcourt. The interest in Harriot's papers reflected in Wallis' letters to Aubrey
in 1683 (MS A 13, 242–5) is perhaps connected with the Royal Society's earlier interest
(Birch, *History*, II, 310 (1669) ). Cf. *B.L.* I, 201 (concerning Davenant).

[1] Aubrey-William Musgrave, 27 Feb. 1684/5, R. T. Gunther *ed.*, *Early Science in
Oxford*, XII, 'Dr. Plot and the Correspondence of the Philosophical Society of Oxford'
(Oxford, 1939), 269.
[2] *B.L.* I, 309.    [3] E.g. A-W, 18 June 1672, F 39, 175.
[4] A-W, 15 July 1681, B. 14, 133.    [5] A-W, 29 Aug. 1676, B. 14, 119v.
[6] MS A 10, 65.    [7] *B.L.* I, 329.    [8] Cf. *B.L.* II, 255.    [9] *B.L.* I, 153.
[10] A-W, St John the Baptist's Day 1682, F 39, 365v.    [11] Cf *B.L.* II, 86.
[12] A-W, 23 Feb. 1673/4, F 39, 255.
[13] Cf. A-W, 14 April 1675, F 39, 294, in connection with a manuscript, *Historia
Roffensis*, that he owned.
[14] A-W, 17 Dec. 1679, F 39, 331.

sale of Sir Jonas Moore's mathematical books to Trinity College, Cambridge,[1] and Aubrey was himself glad to present numerous books to the Bodleian, the Ashmolean and to New Inn Hall, Oxford, apart from the collections he gave to Gloucester Hall and to the Royal Society.[2]

Not only did he think that books should be saved from executors and auctioneers and manuscripts be preserved from 'the mercilesse hands of woemen';[3] he also thought that many rare texts were 'fitt to be made Publick'.[4] He hoped Oxford would play a part in this, noting in 1673 that 'severall great Virtuosi complain, that there being so good a Presse, and so many ingeniouse Correctors, that so many MSS and others almost as rare should lye moth eaten, and not be published for the use of the Commonwealth of Learning'.[5] In 1674 he was eager for Merton and Trinity Colleges to print rare astrological treatises, claiming that 'otherwise the heads of houses are sonnes of swine-herds',[6] and he was often involved in encouraging other people to print valuable texts—'the Booke is of great use,' he said of a mathematical work of Nicholas Mercator's, 'and 'tis pitty that such a MSS should lye so long unpublished'.[7] He was ever active in collecting subscriptions for scholarly works,[8] and his motives were similar when, in 1680 and 1696, he was instrumental in having rare pamphlets reprinted to increase their circulation.[9] For comparable reasons he was keen that a scheme for

---

[1] Newton-Aubrey, 22 Dec. 1683, MS A 12, 347, printed in H. W. Turnbull *ed.*, *The Correspondence of Isaac Newton*, II (Cambridge, 1960), 395. Aubrey subsequently tried to persuade Wallis to get Oxford to take the books: Wallis-Aubrey 17 Sept. and 15 Dec. 1683, MS A 13, 243-4. On other, lost, letters between Newton and Aubrey, cf. Turnbull, *ed. cit.*, II, 239, 266-8 (though this is equally likely to have been to Hooke), 269.

[2] See 'Aubrey's Library'.   [3] MS A 3, 10.

[4] MS A 5, 21v. This was of Celtic manuscripts at Hengwrt.

[5] A-W, 15 Nov. 1673, F 39, 234.

[6] A-W, 24 Oct. 1674, F 39, 282v. Cf. A-W, 21 May 1674, T. 456a, 16.

[7] A-W, 15 Sept. 1674, B. 14, 112.

[8] E.g. A-W, Whitsun Eve 1673, 24 June 1673; F 39, 208, 217 (works by Mercator); 22 May 1680, F 39 340 (by Grew: in this and the next case, Aubrey was hoping to get a free copy himself by obtaining enough subscribers); 17 Aug. 1678, F 39, 311 (Pitt's Atlas); A-L, 24 Feb. 1695/6, 12 Nov. 1696; A. 1829, 56, 78 (on Lhwyd's behalf). For other evidence of Aubrey encouraging publication, e.g. his interest in the grammar that Haak had from Germany (A-W, 24 June 1673, F 39, 217, and B. 14, 156 (n.d.) ), and his advice to Guidott to have a charter from the 'Red Book of Bath' (see below, pp. 164, 181) engraved (T.G.c.25, 192).

[9] *Considerations upon the Reputation, Loyalty, Manners & Religion of Thomas Hobbes* (London, 1680) is a new edition of *Mr. Hobbes Considered . . .* (London, 1662), 'which I lately reprinted', as Aubrey told Wood in a letter of 17 Feb. 1679/80 (B. 14, 126). MS

connecting the Thames with the Avon should not be forgotten:
he gave full details of earlier projects and of the present whereabouts of papers connected with them, so that public-spirited men
could revive them.[1]

Such anxiety was characteristic, for much of Aubrey's scholarly
activity consisted merely of recording information that would
otherwise have disappeared. 'You know my Fate has hindred me
from study and reading much, so that I pretend but to little Learning,' he explained to Wood, 'but for what I have donne by way of
Excerpta, and preserving things from being lost, you know best
of any one'.[2] 'Men thinke, because every body remembers a
memorable accident shortly after 'tis donne, 'twill never be forgotten, which for want of registring, at last is drowned in oblivion,'
he explained. 'Which reflection haz been a hint, that by my meanes
many antiquities have been reskued, and preserved (I myselfe now
inclining to be ancient)—or els utterly lost and forgotten'.[3] In 1679
he proposed to the Royal Society 'that there might be a catalogue
made of all the books and treatises written and published by any
members of the Society; which might be more easily done, than if it
should be omitted too long'.[4] Of the alternative, Aubrey was only
too aware: 'I wish I had taken the account of him: but he is lately
dead', is a common regret in his writings,[5] and he put down detail
after detail 'in perpetuam rei memoriam', 'in perpetual memory of
the thing',[6] reflecting 'How these curiosities would be quite forgott,
did not such idle fellowes as I am putt them downe'.[7]

This activity was one of the leading features of Aubrey's career.
'So worthy a Preserver of Antiquities' was Thomas Tanner's view
of Aubrey,[8] an opinion echoed by generations of later antiquaries,
and in his autobiography Aubrey singled out this, apart from his
role as a whetstone, as his most worthwhile occupation.[9] He had

Aubrey 28 is the copy of the first edition used for this; Wood 431b is the copy of the
new edition presented by Aubrey to Wood. Cf. how in a letter to Lhwyd of 29 Dec.
1696 (A. 1829, 86) Aubrey says he recently had some copies printed of Christopher
Love's *Scripture Rules* (i.e. 'for Buying & Selling: sc. a sheet of paper printed on one
side', MS A 10, 57): I have not been able to locate any copies of this reprint. A-W, 15
April 1682, MS A 12, 8, and 15 Aug. 1682, F 39, 369v, mention Aubrey's involvement in
schemes for engraving old maps of Rome; another letter, of St George's Day 1680,
B. 14, 128, mentions a similar project.

[1] MS A 1, 49 f.   [2] A-W, 23 Oct. 1688, Tanner 456a, 34.   [3] *B.L.* I, 18.
[4] Birch, *History*, III, 472 (1679).   [5] MS A 2, 83.   [6] *B.L.* II, 166.   [7] *B.L.* I, 232.
[8] Tanner-Aubrey, 7 March 1692/3, MS A 13, 198v.   [9] *B.L.* I, 39.

been an active antiquary while an undergraduate at Oxford. Some of
his recollections of Rosamund's Bower in Woodstock Park, which
he later put at the disposal of Anthony Wood, dated from 1642—
'the Aug⟨ust⟩ before Edgehill fight'.[1] In 1643, at a cost of twenty
shillings, he employed a hedge-priest named Hesketh, a pupil of
the celebrated artist William Dobson, to make several drawings of
the ruins of the nearby abbey of Osney, which were soon after
demolished,[2] and one of Aubrey's pictures was later published
as the only evidence about the appearance of the abbey.[3] Occasional evidence survives of the antiquarian notes he made during
the Interregnum,[4] not least the details of Charles I's crown that he
transcribed from the 'booke of Sales of the Kings plate & Jewells',
noting 'sic transit Gloria mundi', for which 'Mr Simpson &c: were
much beholding to me when King Charles the Second's Crowne
was made'.[5]

Throughout his life Aubrey was as concerned with preserving
details of antiquities as he was with disseminating knowledge
among scholars, for ' 'Tis all matter of record'.[6] He would have
liked to see a volume published of views of Wiltshire houses which
'would remaine to Posterity, when their Families are *gonne* and their
Buildings ruind by Time, or Fire: as we have seen that Stupendous
Fabrick of Pauls church not a stone left on a stone, and lives now
only in Mr Hollars Etching in Sir W⟨illia⟩m Dugdales History of
Pauls'.[7] In retrospect, he regretted antiquities now destroyed, like
a Roman temple in Surrey, for ' 'Tis pitty a draught had not been

[1] Quoted from notes under the heading 'Paralipomena' on the back fly-leaves of his
copy of Plot's *Oxfordshire*, Ashmole 1722, which are evidently copied from notes dating
mainly from 1667. Cf. Wood, *Life and Times*, I, plate facing 283.

[2] A-L, 2 Sept. 1694, A. 1814, 116 (there were then three). In a letter to Wood of 22
Oct. 1672, F 39, 190v, Aubrey claimed that although most were by Hesketh, one was by
Dobson himself.

[3] See below, p. 149.

[4] Cf. a note on the back cover of his copy of Plot's *Oxfordshire* about the west towers
of Eynsham, which he had seen in 1647, but 'now downe to the ground [1652]', which
proves that he was keeping antiquarian notes at this time, though this copy of them is
later. He was in Monmouth church looking at scutcheons in 1656 (MS A 4, 32v) and he
recalled rescuing one of a series of drawings of castles by Inigo Jones from the hands of
a child in 1656 (T.G.c.24, 198). Cf. *B.L.* I, 39, and below, pp. 94–5.

[5] MS A 3, 5. In 1661, both John Simpson and Francis Simpson were 'jewellers in
ordinary' to the King.

[6] A-L, 27 March 1694, A. 1814, 109. This was of his hope that the Aubrey family
would be mentioned in the new edition of Camden's *Britannia*.

[7] MS A 2, 177v. The illustrations to Dugdale's book were by Wenceslaus Hollar, the
famous Bohemian engraver.

taken of it when 'twas entire'.[1] And he was always interested in recording finds of coins and other such antiquities, noting of a place in Gloucestershire where coins were often dug up, 'Mr. Kingscot the Lord of the mannour hath great plenty, and hath their names book't, which is a good way: I wish others would doe the like'.[2]

'Me thinks, it shewes a kind of gratitude, and good nature, to revive the pious and charitable Benefactors since dead & gonne', Aubrey reflected,[3] and his passion for all sorts of relics of the past was like that of topographical writers such as John Leland, William Camden, John Stow and their followers in the sixteenth century and his own,[4] among whose heirs he was proud to count himself. His topography of Surrey, in particular, is very similar to those of the sixteenth-century chorographers, full of miscellaneous information about families and local worthies, fairs, ponds, charities, rivers, bridges, seats, etymologies and monumental inscriptions. When, in his *Naturall Historie of Wiltshire*, he wrote 'A Digression' concerning the Earls of March, he sounded almost like Leland in his admiration for roof bosses showing the face of Queen Isabel, 'perhaps the only remayning effigies of that beautifull Queen', and for a Latin bible, 'the fairest that ever I saw'.[5] He used and admired the works of Camden, and on at least one occasion was misled because 'I could not in modesty, but jurare in verba tanti Viri', 'trust in the words of such a man'.[6] He was also deferential to the 'curious enquiry' of Stow,[7] whose writings he had first encountered when a freshman at Oxford,[8] even omitting an account of Southwark from his original description of Surrey because he considered Stow's adequate.[9] He also owed something to John Weever's *Ancient Funerall Monuments*, a collection of memorial inscriptions and similar antiquities published in 1631,[10] and he was glad to quote and, 'by his good favour',[11] to correct and supplement Thomas Fuller's *History of the Worthies of England* (1662), another product of the same tradition of topographical investigation, which combined a description of the

[1] T.G.c.25, 108v.    [2] Ibid., 130v.    [3] MS A 3, 11v.

[4] See T. D. Kendrick, *British Antiquity* (London, 1950), and F. J. Levy, *Tudor Historical Thought*, esp. ch. iv.

[5] MS A 2, 113.    [6] MS A 4, 7a.    [7] Ibid., 21v.

[8] Cf. MS A 3, 96, where he refers to an old edition of Stow which he was shown by Sir Charles Snell.

[9] MS A 4, 5a. He added a survey of Southwark in the 1690s.

[10] For example, he used Weever to recover obliterated inscriptions: ibid., 16.

[11] MS A 2, 2v.

'native and peculiar commodities' of each county of England with
an account of its great alumni.

Aubrey's concern to preserve combined with his truly Baconian
eagerness to collaborate in his enthusiasm for 'the good designe of
a natural History'.[1] This equally Baconian project, part of the aim of
scientists of his age 'to make faithful *Records*, of all the Works of
*Nature*, or *Art*, which can come within their reach',[2] received a
new impetus in the late seventeenth century, gaining a topographical application that allowed it to benefit from the enthusiasm for
antiquarian topography of the previous century. Dr. Robert Plot,
first Curator of the Ashmolean Museum at Oxford, whose *Natural
History of Oxford-shire* (1677) was chiefly influential in popularising local natural history, made it clear that his history of 'Naturall
and Artificiall things' was intended to supplement the 'Civil and
Geographicall Historys' already done;[3] but he was careful to have
the arms of the gentry engraved on the maps issued with his
*Oxfordshire* and his *Staffordshire*, maps that were widely circulated
in their respective counties,[4] and others hoped for patronage and
assistance from such sources.[5] In Aubrey's case, natural history
and antiquarian topography overlapped. Though he claimed to have
begun his *Naturall Historie of Wiltshire* in 1656,[6] and though he
drew up a collection of 'the Naturall History, only' of Surrey
for Plot in the 1670s,[7] he included natural as well as antiquarian
information in the manuscript of his *Wiltshire Antiquities*, and in his
*Surrey* notes on springs and soils, flora and fauna and minerals,
jostled with more miscellaneous information which he set down
'tumultuarily as if tumbled out of a Sack, as they come to my hand,
mixing Antiquities and Naturall things together'.[8]

In natural history, Aubrey was eager not only to preserve information, but to see this organised. He quoted Sir Christopher

---

[1] Paschall-Aubrey, 18 Jan. 1675/6, MS A 13, 6.   [2] Sprat, *History*, 61.

[3] Robert Plot, *Plinius Anglicus sive Angliae Historia naturalis ac Artium* (Society of
Antiquaries MS 85), 2. This MS prospectus is addressed to the Lords, Knights and
Gentlemen of Oxfordshire, and Plot evidently sent similar prospectuses to others: for
example, in Royal Society Classified Papers 22 (1) 12 is a copy by Oldenburg of an
almost identical one addressed to the Vice-Chancellor and University of Oxford.

[4] Cf. C. King-Plot, 26 March 1684, *Early Science in Oxford*, XII, 216.

[5] Cf. Paschall-Aubrey, 1 July 1684, MS A 13, 66v, where he hopes for assistance in
collecting materials for a natural history of Somerset from 'the greatest familyes', and
Cole-Plot, 25 March 1685, *Early Science in Oxford*, XII, 285, hoping for help from the
'principall Gentlemen'.

[6] See below, p. 95.   [7] See below, p. 72.   [8] MS A 4, 31.

Wren's wish 'that an Act of Parliament were made, for Ministers &
the Church-wardens to enter into their Register-booke all extraordinary Remarques, that shall happen in their Parishes, and then
we might be furnished with good Naturall Histories'.[1] In 1675 he
told Wood that 'I have sett a worke newly on foote, and with much
applause, in having gott the Chancery office to engage Attornies
(fitt) in every County of England & Wales pro Account of Husbandry and Huswifry'.[2] He desired that a 'Botanique Survey' of
Wiltshire should be carried out by the local apothecaries, which
'would not be very troublesome' since 'their Profession leades them
to an acquaintance of Herbes' in any case,[3] and in 1671 he considered
helping Sir William Petty with a related project, a 'Reg⟨iste⟩r
Generall of people, Plantations, & Trade of England' which would
'give the King a true State of the Nation at all times'.[4]

Aubrey was also a party to the issue of a printed set of *Queries
in Order to the Description of Britannia* which John Ogilby circulated in 1673,[5] after they had been 'considered of at severall
meetings' by Aubrey, Wren, Hooke, Ogilby, Gregory King, herald
and pioneer of social statistics, and Sir John Hoskyns, a friend of
Aubrey who was later President of the Royal Society.[6] These
sought information on a wide range of topics, from the houses of the
nobility and gentry to 'Places where Battles have been', from 'Waters,
Springs and Baths' to mines of metals and minerals, the division
of land between arable and pasture, 'Extraordinary *Accidents,
Calamities* and *Casualties*' and '*Improvements* in *Husbandry, Mecha-
nicks, Manufactures, &c.*' Aubrey later circulated 'Naturall Queres',[7]
like Plot and other natural historians.[8] He received help for his

---

[1] Wood F 49, 39v, the verso of the original cover of Aubrey's *Surrey*.

[2] A-W, 25 Feb. 1674/5, F 39, 292. Nothing more is heard of this.

[3] MS A 1, 104.

[4] MS A 26, 13v–14v (printed in *The Petty Papers*, I, 171–2). There is no evidence that
anything came of this.

[5] MS A 4, 243 and 244 comprise two separate printings of these queries, which differ
in their wording, which is more elaborate in the second. The first one does not mention
Ogilby. The second is presumably a revised version of the first, though there is no
direct evidence of this.

[6] Aubrey has written this on the second set of queries, MS A 4, 244. On the first he
wrote 'My name to be putt to those Counties, which I describe'. I have taken some
quotations from each set.

[7] Aubrey-Musgrave, 27 Feb. 1684/5, *Early Science in Oxford* XII, 269; these were
connected with his *Naturall Historie of Wiltshire*.

[8] There are specimens of Plot's printed queries of 1674 and 1678/9 in Ashmole 1820a,
222–3 and 224–5. For evidence of Aubrey helping to circulate Plot's queries, cf. Tyson-

*Naturall Historie of Wiltshire* from Sir James Long, a close friend who lived locally and whose letters he quoted at length,[1] from Mr Hayward, a local apothecary who 'eagerly espouses this Designe',[2] and others,[3] and he valued the 'considerable Remarques' that he gathered by such means, 'many whereof will be utterly lost to posterity, without I stitch them together'.[4]

Aubrey was delighted to put his 'collection of the naturall mirables of England'[5] at the disposal of others. His notes on Surrey had been made for Ogilby, who had employed Aubrey to survey this and other counties in 1673 as part of the project for 'the Description of Britannia' that had involved the printed queries.[6] And when Ogilby declined to use the *Perambulation of Surrey* (which in any case primarily reflected Aubrey's own interests), preferring to use 'what scraps he can get out of bookes or by heere say',[7] Aubrey kept it because ' 'tis pitty it should be lost'.[8] He reacted typically to learning that Plot intended a Natural History of England. 'I am right glad to heare of Dr Plott's designe,' he wrote to Wood in 1674, 'it agrees so much with my Humour. I can much assist him in it: having a good Penus naturalis ⟨store of natural history⟩ of my owne Collecting: which I dayly augment'.[9] When he saw Plot's synopsis of his planned history, he set to work to transcribe out of his 'apparatus for a Description of Wilts' all his natural observations.[10] He did the same for Surrey—the original manuscript of 'the Naturall History, only' that he sent to Plot still survives[11]—and he

---

Plot, 26 Feb. 1680/1 and 10 Nov. 1683, in *Early Science in Oxford*, XII, 2, 45, and A-W, 13 Jan. 1680/1, F 39, 351, and 19 March 1680/1, B. 14, 129.

[1] Esp. Long-Aubrey, 11 March 1686/7, MS A 12, 283-4, quoted in MS A 1, 129. Long's letters are also quoted in ibid., 30v, 145; MS A 2, 85, etc.

[2] MS A 1, 103v.

[3] E.g. Hanson, ibid., 43v, 52, 107v, 120, 171; MS A 2, 114v.; Mariet, R.S. MS 92, 39; Scot, MS A 2, 170 (actual letter to Aubrey of 3 April 1689 inserted).

[4] A-W, 27 Oct. 1687, F 39, 392v.    [5] A-W, 10 March 1672/3, F 39, 258.

[6] Cf. A-W, 12 Aug. 1672, F 39, 181, and 10 Aug. 1673, F 39, 221v, which shows his intention of continuing into Sussex and then Berkshire or Oxfordshire. MS A 4, 226 f., comprises 'Memoires of some Excursions in Sussex', evidently mainly the result of accidentally straying across the border while perambulating Surrey.

[7] A-W, 11 Oct. 1673, F 39, 231.

[8] A-W, Morrow after St Matthew's Day 1673, F 39, 229.

[9] A-W, 24 Oct. 1674, F 39, 282. On Plot's original intention to survey the whole of England, cf. his *Oxfordshire*, 157, 186.

[10] Aubrey-Petty, 17 July 1675 (see above, p. 32, n. 6). Aubrey did this 'with the assistance of Sir James Long'.

[11] Now MS A 4, 235 f. because Plot later returned it to Aubrey at his request (cf. A-W, 3 Aug. 1691, F 39, 429v).

also produced 'a sheet or two of other counties'.[1] Plot saw Aubrey's *Adversaria Physica* as well, from which he made profuse notes in his *Analecta*;[2] he quoted 'Mr. *Aubrey's* notes' in his *Oxfordshire*;[3] and Aubrey gave him more information in 1684.[4] Throughout his life Aubrey was proud to offer information to scientists like Martin Lister[5] or John Ray; Ray asked Aubrey to watch for 'any thing extraordinary relating to naturall history or experiment' when he journeyed into Wales in 1687,[6] and he gratefully acknowledged information provided by Aubrey in his great botanical collection, the *Synopsis methodica stirpium Britannicarum*.[7]

A contemporary described Aubrey as 'Vir Publico Bono magis quam suo natus', 'a man born rather for the public advantage than his own',[8] and his humility and omnivorousness made him an ideal research assistant. This was the role he played in perhaps his best-known intellectual venture, the biographical researches that he made for use in Anthony Wood's two great antiquarian works on Oxford, the *History and Antiquities of the University of Oxford* (1674) and *Athenae Oxonienses* (1691–2).[9] Aubrey met Wood in 1667, and his researches on Wood's behalf took much of his time for two decades: indeed, his collaboration with Wood was crucial in turning his enthusiasm for miscellaneous preservation in the direction of biography, which had previously been a relatively minor interest,[10]

---

[1] A-W, 27 Nov. 1675, T. 456a, 19. Cf. A-W, Twelfeday 1675–6, B. 14, 116. These papers were read to the Royal Society before Aubrey sent them to Plot: cf. below, pp. 95, 138.

[2] See 'A Note on *Analecta*'.    [3] Plot, *Oxfordshire*, 99.

[4] Aubrey transcribed and gave to Plot on 3 Dec. 1684 the notes that he had made on the back flyleaves of his copy of Plot's *Oxfordshire* (Ashmole 1722), as he there notes. F 39, 152 is a leaf of notes on Potter's dividing compasses given to Plot by Aubrey.

[5] See below, p. 113.    [6] Ray-Aubrey, 15 Feb. 1687/8, MS A 13, 172.

[7] *Synopsis* (third edition, London, 1724), 131. This refers to information given to Ray by Aubrey in a letter of 5 Aug. 1691 (Ray, *Letters*, 250). Cf. Aubrey-Ray, 15 Dec. 1692, ibid., 269, and Ray's acknowledgements in letters to Aubrey of 17 Aug. 1691 and 20 Dec. 1692, MS A 13, 173, 177.

[8] (Richard Blackbourne), *Thomæ Hobbes Angli Malmesburiensis Philosophi Vita* ('Carolopoli', i.e. London, 1681), 187.

[9] Another project with which Aubrey assisted was Christopher Wase's Inquiry into the Free Schools of England. Cf. Wase-Aubrey, 20 Aug. and 7 Oct. 1673, MS A 13, 246–7, and A-W, n.d., 16 Sept. 1673, New Year's Day 1673/4; F 39, 126, 223v, 250; and 21 May 1674, T. 456a, 16.

[10] On his life of Bacon, see above, p. 44. *B. L.* 11, 116, has a song recorded in 1656, and it is likely that Aubrey had collected a certain amount of biographical information with other antiquarian material before 1667, which he perhaps inserted in the lost 'Liber B' (see 'Aubrey's Lost Works').

and it was to Wood that he addressed most of what he now discovered.

Wood was an eminently suitable task-master for Aubrey, for his
concern for preservation was as strong as Aubrey's: ' 'tis pitty
that such an opportunity of remembering so worthy a person should
for want of so small labour, be omitted' was his cry[1] as well as
Aubrey's, and he too was glad to preserve information about old
authors 'to commend them to posterity'.[2] The story of Aubrey's
association with Wood has been told by Anthony Powell, and Wood
often stressed how much he owed to Aubrey. 'I profess unless yo
help me to some searches of them I shall be at a great loss', he
would write of biographical data he needed,[3] and 'I speake in my
conscience (for I have told other men of it already) that I have
had, & shall have more from yo as to those things then all other
people besides whatsoever'.[4] Aubrey's enthusiasm was immense:
'I wish I were as able as willing, to serve you', he wrote,[5] and he
frequently complained when others were less keen than he was—'I
am sorry to find such slacknesse in great men for carrying on so
publique a worke'.[6]

'Surely my starres impelled me to be an Antiquary, I have the
strangest luck at it, that things drop into my mouth', he wrote,[7]
and he emphasised the new potentialities for collecting accurate
biographical information provided by the coffee-houses, apart
from his own ease due to his 'longaevous' family and his wide
acquaintance.[8] He was indefatigable, and on Wood's behalf he
'dun'd ... unmercifully'[9] all sorts of informants for details of the
birth, employments and preferment, writings, epitaph, and place
and date of burial of Oxford men.[10] His energy in pursuing complete

---

[1] Wood-Aubrey, 10 Nov. 1671, MS A 13, 263.    [2] Id., 23 Sept. 1671, T. 456a, 12.
[3] Id., n.d. (1673), MS A 13, 261 (a fragment).
[4] Id., 10 Nov. 1671, ibid., 263. Wood evidently paid Aubrey for some of the researches he did (cf., e.g., A-W, 27 Jan. 1671/2, 23 Jan. 1674/5; F 39, 163, 284). The
extent of Wood's debt to Aubrey is shown by collation of *Brief Lives* with Wood's
*Athenae*: his lives, for example, of Francis Potter or Seth Ward are virtually epitomes of
Aubrey's (Bliss *ed.*, *Athenae Oxonienses*, III (London, 1817), 1155 f. and IV (London,
1820), 246 f.).
[5] A-W, 9 March 1674/5, B. 14, 115.    [6] A-W, 17 Nov. 1670, F 39, 128.
[7] A-W, 12 Feb. 1671/2, F 39, 166.    [8] A-W, 15 June 1680, *B.L.* I, 10.
[9] A-W, 10 March 1672/3, F 39, 258 (of Boyle).
[10] Aubrey's letters to Wood occasionally refer to Wood's 'Method, in writing' given
to potential informants when requesting biographical information (7 April 1671,
F 39, 199), and Hobbes, for instance, continued his *Life* 'but I question whether exactly
donne after your excellent Method, and way' (New Year's Day 1679/80, F 39, 335). A

and accurate information was remarkable: his letters to Wood show him trying source after source after first drawing a blank,[1] or returning again and again in search of an elusive informant. 'I beleeve I have been 10 times at Ob⟨adiah⟩ Sedgewicks sonnes chamb⟨er⟩ & cannot meet with him,' he wrote, when seeking information about that Puritan divine; 'I think people are afrayd of bugbeares'.[2] Moreover the sources of his information were often the best available: some of his knowledge of great contemporaries he had 'from his owne mouth this day';[3] some he obtained from their sons,[4] widows[5] or nephews;[6] and he was prepared to go to people he had not met before if they could tell him things that no one else could.[7] He constantly sought accurate dates of birth and death from parish registers and epitaphs—'Chronologie is the prettiest Trap or gin to catch a Lyer in that can be'[8]—and his aspiration to accuracy in his biographical collections is shown even by his care to change adjectives so as not to be guilty of overstatement.[9]

## The Author

Aubrey was delighted to serve Wood's 'living & lasting History',[10] and happy enough for his name merely 'to remayne for ever there like an unprofitable elder or ewe-tree on some Noble structure'.[11] For his humility as a scholar made him diffident about his own skill as an author, and he was always anxious to enrol the help of an

---

specimen of Wood's written enquiries, sent via Aubrey to Evelyn, survives among the Evelyn papers at Christ Church, Oxford (a loose paper in a folder numbered MS 543); it requests details of birth, education, employment and writings (and also has some queries concerning other local people).

[1] For example, the search for Raleigh's epitaph in Aubrey's letters to Wood of 9 Aug. 1671, 27 Oct. 1671, 12 Feb. 1671/2, 31 Jan. 1673/4, Die Annunciationis 1673, 19 June 1675 (F 39, 135, 141, 166, 252v, 259v, 299), or for Dee's burial place, 6 July 1672, 22 Oct. 1672, 18 Jan. 1672/3 (F 39, 178v, 190, 192).

[2] A-W, Jan. 1673/4, F 39, 253.  [3] A-W, 23 June 1674, F 39, 275 (of Petty).

[4] E.g. A-W, 11 Nov. 1668, B. 14, 82 (Digby), St John the Baptist's Day 1682, F 39, 365 (Clarendon).

[5] E.g. F 46, 67v (Davys).

[6] E.g. A-W, 27 Oct. 1671, F 39, 142v (Allen), 8 Jan. 1667/8, B. 14, 80 (Owen).

[7] Cf. A-W, 21 June 1681, F 39, 354v.  [8] Loc. cit.

[9] This is evident from *Brief Lives*, which he had opportunities to revise, rather than the letters to Wood, which he did not. Cf. H. Darbishire *ed., The Early Lives of Milton* (London, 1932), xxxviii. For other examples of alterations making his text more precise, e.g. *B.L.* I, 230, 261.

[10] A-W, 2 Sept. 1671, F 39, 138v.  [11] A-W, 19 Aug. 1672, F 39, 183.

'Aristarchus' in 'methodizing' his papers.[1] His topographical collections for Wiltshire were, as he explained, 'occasionally made', and 'perhaps may some time or other, fall into some Antiquaries hands to make a handsome worke of it'.[2] If Wood finished what he had begun, he 'might make as good a worke of it' as Sir William Dugdale's *Antiquities of Warwickshire*, on which it was consciously modelled,[3] and his Surrey collections would be 'a peice not contemptible' with a little of Wood's supervising.[4] With his natural history, he not only lent Plot his papers but tried to persuade him to undertake natural histories of Wiltshire and Surrey using his materials, and it was only after he had 'importuned' him twice that he was persuaded 'to finish and publish what I had begun'.[5]

But Aubrey's modesty was not so great that he entirely deprecated his ability as an author, and he came more and more to see that he could make a contribution to scholarship that no one else would, even though he often came to realise this only through projects in which he had originally intended only to help others. Despite his diffidence about the merits of his *Wiltshire Antiquities*, he finished it '(in good part)' in 1671,[6] explaining to Wood 'I do not know how or why, methinkes, but I have a kind of divine impulse to have it donne; no body els will doe it. & when tis donne none of these parts will value it, but the next generation I hope will be lesse brutish'.[7] His resolve to complete it was strengthened by the knowledge that he was about to leave his ancestral Wiltshire home, an awareness which also led him to complete his *Designatio de Easton-Piers* and other minor works.[8]

By 1672 his '*Templa Druidum* & Chorographia Antiquaria [or Miscellanea Antiq⟨uaria⟩]', the two main components of what was later to become his *Monumenta Britannica*, were ready for the press, and John Locke was 'much importunate' with Aubrey to print them, even offering to 'be at the chardge himselfe'.[9] Others were

---

[1] Cf. A-T, 4 May 1693, T. 25, 39.  [2] MS A 3, 10.
[3] A-W, Whitsun Eve 1671, F 39, 133. Cf. A-W, 27 Oct. 1687, F 39, 392.
[4] A-W, 4 Nov. 1673, T. 456a, 14.  [5] MS A 1, 6–7. Cf. MS A 4, 30v.
[6] *B.L.* I, 42.  [7] A-W, 17 Nov. 1670, F 39, 128.
[8] It is interesting that the *Designatio* (MS A 17) is one of Aubrey's most 'finished' manuscripts. The *Idea Filioli seu Educatio Pueri* also dates from this period (see p. 50, n. 11), and so do *The Countrey Revell*, Aubrey's lost play and his lost literary work on the Wiltshire countryside (see 'Aubrey's Lost Works').
[9] A-W, 3 Feb. 1672/3, F 39, 196. Aubrey claimed to be 'very intimate' with Locke (A-W, 28 Nov. 1671, F 39, 147), who borrowed 'Templa Druidum' for Shaftesbury and himself to read in 1672 (cf. A-W, 4 Nov. 1673, T. 456a, 14, when it was still at the

equally enthusiastic, including Sir Thomas Browne, who assured
Aubrey that 'Sir your friends who persuade you to print your
Templa Druidum &c do butt what is fitt & reasonable'.[1] Nothing
came of this, however, partly because of Aubrey's involvement with
Ogilby the next year.[2] Similarly, when it became clear that his notes
on Surrey would be useless to Ogilby, Aubrey considered publishing
them as a serious work in their own right,[3] and in 1675/6 he showed
the manuscript to John Evelyn, who read it 'Whith incredible
satisfaction ... It is so Usefull a piece; and so obliging, that I
cannot sufficiently applaude it'.[4]

In these works, apart from the help that he had from a whole
range of 'Persons of quality, and worthy of Beliefe'[5] and more
transient informants like 'old Mr Rob: Bignol, neer 80. a sensible
person',[6] Aubrey was as delighted to accept the assistance of
colleagues like Plot and Wood as he was glad to help them with
theirs. Plot provided an account of the strange discoveries of grave-
diggers at Woking, which Aubrey inserted into the manuscript of
his *Surrey*.[7] For his *Wiltshire Antiquities* he sought information
from Oxford sources from Wood,[8] and for the 'Chronologia Architectonica' that he attached to it he asked him about the dates of old
buildings.[9] In the 1670s Aubrey also undertook an astrological
study, some of the results of which appeared in his *Collectio
Geniturarum*, and for this he requested exact birth dates from Wood,
which Wood saw little point in recording.[10] Moreover though during
the 1670s Aubrey apparently collected biographical data exclu-

---

Lord Chancellor's). Locke was still interested in the *Monumenta* at the time of Aubrey's
death (cf. A-L, 12 Nov. 1696, A. 1829, 78), and he sent measurements of Hautwell's
Coit for it in 1694 (Locke-Aubrey, 18 May 1694, MS A 12, 258). Cf. M. Cranston in
*Notes and Queries* CXCV (1950), 552-4, and CXCVII (1952), 383-4.

[1] Browne-Aubrey, 14 March 1672/3, MS A 12, 51v (printed in G. Keynes *ed.*,
*The Works of Sir Thomas Browne* (London, 1964), IV, 376). Aubrey also refers to his
hopes to print these works in MS A 4, 238, and in a letter to Wood of 15 Nov. 1673,
F 39, 234. Cf. also A-W, 9 March 1674/5, B. 14, 115, and 22 May 1680, F 39, 340.

[2] A-W, 4 Nov. 1673, T. 456a, 14. A-W, 11 Oct. 1673, F 39, 231v, shows that he hoped
that it might have been incorporated in Ogilby's *Britannia*.

[3] A-W, Morrow after St Matthew's Day 1673, 11 Oct. 1673; F 39, 229, 232.

[4] Evelyn-Aubrey, 8 Feb. 1675/6, MS A 4, 28.    [5] T.G.c.24, 78.    [6] MS A 4, 143v.

[7] Ibid., 164. Cf. Plot-Aubrey, Feb. 1675/6, MS A 13, 137.

[8] E.g. MS A 3, 98, 'q⟨uaere⟩ A. Wood de hoc', or A-W, 27 Oct. 1671, F 39, 142v, etc.

[9] A-W, 7 Aug. 1669, F 39, 123. Cf. MS A 3, 2a f.

[10] See below, p. 121. Cf. e.g. A-W, 14 March 1671/2, F 39, 169, 15 Sept. 1674, B.
14, 111, 24 Oct. 1674, F 39, 282v.

sively for Wood's use, in 1680 even this changed, as he suddenly
realised that he had merits as a biographer himself.

The spur to this was evidently the life of Hobbes which Aubrey
found himself responsible for publishing after Hobbes' death in
1679. Though at first Aubrey intended merely to publish the prose
life that Hobbes had written himself with brief additions bringing
it up to date,[1] his additions became a sizeable work in their own
right—'I did not think I could have been so copious,' he noted with
surprise.[2] Aubrey set down all sorts of intimate details about Hobbes
—for 'nobody knew so many particulars of his life as myselfe'[3]—
and though he intended 'upon review, to retrench what was super-
fluous and triviall', seeking the advice of 'some friends of mine (who
also were of Mr. Hobbes's acquaintance) whose judgements I much
value', they advised him 'to let *all* stand'.[4]

To help translate these steadily growing notes into Latin, Aubrey
sought the help of an 'Aristarchus', and this was the only work for
which he ever succeeded in finding one. At first he hoped that Sir
George Ent, a distinguished physician and a close friend, might
assist.[5] But he was unable to, so Aubrey turned to Richard Blackbourne, another doctor, who 'practises but little; studies much. a
Generall Scholar. prodigious memorie: sound judgment; but 30
years old now.'[6] Not only was Blackbourne 'one of the best schol⟨ars⟩
in London of his age' and 'a mighty read man'; he was also a
'φιλο Hobbist', who 'hath harried all Mr. H⟨obbes'⟩ adversaries'.[7]
He agreed to 'make use of all my supellex; doeing me the right to

---

[1] Cf. A-W, 17 Dec. 1679, F 39, 331. Aubrey had promised Hobbes that he would
publish his life in 1667 (*B.L.* I, 17), but there is no evidence that he did anything about
it until Hobbes' death. The reprint of *Mr. Hobbes Considered* (see above p. 66, n. 9)
also dates from this episode immediately after Hobbes' death.

[2] A-W, 10 Feb. 1679/80, B. 14, 125. By this time he was engaged on a third draft
(cf. A-W, 12 Feb. 1679/80, *B.L.* I, 19). He had completed an earlier draft, 'above a
whole sheet: every page close written' by mid-January (A-W, 17 Jan. 1679/80, F 39,
337–8).

[3] *B.L.* I, 17–8.

[4] *B.L.* I, 18–19. Of these friends, Aubrey names Petty and Wood in a letter to Wood
of 27 March 1680 (B. 14, 131. Cf. A-W, 7 March 1679/80, T. 456a, 23). When Wood
saw the 'Supplementum vitae Thomas Hobbes', as it was then called, he endorsed it
'What need you say Supplimentum? pray say the life of Thomas Hobbs', and Aubrey
obediently changed it in the MS (*B.L.* I, 17).

[5] A-W, 17 Dec. 1679, F 39, 331.

[6] A-W, 21 June 1681, F 39, 354v. Aubrey had also considered Pigott (A-W, St John
the Evangelist's Day 1679, F 39, 327v) and 'Dr Char . . . ' (mutilated; probably Charleton) (10 Feb. 1679/80, B. 14, 125).

[7] A-W, 10 Feb. 1679/80, B. 14, 124v–5.

quote me',[1] and he produced a Latin life in 'delicate Style' (' 'tis as if Mr Hobbes's soule were come into his body'),[2] which was published late in 1680.[3]

But, significantly, in this one work for which Aubrey actually found an 'Aristarchus', the enthusiasm reflected in his letters to Wood when Blackbourne undertook the project soon showed signs of wear. 'I suffer the grasse to cutt under my feet,' he complained, for 'Dr Blackbourne will have all the Glory'.[4] Subsequently he criticised Blackbourne because he was 'carelesse of my papers, and keepes them not cleane',[5] and an even more serious disagreement arose, about the very function of biography. For Aubrey's views differed entirely from those of Blackbourne and his advisers, John Dryden and Lord John Vaughan, another man of letters, and he articulated his dissatisfaction in his letters to Wood in 1680. Not only, Aubrey complained, would Blackbourne put the life 'in the *High-Style*';[6] worse still, he falsified detail 'because it would make a better picture'[7]—'there will be the trueth, but not the whole'.[8] Blackbourne, 'a great judge, & consequently magisteriall', was 'much against Minutiae',[9] and he and Dryden felt that Aubrey was too inclusive: 'for the compiling' they agreed to omit such details as the fact that Hobbes had been a page.[10] 'Now I say the Offices of a Panegyrist, & Historian, are much different,' Aubrey wrote. 'A Life, is a short Historie: and *there* minutenes of a famous person is gratefull. I never yet knew a Witt (unles he were a piece of an Antiquary) write a proper Epitaph, but leave the reader ignorant, what countryman &c: only tickles his eares with Elogies'.[11] 'Pox take your orators and poets, they spoile lives & histories,' he later exclaimed to Wood. 'The Doctor says that I am too minute; but a hundred yeare hence that minutenesse will be gratefull', and he hoped 'to gett all my originall papers into my hands, & then

---

[1] Loc. cit.   [2] A-W, 7 March 1679/80, T. 456a, 23.

[3] Wood received his copy of the work, *Thomæ Hobbes Angli Malmesburiensis Philosophi Vita*, at Weston on 6 Nov. 1680 (cf. his note in his copy, presented to him by Aubrey, Wood 434). Aubrey's part in the project is acknowledged on sig. B4v and p. 187. Though one dedicatory verse is signed 'Jo. Awbrey' (A8v), it was not in fact by him (cf. Wood's note on that page of his copy and A-W, 3 Nov. 1680, F 39, 350).

[4] A-W, 27 March 1680, B. 14, 131.   [5] A-W, 3 Nov. 1680, F 39, 350.
[6] A-W, 22 May 1680, F 39, 340.   [7] A-W, 3 Nov. 1680, F 39, 350.
[8] A-W, 27 March 1680, B. 14, 131.   [9] A-W, 7 March 1679/80, T. 456a, 23.
[10] A-W, 27 March 1680, B. 14, 131. Dryden's attitude here contrasts with the emphasis on the value of trivialities in his 'Life of Plutarch'.
[11] Loc. cit.

I will transcribe a faire Copie to be preserved in your hands'.[1]

It can hardly be coincidental that it was just at the time when he was writing the life of Hobbes, and when Blackbourne's treatment of it was making him express this theory of biography, that Aubrey began his famous *Brief Lives*. He had been becoming restive about the limitations of Wood's scheme for some time, though he always remained gratefully aware that he would never have begun his biographical collecting without Wood's stimulus.[2] 'You have me thinkes curtaild some eminent men's Lifes too much, e.g. James Harrington Esquire, an eminent person & writer: the like Sir Hen⟨ry⟩ Blount,' he had written, after the appearance of the *History and Antiquities of the University of Oxford*,[3] and 'You are blamed (as I feared you would be) for leaving out living Writers'.[4] Earlier he had told Wood 'me thinkes you should mention Viri Illustres though not Writers';[5] he also wanted to record details of Cambridge as well as Oxford men, 'which may be of use hereafter there'.[6] Such worries, added to his discovery of his biographical ability through the Hobbes life, are the background to his departure in February 1679/80 from his earlier practice of merely pouring out biographical information in his letters for Wood to sort out and use. Instead, he now wrote a series of *Lives* of eminent men, mainly contemporaries.

As he explained in a letter to Wood of 21 February 1679/80, 'It came into my mind Sunday last taking a pipe of Tobacco in my chamber (my hand now being-in) to write my hon⟨oure⟩d friend Sir W. Petty's life, which will be a fine thing, & which he shall peruse himselfe, & then it shall be left with your Papers, for Posterity hereafter, to read [published]'.[7] In February he also did lives of Wren, Hooke, Pell, Bacon ('neer 2 sheetes untouch't by anyone'), and Dr William Aubrey, his grandfather.[8] By 27 March 1680 he had made a 'Kalendar' of fifty-five persons whom he hoped to write about and he sent Wood a list of the lives he had completed, including those of Sir Walter Raleigh, William Harvey, Sir John Suckling,

---

[1] A-W, 22 May 1680, F 39, 340.  [2] Cf. *B.L.* I, 10.
[3] A-W, 15 Sept. 1674, B. 14, 111.  [4] A-W, 6 Aug. 1674, F 39, 280.
[5] A-W, 18 Jan. 1672/3, F 39, 192.  [6] A-W, Jan. 1673/4, F 39, 253.
[7] A-W, 21 Feb. 1679/80, B. 14, 127. Cf. 17 Feb. 1679/80, B. 14, 126.
[8] A-W, 21 Feb. 1679/80, B. 14, 127. Aubrey also mentions that 'I lodged 5 yeares since with Mr Ashmole, a sheet of Minutes of Jo⟨hn⟩ Dee, who was my gr⟨eat⟩ gr⟨and⟩ f⟨ather⟩ Dr. W. Aubrey's great acquaintance and Cosen', and refers to his hope to obtain material on the first Earl of Cork from the Countess of Thanet.

Edward Davenant, Edmund Waller, Thomas Randolph, William Camden, William Oughtred and Lord Falkland,[1] while by 22 May he had done sixty-six, 'a booke of 2 q⟨uire⟩s close written'.[2]

He expected Wood to use these lives—indeed they are sometimes addressed to him[3]—but he came increasingly to value them in their own right rather than merely as a quarry for others, intending them to be preserved after Wood had consulted them, and he tried to make them like formal biographies: he gave the longer lives a regular structure, with date of birth followed by a short account of the subject's family, an outline of his career, a description of his appearance, an analysis of his character, and a list of his writings.[4] He continued to add to the *Lives* in the 1680s, and in 1690 he began a series of 'Lives of our English Mathematical Writers' that he evidently conceived almost as a brief history of English mathematics.[5]

When he sent the first batch of the *Lives* to Wood in June 1680, he noted that ' 'Tis pitty that such minutes had not been taken 100 yeares since or more: for want wherof many worthy men's names and notions are swallowd-up in oblivion'.[6] He remarked, too, 'What uncertainty doe we find in printed histories?' and his *Lives* differed from Wood's not least because he was able to include information that Wood was unable to use for fear of scandal, for he knew that 'these *arcana* are not fitt to lett flie abroad, till about 30 yeares hence; for the author and the persons (like medlars) ought to be first rotten'. His *Lives* contained 'the trueth and, as neer as I

---

[1] A-W, 27 March 1680, B. 14, 130v-132v. He also 'could afford to putt-in' Kettell.

[2] A-W, 22 May 1680, F 39, 340.     [3] E.g. *B.L.* I, 311.

[4] A similar structure is found in, for instance, Gilbert Burnet's *Life and Death of Sir Matthew Hale* (1682). Aubrey's precise model is unknown, though it certainly represents an attempt at orthodoxy: except in one case (see below, p. 225), Aubrey only cites other biographical works (notably Fuller's *Worthies*) as sources of information. Though exhaustively discussed in N. P. Barker, 'John Aubrey's *Brief Lives*' (Minnesota Ph.D., 1966), esp. ch. II, earlier writings are virtually irrelevant to Aubrey's activity as a biographer, which clearly grew out of his general anxiety to preserve information: his attacks on the irresponsibility of 'wits' parallels his feeling that he must complete his topographical description of Wiltshire since 'no body els would doe it *throughly* like an Antiquary' (A-W, I April 1672, B. 14, 92), and he always put minuteness before literary form. On the general background of 'Renaissance individualism' against which Aubrey's curiosity about biographical particulars should be seen, cf. J. L. Clifford, *Biography as an Art* (Oxford, 1962) and D. A. Stauffer, *English Biography before 1700* (Cambridge, Mass., 1930).

[5] The title-page, dated 1690, is MS Aubrey 8, 69. Cf. *B.L.* I, 15-6. By scattering them alphabetically, Clark unfortunately hides Aubrey's intention.

[6] A-W, 15 June 1680, *B.L.* I, 11-12.

can and that religiously as a poenitent to his confessor, nothing but the trueth: the naked and plaine trueth, which is here exposed so bare that the very *pudenda* are not covered, and affords many passages that would raise a blush in a young virgin's cheeke'.[1]

But apart from the odd, scurrilous and obscene stories that he recorded, posterity can be grateful for the minutiae that he set down, for which there had been no place in Wood's scheme, of the looks, habits, characteristics and sayings of famous men. 'I doe not here repeat any thing already published (to the best of my remembrance)', he claimed,[2] and he was glad to preserve such information if only 'for the rarity's sake'.[3] In their spontaneity and verisimilitude, Aubrey's *Lives* look forward to that classic of intimate biography of a century later, Boswell's *Life of Johnson*. Indeed, literary antiquaries like Edmund Malone who rediscovered them in the late eighteenth century deliberately compared them with that work, which 'highly as ... ⟨it⟩ is admired at present, to posterity, it will be still more valuable and interesting';[4] Aubrey's reputation as a writer has been mainly based on them ever since.

It is therefore appropriate that Aubrey's discovery of his ability as a biographer in 1680 heralded a new persistence of authorship in the following years. In the early 1680s he consolidated his earlier notes on education into his *Idea of Education of Young Gentlemen*. In 1685, when Plot had declined to make use of his notes on natural history, he set to work to construct from them a *Naturall Historie of Wiltshire* comparable with Plot's work on Oxfordshire. He modestly explained in his preface how, 'Considering therefore, that if I should not doe this myselfe my papers might either perish; or be sold in an Auction, and somebody els (as is not un-common) put his name to my Paines: and not knowing any one that would undertake this Designe whilst I live, I have tumultuarily stitch'd up what I have many yeares since collected'.[5] But it is in fact a self-conscious and elaborate work, in contrast to the somewhat rudimentary notes

<hr/>

[1] Loc. cit.    [2] Loc. cit.

[3] A-W, Vigil SS Peter and Paul 1681, F 39, 397. There is no evidence for any deliberate selection of details by Aubrey: they are apparently entirely miscellaneous.

[4] Malone in Bodleian MS Eng. Misc. d. 27, 170v. On the rediscovery of the lives at this time, see M. Hunter, 'The bibliography of John Aubrey's *Brief Lives*', *Antiquarian Book Monthly Review* 1 (Feb. 1974), 6 f. Aubrey apparently had no influence on biographical writing in the eighteenth century, when a 'theory' of biography like his was articulated quite independently by Roger North, Boswell, Johnson and others (cf. Clifford, *Biography as an Art*).

[5] MS A 1, 7.

that had evidently formerly comprised his writings on natural history.[1] Between 1686 and 1689 he spent a great deal of time searching classical authors for precedents for the folk-customs and superstitions that he had long observed during his field-work, using them to compile his *Remaines of Gentilisme and Judaisme*.[2] Moreover in the late 1680s he also began a treatise on place-names, which, perhaps significantly, is somewhat insubstantial in content, but has all the apparatus of a finished book, including title-pages and preface.[3] At this stage in his career, Aubrey's concern for book-making had almost outrun his will to collect.

The 1680s and 1690s also witness a growing mistrust of his colleagues and their use of his materials, and an increasing possessiveness about his own works, perhaps partly inspired by his close friend Hooke, whose jealousy of Newton and others is notorious.[4] Referring to a proposal in a letter from Andrew Paschall that he should collect educational theories so that a friend of Paschall's could apply them, Aubrey sourly noted: 'A wise Proposall! I must beat the Bush, and another must catch the Bird'.[5] He apparently also became rather bitter about Plot's use of his works: 'I did not think that there had been so much trueth in Mr. R. Sheldons advice to ⟨me⟩ sc: lend not your MSS. how ungratefully Dr Plott hath used me!'[6] Aubrey even quarrelled with Wood, who, fearing prosecution for libellous information supplied by Aubrey, 'gelded' several leaves from the manuscript of *Brief Lives* in 1692, an act of 'Ingratitude' that Aubrey never fully forgave.[7] His feelings were exacerbated by Wood's failure to acknowledge the immense pains that he had taken in gathering material for the *Athenae Oxonienses*.

[1] Cf. below, pp. 100–101.

[2] The title-pages of the three parts are dated February 1686/7, October–December 1688 and 25 March 1689. Cf. *T.P.W.*, 401.

[3] *An Interpretation of Villare Anglicanum*; the preface is dated 31 Oct. 1687 (MS A 5, 19v). He copied out a list of the place-names of England from Sir Henry Spelman's gazetteer *Villare Anglicum* (1656) and began to interpret them, but it is very incomplete. The annexed 'Villare Scoticum' has only five entries, and the 'Villare Hibernicum' (dated 1691, MS A 5, 107) only one (for these he used printed lists of names from maps by Morden and Visscher). Nicolson's opinion of the work was rather inflated: he speaks of the 'mighty Improvements' made by 'the Industrious and Learned Mr. *Aubrey*' in *The English Historical Library* (second edition, London, 1714), 7.

[4] Cf. Margaret Espinasse, *Robert Hooke*, ch. I, and F. E. Manuel, *A Portrait of Isaac Newton*, ch. VII. Hooke actually had Aubrey write a letter to Wood outlining his achievements which he went through and emended himself (*B.L.* I, 412 f.).

[5] Wood F 46, 327: a note by Aubrey on a letter from Paschall of 20 April 1688.

[6] T.G.c.25, 95av. Sheldon was an antiquary friend.

[7] *B.L.* I, 13, though cf. A-L, 10 Oct. 1694, A. 1814, 117.

'You will see by my Lives, how much I have obliged my friend Anthony,' Aubrey told Thomas Tanner,[1] but in fact few ever saw Aubrey's manuscripts or his letters to Wood, and 'the consumate ingratitude and impudence of Anthony Wood' in using Aubrey's work as if it were his own[2] was only discovered by antiquaries a century later.

Aubrey's jealousy for his writings even inspired him to unjust suspicions of those whom he had allowed to consult his notes. His worries about Plot's use of his papers included the rather unreal fear that Plot would try to get money by exploiting secrets recorded in them that Aubrey hoped to use himself.[3] And in 1692, when John Ray published his *Miscellaneous Discourses Concerning the Dissolution and Changes of the World*, Aubrey claimed that his ideas were plagiarised from those of Hooke recorded in 'An Hypothesis of the Terraquious Globe' in the *Naturall Historie of Wiltshire*, which Ray had borrowed, considering it 'a right Presbyterian trick'.[4] But in fact Ray's theories differed from Hooke's and he had undoubtedly worked them out for himself.[5] At this stage in his life Aubrey's suspicions were almost getting out of hand: 'I would have a man hanged should print anothers booke under his owne name,' he stoutly maintained in 1694,[6] and in 1695, when Benjamin Woodroffe, Master of Gloucester Hall, Oxford, claimed the credit for discovering a medicinal spring that he had heard of from Aubrey, Aubrey wrote 'Lord! what snatching & catching there is of other mens discoverys'.[7]

Such were Aubrey's feelings when he was approached in connection with one of the grandest antiquarian projects of the century, the preparation of an augmented edition of Camden's *Britannia* under the supervision of Edmund Gibson, a young Oxford scholar who was later to be Bishop of London.[8] Gibson, Tanner and

---

[1] A-T, 1 June 1693, T. 25, 49.

[2] Malone's note on Aubrey's life of Penn in Bodleian MS Eng. Misc.d.27, 137v.

[3] See below, p. 110, n. 13.     [4] A-W, 13 Feb. 1691/2, F 39, 438.

[5] On Ray's geological ideas, which were less radical than Hooke's and Aubrey's, see C. E. Raven, *John Ray, Naturalist* (second edition, Cambridge, 1950), esp. ch. XVI, and the works referred to on p. 58, n. 5. Aubrey's view about Ray's supposed plagiarism probably owed something to Hooke, as apparently did his view that Steno stole his geological ideas from Hooke, which was equally unjust: cf. V. A. Eyles, 'The influence of Nicolaus Steno on the development of geological science in Britain', *Acta Historica Scientiarum Naturalium et Medicinalium* XV (Copenhagen, 1958), 173 f.

[6] A-W, 6 July 1694, F 39, 277.     [7] A-W, 2 Sept. 1695, Wood F 51, 11v.

[8] Cf. Stuart Piggott, 'William Camden and the *Britannia*', *Proceedings of the British Academy* XXXVII (1951), 209 f.

Edward Lhwyd, Plot's successor as Curator of the Ashmolean and himself an eminent naturalist and antiquary, were all anxious to use Aubrey's *Monumenta Britannica* in preparing it. Aubrey was, perhaps not unreasonably, afraid that he would 'loose the Credit of it and the creame would be skimmed to imbelish that Designe. and then who would *buy* or *print* my Collections?'[1] Lhwyd tried to pacify him: 'I can not in the least blame your caution in communicating your Monumenta Britannica,' he wrote, but 'this I had not desired, but that I thought one or two pages of your three volumes, might be made use of (under your name), without any prejudice to the work';[2] he also promised that 'if you are pleas'd to communicate, I shall be carefull to doe you right, and not rob you of any part of that honour and thanks that is due to you from the curious and ingenious'.[3] Tanner also assured Aubrey that 'nothing can raise the expectation of the World more, than to quote two or three curious Remarks out of a book with respect to the Author',[4] and Aubrey was eventually 'contented to have some Excerpta of my MSS [with mention of me] printed in the Britannia',[5] relying on Gibson's 'Integrity & virtue'.[6]

Worries about plagiarism none the less continue in his correspondence with his Oxford friends in these years, even concerning projects which he realised he would never be able to complete himself and therefore delegated to others. Tanner, who undertook the completion of the *Wiltshire Antiquities* with Aubrey's brother William, assured him that 'I shall scorn to be like *Ant⟨hony⟩ Wood*, viz. make use of your papers and acquaintance and at last not afford you a good word', and (echoing Aubrey's request) he promised that the originals would be sent to the Ashmolean 'that posterity may see how just we have been to the memory of your pains'.[7] Even when he asked Edward Lhwyd to finish the *Interpretation of Villare Anglicanum* for him, Aubrey requested him to 'doe me the Right, to make mention of me' and preserve the original,[8] and he was always worried about which of his friends and helpers should get the benefit of the works that he entrusted to them.[9]

[1] A-L, 19 Oct. 1693, A. 1814, 100.   [2] Lhwyd-Aubrey, 16 Nov. 1693, MS A 12, 250.
[3] Id., 13 Oct. 1693, ibid., 248.   [4] Tanner-Aubrey, 26 Dec. 1693, MS A 13, 204.
[5] A-T, 6 Feb. 1693/4, T. 25, 118.   [6] A-L, St David's Day 1693/4, A. 1814, 107.
[7] Tanner-Aubrey, 16 May 1693, MS A 13, 200. Aubrey made the request in a letter to Tanner of 4 May 1693, T. 25, 39.
[8] A-L, 21 April 1691, MS A 5, 2.
[9] Cf. A-L, 27 March 1694, A. 1814, 110 (concerning Lhwyd and the *Naturall Historie of Wiltshire*); A-T, 14 Oct. 1693, T. 25, 94 (concerning Tanner and William Aubrey and

This jealousy about the value of his work was combined with a growing concern, from the 1680s onwards, that his papers should be safely preserved, and that they should be in a form in which they would be useful to posterity even if not to his own generation. The first impulse seems, appropriately, to have been associated with the newly composed *Lives* in 1680. When he wrote to Wood on 22 May of that year describing the work, he added, 'I have lately been very ill of a cold, and being one day taken with a Lipothymie, fainting away, as soon as I came to my selfe in the first leafe of the Booke aforesaid, I writt that my Will & humble request was, that those Minutes should be safely transmitted to you.'[1] Subsequent events, like the death of John Collins and other close friends in 1683,[2] intensified his feeling 'that we are all mortall men, & that we must not loose Time',[3] and other incidents, like the near loss of his *Naturall Historie of Wiltshire* when the box in which it was travelling to Andrew Paschall in Somerset was broken to splinters,[4] increased his anxiety about the fate of his manuscripts. ' 'Tis pity they should be putt under pies, as the Bishop of Sarum's were . . . I see what becomes of Mens writings when they are deceased', he reflected,[5] and his long experience of the misfortunes befalling the life's labours of others inspired him to unique efforts to ensure that his own works survived.

'Now what shall I say, or doe with these prety collections?' he asked Wood in 1687. 'I thought to have made Mr R. Hooke my Executor to publish them if I dye before I doe it my selfe: but he hath so much to doe of his owne, that he will not be able to finish. & you know how Dr Plott served me. I shall write them legibly: and if you survive me, you would be more carefull of them than any body els. Mr Elias Ashm⟨ole⟩ growes old, & sickly'.[6] But the dangers of leaving them to any private person increasingly dawned on him: 'You are not very young, & a mortall man,' he told Wood, '& when you dye, then your Nephew stoppes Gunnes with them'.[7]

the *Wiltshire Antiquities*); and, e.g., F 39, 400 (a note by Aubrey on the back of a letter to him of 31 March 1690 from 'G.M.') about Wood getting profit from publishing Aubrey's papers.

[1] A-W, 22 May 1680, F 39, 340. Cf. *B.L.* 1, 9–10.
[2] A-W, 26 Jan. 1683/4, B. 14, 137.      [3] A-W, 15 April 1682, MS A 12, 8.
[4] A-W, 17 Aug. 1685, F 39, 375.
[5] A-W, 24 April 1690, F 39, 402v–3. This was of Aubrey's collection of letters, MS A 12–13.
[6] A-W, 27 Oct. 1687, F 39, 392v.
[7] A-W on a letter of G.M. to Aubrey of 31 March 1690, F 39, 400.

Instead he resolved to copy Ashmole, who had presented his collection of rarities to the University of Oxford to be housed in a museum named after him over a decade before. He and others now advised Aubrey that this was the best home for his collections, and Aubrey resolved 'by all meanes to secure them in the Musaeum: which (I grant) would be safe'.[1] In the Ashmolean he could be sure that they would never be 'cast away as Rubbish',[2] and for the last seven years of his life he was resolved to send everything there. His quarrel with Wood in the 1690s was intensified by his frenzied concern for the fate of his works and the rarities he had collected, such as the drawings he had had made of the ruins at Osney, 'which I have ten times over desired him to putt into the Museum. for when he dies, it will be lost and torne by his nieces children'.[3]

But before they went to the Ashmolean, the manuscripts needed retranscription and reorganization. As he told Wood in 1689, 'my Minutes were so confused, & so interlined &c.: that (as you say) had I not donne it in my life time they would have signified nothing'.[4] He embarked on a lengthy programme of recopying his works in a form suitable for the printer or posterity, spurred by friends like John Evelyn and Charles Howard, another Surrey virtuoso, who were both keen that Aubrey should leave his *Perambulation of Surrey* 'as intelligible [sc. in Manuscript] as well as my Lawsuite & troubles will give me leave'.[5] Between 1688 and 1692 Aubrey transcribed his *Monumenta Britannica*, his *Naturall Historie of Wiltshire* and his *Perambulation of Surrey*,[6] thus preserving, he hoped, 'many good Remarques, that deserve not to be buried in Oblivion'.[7] In 1690/1 he told Wood 'I have now donne my Naturall Hist⟨orie⟩ of Wilts within 3 chapters. So that I am now contented to resigne up my animula, when it shall please God to call for it';[8] but he would have 'methodized' his *Surrey* and other works more had he not dreaded the 'drudgery of another transcribing',[9] and he was still hoping to retranscribe his *Idea of Education* in 1696/7.[10]

He was doubtless encouraged in this labour by the enthusiasm

---

[1] Loc. cit.   [2] A-W, 23 Jan. 1693-4, Wood F 51, 8.
[3] A-L, 2 Sept. 1694, A. 1814, 116.   [4] A-W, St Peter's Day 1689, F 39, 386.
[5] A-L, 29 March 1692, A. 1814, 99.
[6] He had completed the *Monumenta* by October 1689 (cf. A-W, 24 April 1690, F 39, 402), the *Naturall Historie of Wiltshire* by August 1691 (A-W, 3 August 1691, F 39, 429) and was hoping to finish *Surrey* in May 1692 (A-W, 19 May 1692, T. 456a, 40).
[7] MS A 4, 31.   [8] A-W, 1 Feb. 1690/1, F 39, 414v.   [9] MS A 4, 31.
[10] A-L, 26 Jan. 1696/7, A. 1814, 118.

with which his works were received by those who now read them. Ray perused the *Naturall Historie of Wiltshire* 'with great pleasure & satisfaction. You doe so mingle *utile dulci* ⟨the useful with the pleasant⟩ that the book cannot but take with all sorts of Readers.'[1] The *Adversaria Physica* he read twice for the 'variety and curiosity of the Matter & observations';[2] indeed it was his praise that made Aubrey resolve to send it to the Ashmolean with his other papers, for formerly he had considered it 'not worthy to be conserved in so sacred a Repository'.[3] Evelyn, Tanner, Lhwyd, Thomas Gale, the scholarly High Master of St Paul's School, and others annotated his newly transcribed works, as he proudly noted on their title-pages, evidently considering that this added to their value.[4]

The Earl of Abingdon had a transcript made of the *Remaines of Gentilisme*;[5] another of Aubrey's patrons, the Earl of Pembroke, read the *Idea of Education* 'all over, & excerped some things';[6] and William Fanshawe also read this 'most excellent treatis', which, he told Aubrey, 'if you pleas to perfect & send abroad: posterity will be obliged to celebrate your name with more respect, then any of the past greate men whoe first civilizd & cultivated rude & untaught mankind'.[7] Benjamin Woodroffe saw the *Idea* too,[8] and Evelyn, whose perusal Aubrey claimed to value more than anyone else's,[9] paid this and Aubrey's other works the compliment of making lengthy extracts in his commonplace books.[10] Above all, the Royal

---

[1] Ray-Aubrey, 22 Sept. 1691, MS A 13, 174.     [2] Id., 24 Aug. 1692, ibid., 176.

[3] A-L, 4 May 1693, A. 1814, 91. It was not at first in the catalogue of Aubrey's writings in MS A 5, 123v, and is added in Lhwyd's hand. (Cf. A-L, 4 Feb. 1692/3, A. 1814, 102).

[4] E.g. T.G.c.24, 20. Evelyn annotated *Surrey, Nat. Hist. Wiltshire, Gentilisme*, and Book IV of *Monumenta*; Gale annotated *Surrey, Nat. Hist. Wiltshire, Monumenta;* Kennett, *Gentilisme*; Lhwyd, *Surrey, Monumenta*; Ray, *Nat. Hist. Wiltshire*; Tanner, *Nat. Hist. Wiltshire, Wiltshire Antiquities, Monumenta*; B. G. Cramer, *Gentilisme*. There are occasional notes by others (e.g. Ashmole in T.G.c.24, 271, 274v; John Beaumont in MS A 4, 102v) and others read manuscripts without marking them (e.g. Hoskyns had *Nat. Hist. Wiltshire* at one stage: A-T, 4 May 1693, T. 25, 39).

[5] A-T, 4 May 1693, T. 25, 39. It cost £3. He also wanted a transcript of part of the *Monumenta*: A-W, 5 July 1690, F 39, 405v.

[6] Aubrey-Henley, 27 Feb. 1693/4, MS A 10, 2.

[7] Fanshawe-Aubrey, 7 Aug. 1691, MS A 12, 115.

[8] Cf. A-L, 18 July 1695, A. 1829, 25v: 'I would have my *Idea* sent speedily to Dr Woodroff'; Woodroffe-Aubrey, 21 July 1695, MS A 13, 273: 'I long to see your method.'

[9] Aubrey-Evelyn, 15 May 1692 (see p. 55, n. 5).

[10] Evelyn's notes from the *Idea* will be found in Christ Church Evelyn MSS 36, 680 f., and 38 (unpaginated leaves at end). MS 173 is a volume entitled *Adversaria* which Evelyn began for his notes from the *Naturall Historie of Wiltshire*. He added notes from *Gentilisme*, and also 'some particular notes in my Travells', etc. MS 38 also has a

Society did Aubrey the honour of having a transcript made of his *Naturall Historie of Wiltshire* in 1690-1, a unique and extraordinary gesture showing their esteem for it, which cost them the considerable sum of seven pounds;[1] they also claimed to be 'utterly against' his sending his papers to Oxford,[2] which he doubtless also found flattering.

His friends were no less importunate for Aubrey to publish his writings. Thomas Tanner bewailed 'the notorious misfortunes that usually attend posthumous papers',[3] while Ray felt that the *Adversaria Physica*, the *Perambulation of Surrey* and the *Naturall Historie of Wiltshire* were all worth publishing.[4] Aubrey was encouraged to print his *Monumenta Britannica* by Ray, William Nicolson, the learned archdeacon of Carlisle, and many others:[5] 'I long to have your Book in the presse,' wrote Lhwyd.[6] The *Monumenta* did, in fact, come quite near to being published: proposals were distributed and subscriptions collected in 1693,[7] and Aubrey became quite sanguine in his hopes for its appearance; but this was never to come about.[8] Aubrey's letters mention vaguer plans for getting his

---

copy of Aubrey's 'The proportions of severall languages, ingredient in our English', copied from the *Monumenta* (T.G.c.25, 239-41).

[1] A-W, 5 July 1690 and 3 Aug. 1691; F 39, 405v, 429. It was made by B. G. Cramer, Clerk to the Society (cf. MS A 2, 124a, where Aubrey tells him what to transcribe). It is now Royal Society MS 92.

[2] A-L, 4 May 1693, A. 1814, 91.

[3] Tanner-Aubrey, 16 May 1693, MS A 13, 199.

[4] Ray-Aubrey, 20 Dec. 1692 and 4 July 1693, MS A 13, 177, 178. Cf. A-L, 4 Feb. 1692/3, A. 1814, 102.

[5] A-L, 12 Nov. 1696, A. 1829, 78.

[6] Lhwyd-Aubrey, 2 March 1692/3, MS A 12, 241.

[7] Copies of the *Proposals* survive in Wood 658, nos. 780, (dated by Wood 10 April 1693), 811 and 811*. References to their distribution and the collection of subscriptions will be found in the following letters, all of early 1693: from Aubrey to Tanner, T. 25, 30, 39, 49; to Lhwyd, A. 1814, 90 and 91; to Wood, Wood F 51, 5; to Aubrey from Bathurst, MS A 12, 23v; Holder, ibid., 168; Lhwyd, ibid., 245; Paschall, MS A 13, 85; Ray, ibid., 178; Tanner, ibid., 194-5, 198, T.G.c.24, 19; D. Danvers-Aubrey, MS A 12, 92, of 12 Oct. (no year), which apologises for his failure to obtain subscribers, is presumably a late-comer.

[8] The chronology of the plans for publishing the *Monumenta* seems to be as follows. In 1692 Aubrey tried to find a London bookseller to publish the work (cf. e.g. A-W, 19 May 1692, T. 456a, 40); but none was willing to undertake so expensive a book, so Aubrey resolved early in 1693 to publish it by subscription at Oxford (A-L, 4 Feb. 1692/3, A. 1814, 102). Proposals were thereupon issued and subscriptions collected. Unfortunately, however, the proposals for Gibson's *Britannia* were also issued in April 1693 (Cf. Wood 658, no. 806), and the market was evidently insufficient for two large books with similar titles. By 19 July, as Aubrey told Tanner in a letter of that date

*Naturall Historie of Wiltshire* printed, perhaps involving Lhwyd, but they did not get very far.[1] In the event, the only work published before Aubrey's death was a compilation of papers on supernatural topics, *Miscellanies* (1696), which at least some people hoped would 'meet with good encouragement for the worthy Authors sake',[2] and which achieved a second edition in 1721.

The rest of Aubrey's works were saved by his determination to have them preserved in a 'publick Repository'.[3] By the time he died in June 1697 he had sent to the Ashmolean most of his manuscripts, together with numerous printed books, antiquities and other objects, as was gratefully recorded in the Register of Benefactors to the Museum, and in a prominent inscription in gold letters on a blue ground over the door to its library.[4] Almost all his manuscripts and books have remained at Oxford ever since. Two of his works, which were not in his possession when he died, remained outside libraries for longer. His *Remaines of Gentilisme* was in the hands of White Kennett, an antiquary who was later Bishop of Peterborough, and it went with his manuscripts to the Lansdowne collection and the

---

(T. 25, 66), 'I have gott yet but 112 subscriptions', which was apparently not enough, 'so that I presume, I must try if the University will print it, affording me a competent number of Copies'. By the summer of 1694, however, it was clear that this too was impossible (A-L, 24 May 1694, A. 1814, 113), and in September Aubrey was wondering if Sir John Aubrey would pay for the publication of 'Templa Druidum', which would advertise and pay for subsequent parts (A-L, 2 Sept. 1694, A. 1814, 116). In 1695 Aubrey went back to the London booksellers (A-W, 11 Aug. 1695, Wood F 51, 9v), and in August he came to an agreement with Awnsham Churchill (Aubrey-Halley, 31 Aug. 1695, *T.P.W.*, 459; cf. Churchill-Tanner, 31 Aug. 1695, Tanner 24, 58). But although Aubrey complained about how long Churchill was keeping the manuscript without publishing it in November 1696 (A-L, 12 Nov. 1696, A. 1829, 78), it remained unpublished in his hands.

[1] A-T, 4 May 1693, T. 25, 39, mentions Aubrey's intention of depositing it with Arthur Charlett, Master of University College, 'or Queens Coll⟨ege⟩: to be printed at leisure at Oxon', but A-T, 14 Oct. 1693, T. 25, 94, and A-L, 27 March 1694, A. 1814, 110, want Lhwyd to oversee its publication.

[2] Archer-Tanner, 22 April 1695, Tanner 24, 29v; but he added ' 'tis more than I can well hope for'.

[3] A-W, 8 Nov. 1692, F 39, 437.

[4] The inscription is reproduced as plate 17; the entry in the Benefactor's Book is printed in Powell, *John Aubrey and his Friends*, 206. Apart from his manuscripts, Aubrey presented to the Ashmolean books from his library (see 'Aubrey's Library'), mathematical instruments (cf. above p. 43, n. 5), mineralogical specimens (cf. A-L, 18 July 1695, 24 Feb. 1695/6, A. 1829, 25, 56), pictures and Roman coins etc. (cf. Plot-Aubrey, 8 Oct. 1688, MS A 13, 140; on the pictures see Powell, op. cit., 217–18, and on the Roman antiquities, Britton, *Memoir of John Aubrey*, 84: in Britton's time they still survived, but my enquiries at the Ashmolean have failed to locate them).

British Museum.[1] *Monumenta Britannica* was in the hands of Awnsham Churchill, the publisher, who had bought it from Aubrey with a view to publishing it; it remained in the hands of his descendants throughout the eighteenth century and reached the Bodleian Library only in 1836. Several works have disappeared: 'Liber B' of the *Wiltshire Antiquities*, which was borrowed from the Ashmolean by Aubrey's brother William in 1703 and never returned;[2] *Religio Naturalis*, or *Hypothesis Ethicorum & Scala Religionis*, which may have been in the possession of Dr Edward Waple, a London divine with scientific interests;[3] and *A Collection of Approved Receipts*, the *Adversaria Physica* and some minor literary works.[4]

Apart from these unfortunate lacunae, Aubrey's surviving manuscripts provide a conspectus of the bulk of his intellectual concerns, deliberately bequeathed by him to posterity. Though, after the interest in them aroused in the 1690s, most of them were little known even in antiquarian circles for nearly a century,[5] they remained in Oxford to be rediscovered by later scholars. They form the main subject-matter of this book, together with Aubrey's letters to his friends, many of which have survived, particularly in the collections of Wood, Tanner and Lhwyd. But other letters are lost, and the endorsement in the early eighteenth century even of one that survives—'papers not very materiall, & may be used for

---

[1] Now British Library MS Lansdowne 231. It may have been only partly accidental that this never reached the Ashmolean: in a note on the back of a letter from Lhwyd, MS A 12, 251v, Aubrey noted that it 'would not be fitt to leave to the Critiques of the University'; he felt that it was 'too light' (A-L, 27 March 1694, A. 1814, 109). The absense of *Hypothesis Ethicorum* may also not be entirely coincidental, for Aubrey thought it 'not fit to be exposed' (A-W, St. Peter's Day 1689, F 39, 386).

[2] Cf. Jackson, 'Lost Volume of Aubrey's MSS', *Wiltshire Archaeological and Natural History Magazine* VII (1862), 76 f. William Aubrey also had the manuscript of the *Miscellanies*, which has also not survived: cf. W. Aubrey-Tanner, 27 Oct. 1699, Tanner 21, 174.

[3] Cf. his *Epistola ad Regiam Societatem Londinensem de Nuperis Terrae Motibus* (1693). Powell, *John Aubrey and his Friends*, 292, is mistaken in claiming that he assisted Aubrey in compiling the *Miscellanies*; the phrase 'with Dr Waple' in the list of Aubrey's works in MS A 5, 123v, merely means (like other similar references) that certain of Aubrey's MSS were then in Waple's hands.

[4] On all these, see 'Aubrey's Lost Works' and 'A Note on *Analecta*'.

[5] The *Monumenta*, however, which was in private hands, was well known: see below, p. 206. The Ashmolean MSS were apparently occasionally consulted, but they were hardly known until *Brief Lives* were rediscovered in the late eighteenth century: cf. above, p. 82, n. 4. The manuscripts and books were transferred from the Ashmolean to the Bodleian in 1860.

necessary uses'[1]—is an ominous reminder of the prescience of Aubrey's desperate concern to preserve his work, 'to make my owne hands my Executors'.[2]

[1] B. 14 146v     [2] A-L, 2 Sept. 1694, A. 1814, 116.

# CHAPTER TWO

# *Science, Technology and Magic*

Aubrey's two most important scientific works, his *Naturall Historie of Wiltshire* and his *Adversaria Physica*, were both mainly descriptive, collections of observations of all kinds of natural phenomena. In this they were not unusual, for in his generation, heavily influenced by Bacon, many were glad to accumulate information, often merely as materials for others more expert to interpret. 'Every man has his delight; ingenious information is mine,' wrote Sir John Hoskyns, a keen member of the Royal Society, whose profuse letters to Aubrey outlined his views on the proper programme of natural history;[1] but he felt that 'meere compiling will content mee', leaving the work of interpretation to others.[2] Andrew Paschall, the 'chief undertaker'[3] of a design for writing the natural history of Somerset, modestly claimed that 'the top of what we aim at is onely to do all we can to prepare & preserve materials for some other person who may be heerafter inclined & able to do that work'.[4] Even Robert Plot's published natural histories were more praised by those, such as Ray,[5] who used them as quarries for investigations of more specialised topics, than as important scientific exercises in their own right.

But some saw the collecting of information as valuable for its own sake, wanting to 'gain all the Knowledg that is worth getting' about Britain,[6] in the hope, perhaps somewhat simple-minded, that 'the more we know of these *Islands*, the better, I presume, may they be manag'd'.[7] Plot conceived his enterprise as a serious scientific project, a history of 'Naturall Bodys, and manual Arts, found or

---

[1] Hoskyns-Aubrey, 20 Feb. 1674/5, MS A 12, 215. MS A 12, 197 f. comprise his letters to Aubrey of the early 1670s outlining his proposals for a natural history of England; he regretted, however, that 'I would bee glad to view places in your company but considering my selfe can say or thinke or doe noe more than writing soe' (21 Aug. 1672, ibid., 204v).

[2] Id., 16 March 1677, ibid., 220; in this case, Robert Morison.

[3] Birch, *History*, IV, 316 (1684).

[4] Paschall-Aubrey, 18 July 1684, MS A 13, 67. He hoped Plot would do it.

[5] E.g. *Synopsis Methodica Stirpium Britannicarum* (London, 1690), a3.

[6] John Houghton, *A Collection for the Improvement of Husbandry and Trade*, II, no. 25 (20 Jan. 1692/3).

[7] Ibid., I, no. 3 (13 April 1692).

practised within the Kingdom of England and Dominion of Wales'.[1]
He could quote in justification Bacon's dictum that natural history
'is used either for the sake of the knowledge of the particular things
which it contains, or as the primary material of philosophy and the
stuff and subject-matter of true induction',[2] and such views were
frequently echoed by scientists at the Restoration, even the most
sophisticated, like Hooke.[3] But a rather more superficial earlier
attempt of the same kind as Plot's, Joshua Childrey's *Britannia
Baconica: or, The Natural Rarities of England, Scotland & Wales*
(1661), illustrates well how pure description could be seen by the
ardent Baconian as the only proper concern of the scientist—thus
moving even further towards losing the balance between induction
and mere accumulation that sometimes seemed precarious in the
scientific writings of Bacon himself.

Childrey's chief end, he claimed, was 'to serve the *Commonwealth
of Learning*, which much wants such *Histories* as this to be written,
and laid as a sure *Foundation*, whereon to build those *Axiomes* that
make us *true Schollars*, and *knowing men* in *Philosophy*'.[4] What is
particularly revealing is Childrey's apology for his occasional lapses
into theory, for he despised the Aristotelians and 'the pest of
Learning . . . that men first fancy Opinions and Axiomes to themselves, and then by the help and art of Distinguishing, wrest and fit
particular Instances and Observations to them'.[5] As he saw collecting materials as the primary function of natural philosophy, so he
felt bound to apologise that 'I have here and there attempted to give
the Causes of the *Raritie* I relate, having the example of my Lord *B.*
for my authority, who in his *Sylva Sylvarum* hath the like excursions ever and anon into the *Ætiology*'. But he hastened to 'confess,
that such kind of writing is a little too bold yet, before the *Histories*
of *Art* and *Nature* are compleatly done'.[6]

Childrey's contribution to this project had been, in 1658, to take
paper-books and fill them with observations of natural history,[7]
and Aubrey's motives were doubtless similar when, in 1654, he

---

[1] Plot, *Plinius*, 1.    [2] *Parasceve*, 2, in Bacon, *Works*, IV, 254.
[3] Cf., e.g., Hooke, *Works*, 18.    [4] *Britannia Baconica* (London, 1661), Blv.
[5] Ibid., B2v–3.
[6] Ibid., B2–B2v. Aubrey quotes Childrey (e.g. MS A 1, 28v, 32, 53; R.S. MS 92, 39)
but there is no evidence that Childrey had any seminal influence on him, or of when he
discovered the work.
[7] Cf. Childrey-Oldenburg, 12 July 1669, *The Correspondence of Henry Oldenburg, ed.*
A. R. and M. B. Hall, VI (Madison, 1969), 108.

'began to enter into pocket memorandum bookes philosophicall and antiquarian remarques',[1] and, in 1656, began his *Naturall Historie of Wiltshire*, which, 'for ought I know', was the first essay of its kind in the nation.[2] It is certainly significant that it was through the work of another active Baconian of the 1650s, Ralph Austen, that he recalled Bacon's dictum 'That the Writings of Speculative men upon active matters, seemes to men of experience, to be but dreames & dotage: And that it were to be wished (as that which would make Learning indeed solid & fruitfull) that *active* men would or could become writers'.[3] This Baconianism of the Interregnum is the background to Aubrey's scientific works.

None of Aubrey's scientific manuscripts of the 1650s survive, but this is only because he continued to add to the books that he began then throughout his life. His *Adversaria Physica*, which by 1692 was 'fol⟨io⟩ an inch thick',[4] evidently developed from the 'observations' that he gleaned 'even travelling (which from 1649 till 1670 was never off my horsback)'.[5] Though it is now lost, some indication of its content in the 1670s is available from the substantial notes from it that Robert Plot made in his *Analecta* in 1675/6, and the shorter extracts by Henry Oldenburg preserved among the Classified Papers of the Royal Society.[6] The *Naturall Historie of Wiltshire*, though now surviving only in the form in which Aubrey cast it in 1685, incorporates material accumulated over thirty years, and some idea of the form of Aubrey's earlier Wiltshire notes, whose content overlaps totally with the finished book, can be gained from a paper on springs in Wiltshire that he read at the Royal Society in 1668 and from his more general observations on Wiltshire read there in 1675–6 and subsequently copied by Oldenburg for its archives.[7]

In fact, Aubrey's scientific interests do not seem to have changed

---

[1] *B.L.* I, 39.   [2] MS A I, 6.

[3] Aubrey quotes this passage from 'L⟨or⟩d B⟨acon⟩ in his Advancement of Learning' on an old document used for mathematical calculations in Worcester College MS 5.4 (unpaginated; it is the third leaf after the title-page 'Algebra Literalis') and then wrote 'q⟨uaere⟩ pag⟨inam⟩: π⟨αρὰ⟩ χορογραφ⟨ίαν⟩ Antiquariam' (cf. T.G.c.24, 138, where he quotes it as from Bacon's *Instauratio Magna*); 'V⟨ide⟩ Austins little treatise of Fruit trees in study at Chalke' (i.e. R. Austen, *Observations upon some part of Sr Francis Bacon's Naturall History as it concernes, Fruit-trees, Fruits, and Flowers* (Oxford, 1658), who cites Bacon thus in 'To the Reader'; I have not located the source of the quotation).

[4] A-L, 4 Feb. 1692/3, A. 1814, 102.   [5] *B.L.* I, 42.

[6] See 'A Note on *Analecta*' and *T.P.W.*, 336 f.

[7] Cf. *T.P.W.*, 324 f. and 333 f. On the former, cf. Birch, *History*, III, 271 (1675), 272 (1675/6). These notes were in fact the observations that he had written out for Plot:

much throughout his life, though he naturally became better informed on specific topics.[1] Observations in the *Adversaria Physica* and *Naturall Historie of Wiltshire* show that already in the 1650s, and even the late 1640s, he was collecting information about diseases and cures,[2] human prodigies,[3] inventions,[4] medicinal waters,[5] overlapping rainbows,[6] hurricanes[7] and echoes.[8] His contributions at meetings of the Royal Society from the 1660s onwards, which were recorded in the minutes published in the eighteenth century by Thomas Birch, indicate similar interests. He showed the Society the inventions of his friend Francis Potter;[9] he communicated astronomical observations that he had made[10] and cited evidence concerning the processes of vegetation and fermentation;[11] but most of his contributions concerned local observations of natural phenomena, improvements in husbandry, and recipes. He was interested in the behaviour of tides,[12] in winds,[13] fogs[14] and earthquakes,[15] in 'monstrous productions', animal and human,[16] in fossils,[17] in clay and iron ore[18] and in medicinal waters.[19] He reported that liming of the ground was bad for wool,[20] told of an antidote against poisons[21] and even mentioned a way of making excellent beer without hops.[22]

---

cf. A-W, Twelfeday 1675/6, B. 14, 116. On the latter, which were evidently copied by Oldenburg at the same time, cf. *T.P.W.*, 454.

[1] For example, his relative ignorance about fossils in MS A 3, 90v and *Analecta*, 119, where he has to ask Hooke the name of belemnites, or *Analecta*, 165, where he speaks of ammonites as 'great plenty of stones like Snakes or Lamprices rolled up like a scroll: but all want heads', compared with the chapter 'Of formed Stones' in MS A 1, 84 f.

[2] *Analecta*, 207X.    [3] MS A 1, 156, 158.    [4] Ibid., 164.

[5] Ibid., 37. Cf. MS A 4, 180.    [6] *Analecta*, 203, and R.S. MS 92, 38.

[7] R.S. MS 92, 34.    [8] MS A 1, 29.    [9] Cf. p. 64, n. 1.

[10] Birch, *History*, II, 273 (1668) and 349 (1668/9). Cf. *T.P.W.*, frontispiece, and Aubrey-Boyle, 15 March 1665, Boyle, *Works*, VI, 544.

[11] Birch, *History*, I, 212, 233-4 (1663), IV, 209 (1683).

[12] Ibid., II, 121, 127 (1666), IV, 469 (1685/6).

[13] Ibid., III, 122 (1673/4). Cf. Copy Journal Books VII, 251 (1690).

[14] Birch, *History*, IV, 81 (1681).    [15] Ibid., IV, 220 (1683).

[16] Ibid., IV, 41, 43 (1680).    [17] Ibid., IV, 511 (1686).

[18] Ibid., III, 271 (1675/6), IV, 81 (1680).

[19] Ibid., II, 272 (1668), IV, 186 (1682/3). Cf. Copy Journal Books VIII, 338 (1696).

[20] Birch, *History*, I, 246 (1663).    [21] Ibid., III, 423 (1678).

[22] Ibid., I, 422 (1664). He also contributed on antiquities (ibid., I, 272 (1663), II, 455 (1670), 462 (1670/1)), hydrostatics (Aubrey-Boyle, 15 March 1665, Boyle, *Works*, VI, 544) and mathematics (Copy Journal Books VIII, 101 (1692) ). For other references to Aubrey's contributions to the Society's discussions in Birch, see the list in G. E. Scala, 'An index to the proper names in Thomas Birch, *The History of the Royal Society*', *Notes and Records of the Royal Society* XXVIII (1974), 265. See also Copy Journal Books VII, 145 (1688), 215 (1689), VIII, 5 (1690), 82 (1691), 94, 214-15 (1692), IX, 3 (1696).

These were exactly the kind of subjects that Aubrey was concerned with in his scientific writings—indeed many of these observations were inserted into his *Naturall Historie of Wiltshire*—and such topics continued to interest him till the time of his death. He was still studying springs in 1695, garrulously repeating to his correspondents his earlier views on the subject;[1] and in collecting minerals in 1695/6 he cited Robert Hooke's observations on the subject that he remembered from twenty-five years before.[2]

Though it was not in the nature of descriptive works like Aubrey's to contain much theory, his passing comments on the phenomena that he recorded illustrate the wide range of scientific theories that interested him and which he hoped that the evidence he was amassing would illuminate. The author with whom he had most in common was, perhaps not surprisingly, Bacon. His curiosity about such topics as the activity of nitrous salts and the effect of climate and diet in lengthening or shortening life has much in common with Bacon's scientific ideas, particularly those expressed in his *History of Life and Death*, and he often cited Bacon's views on such matters.[3] His association with Thomas Willis and other scientists in Oxford in the Interregnum left him with some curiosity about fermentation and its potentialities,[4] and he owned and annotated a copy of Sir Kenelm Digby's influential *Discourse concerning the Vegetation of Plants* (1661), showing in his notes his curiosity about the explanation of fertility, the possibility of equivocal generation and other subjects.[5]

For information on particular points, Aubrey quoted eclectically from a wide range of scientific opinion. Robert Hooke frequently appears as a source of information and hypothesis in Aubrey's

[1] A-W, 11 Aug. 1695, Wood F 51, 10, and Aubrey-Halley, 31 Aug. 1695, *T.P.W.*, 361.

[2] A-L, 24 Feb. 1695/6, A. 1829, 56.

[3] E.g. MS A 1, 60, *Analecta*, 202x, *B.L.* 1, 84, 348. His views are often similar to Bacon's even when he does not actually quote him. But Aubrey was not slavishly dependent: he occasionally criticised Bacon's observations and conclusions (e.g. MS A 1, 78v, *Analecta*, 210), and they disagreed, for instance, on whether or not nitre ensured longevity (cf. Bacon, *Works*, v, 274, and Aubrey in MS A 1, 60, and R.S. MS 92, 29).

[4] He quoted Willis in MS A 2, 100v and *Analecta*, 211, 220x, and his views on the potentialities of fermentation are shown, for instance, by his consideration of whether madness was caused by a fermentation of the brain (*Analecta*, 218x). But Willis' influence on Aubrey was apparently relatively small compared with Bacon's; even the interests shown by Aubrey in his copy of *De Fermentatione* (cf. above, p. 44) were connected with preoccupations he shared with Bacon, while the interest in the medicinal qualities of fresh earth shown in his copy of Sanctorius' *Ars de Statica Medicina* (Wood 850) is similar to Bacon, *Works*, v, 274–5.

[5] Aubrey's copy, obtained in 1662, is now Ashmole 1590. He mentions Digby, e.g., in MS A 1, 66v, 67v, *Analecta*, 254.

7

scientific manuscripts. Aubrey had immense faith in Hooke's scientific ability, and he asked him to explain various phenomena that he found puzzling: 'Desire Mr Hook to enforme me the manner, how the Clowdes are sometimes kept up high [in Mist] and some times fall downe to the Earth in raine? which, though obvious enough, yet He can make a clearer explication of it, than any I have yet seen'.[1] But, despite their close association, Hooke did not dominate Aubrey's preoccupations, nor was he Aubrey's only source of scientific advice. His 'Quere's for the tryall of Minerall Waters' were drawn up by Sir William Petty;[2] he also obtained information from eminent scientists like Robert Boyle[3] and John Ray;[4] and he often quoted his old scientific mentor, Francis Potter.[5] But he also cited the opinions of the more amateur —his friend Robert Good's view that the petrification of sticks proved the Aristotelians wrong;[6] Sir John Hoskyns' theory on how nitrous vapours 'cruddled' the air;[7] or Edmund Wyld's opinion about the 'fixt salts' of vegetables.[8] There is even greater variety in the books that he cited, or intended to consult (for it is striking how often he instructs himself to 'vide' them to confirm theories that he had found out in other ways, rather than as original sources). He mentions old classics like Georgius Agricola's famous *De Re Metallica* (1556), which he hoped would provide information about mines,[9] and he referred to the herbals of Gerard and Parkinson about plants.[10] But he also knew the work of Descartes and Hobbes— he hoped that they might reveal the cause of halos[11]—and he cited articles in the *Philosophical Transactions* on such topics as the physical explanation of prodigious births.[12]

The *Adversaria Physica* was merely a compilation of information that seemed to him significant in terms of such theories, or interesting for other reasons, a sort of scientific common-place book in which he entered all sorts of observations with only spasmodic grouping. Its contents ranged widely, both in subject-matter and

[1] R.S. MS 92, 30. Cf., e.g., MS A 1, 17, 39; MS A 2, 160v; *Analecta*, 199, 216–7x, 263.

[2] MS A 1, 45. They were abridged from the observations on mineral waters of Duclos, physician to the French king.

[3] E.g. ibid., 42–3; MS A 3, 22; *Analecta*, 259, 273.       [4] See below, p. 133.

[5] E.g. MS A 1, 67v, 106v, 146v, 147v; MS A 2, 66; *Analecta*, 199–202, 203x, 271.
[6] MS A 1, 42.    [7] R.S. MS 92, 32.    [8] MS A 1, 116v.    [9] See below, p. 117, n. 7.

[10] Gerard: MS A 1, 11, 14v, 106v, 109v; Parkinson, ibid., 106v, 111, 112.

[11] *Analecta*, 204, Cf. 207, where he intended to consult Hobbes' *De Corpore*, and 202, 205, 220, where he quotes information and opinions from Hobbes.

[12] MS A 1, 158.

sophistication—from notes on mundane topics like altering the colour of tulips by putting brimstone and size on their roots[1] and observations such as 'Memorandum the women give to young turkeys spiders for a Cordiall',[2] to a note on an experiment devised by Francis Potter, using 'a paire of scales golden in a boat or ship to see whether the lances plays parallell, or fly frome one another: for proofe or confut⟨ation⟩ of the hypothesis of Copernicus'.[3] He recorded all sorts of phenomena, that 'almost all at Bedlam have black haire'[4] or that those who had smallpox first in a family had it least—in which he came close to observing the principle of innoculation[5]—and in many cases he tried to probe at the explanation of them: 'when the ordure swimmes, the person is not in right health. the cause of its swimming is the repletion of wind'.[6] But in others, as was not unreasonable in a descriptive work of this kind, there is an element of pure curiosity. 'It were an incomparable pleasure to know what is in the middle of a mountaine or great hill,' he wrote, telling how he had been a quarter of a mile underground at Cheddar,[7] and he included all sorts of entirely miscellaneous material.

The *Naturall Historie of Wiltshire* also has a heterogeneous streak. Here too there is an element of pure unreflective admiration —the variety of plants in Wiltshire impressed him for the 'Entertainment' they gave[8]—and here too Aubrey found it difficult to resist recording almost any natural phenomenon that seemed to him significant or curious. The chapters contain much miscellaneous information, like that on Wiltshire rivers, which ranges from their etymology to their excellent trout, from subterranean rills to the project for a canal: and that reminded him to insert an account of the best way of digging a canal, out of his *Surrey*.[9] In other chapters he incorporated matter which, though 'not absolutely pertinent to this chapter, yet, the Booke being now exceeding scarce, the Reader may be pleasd to take in good part',[10] and he wrote about cures by 'the fruit of the Penguin in Tabago' merely 'for the rarity of it'[11] and about the 'Great bell of Mosco' 'for curiosities sake'.[12]

But unlike the entirely heterogeneous *Adversaria Physica*, the *Naturall Historie of Wiltshire* was more single-mindedly devoted to

[1] *Analecta*, 213x.   [2] Ibid., 274.   [3] Ibid., 273.   [4] Ibid., 136.   [5] Ibid., 207x.
[6] Ibid., 268.   [7] Ibid., 264.   [8] MS A 1, 106.   [9] Ibid., 47 f.   [10] Ibid., 104v.
[11] Ibid., 116.   [12] MS A 2, 80v.

a series of themes, and Aubrey carefully selected material from the
*Adversaria* to illustrate them. They were not exclusively Wiltshire
ones, for Aubrey seems to have conceived of his *Wiltshire* as a kind
of compendium of his scientific interests, and he deliberately
included a good deal of material from outside the county. 'For want
of good Echo's in this County,' he explained, 'I will entertain the
Reader with some in other places', and he proceeded to quote
examples in Gloucester, Hereford and Scotland.[1] Elsewhere he
illustrated points with evidence from Cheshire,[2] Snowdon,[3] and
even Naples,[4] and the title-page shows that he originally intended
to annex to the manuscript 'Observables of the same kind in the
county of Surrey and Flintshire'.[5] He also inserted as 'a Digression'
'An Hypothesis of the Terraquious Globe', his theory of the early
history of the world based on the ideas of Robert Hooke;[6] he
prefaced the work with a more general study of 'Chorographia
super- et subterranea naturalis', 'natural chorography above and
below ground';[7] and he may have intended to add an appendix
giving more information about echoes, reflections and similar
phenomena than he had been able to insert in the book itself, using
drawings that he had made in 1663.[8]

   Basically, however, the *Naturall Historie of Wiltshire* was conceived as a survey of the natural phenomena of Aubrey's native
county, and when he came to compile it in its present form in 1685
he had seen Robert Plot's seminal *Natural History of Oxford-shire*.
Plot's influence on Aubrey's natural history was important in terms
of arrangement rather than subject-matter. Aubrey had begun his
*Wiltshire*, and was collecting material of the kind that interested
him throughout his life, long before he met Plot—indeed it is clear
that he had collected much of the material that he used for his
*Wiltshire* before his absconding in 1671.[9] But what evidence there is
suggests that the arrangement of these notes was haphazard;[10]
only in the paper on Wiltshire springs read at the Royal Society
in 1668 and another on winds given there in 1673 did he attempt a

---

[1] R.S. MS 92, 41.     [2] Ibid., 37.     [3] Ibid., 28.     [4] Ibid., 37.
[5] MS A 1, 3v. In MS A 2, 152–3, he inserted 'Remarques taken from Henry Milbourne
Esq concerning Husbandrie Trade &c in Herefordshire &c.'.
[6] MS A 1, 87 f. See also above, p. 58.     [7] See below, p. 113.
[8] This seems to be the implication of MS A 1, 28.
[9] Cf. above, p. 82, and below, p. 132.
[10] The lack of any other arrangement for the notes is suggested by his insertion of
some of them topographically among antiquarian notes in his *Wiltshire Antiquities*,
evidently before he had conceived the present *Naturall Historie*.

thematic arrangement.[1] In his *Naturall Historie of Wiltshire*, however, he consolidated this attempt to deal with natural phenomena in classes, inspired by Plot's classification of the natural things of Oxfordshire into discrete chapters.[2] But he was not a servile copyist. He followed some of Plot's chapter divisions, but he did not limit himself to as few, nor did he sub-classify his material as rigorously as the methodical Plot, using the chapters more as convenient headings for the different kinds of phenomena he had collected. Some of his additional chapter titles were evidently derived from the 'Catalogue of Particular Histories' appended to Bacon's *Preparative towards a Natural and Experimental History*;[3] others he invented himself; and others seem to link his work with earlier and more omnivorous topographical descriptions like William Harrison's *Description of England* (1577) and the county surveys written under its influence.[4]

The first chapter, on 'Air', ranged from winds and mists to sounds, meteors and storms. He devoted an entire chapter to the medicinal springs of the county and another to rivers, whereas Plot had a single chapter 'Of Waters'. Like Plot, he described the different soils, the various minerals and their location, and stones and 'formed stones'. An inventory of plants and trees (like Plot's 'Of Plants') was followed by a description of the beasts, fishes, birds, reptiles and insects of Wiltshire, each in a separate chapter, whereas Plot had included all in 'Of Brutes'. Under the heading 'Men and Woemen', like Plot, he described numerous strange

---

[1] *T.P.W.*, 333 f. and 357 f.

[2] MS A 21, 86–7, is a fragment of the notes made by Aubrey on Plot's *Oxfordshire*, evidently when he was in the process of compiling his *Naturall Historie of Wiltshire*. Plot's division of his matter into ten chapters may have been a deliberate allusion to the ten centuries of Bacon's *Sylva Sylvarum*. His division of subjects, Air, Waters, Earth, etc., however, is not found in Bacon, and is evidently Plot's characteristically methodical rationalisation of Pliny's subject-divisions (which are similar, but more numerous and less well arranged): Plot claimed that the division of subject-matter in his *Plinius Anglicus* (which is similar to that in *Oxfordshire*) was 'drawne up after the method of Pliny's naturall History' (Plot, *Plinius*, 2). Pliny's influence on Plot was important: in his *Plinius Anglicus* he frequently speculates whether phenomena mentioned in Pliny were to be found in England. The influence of Pliny on Aubrey was smaller: his notes to his copy of Pliny's *Naturalis Historiae Tomi Tres* (Lugd. Bat. 1669, Ashmole D 19–21) were apparently made after he had written his *Naturall Historie of Wiltshire*, and they show him hunting for analogues for material that he had already collected. Earlier evidence of Aubrey's acquaintance with Pliny is hard to find.

[3] E.g., those on fishes, birds, wool, architecture, gardening, agriculture. Cf. Bacon, *Works*, IV, 265 f.

[4] Cf. T. D. Kendrick, *British Antiquity*, 141, 160.

births and deaths and other 'unnatural things and things praeter Naturam'[1] that he and his colleagues hoped could throw light on the development of life; he also inserted an entire chapter of 'Diseases and Cures' and a page of 'Observations on Parish Registers, according to the way prescribed by the Honourable Sir W⟨illia⟩m Petty Knight'.[2]

Though its chapters are more numerous and somewhat more miscellaneous, this first part of the book is recognisably similar to Plot's *Oxfordshire*. The second part, however, is rather more independent. Plot had included chapters 'Of Arts' and 'Of Antiquities', and the former partly overlapped with Aubrey's chapters on 'Arts Liberall & Mechanicall', gardens, agriculture and architecture, in which he described a wide variety of buildings in Wiltshire, from Stonehenge to Longleat, 'the most august Building in this Kingdome'.[3] But Aubrey had nothing to correspond with Plot's 'Of Antiquities', presumably because he had already devoted his separate 'Templa Druidum' and 'Chorographia Antiquaria'—the two chief components of his *Monumenta Britannica*—to such topics.[4] Instead he included several chapters on miscellaneous subjects that are somewhat reminiscent of earlier county descriptions like Richard Carew's *Survey of Cornwall* (1602) or George Owen's unpublished *Description of Pembrokeshire*—from 'Worthies' and 'The Grandeur of the Herberts, Earles of Pembroke' to 'The Downes' (which included a section of 'Pastoralls'), 'Faires & Markets', 'Hawkes & Hawking', and 'Seates'.

The phenomena which Aubrey thought it proper to introduce into his *Naturall Historie of Wiltshire* included the supernatural as well as the natural, artificial and human. He devoted sections to witchcraft, apparitions, divine impulse, fatalities of families and places, and portents (which came in the middle of the chapter on 'Air').[5] Some of the examples that Aubrey cited were 'Impostures',[6]

---

[1] Plot in *Analecta*, 172.    [2] MS A 1, 168.    [3] MS A 2, 80.

[4] For evidence that Aubrey himself thought that these held a position in relation to his *Naturall Historie* similar to Plot's chapter 'Of Antiquities', see below, pp. 192–3. The list of contents in MS A 1, 25v, however, mentions a chapter on 'Antiquities and Coines' which never materialised.

[5] Witchcraft, apparitions, and divine impulse were part of the chapter 'Accidents, &c.' (R.S. MS 92, 363–6); these sections, and 'Fatalities of Families and Places' (ibid., 355–7) were removed from the Oxford MS of the work, as were all but the last few pages of the chapter on 'Air' (R.S. MS 92, 27 f.), although the part devoted to portents was only a small part of what was removed.

[6] R.S. MS 92, 263, and MS A 2, 172–3.

but more were not. He wrote about a witch in Chalke parish in the 1670s, who 'would vomit crooked pinnes, and some times have strange Fitts'.[1] He cited the experience in about 1671 of Father Symonds, a Jesuit priest, who said that he had seen a spectre while riding home late one night and whose testimony Aubrey (though sceptical) considered corroborated by the behaviour of the horse, 'that trembled and sweat, when He came home, and continued so the next day, and would not eat his Oates'.[2] He quoted Machiavelli, 'who was no superstitious Man', 'that before great changes in Government there doe many times happen Portents', after giving examples;[3] and, having mentioned a number of long-lived families and some unlucky ones, including his own, he speculated on the potentialities of exorcism.[4]

At the end of his life, Aubrey removed these notes from his *Naturall Historie of Wiltshire* and developed them, with separate materials, into a book entitled *Miscellanies*.[5] But it is significant that they began their career as part of his *Naturall Historie of Wiltshire*, the compendium of his scientific interests. Moreover the material on similar subjects which he added had been collected, in Surrey in 1673, for instance, with natural phenomena;[6]

---

[1] R.S. MS 92, 364.     [2] Ibid., 365. Symonds 'officiated then at Garesdon'.
[3] Ibid., 39. He cited Machiavelli's *Discorsi della prima deca di Tito Livio*.
[4] Ibid., 355 7.
[5] These sections were removed from MSS A 1–2 and 'inserted in my Hermetique Philosophie' (MS A 2, 2) after the work had been copied by Cramer and read by Evelyn (they were all present when he made his notes on it in Christ Church Evelyn MS 173, which was after 4 Feb. 1692/3: cf. A-L of that date, A. 1814, 102). The other chief components of 'Hermetique Philosophie' were '3 Diatribes, sc. Day-fatality which is at the Museum: 2ndly a Collection of Omens. 3rdly a collection of divine Dreames from vertuous & learned persons of my acquaintance, fide digni' (A-T, 1 June 1693, T. 25, 49). These had formerly been attached to 'Στρώματα' (cf. T.G.c.25, 150), which was now added to *Monumenta Britannica* (see below, p. 157), and at the time of the letter to Tanner just quoted he was considering attaching them to *Gentilisme*. By 1 March 1693/4, however (A-T, T. 25, 127), Aubrey had decided to write a 'Treatise of *Hermetique Philosophie*', proposals for which were in circulation early in 1695 (cf. Archer-Tanner, 22 April 1695, Tanner 24, 29). On the sources of the *Miscellanies*, see also *T.P.W.*, 368 f. Aubrey mentions his 'Dreames' in a letter to Wood of 23 Oct. 1688 (T. 456a, 35), and this was presumably related to 'Mr. Aubry's Collection of dreames, phantasmes, Instincts &c:' from which Ashmole made notes in British Library MS Sloane 3846, 114v–115v. It is puzzling, however, that some matter appears there that is not in the *Miscellanies*, and there does not seem to be any obvious principle of selection.
[6] E.g. the information from Mr Pacy, *Miscellanies*, 145–6, and the dream of Archbishop Abbot's mother (ibid., 58. Cf. MS A 4, 108–9). The latter story is marked with a φ in MS A 4, the sign Aubrey used to designate natural historical information, as is his

much came from informants, including Wren, Paschall, Evelyn and the astronomer Edmond Halley, who also told Aubrey about natural things;[1] and some cases had originally been recorded in his *Adversaria Physica*, including omens concerning Charles I.[2] From these and other sources Aubrey had amassed information on all kinds of occult phenomena, from magic to visions and transportation by an invisible power. The *Miscellanies* contained stories of premonitory dreams, of the 'divine impulse' of such well-known figures as Cromwell,[3] of 'knockings' that Aubrey had experienced himself,[4] and of the information learnt by Richard Napier, the early seventeenth-century astrologer and doctor, in converse with spirits, on topics like 'Religion, Transubstantiation &c.', as well as cures for his patients' diseases.[5]

## Useful Knowledge

The *Miscellanies* is thus basically a descriptive work, a record of supernatural phenomena complementing Aubrey's works on natural history, his *Naturall Historie of Wiltshire* and *Adversaria Physica*. But, though the material is presented in it in a beguilingly non-committal way, suggesting a curiosity about 'whether there was something in it' reminiscent of more recent collections of anecdotes about ESP, there is more to the *Miscellanies* than this. For in other ways it can be seen as a manifestation of a strong practical interest in interpreting and manipulating the supernatural which Aubrey had had at least since the 1670s,[6] and which is evidenced in other texts. He expressed concern in his letters to Wood when

---

account of a stream that only issued when 'some thing strange' occurred in the nation (ibid., 83).

[1] *Miscellanies*, 60, 62, 87, 149 f., etc.

[2] *Analecta*, 114 and 204–5x; *Miscellanies*, 39 and 38.

[3] *Miscellanies*, 117–18.     [4] Ibid., 121–2.     [5] Ibid., 169–70.

[6] Cf. also Aubrey's astrology, below, pp. 118–19. It is interesting in this connection that the letters on occult topics from Sir John Hoskyns quoted below (p. 141) date from this period, and some of them, especially that of 4 Sept. 1672 (MS A 12, 205) read as if they were replies to letters in which Aubrey asked Hoskyns what he thought of these subjects. I have deliberately refrained from emphasizing the evident intensification of Aubrey's practical concern with the occult in the 1670s. The surviving evidence concerning his scientific interests is so heavily weighted towards the period from the 1670s onwards that negative conclusions about his earlier interests are extremely hazardous. For evidence of his earlier interest in the occult, though of a descriptive rather than a practical kind, see below, p. 210.

6. A selection of the books and manuscripts presented by Aubrey to Gloucester Hall, now in the library of Worcester College, Oxford

OVERLEAF

7. The title-page of the manuscript of Aubrey's *Perambulation of Surrey*, showing his formal presentation of the works that he recopied in his later years

8. A page of the manuscript of Aubrey's *Naturall Historie of Wiltshire*, with a pressed flower inserted and with annotations by John Ray

A

PERAMBULATION

of SURREY

Anno Dm 1673. [left unfinished].

By

Mr John Aubrey R.S.S.

Persius. Sat. 1.
Quis leget hæc? — Vel duo, vel nemo. /

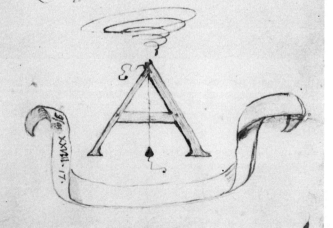

Clowdberries [ vaccinium nubis. Gr. χαμαιμαλα ⊙ ] in
Westmorland. Knootberries vulgo, neer Fountaines abby
and the like upon other high hills, thereabout, like
a Mulberry. vid. Gerard.
Knootberry & Cloudberry are all one. See Ger. emac. p. 1630.

On ye Rocky Mountaine above Nestor-
-dale in ___ Yorkshire Aug 1667.
'Tis a sort of Moss, which growes also
in Scotland.

Gnaphalium
longifolium
humile ramo-
sum capitulis
nigris

Old Captain Tooke of ...... in Kent [ nat 9 Aᵒ. 1588 ]
1672
told me, that Cherries were first brought into Reat
the Hen: 8. who being ___ in Flanders, & liking the
Cherries, his Gardiner brought them thence, and propagated
them in England, particularly in Kent, wʰ soile is most
proper for them. quære plus de hijs of Capt. Tooke.

Mr Stowe in his Chronicle records, that in ye
time of Hen: VIII. a Basket of Pearmaines was presented
by ...... to Cardinal Wolsey.

Hoppes, a great comodity in Kent, most of any part of England: they
...... say it is not above sixty yeares that they have taken to it: but Captain
Tooke sayeth about fourescore yeares [ now 1672 ]

9. A page of the manuscript of Aubrey's *Brief Lives* showing an example of a biography written around the horoscope of its subject

he had been troubled about him in his dreams,[1] and he noted in his *Idea of Education* that 'Collerus [German] in his booke of Agriculture, saies, that they doe every morning tell their Dreames: and that they doe find it significant and usefull. secundum Virgilium in Æneid⟨i⟩

'—et habent in somnia pondus'

'They consider there to be significance in dreams'.[2]

The seriousness with which he took visions in crystal is shown by his additional note: 'Also let those (or the most innocent and Angelicall vertuouse youths) looke into Berills, or Crystalls. quod NB'.[3] What is more, in 1674 Aubrey transcribed a copy of the *Clavicula Salomonis*,[4] a magical treatise which has been described as 'the fountainhead and storehouse of Quabalistical Magic ... ever valued by occult writers as a work of the highest authority'.[5] From it he could learn how to perform magical rites, with full details of all the necessary equipment, conjurations and prayers, how to carry out 'experiments' of sympathetic magic, or how to make magical pentacles capable of contradicting the laws of nature.

This manuscript shows Aubrey in the mainstream tradition of magic. That he did not copy the text as a curiosity is shown by the several pages of additional recipes and invocations that he added at the end, endorsing several 'this hath bin oftin proved' or 'probatum est', and demonstrating his intention of practising them by such notes as 'q⟨uaere⟩ the dos⟨age⟩ of this powder'.[6] He had consulted various magical treatises,[7] and from them quoted profuse

---

[1] A-W, 2 Jan. 1672/3, B. 14, 94.

[2] MS A 10, 114. He evidently knew of this book through Dr Luke Ridgeley: see above, p. 23, n. 1.

[3] Loc. cit.    [4] MS A 24.

[5] S. M. McG. Mathers *ed.*, *The Key of Solomon the King* (London 1889, reprinted 1972), vii.

[6] MS A 24, 89. The additional recipes are on fols. 85 f.

[7] He used magical manuscripts owned by Henry Coley (ibid., 100v), by 'Mr Hitchcock, a Clerk at the Rolls Office' (92v), and presumably also by Ashmole (cf. *Miscellanies*, 166, 169–70, though he is not mentioned in MS A 24). He also cites in MS A 24 (passim) Scot's *Discovery of Witchcraft*, in the London 1651 edition (of which Ashmole owned a copy: Ashmole 549), as his page references show. Few of his spells and recipes can, however, be identified as coming from there: e.g. the invocation 'To make a Spirit appear in a Chrystall glasse' on f. 98 appears in almost identical form in Scot's *Discovery* (London 1651), 304–5, but this was not Aubrey's source, for he writes 'I beleive this is in Scot, which see'. It is curious that there is no overlap between the magical recipes in MS A 24 and those in the *Miscellanies*. For the background to Aubrey's magical interests, cf. K. Thomas, *Religion and the Decline of Magic* (London, 1971), ch. VIII.

incantations. By invoking Christ in his most powerful attributes he hoped to see in a crystal glass 'these spirits—Alkates, Walkates, Mioron, Micriton, Balko and Bosko', and to discover from them 'the trueth without faile of all things doubtfull and of theft, man-slaughter, treasure hidden in the ground, what sp⟨irit⟩ keepeth it, of the state of thy friends, wheresoever they be, and of secret things lost whether you shall have them or not'.[1]

He also copied out numerous magical recipes, to test virginity, for instance,[2] or 'To make a man Gunne-proofe': 'Write these characters + Zada + Zadash + Zadathan + Abira + in virgin paper [I beleeve parchment] carry it always with you, and no gun-shott can hurt you'.[3] 'If you will not beleive,' he continued, concerning a similar recipe, 'hang the ring in a string about a Cocks neck, and shoot at him with a bowe or gun loaded with a bullet, and you will find the experiment true.'[4] To win at cards you should wear a ring containing the ashes of two dice bought and burnt in the Devil's name, and Aubrey noted a story told by his uncle, Thomas Danvers, about a gamester with a magical bracelet with which 'he won a good while to a miracle at last lost & sent for 3d of Rattsbane which he dranke in a cup of ale & so poysoned himselfe'.[5] There were numerous other recipes, many of them involv-ing practices close to those cited in the *Clavicula*, with Hebrew hieroglyphs written out in bat's blood, or magic sigils dedicated to particular planets, or the burning to powder of the hearts of black dogs, white hens or turtle-doves in the odour of frankincense and myrrh.

Though it is impossible to know whether Aubrey actually carried out these recipes, or what happened if he did, there can be no doubt that he valued them because they might work, that his motive in compiling his magical collection was utilitarian. This streak of practicality is also very prominent in his natural history. For, though the purely descriptive element in it is important, it is sometimes almost overwhelmed by an emphasis on exclusively useful knowledge. There is almost a tone of regret in his observation that 'Lead, tin and iron may be all turned into Vitriol: and vice versâ: but without any profit: However it is experimentum Luci-ferum', 'an experiment of light',[6] and criteria of usefulness leaven the lump of what would otherwise be purely miscellaneous infor-

---

[1] MS A 24, 87.    [2] Ibid., 88.    [3] Loc. cit.    [4] Ibid., 88v.    [5] Ibid., 89v.
[6] MS A 1, 76.

mation in both the *Adversaria Physica* and the *Naturall Historie of Wiltshire*, for thus he often judged the relevance of material to his theme.

He attempted an inventory of Wiltshire plants, 'that we might know our Store: and whither to repaire for them for medicinall uses', and his list proudly detailed those that were sought after by dyers and watchmakers.[1] Similarly, freestone was the 'best kind of stone' in the county,[2] and he paid special attention to the earth used by fullers,[3] to blue clay that might be employed for porcelain,[4] and to 'the toughest & therefore the best Oakes for building of Shipps'.[5] The chapter on springs in his *Wiltshire* is merely a list of sites with a description of experiments concerning their curative properties, and he apologised that 'this Countie cannot boast much of Mineralls: it is more celebrated for Superficiall Treasure'.[6]

Parts of Aubrey's works degenerate to mere lists of recipes, giving them at times the air of earlier collections of useful nostrums like the *Jewell House of Art and Nature* by the Elizabethan Sir Hugh Plat. 'First make the water boyle & then put in the Egge & it will not be hard' was one piece of advice he thought worthy of the *Adversaria Physica*,[7] and the chapters on plants, beasts and 'Diseases and Cures' in his *Wiltshire* are full of useful recipes, from cures for sciatica[8] to lotions to kill the lice in children's hair,[9] which he had learnt from a wide range of informants. Thus the Dutch scientist Theodore Haak told him 'that take an Eele, and draw it, and skinne it, and roast it, (but without basting) The Dripping of it putt into the Eare wonderfully helps Deafnesse: e.g. a Woman that could not heare a Drum beat, was cured by it, & heard perfectly: but Memorandum, he saies, it putts one into intollerable paine, for some time; as if ones head would tear in pieces. He intends to use it himself.'[10]

The agricultural sections of Aubrey's works are equally replete with practical information and advice. He inserted into his *Naturall Historie of Wiltshire* 'Some Excerpta, out of John Norden's Dialogues. though they are not of Wiltshire, they will doe no hurt here: and if my countrey-men know it not, I wish they might learn'.[11] He also included much piecemeal advice, like the information that

---

[1] Ibid., 104 f. He later erased 'for medicinall uses'.   [2] Ibid., 77.   [3] Ibid., 57.
[4] Ibid., 56.   [5] *Analecta*, 62.   [6] MS A 1, 70.   [7] *Analecta*, 274.   [8] MS A 1, 132.
[9] Ibid., 109.   [10] Ibid., 137v.
[11] MS A 2, 90. Aubrey's copy of this work is Wood C 20.

pigs let loose in a corn field would eat the weeds in preference to the young corn, on the authority of a neighbour, 'a sober discreet person & worthy of beliefe'.[1] Related to Aubrey's hope to improve agricultural practice was his interest in inventions. Some surviving notes that he made in connection with discussions at the Royal Society deal with various ingenious devices, from machines for sowing corn and carts with only one wheel to devices for flying and ships with fins. They show that he sought means 'that the soweing and harroweing may bee but one and the same labour' and considered such technical problems as 'whether a Parabolicall built vessell is not best both for sayling and strength as well as stowage'.[2]

This obsession with practicality overlapped with the descriptive element in Aubrey's natural history, for his eagerness to record recipes merged with an interest in giving details of agricultural improvements and when they had been made. The chapter in his *Wiltshire* entitled 'Agriculture & Improvements'[3] ranges from recipes to histories of the use of cinquefoil, of marl and of burning the stubble, when each was introduced and where. The overlap of the descriptive and the practical is shown by Aubrey's account of vineyards recently established in Wiltshire. In it he not only told who had made them and where, but also recorded 'that the Navarregrape is the best for our Climate' and 'that the Hills by Cannings are proper for Vinyards: and so about Lavington', on the authority of Sir William Basset, the local landowner who had made the 'best' one.[4] Aubrey also devoted space to 'Mechanicall Arts' including 'Cloathing',[5] 'Maulting and Brewing'[6] and 'Inventions and Engines,'[7] and he noted numerous fruits of human ingenuity, from the excellent bath constructed at Bayworth by Hannibal Baskerville, a local antiquary,[8] to an 'ingeniose' machine for grinding colours, involving a windmill which drove twenty-nine small mills, that he had seen in Surrey.[9]

Ingenuity and improvement were, indeed, themes close to Aubrey's heart. He quoted Gabriel Plattes, a writer on husbandry and mining associated with Samuel Hartlib, that 'he that can find out

[1] MS A 2, 103v.

[2] MS A 21, 54v, 57–9. Cf. MS A 12, 5, evidently a paper by Aubrey suggesting to the Royal Society a boat cranked with wheels.

[3] This is the title it is given in the contents list in MS A 1, 25v. The chapter itself is MS A 2, 83 f.

[4] MS A 2, 86.    [5] Ibid., 64–5.    [6] Ibid., 103.    [7] Ibid., 66–7.    [8] *Analecta*, 106–7.
[9] MS A 4, 26.

an improvement in Husbandry doth more good to the Common-wealth, than he that founds 100 Almeshouses. It is the most usefull & innocent profession that is'.[1] His comparable concern for inventors in his *Wiltshire* was linked to his idolatry of successful entrepreneurs like Richard Foley and Thomas Firmin in his *Idea of Education*,[2] and in his *Brief Lives* he was anxious that Mr Ingelbert should be remembered, 'the first inventor or projector of bringing the water from Ware to London': Sir Hugh Myddleton provided the capital and took the credit, but for 'that most usefull invention', 'there ought to have been erected a statue for the memory of this poore-man from the city of London'.[3]

Aubrey was particularly fascinated by men who had made their fortune by such means as soap-making[4] or exploiting pilchards[5] or alum,[6] and he proudly recounted how he himself had told a local landowner about marl that he had found, who thereupon improved by it.[7] The possibility of profiting by his discoveries in natural history was constantly in Aubrey's mind, particularly in connection with medicinal springs, which he investigated indefatigably. 'Deo gracias', he marked his notes when he found such sites,[8] and the waters that he discovered at Seend in Wiltshire he advertised in a London almanac,[9] intending eventually to provide a 'handsome convenient House of entertainment' and a 'fine Bowling green' for the enthusiastic water-drinkers whom he expected to attract.[10] His hopes for profit received a more sustained exposition in a little volume entitled *Faber Fortunæ*, which he headed with Paracelsus' 'verse, & Motto', 'Alterius non sit, qui suus esse potest', 'let him

---

[1] *Analecta*, 224. This is paraphrased from Gabriel Plattes, *A Discovery of Infinite Treasure, Hidden since the Worlds Beginning* (London, 1639), alv. He also quotes Plattes in MS A 26, 10.

[2] MS A 10, 143 and 145, where he also cites almost the same passage from Plattes as that just noted, introducing it with 'H. Plattes in his Superficial Treasure saies', evidently confusing Plattes with Sir Hugh Plat.

[3] *B.L.* II, 1. But cf. J. W. Gough, *Sir Hugh Myddelton* (Oxford, 1964), 32–3, who considers that Ingelbert deserved no credit.

[4] MS A 26, 10v.     [5] Ibid., 9v.     [6] *Analecta*, 189–90. Cf. *B.L.* I, 159.

[7] MS A 1, 32.     [8] Ibid., 44.

[9] I have not been able to find this advertisement, which he claims to have inserted in Coley's almanac 'about 1681': cf. MS A 1, 35v, where he gives an MS copy of the advertisement, which he says was composed by Richard Blackbourne. In *B.L.* 1, 40 (a passage dating from the early 1680s), he says that he advertised it in Lilly's almanac, not Coley's, but I have searched for it in vain in Lilly's almanacs of this period too.

[10] MS A 26, 4. He had shown the water to the Royal Society in 1669, but though the waters were in general use by 1688 (MS A 1, 35–6), Aubrey's grandiose scheme came to nothing.

not be beholden to another, who is able to be self-sufficient'.[1] In it he recorded all sorts of potential sources of wealth that he had met with in his travels. He had found coal in Surrey which he hoped 'to gett a Patent to digge for';[2] he knew of iron and tin in Wiltshire,[3] lead in North Wales,[4] copper in Flintshire, Shropshire and Wiltshire,[5] antimony in Somerset and near Plymouth[6] and silver and gold elsewhere.[7]

Such information rubbed shoulders in the little book with more miscellaneous and wilder schemes—from plans to search the records of the Rolls for unused patents[8] or to claim land embezzled by the Fishmongers Company,[9] to purely hearsay accounts of the possibilities of extracting silver from English tin, like the German who made his fortune by it and built a monastery with the proceeds.[10] Many of his projects were characteristically far-fetched; his knowledge of the whereabouts of some commodities was as vague as '*somewhere in* Herefordshire',[11] and some of the facts that he felt the need to record indicate that he had little grasp of the practical difficulties of exploiting his discoveries.[12] But it is interesting that even in this book, in which Aubrey became unwontedly secretive in the prospect of profit,[13] he recorded schemes of more than merely

---

[1] MS A 26, 1. The present MS dates from the 1690s, and it contains an accumulation of potential schemes that Aubrey can hardly have hoped would prove practicable. On the Baconian associations of the 'Faber Fortunae' theme, cf. R. C. Cochrane in *Studies in the Renaissance* v (1958), 176f.

[2] Ibid., 2.  [3] Ibid., 3, 4.  [4] Ibid., 8v, 'from Mr Million'.  [5] Ibid., 3.  [6] Loc. cit.

[7] Ibid., e.g. 5, 6, 6v.  [8] Ibid., 5v.  [9] Ibid., 2.  [10] Ibid., 7.  [11] Ibid., 6v.

[12] He cited Mr Martin, a jeweller, concerning the elementary fact that refiners washed the dust of their gold and silver ore on a striated wooden platter (ibid., 13). That he was not even particularly expert on farming is suggested by his reference to 'the shareboard (I thinke they call it)' (*Analecta*, 273). The invalidity of Aubrey's optimistic assumption that all would favour his improving schemes is shown by the dislike of owners of wells for the crowds that the discovery of their medicinal properties brought (cf. A-W, 11 Aug. and 2 Sept. 1695, Wood F 51, 10, IIV, and A-L, 24 Feb. 1695/6, A. 1829, 56).

[13] There is a slight ambivalence in all of Aubrey's writings on natural history, between a hope to propagate useful information and a desire to keep it secret so that he could profit from it personally. In a letter to Hooke of 6 Nov. 1695, Aubrey told him of a spring near Lantrithid with medicinal virtues, which a divine was hoping to keep secret 'but I will try to have them disclosed' (British Library MS Sloane 1039, 108). Yet it was also in the 1690s that he was suspicious of Plot because he was afraid he would exploit secrets that Aubrey had recorded in his MSS—notably, presumably, the account of a treasure-trove of minerals excavated at Worplesdon in Surrey, which is headed 'Secretum. quod bene vertat' in MS A 4, 170 (cf. A-W, St Peter's Day 1689, F 39,386). A-W, 24 April 1690, F 39, 402v, requests Wood to prevent Plot and others from seeing a passage in Aubrey's *Monumenta* concerning the possibility of clearing rocks from the Bristol Avon, 'because I may sometime or other gett money by it' (cf. T.G.25, 134v, 137).

personal interest, as 'That we may be furnished with Pitch and Tarre from Scotland without being beholding to the Suedes: also for Masts'—thus expressing a hope for national self-sufficiency in raw materials typical of his mercantilist age.[1] Aubrey's studies of natural history went with a profound faith in their use to the national interest, and it is interesting that his library contained several pamphlets by mercantilist writers like Henry Slingsby[2] and Thomas Firmin,[3] proposals for a land registry[4] or for banks[5] and tracts concerning many other projects.[6]

For he was not alone in stressing the practical benefits of the kind of investigations in which he was engaged. Robert Plot also claimed that in his account of the natural things of Oxfordshire he 'treated only of such as eminently ... were some way or other useful to *Man*',[7] and he stressed the 'great Advantage' to be reaped from the mines he found in his travels.[8] Agricultural improvement was encouraged by that active organ of the Royal Society, the Georgical committee, of which Aubrey was a member, which sent printed enquiries to the provinces in the manner of compilers of natural history.[9] It was also symptomatic that Aubrey inserted into his *Naturall Historie of Wiltshire* papers on husbandry by Adam Martindale and John Flamsteed that had been published in the *Collection of Letters relating to Husbandry and Trade* of John Houghton, another member of the Society with similar interests.[10]

[1] MS A 26, 4v.

[2] Ashmole 1630, 'A Discourse Concerning the Establishing a well govern'd Trade and Traffick upon our owne Foundation', an MS, inscribed 'Sum Johanni Aubrii. Maii 15to 1660'.

[3] Ashmole 1672 (10), *Some Proposals for the Imployment of the Poor* (London, 1681). This was presumably the book 'of setting the poor to worke' that Aubrey referred to on f. 1 of MS Aubrey 20, which comprises two tracts by Henry Milbourne, on the ordering of the poor and on the decay of rents, to which he intended to annex 'Mr Fourmin's Essay'. Aubrey obtained these Milbourne MSS in 1659.

[4] Ashmole 1672 (17), Nicholas Phillpott, *Reasons & Proposalls for a Registry* (London, 1671).

[5] There are several tracts on this subject in Ashmole 1065 and 1672.

[6] E.g. tracts on making salt-water sweet in Ashmole D 60 and Ashmole E 39. For other projecting pamphlets in Aubrey's library, see the list in Powell, *John Aubrey and his Friends*, Appendix B: most, however, are in the volumes of tracts (especially Ashmole 1065, 1672), the contents of which are unfortunately not separately listed there.

[7] Plot, *Oxfordshire*, 69.

[8] Plot's letter to Fell (n.d.), Bodleian MS Jones 17, item 12, printed in R. T. Gunther ed., *Early Science in Oxford*, XII, 335 f. The quotation is from page 337.

[9] Cf. R. Lennard, 'English agriculture under Charles II: the evidence of the Royal Society's "Enquiries" ', *Economic History Review* IV (1932), 23 f.

[10] MS A 1, 58, and MS A 2, 96, 109 (Martindale), 105 f. (Flamsteed).

It is indeed revealing that the earliest English specimen of the genre of a natural history of a particular area topographically defined, Gerard Boate's *Irelands Naturall History* (1652), had been published by Samuel Hartlib, and that it reflects Hartlib's practical preoccupation with husbandry and with mining iron and minerals, which he urged should be employed 'For the Common Good of *Ireland*, and more especially, for the benefit of the Adventurers and Planters therein'.[1] The same motives were echoed thirty years later in the letters to Aubrey of his Somerset friend, Andrew Paschall. Paschall was particularly interested in investigating such natural things as, 'if well prosecuted may turne to a publick benefit',[2] and when in 1685 plans were made to mine ores discovered in Somerset and shares were sold, it was promised that the first ten shares of the clear profit would be consecrated to God and to 'the promoteing of useful Knowledge particularly in this Country'.[3] 'None alive (not the K⟨ing⟩ & P⟨arliament⟩) will deny assistance if requisite,' Sir John Hoskyns confidently asserted in a similar connection, ' 'tis the worlds interest',[4] just as Plot emphasised how his work would contribute 'to the great benefit of Trade, and advantage of the People'.[5]

## The Quest for Rules

This emphasis on the practical benefits of scientific knowledge, this blatant claim to investigate only such natural phenomena as seemed useful to man, if rigorously pursued, might have made books like Aubrey's little more than collections of nostrums, remedies and eulogies of projectors, spiced only with irrelevancies of miscellaneous description that he lacked the will-power to exclude. As John Houghton put it, 'I shall greatly (although not altogether) avoid *speculation*, and chiefly mind those things that tend to *useful Practice*'.[6] But though such utilitarian single-mindedness is an element in Aubrey's natural historical notes, it is not the

---

[1] *Irelands Naturall History*, title-page.

[2] Paschall-Aubrey, 29 June 1683, MS A 13, 62.

[3] Id., 15 May 1685, ibid., 74. Aubrey was involved in this scheme, which proved abortive when his patron, the Earl of Abingdon, failed to provide capital.

[4] Hoskyns-Aubrey, 20 Feb. 1674/5, MS A 12, 215v. This was of his scheme for a study of English agriculture.

[5] Plot, *Plinius*, 2.

[6] *A Collection for the Improvement of Husbandry and Trade*, I, no. 3 (13 April 1692).

only theme that redeems his works from being mere collections of curiosities. For, although 'experimenta lucifera' played so small a part in his investigations, there was one kind of general rule that he was interested in establishing and testing in his investigation of natural things. Like Plot and other early members of the Royal Society, he hoped that a study of a wide range of diverse phenomena would make it possible to understand the reasons for their diversity and, perhaps, to control them.[1] Thus Sir John Hoskyns advocated 'a physicall survey, e.g. what soyle, what temper, how early things ripen, how healthy the inhabitants & of what looke or aire (as they call it) what fruits the land is most given to & what increase &c . . . there is in all these things difference enough to yield matter of distinction & the knowledge is usefull & exceeding pleasant'.[2]

'There is no Nation abounds with greater varietie of Soiles, Plants, & Mineralls, than ours: and therfore it very well deserves to be surveyed,' Aubrey explained in the preface to his *Naturall Historie of Wiltshire*,[3] and already by 1670 he could claim that 'between S. Wales & the French Sea: I have taken an account of the severall earths, & naturall observables in it, as the nature of the plants in the respective soyles, the nature of the cattle thereon feeding, & the nature of the Indiginae'.[4] These widespread investigations were the basis of the most thematic of Aubrey's scientific writings, his 'Chorographia super- et subterranea naturalis', 'Natural Chorography above and below ground', which he sent to Martin Lister in 1684[5] in connection with a paper advocating a geological survey of Britain that Lister read at the Royal Society.[6] Aubrey subsequently prefixed it to his *Naturall Historie of Wiltshire* by way of justification, showing the sort of conclusions to which he hoped natural historical studies might lead, alluding back to its theme in the text of the book.[7]

[1] Cf., e.g. Plot in *Analecta*, 3, or Birch, *History*, IV, 143 (1682), where Plot spoke at the Royal Society of the varieties of sheep in different parts of England, or ibid., IV, 185, 199, etc. (1683), where he presented samples of various earths. For the Royal Society in general, e.g., Boyle's 'General Heads for a *Natural History of a Countrey*, Great or small', *Philosophical Transactions* I (1666), 186 f., or Sprat, *History*, 156, 191, 219, 385 f.

[2] Hoskyns-Aubrey, n.d. (?1672), MS A 12, 212v.

[3] MS A 1, 5. Aubrey used the same argument in recommending travel in his educational proposals: MS A 10, 79.

[4] A-W, 17 Nov. 1670, F 39, 128v.

[5] Cf. *T.P.W.*, 447–8 and 311 f. I have used the slightly fuller version in MS A 1.

[6] 'An Ingenious proposal for a new sort of *Maps* of *Countrys*, together with *Tables of Sands* and *Clays* . . . ', *Philosophical Transactions* XIV (1684), 739 f.

[7] E.g., he alludes back to the 'Chorographia' at the beginning of the chapter on

The 'Chorographia' is a study of the differences in soil, flora and fauna, in climate, and in the healthiness and humours of the inhabitants all over England. He noted where chalk, and where other soils, began and ended, and advocated the preparation of maps showing this and the use of lands in different areas.[1] He recorded the plentifulness of wormwood, the tallness of the corn and the length of the leaves of the wych-hazels in Yorkshire;[2] the commonness of hornbeam in Hertfordshire and its rarity in the West;[3] the varying colours of cattle and the size of their horns in different counties;[4] and the fact that whereas cattle were larger in Yorkshire than in the south, hares, pigeons and blackbirds were smaller.[5] He also considered the similarities and differences of the humours of the inhabitants of Norfolk, Devon, Cornwall and Yorkshire[6]—the latter, for instance, unusually tall and long lived, 'their skin, a kind of horse skin',[7] and their manners 'subtile & wary; no fooles'.[8]

But what interested Aubrey most was how such phenomena affected each other, and from the observations that he had made in his fieldwork he evolved a homespun theory of environmental determinism similar to those of ancient writers like Hippocrates, Theophrastus and Vitruvius, but which he evidently hoped to refine by adding precise, local observation.[9] Where there was a great variety of earths, 'a priori', he considered, there would be many sorts of plants,[10] and he carefully noted correlations of soil, flora and fauna. Cloud-berries, he remarked, were found on high hills,[11] and cowslips often in conjunction with clay.[12] He noted that sheep had horns in some areas but not in others, observing 'quippe solo natura subest', 'to be sure, the nature is subject to the soil',[13] for elsewhere the colour of cattle was sometimes paralleled by that

---

'Men & Woemen' (MS A 1, 151), and on the title-page of the chapter on springs (ibid., 31) he cites Hippocrates on the connection between the health of the inhabitants and the local waters.

[1] Ibid., 14, 19; cf. MS A 2, 115. There is no reason to assume that Aubrey derived this idea from Lister (art. cit., p. 113, n. 6).

[2] MS A 1, 15.    [3] Ibid., 16.    [4] Ibid., 25.    [5] Ibid., 16.    [6] Ibid., 15, 16, 24.

[7] Ibid., 15. Aubrey subsequently erased this sentence, presumably to avoid giving offence.

[8] Ibid., 16.

[9] Aubrey quotes Theophrastus in R.S. MS 92, 28, and Vitruvius in MS A 1, 20v. For a survey of such ideas, see C. J. Glacken, *Traces on the Rhodian Shore* (Berkeley and Los Angeles, 1967).

[10] MS A 1, 104.    [11] Ibid., 14v.    [12] Ibid., 106.    [13] Ibid., 137. Cf. 21, etc.

of rabbits in the same area.[1] He even applied the treatment to people: 'Wood sorrell & such acide herbes naturally produced in clay sandes, make an acidenesse in theire complexions, fire theire spirits, makes them lazie and contemplative & Venerous'.[2] Regional differences of pronunciation 'must proceed from the earth, or aire or both',[3] and good singing could be correlated with the rich soils on which people lived: 'Memorandum,' he noted while at Lingfield in Surrey, 'they doe sing very well in this Parish-church: as they doe in N. Wilts & Gloucestershire, Woodsere-countreys.'[4] It all seemed rational enough: 'Plants are made by the earth, by them we are nourisht',[5] just as the excellence of mutton naturally depended on grazing,[6] and it was similarly only to be expected that the sharper, more nitrous air of hill-countries would make their inhabitants 'more vigorous & couragious'.[7]

He took his analysis to remarkable lengths: 'Tewkesbury-vale, & Evesham-vale, breeds fair lusty, tough people. At Huntley in Gloucestershire, the nature of the people breakes with the soile: which there the sand leaves: and the wett woodsere soile comes-in, and so the north part of Wiltshire. In the sandy parts the natives are of ruddy complexion, hazel or blacke eied, quick &c.: the other slow, pale, long visaged, drawning voice, spightfull, & ex consequente inhospitable, always cold in their feet, envious, malicious, Bigots, & witches, according to the saying, you may as soon breake your neck, as you thirst among 'em: è contra, in Herefordshire they will aske strangers as they ride along by their houses, invite them to drinke'.[8] He even hoped to test his views: 'in Wales people are generally black eyed examine better the composition of theire earth'.[9] He was fascinated by the story of a great Physician who 'would undertake, by Dyet, to make any man a Coward in six weekes',[10] and he noted: 'Quaere if Aborigines of one Countrey being transplanted to another, will not after some generations degenerate, or the contrary, according to the soile? ... 'Tis sayd that the English after they have lived a matter of seaven yeares in Ireland; become as lazy as the Irish'.[11]

[1] Ibid., 25.   [2] *Analecta*, 173X.   [3] MS A 1, 23v.   [4] MS A 4, 68.
[5] MS A 1, 21.   [6] Ibid., 136v.   [7] Ibid., 21. Cf. R.S. MS 92, 29.
[8] MS A 1, 10v.   [9] *Analecta*, 260.
[10] MS A 1, 21. He found the story in Sir William Temple's *Observations upon the United Provinces* (London, 1673), 157, which he slightly misinterprets in claiming that it was 'a great Physician of Holland'; Temple says 'a great Physician among us.'
[11] MS A 1, 20. But on f. 19v Aubrey noted the excellence of Irish memories.

But he had a further motive, and this was the hope that by understanding the reasons for natural diversity, it could be turned to man's advantage—a prospect that practically minded investigators like him were bound to find attractive. He was always anxious not only to record where the best of any natural commodity was found—for instance, that oaks were tougher north of the Severn than south of it[1]—but also to try to find out why this was so in terms of habitat, noting that stonebrash made good barley land,[2] or that 'Clay-ground is proper for Quince-trees'.[3] He also tried to apply observations made in one area to others. Noting the 'excellent sand ... for Vitrification' in North Wiltshire and Berkshire, he wondered if 'the Sand of Ryegate in Surrey may be as good for glasse worke. q⟨uaere⟩',[4] and his French travels allowed more cosmopolitan comparisons still. In his notes on the springs at Minety in Wiltshire he entered 'A Wish. When I experimented these waters I wish't that some ingeniose English man would experiment the waters at Colbec in France, where the best Felts are made: and they can make them no where els by reason of that water. if one knew what impregnated the water, one might ⟨find⟩ some other of the same vertue, and so improve that manufacture in England &c: and make a small village a flourishing Towne'.[5]

Whenever he noted diversity, he was eager to discover which was preferable—even whether the sickles used for reaping in Surrey were more efficient than the reap-hooks used elsewhere[6]—and in the case of cheese-making he planned a comparative survey of the art in England, with an eye to transferring better practices from one area to another. 'Insert the way of makeing Cheese in North Wilts: and in Cheshire: Suffolk (the worst). Banbury: why made so thin? & why, were it not better that N. Wilts should make their cheeses thicker? e.g. Warwicksh⟨ire⟩ & Cheshire? they make them but an inch thick & ... diameter. Compute the quantity, & value (praeter propter) of the Cheese sold at the eminent Cheese-marketts: viz. Marle-borough: Chippenham: & Tedbury in Gloucestershire'.[7] He had discovered that areas like North Wiltshire, with their 'sower' herbage,[8] made good cheese, and he hoped that in the similar red, clay, woodsere ground of the Surrey Weald they could, 'if they had the art of the N. Wilts Huswives', do equally well,

---

[1] Ibid., 11.　　[2] Ibid., 10.　　[3] Ibid., 56.　　[4] *Analecta*, 180.
[5] MS A 3, 21; cf. MS A 1, 41.　　[6] MS A 4, 209.
[7] MS A 2, 102. The omission is Aubrey's.　　[8] MS A 1, 10.

'whereas the Cheese here is very ordinary: white, spungie, and porous'.[1] Subsequently he noted the lack of salt in the wealden clay, and hoped that the cheese could be improved by adding vitriolate salt to the milk, to help coagulation.[2]

In his 'Chorographia' Aubrey was equally practical concerning correlations between geology and vegetation, for he hoped that certain trees could be identified as 'markes of minerals'.[3] Perhaps rather in the way that he had become used to identifying medicinal springs by finds of iron ore[4] or by the ochre colour of local streams, 'which gives us a Hint for such a discovery',[5] he hoped to find similar 'Symptoms of Subterranean Treasure',[6] and he surpassed his contemporaries in his efforts along these lines.[7] Hazel was a 'signature' of freestone;[8] so was betony, and yew trees seemed to be 'another dignostique';[9] *terre vert* indicated copper;[10] and oaks and iron 'seeme to have a kind of Cognation'.[11] He suspected that holly and oaks went with coal, quoting the opinion of William Oughtred, the famous mathematician, that this was so,[12] and when he learnt that they were found in plenty near the 'famous Coaleries of Durham & Newcastle', he decided that his friend Sir James Long 'may very well hope to find coale in the North part of Draycot estate: for the symptomes abovesaid both of Hollyes & oakes'.[13]

The intensely practical inferences that Aubrey hoped to make in his 'Chorographia' can be paralleled in the other subject where he can be observed consistently collecting information over many years in an attempt to test and refine rules—Astrology. 'The Transits of the Planets by their Radicall places & Aspects are worth any gentl⟨eman's⟩ serious observation,' he wrote,[14] for he believed that astrology could give a great deal of useful information. It

[1] MS A 4, 126.    [2] Ibid., 210. Cf. *Analecta*, 180.    [3] *T.P.W.*, 346.
[4] MS A 1, 35.    [5] MS A 4, 68.    [6] *T.P.W.*, 346.
[7] Neither Gabriel Plattes' *A Discovery of Subterraneall Treasure* (London, 1639) nor Boyle's 'Articles of Inquiries touching *Mines*', *Philosophical Transactions* 1 (1666), 330 f., attempt precise correlations like Aubrey's; nor, indeed, did Agricola's *De Re Metallica* or Aldrovandus' *Musaeum Metallicum*, though Aubrey intended to see what information they gave on this point (MS A 1, 69v).
[8] MS A 1, 10.    [9] MS A 4, 209.    [10] MS A 1, 8v.    [11] Ibid., 11.
[12] *Analecta*, 167. Cf. MS A 1, 11.    [13] *Analecta*, 164.
[14] MS A 23, 66: a paper in Aubrey's hand entitled '⟨J.⟩ Hoskyns. Esq usefull memorandums, partly for Confirmation of the Geniture'. It is not possible to give an adequate explanation of the astrological terminology used by Aubrey and his friends here. Of the most common terms, 'transit' and 'aspect' denote relations between the planets in the horoscope. For further details, see James Wilson, *A Complete Dictionary of Astrology* (London, 1819).

provided rules, he thought, by which one could judge the good or ill
fortune of a father by the horoscope of his first son;[1] for discovering
whether a child was of your own begetting and if it would be male
or female;[2] or 'to direct us to what Professions, (or Callings)
Children are by nature most fitt, or most enclined to', a principle
that he incorporated in his *Idea of Education*.[3]

From the 1670s onwards, Aubrey's manuscripts show him constantly thinking about astrology, 'for we are governed by the planets,
as the wheeles & weights move the Index of the clock'.[4] In his
almanacs he noted his moods in relation to the movements of
the planets—'melancholy sans cause',[5] 'dejected & dispirited',[6]
'Indiff⟨erent⟩',[7] or 'good, jolly',[8] and he took the horoscopic
predictions that he had cast each year very seriously. These were
mainly done by his friend Henry Coley, with whom he sometimes stayed in the 1670s, one of the most eminent astrologers of
Restoration England, and the adopted son of William Lilly, the
high-priest of the art during the Interregnum. Coley told Aubrey
when to act warily, which months appeared 'very calm', which
were 'of great Caution', so that Aubrey should act warily, and so on,[9]
and it may even have been such predictions that dissuaded Aubrey
from his schemes for emigration.[10] 'Forewarn'd Forearm'd' was
Coley's cheerful view,[11] and Aubrey quoted William Lilly that his
almanacs and his *Anima Astrologiæ: or, a Guide for Astrologers*
(1676) gave 'the true Key of understanding generall accidents, i.e.
Mundane affairs'.[12]

[1] *Gentilisme*, 278.

[2] MS A 23, 2. He told himself to 'v⟨ide⟩ in Haly . . . ' to discover this: i.e. presumably
the Latin translation of the astrological treatise of Alí Ibn Abí Al-Rajjal, of which
Ashmole had three printed copies (Ashmole 441, 442, 572), all formerly owned by
William Lilly.

[3] MS A 10, 144.      [4] A-W, 14 May 1673, F 39, 206.

[5] Ashmole D 60(4), Lilly's *Merlini Anglici Ephemeris* for 1675, C8.

[6] MS Aubrey 33, Lilly's *Merlini Anglici Ephemeris* for 1673, C1v.

[7] Ibid., C5v.      [8] Ibid., C4.

[9] MS A 23, 112. These predictions, from 1672 onwards, are all in MS A 23. Aubrey
shared with Coley his interest in mathematics as well as astrology: he told Wood that
'no man can love learning mathematicall more than he does' (A-W, 14 May 1673,
F 39, 206).

[10] MS A 23, 107v, 109 (1672/3).      [11] Ibid., 112v.

[12] MS A 12, 213v (a note on the back of a letter from Hoskyns of 22 Nov. 1673). Aubrey
actually says 'his Prophetical Merlin & Guido Bonat⟨us⟩'. Lilly's almanacs were called
*Merlini Anglici Ephemeris*, and his *Anima Astrologiæ* was largely a translation of Guido
Bonatus and Cardan. Aubrey's copy of the latter work is now Worcester College E x 6;
at the end of it are some autobiographical and other notes by him.

It is almost certainly significant that Aubrey's active concern with astrological predictions apparently dates only from the 1670s, for astrology must have appealed to him by offering a rational explanation of his misfortunes at the time of their climax. It never involved a fatalism contradictory to the preoccupation with worldly success shown by his *Faber Fortunæ*: Coley, when casting Aubrey's horoscope, was adamant that 'However Let him not wholly Confide in these Astrological Conjectures but rather strive to Baffle a Bad Fate'.[1] But explanation was none the less welcome. Thomas Flatman, amateur astrologer as well as poet, found that Aubrey's horoscope agreed exactly with his misfortunes;[2] Charles Snell, who often corresponded with Aubrey on astrological subjects, similarly claimed that the indications of the stars did 'well describe your person, and prognosticate your fate';[3] and Henry Coley elaborately diagnosed Aubrey's horoscope: 'The position of Cauda Draconis upon the Cusp of the Ascendant, which sometimes & Indeed Generally shows the Native will be subject to Calumny & Troubles in the Course of his life, & here the more Confirmed by reason of the aforesayd Configurations, which also never faile of giveing a defect in the Elocution (which All Authors unanimously Confirme) and not only so but Superlative vexations in Matters Relating to Marriag, or great Discords if so united; besides wondrous Contests in Law suits, of all which vexations I suppose the Native hath had a Greater portion than ever was desired, the Consideration of which is no small Argument to confirme the truth of Cœlestial Influences having beene verifyed not only in this, but (almost) Innumerable Genitures.'[4]

Everything is there: horoscopes accounted for Aubrey's stutter, his marital troubles (though, Coley assured him, women should in general be kind),[5] even his curiosity about antiquities, his 'Fancy for drawing & Painting'[6] and his desire 'to Inspect all things that are Learned or Ingenious'.[7] It all fitted so well that it is not surprising that he tried to repeat it on a larger scale, and one of his aims in collecting the biographical data that he used in *Brief Lives* was to collate human life with its astrological circumstances. He commended the 'Proposalls for the advancement of Astrol⟨ogy⟩' made in the 1671 almanac of John Gadbury, another prolific astrologer.[8]

---

[1] MS A 23, 107v.    [2] Flatman-Aubrey, 6 Sept. 1670, MS A 12, 116.
[3] Snell-Aubrey, 12 July 1677, MS A 13, 189.    [4] MS A 23, 104v.
[5] Ibid., 86v.    [6] Ibid., 106.    [7] Ibid., 86.    [8] A-W, 17 Nov. 1670, F 39, 128v.

Gadbury advocated a grand programme of astrological research by a whole team of workers, and one of these was 'to observe the *Nativities* of all sorts, *viz.* of *violent* or *peaceable* Lives or Deaths, of *Brevity* or *Longevity*, of *handsom* or *mishapen* persons, of *Twins*, of such as are *eminent* in any Faculty, whether of Law, Physick, Heraldry, Philosophy, Musique, the Mathematiques, Martial Discipline, Government of Kingdoms or Cities; of great *Riches*, and extreme *Poverty*; of *Melancholy* people, whether proceeding from *Love*, or *Devotion*: and lastly, of such as are subject to the *Gout*, *Stone*, *Palsey*, loss of limbs, *&c.* And then to draw up their *Observations* into *Axioms* or *Aphorisms*, putting them into certain and distinct *Classes*, as the several *Subjects* shall require; and communicate them for *Publique* good'.[1]

Aubrey's *Brief Lives* are full of piecemeal observations on such topics. He noted the correlation between events and astrological ill-hours,[2] and, indeed, he recorded that in 1673 he told his patron the Earl of Thanet that if any good came of an embassy that started just at the time of an opposition of Saturn and Mars (the worst of all possible conjunctions of the planets), 'I would never trust to astrologie again'.[3] He thought that Hobbes owed his importance to having 'a *satellitium* in his ascendent', for 'it is a maxime in astrologie' that such people were unusually eminent.[4] He saw from 'the Sun and Aries being in the second house' that Erasmus was not born to be a rich man.[5] He reported that Edmund Waller, the poet, could versify easily only 'when his Mercurius and Venus are well aspected',[6] while Cardinal Wolsey, he believed, 'had Taurus ascending with the Pleiades, which makes the native to be of a rough disposition'.[7] He recorded 'accidents', significant events in a man's career, in order to rectify their nativities,[8] and he was sometimes prepared to speculate from their character as to the planetary influence under which they were born: he thought it must be Saturn that made Thomas Gore, High Sheriff of Wiltshire, so 'damnable covetous, and narrow souled',[9] and when he wrote about Colonel Ludlow, the regicide, he instructed himself 'V⟨ide⟩ the Reg⟨iste⟩r for his Nativity, or if possible to gett his true Geniture

---

[1] Ἐφημερίς: *or, A Diary Astronomical, Astrological, Meteorological For the Year of Grace 1671*, A 5v.
[2] *B.L.* II, 2.    [3] *B.L.* II, 8.    [4] *B.L.* I, 328.    [5] *B.L.* I, 248.    [6] *B.L.* II, 275.
[7] *B.L.* II, 310.    [8] E.g. A-W, 30 May 1674, F 39, 274.
[9] A-W, 14 May 1673, F 39, 206.

for the sake of Astrology, to see under what rugged aspects of Saturn and Mars he is under. Apocalyptically mad'.[1]

The biographies in the *Brief Lives* manuscripts are often written around horoscopes,[2] showing that these were more than mere appendages to his narrative, and another of Aubrey's manuscripts, his *Collectio Geniturarum*, compiled in the 1670s, is merely a series of horoscopes.[3] He explained to Wood, whose help he hoped to recruit for the project, that he hoped to find out 'exactly' the birth-dates of people, especially those 'famous in Learning, Wealth, Valour &c.',[4] evidently hoping to work out a sort of determinism. In his *Collectio*, he remarked briefly on the characteristics of each of the subjects: 'a very blockhead',[5] or 'a swindging lustie woman',[6] or 'she haz a solar face: and thrives well, & has a good sound judgement';[7] he paid particular attention to the Shirburne brothers, identical twins, 'both excellent scholars; and excellent poets'.[8] In 1681 he spent hours with Elias Ashmole making 'a collection of Nativities of learned men, beyond expectation, out of old English Astrologers that lived, above a hundred yeares since', manuscripts that Ashmole had had from William Lilly.[9] By such means, or, in the case of his contemporaries, by obtaining the most reliable information *'from their owne mouthes'*, he hoped 'to gett a supellex of true genitures . . . which the astrologers may rely on',[10] and thus he hoped to do much 'for the sake and improvement of Astrologie'.[11]

## Aubrey's World View

It is interesting that in astrology as in chorography, Aubrey hoped to establish determinist explanations of human behaviour, whether by observing the planets or by trying to make general rules about the effects of soils, plants and animals on each other and on man. It is still more interesting that for Aubrey astrology overlapped with natural history, determinism by the stars could not always be separated from the effect of the environment. He considered the people of

[1] MS A 3, 177.
[2] Cf. plate 9, from MS Aubrey 6, 5v, and, e.g., ibid., 39 (Oughtred), 49v (Tonge), 60 (Potter), 98 (Partridge), 99 (Digby); MS Aubrey 7, 3 (Aubrey), 12 (Bovey).
[3] MS A 23. It is dated 1677 on the cover, but Aubrey began it slightly earlier: cf. f. 8.
[4] A-W, Wednesday in Whitsunweek 1671, F 39, 131.
[5] MS A 23, 22.     [6] Ibid., 48v.     [7] Ibid., 46v.     [8] Ibid., 73v.
[9] A-W, 20 Dec. 1681, B. 14, 134v. Aubrey's notes survive as MS A 23, 121a.
[10] *B.L.* I, 9.     [11] A-W, 15 Sept. 1674, B. 14, 111.

North Wiltshire 'something heavy, and melancholy, as under Capricorn',[1] but elsewhere he connected their humours with the 'dirty, clayy countrey' in which they lived.[2] He listed 'Accidents to rectifie the Horoscope of Malmesbury by', including the time of year of plagues and the exact times of the capture and recapture of the town in the Civil War, evidence similar to the material on 'fatality' that he put in his *Naturall Historie of Wiltshire* and *Miscellanies*.[3] His belief that the local influence of particular planets could explain religious enthusiasm parallels his interest in geological topography: 'The Astrologers, and Historians write that the Ascendent of Oxford is Capricornus, whose Lord is Saturne, a Religious planet, & patron of Religious men. If it be so, surely his influence runnes all along through North Wilts, vale of Glostershire and Somersetshire. In all changes of Religions they are more zealous then other where. e.g. in the time of the Rom⟨an⟩ Catholique religion, there were more and better Churches and Religious Houses founded than any other part of England could shew: and now they are the greatest Fanaticks, even to spirituall madness. e.g. the multitude of Quakers & Enthusiastes.'[4]

Aubrey's chorography and astrology constantly interconnected. He was interested to know not only what vegetation was associated with minerals, but also 'to what part of the heavens' stones on the surface pointed, for 'the Mineralists take Indications by it'[5]—just as in his magical manuscript it was important to use spring water running towards a certain part of the heavens.[6] He was anxious to insert astrological data about Siamese twins in his *Naturall Historie of Wiltshire*,[7] and when, in 1692, Edward Lhwyd reported the curious phenomenon of a child born with an ear of rye in its side, Aubrey requested the exact time of the child's birth on Gadbury's behalf.[8] In his *Collectio Geniturarum* he copied out an elaborate table of the mutation of airs in terms of the aspects of the planets.[9] He also approvingly noted Camden's claim that the plagues

---

[1] MS A 3, 116v. This was of the people living around Hartham.          [2] MS A 1, 21.
[3] MS A 3, 36v.     [4] MS A 1, 22.     [5] Ibid., 82.     [6] MS A 24, 85.     [7] MS A 1, 156.
[8] A-L, 20 Feb. 1691/2, A. 1814, 97. Lhwyd was unable to provide the information (Lhwyd-Aubrey, 3 April 1693, MS A 12, 243). Aubrey had earlier reported the case to Ray (Aubrey-Ray, 21 Jan. 1691/2, Ray, *Letters*, 251–2 (an extract)) and to the Royal Society (Copy Journal Books VIII, 94 (1691/2)) without the astrological overtones.
[9] MS A 23, 5–6. It is interesting that Aubrey inserted these natural astrological observations in his *Collectio Geniturarum*. Since he made no attempt to separate natural and judicial astrology, neither have I.

of London could be correlated with the position of Saturn,[1] just as he used information about the occurrence of plague at regular intervals from John Graunt's *Observations on the Bills of Mortality* as evidence of 'fatality', together with other evidence of supernatural interference in human affairs, in the *Miscellanies*.[2]

Such interconnections give a clue to discovering how Aubrey considered that the world worked. They make sense in terms of the kind of view of a world full of spirits and non-mechanical causes, of correspondences between the celestial spheres and the sub-lunar world, held by most people in the sixteenth century and earlier and strengthened by sixteenth-century neo-Platonism, but which was being replaced in his period by a more rigorous mechanist approach. Aubrey inherited many of his ideas from sixteenth-century thinkers, as he was aware in some instances. The case of the Siamese twins that interested him in his *Naturall Historie of Wiltshire* had been recorded by the Italian scientist, Jerome Cardan, when he was in England;[3] the table of planetary aspects was evidently compiled by Johann Schoner, professor of mathematics at Nuremburg in the early sixteenth century and author of several influential astrological works;[4] and he quoted similar writers of the last century and his own as authorities on various specific occult topics.[5] But many of his ideas were unconsciously derived from such sources, and he was ignorant of the intellectual ramifications of many of his theories.[6]

---

[1] MS A 23, 8. Cf. *B.L.* I, 145. Aubrey claimed that the reference was in Camden's *Britannia*, 'somewhere about the middle', but I have been unable to locate it.

[2] *Miscellanies*, 33.

[3] Aubrey also quoted Cardan on dreams in his *Miscellanies*, passim: cf. his marginal markings in his copy of Cardan's *Somniorum Synesiorum, Omnis Generis Insomnia Explicantes Libri IIII* (Basle 1562), Ashmole D 50, which he was given by William Holder in 1693.

[4] Aubrey wrote 'Jo⟨hannes⟩ Schoner' on it.

[5] For instance, he quoted Caspar Peucer on divination (MS A 1, 11v) and David Origanus on astrology (*B.L.* I, 246, 328: Aubrey's copy of his *Nova Motuum Coelestium Ephemerides* (1609) is now Worcester College E π 2), and he instructed himself to seek details from Agrippa on magic sigils (*Gentilisme*, 250) and other occult topics (cf. a note on the fly-leaf of Worcester College QQ 9 14, a work on geomancy by de Pisis, which he cites in *Gentilisme*, 212). At the beginning of his *Miscellanies* (p. 1), Aubrey recommended for 'those, who desire to know more of Things of this Nature', Comenius' *Lux è Tenebris* (1655) and a work called *Histoire Prodigieuse* by Père Arnault. Comenius' work is rather different from Aubrey's, more concerned with explicitly spiritual, religious visitations; I have been unable to locate the book by Arnault.

[6] He very rarely quotes authorities on the intellectual ramifications of such details: his quotation from the fourth-century neo-Platonic writer Iamblicus on the power of words (*Miscellanies*, 142–3) is almost unique. It is perhaps symptomatic of his ignorance that in claiming that Stonehenge was a heptagon (cf. below, p. 187), he added

The author whom he quoted most often on these as on other scientific topics was Bacon, yet his views were not even identical with Bacon's.[1] Though Aubrey's world view belongs to a recognisable context and has much in common with earlier occult writings, it was not dominated by them; his ideas about the interrelationship of natural and unnatural events must therefore be investigated in their own right.

The key to his views on such matters is a chapter in his *Naturall Historie of Wiltshire* entitled 'Accidents &c.',[2] for 'accident' is a primarily astrological term. Yet in this section he included observations of environmental determinism, about moles and rooks living in certain places and avoiding others near by. It was here that he inserted evidence of witchcraft, apparitions and divine impulse, together with stories of a man found alive after being hanged and of wonderful cures by the touch of a seventh son or 'the touch of a dead hand' (sometimes by a man's hand touching a woman and sometimes vice versa).[3] He included, too, examples of the equivocal production of matter, of an oak tree that grew in holy water miles from any other tree, and of cowslips reproduced in frozen cowslip water.[4] One also reads in this section of dogs who warned their

---

only as an afterthought that it might be connected with the seven planets: surely a well-informed neo-Platonist would have postulated some kind of Pythagorean computer!

[1] Both believed, for instance, in the susceptibility of the human spirits to planetary influences, and both were somewhat ambivalent about the power of the imagination (cf. p. 125, n. 3). But Aubrey's views on certain aspects of the occult were less sceptical than Bacon's, for, as his magical treatise shows, he did not entirely mistrust the 'secret' short-cuts that Bacon hoped to supersede by laborious empiricism. Bacon rejected judicial astrology, the use of talismans and astrologically-prepared medicines and other occult activities in which Aubrey dabbled, and he was sceptical on such subjects as astrologically propitious times. For a summary of Bacon's views, see D. P. Walker, *Spiritual and Demonic Magic from Ficino to Campanella*, 199 f. and P. Rossi, *Francis Bacon, From Magic to Science*, ch. 1.

[2] MS A 2, 169 f. and R.S. MS 92, 359 f. (more complete: cf. above, p. 102, n. 5).

[3] MS A 2, 171.

[4] The implication was that the 'essence' of the flower was thus transmitted: cf. K. Digby, *A Discourse concerning the Vegetation of Plants* (London, 1661), 76 f. (and Aubrey's notes on the back cover of his copy, Ashmole 1590). Aubrey also quoted Dr Nathaniel Highmore that the reproduction of trees by frost could be used to 'evince the possibility of the Resurrection of the Body' (MS A 2, 169v, quoting his *Corporis Humani Disquisitio Anatomica* (1651) ). Highmore was a member of the Oxford group of the 1640s and 1650s with which Aubrey had been associated, and Aubrey owned a copy of his *History of Generation* (1651) (cf. A-W, 30 May 1674, F 39, 273) which is now lost; he quotes it in his notes on the front fly-leaf and p. 43 of his copy of Digby. On Aubrey's related curiosity about the spontaneous generation of plants from certain earths cf. MS A 1, 67 (where he quoted Danvers about experiments Bacon had carried out to see what plants were produced by earth dug from 'very deep'), and 114–15v; *Analecta*, 155.

masters of imminent catastrophe or who refused to stay alive after
their masters died, of people who died of fright, and of others who
felt pain in exactly the same place at the same time as others suffered
it.

Clearly Aubrey thought that all these phenomena had some connection with each other, so it is interesting that further examples of
these and similar effects can be found scattered through both his
scientific and occult works. A section of his *Adversaria Physica*
entitled 'Effects of Longing' included the story of William Okeden,
a school-fellow of Aubrey's, whose mother had longed for strawberries while she was pregnant, and who was born with a red spot
on his cheek that bled at strawberry-time when he was about nine
years old.[1] He also told of a woman who gave birth to a one-armed
child after she saw a picture of Siamese twins and claimed that her
child would only have one leg,[2] which he obviously thought could
be attributed to the power of the imagination, a semi-occult concept
which he considered in his *Miscellanies*, quoting Bacon that 'Imagination is next Kin to Miracle-working Faith'.[3] Other examples of
these and related phenomena are reported both in the *Adversaria
Physica*[4] and the *Miscellanies*, which had whole chapters on the
'Impulses' and 'Miranda' of which there are a few examples in
'Accidents &c.',[5] while sometimes it was 'Dreams' that told people
what it was that cured them after they longed for it.[6]

Aubrey evidently took such non-mechanical causes and reactions for granted, and his manner of thinking about interactions
is shown by a passage in which, after citing Bacon on the power of
glances of love and malice, he compared them to chemical reactions

[1] *T.P.W.*, 353. The story appears in *Analecta*, 113, without the heading, and it is
possible that all the headings in Oldenburg's transcript from the *Adversaria Physica*
are his glosses on Aubrey's text rather than part of the text. However, I have treated
them here and on p. 117 as Aubrey's own work.

[2] *Analecta*, 161: she saw 'Lazaro & his brother which grew out of his side'. Cf.
Thomas Bartholinus, *Historiarum Anatomicarum Rariorum Centuriae*, I (Hafniae, 1654),
116–17, and plate.

[3] *Miscellanies*, 130. Though Aubrey attributes this view to Bacon himself, in fact it
is a misquotation of Bacon, *Works*, II, 641: 'Paracelsus, and some darksome authors of
magic, do ascribe to imagination exalted, the power of miracle-working faith'. On the
views of sixteenth-century writers (and Bacon) on the power of the imagination, cf.
D. P. Walker, *Spiritual and Demonic Magic*, who shows how they ranged from the occult
to the 'psychological'. For other remarks by Aubrey on this subject, cf. *Miscellanies*,
89, and R.S. MS 92, 366, where he tends to the latter attitude.

[4] *Analecta*, e.g. 207 (from Dr Samuel Bave), 213X, etc.

[5] *Miscellanies*, 117 f., 129 f. Cf. 37 f. ('Omens').        [6] Ibid., 47 f.; esp. 60–1.

at a distance, adding that 'if an Astrologer had their Nativities, he would find a great disagreement in the Schemes. These are Hyperphysical Opticks, and drawn from the Heavens.'[1] 'The Eye of the malicious Person does really infect and make sick the spirit of the other',[2] and he was going to be sure to guard against it in the relations between masters and boys at his school, for 'A boy will never learn well of a Teacher that hath an Antipathie to him'.[3] Moreover he believed that horoscopes could be used to decide whom one would or would not get on with: he wanted some accidents of Mrs Elizabeth Blount because 'me thinkes she much resembles Gemini & haz an Antipathy to me'.[4]

What is significant is that there was no distinction between Aubrey's views of such reactions and his ideas about more 'natural' ones. For sympathy and antipathy, with the occult calculations that they implied, played a large part in his system of scientific explanation. He conceived an experiment to let holly berries swim in water, 'if one should apply or set a peice of seacoale neer [try it according to all positions] whether one should find any Magnetisme',[5] and it was evidently in these terms that he conceived the 'kind of affinity'[6] that he had observed between holly and coal and its 'effluvium'[7] on his travels. Elsewhere, his theories often seem to take imagery literally in terms of contraries. He actually compared the differing humours of those who lived on either side of the Severn with those of toads and adders, noting that the eyes of the citra-Sabrinians were the colour of a viper's.[8] Following Bacon, he speculated whether 'Youthfull Spirit infused into an old body might turne natures course back againe'.[9] 'By the Rule of Contrarys', he thought that winds from the thyme-scented uplands could cure diseases contracted in moorish areas,[10] and he hoped that the blossoms of fruits would take out their stains.[11] He even recalled a recipe for recovering stale drink from Sir Hugh Plat's *Jewell House of Art and Nature,* and suggested 'try if it may not be a hint, for promoting a Rejuvenescence. e.g. if the blood of a Viper or Adder

---

[1] Ibid., 185. Cf. Bacon, *Works,* II, 653.

[2] Loc. cit. In MS A 10, 11, this view is attributed to Van Helmont. There is, however, nothing specifically Helmontian about it, and Bacon's views, just cited, were almost identical.

[3] MS A 10, 11.　　[4] MS A 23, 29v.　　[5] *Analecta,* 204x.　　[6] MS A 1, 122.

[7] *Analecta,* 164.　　[8] MS A 1, 23.

[9] *Analecta,* 212, quoting 'Canon XIX' from Bacon, *Works,* V, 330.

[10] R.S. MS 92, 30.　　[11] *Analecta,* 205x.

intromitted into the veine of a person whose blood is in the nature of dead drinke, whether it will not excite a naturall fermentation'.[1]

For in Aubrey's world view metaphor actually overlapped with fact, imagery could itself be significant. It is impossible to be sure how metaphorically he was speaking when he claimed that viper eyes indicated good wit,[2] or when he mentioned the hardness and harshness of Welsh plums and cherries in connection with the choleric humour and dark eyes of the inhabitants.[3] This has interesting implications for *Brief Lives*, where he often combined observations of people's appearance and their character, for he believed that physiognomy was an 'infallible Rule, to discover the Indications of pride, Treachery' and other traits,[4] just as physical features of the subject were relevant to astrological predictions.[5] When he wrote about a woman at the siege of Gloucester in the Civil War, a notable markswoman who 'would give money to the Souldiers for a faire shott', he noted 'V⟨ide⟩ her Phisiogn⟨omy⟩ if black or hazell eye or Leonine',[6] and he was thinking in more than purely descriptive terms when he said of Bacon in the *Lives* 'He had a delicate, lively hazel eie; Dr. Harvey told me it was like the eie of a viper'.[7] He carefully noted that Hobbes' complexion and the shape of his head were 'approved by the physiologers';[8] and of Thomas Allam, clerk to Sir John Hoskyns, whose appearance he described with characteristic vividness—'dark hazel eie kind of lowring looke dark-browne haire'—he observed 'a clowd (unlucky) in his physiognomie' and noted, as if it was equally significant, that he was born on the morning that Charles I was beheaded.[9]

Such modes of thought, with theories of sympathy and antipathy and non-mechanical causes and cures, made sense of the combination of interests that Aubrey espoused, and magical remedies cannot have seemed very different from 'rational'[10] ones when they were so conceived. It is not surprising that it was not only in his magical manuscript that Aubrey invoked sympathetic charms—for

[1] Ibid., 258. Cf. Sir Hugh Plat, *The Jewell House of Art and Nature* (London, 1594), 59.

[2] MS A 1, 23.     [3] Loc. cit.     [4] MS A 10, 85. Cf. 118.

[5] For instance, he noted while elucidating the horoscope of Mrs Grace Hooke, Robert Hooke's niece, that she had 'a hairy Mold, on her left pappe': MS A 23, 56.

[6] *Analecta*, 117.

[7] B.L. I, 72. Cf. Samuel Butler's 'leonine-coloured haire', ibid., I, 138.

[8] B.L. I, 347–8.     [9] MS A 23, 101b.

[10] Of some recipes in his *Wiltshire*, Aubrey notes 'it seemes to be a very rational medicine' (MS A 1, 146v).

finding thieves, for instance,[1] or for seducing women.[2] Similar recipes also appear in the *Naturall Historie of Wiltshire*. His recipe for the ague involved boiling an egg in the invalid's urine and leaving it in an emmets' hill, and as the egg decayed the patient was supposed to recover,[3] while 'all manner of Fitts, Convulsions, falling-sickness &c.' could be cured by wearing a small willow branch around the neck on a white silk till it fell off, and then 'no body must touch it, but the party that wore it; and the party, not with his fingers, but with the tongues' (i.e. tongs).[4] On the other hand some of the recipes in Aubrey's magical manuscripts are as 'rational' as those in his scientific ones—such as putting a cold iron bar on barrels to stop beer being soured by thunder (though Aubrey attributed this to Mars' unwillingness to harm his own house).[5] Some recipes actually appear in both the magical and scientific manuscripts,[6] and it was in his magical treatise that he claimed 'So there may be more vertue in plants, then is commonly thought of', continuing 'Memorandum before the Tryall per Duellum the Challenger & Combatant were both to take their corporate oathes, that they had about them neither Spell, nor Herbe &c.'.[7]

Equally predictable was the ease with which Aubrey paralleled the natural with the supernatural. 'As toades are kild with salt & sp⟨irit⟩ of salt: so why may not the Spirits of Saturne be driven away with holy water which is made with salt but best I beleive Astrologically',[8] and elsewhere he elaborated this to consider how bad spirits could be raised and pleased with bad smells like henbane and good ones with pleasant ones like frankincense.[9] 'One says why should one think the Intellectual World less Peopled, than the Material?' he asked,[10] and he quoted Sir Matthew Hale, Lord Chief Justice, 'That whirlewinds, and all Winds of an extraordinary nature are agitated by the Spirits of the Air.'[11] 'On which Notion I reflected at the time of the Fight at Philips-Norton 168⟨5⟩ (The D⟨uke⟩ of Monmouth) being then at the Parsonage at Wyly with the Reverend Rector Mr. Jo: Stevens. Ther were smart showres of Rain fell driven with brisk gusts: but there violent & suddain

---

[1] MS A 24, 85.     [2] Ibid., 87v–88.     [3] MS A 1, 147.     [4] Ibid., 119v.
[5] *Miscellanies*, 147; cf. *Gentilisme*, 258.
[6] E.g. carrying a green elder stick in the pocket while riding to prevent galling: MS A 1, 124, and MS A 24, 94v.
[7] MS A 24, 94v.     [8] *Analecta*, 206x.     [9] *Miscellanies*, 172–3.     [10] Ibid., 173.
[11] R.S. MS 92, 35. Cf. M. Hale, *The Primitive Origination of Mankind* (London, 1677), 36–8.

Whisks of wind were to and fro; as it were chasing on another.' And he quoted Homer 'That in the Engagement between the Greeks & Troians, The Gods sate on Olympus Hill, and lookt on, and were divided in opinion', as if he had been a witness to their interference.[1]

This appeared in the chapter on 'Air' in his *Naturall Historie of Wiltshire*, in which the accounts of selective storms and vindictive meteors were doubtless conceived in similar terms.[2] He was also interested in the sufferings of those who felled a venerable tree 'as if the Hamadryades had revenged the Injury donne',[3] and he noted that the breaking of irons while digging for minerals in Surrey was 'thought by Mr William Lilly [Astrologer] to be by the Sub-terranean Spirits'.[4] In this world where imagery merged with fact and spirits directly influenced things, it is not surprising that the interaction of the planets with mundane affairs, the workings of magic, and the occult phenomena of the *Miscellanies*—from blows invisible to transportation by an invisible power, from visions in crystal to second sight—all had a place which in a mechanised world they were denied.

Of course, Aubrey was not completely uncritical. He was always very careful about his sources when studying the supernatural, going out of his way to quote stories 'credibly told by several Persons of Belief',[5] or to have things vouched for by 'a very understanding Gentleman, and not Superstitious'.[6] 'Quaere de hoc,' he would write of unlikely natural phenomena, 'if it be true 'tis considerable: sed vix credo',[7] and he was ever anxious to unmask such 'vulgar errors' as the story of wyverns in Mount Atlas 'that are as big as Swannes' told by Samuel Purchas in his *Pilgrimes*.[8] He was aware that supernatural phenomena were particularly susceptible to charlatanry: 'where one is true, a hundred are Figments' —'There is a Lecherie in Lyeing: and imposeing on the Credulous'.[9] Henry Coley, he considered, was far from mountebanking, but not so other supposed astrologers;[10] he flatly denied what he read 'in an old Physique booke' of the bodies of people born at certain conjunctions of the planets not consuming in the grave;[11] he inserted the proviso into his study of fatalities of families and

---

[1] R.S. MS 92, 35-6.  [2] Ibid., e.g., 35, 37, 38, 39.
[3] MS A 4, 85. Cf. *Gentilisme*, 196.  [4] MS A 4, 171.  [5] *Miscellanies*, 88.
[6] Ibid., 120.  [7] MS A 1, 141v.
[8] Aubrey's note on a letter from Wyld Clarke from Santa Cruz, 7 July 1687, MS A 12, 76, transcribed in MS A 1, 142v. Cf., e.g., R.S. MS 92, 38.
[9] R.S. MS 92, 366.  [10] A-W, 17 June 1673, F 39, 214.  [11] *Analecta*, 135.

places that the capaciousness of their estates explained the longevity of some families;[1] and, when studying apparitions, he quoted a French saying 'That when a Man has been drunk, Il a veu le Diable'.[2]

He also produced entirely rational explanations of both natural and supernatural phenomena. He attributed Nan Green's sudden vision of light when she was taken down alive from the scaffold at Oxford in 1650, like another case of a similar event, not to a supernatural visitation, but to 'the nerves constringed'.[3] He was aware that epidemics of smallpox had purely natural causes—that in 1654, for instance, he attributed to the dryness of the summer and the resulting muddiness of the waters[4]—and he explained the variety of fertility and healthiness of different areas that he had observed in his 'Chorographia' in terms of the effects of nitrous and vitriolate salts,[5] believing that the mists and nitrous soil of the hills 'shootes Cold, and causeth Dampishnesse, condenseth the aire, hurts the Nerves & gives Aches',[6] and observing that oaks seemed to 'delight' in vitriolate soils and not chalk ones.[7]

But it is characteristic that such piecemeal rationalisations conflicted both with less natural causes suggested elsewhere, and even with each other. Astrological circumstances as well as astringent air could explain illness: a prediction in Aubrey's *Collectio Geniturarum* warned its subject that while he was 'under the moones Direction ad corpus Saturni', he was threatened with 'some cold or moyst distemper as an ague or fever proceeding from phlegme & melancholy or aliquid tale'.[8] Similarly, whereas black eyes could be associated with the drinking of cider and vitriolate waters,[9] fair hair might be due to the position of Aries and Mars in the horoscope;[10] and while the absence of snakes from certain areas was because 'the Nitre in the Chalke is inimique to them',[11] moles and rooks avoided certain parts due to more unnatural 'Accidents'.[12] It is, in any case, difficult to see what 'natural' explanations of cures could have been adduced if the plants they used had 'little or no Vertue' if not gathered 'according to the Rules of Astrology',[13] or if ash wood would cure bleeding only if cut 'at the very houre & minute when

---

[1] *Miscellanies*, 28.   [2] R.S. MS 92, 365.   [3] *Analecta*, 214x.   [4] Ibid., 207x.
[5] Esp. MS A 1, 60, and see above, pp. 97, 114-15.   [6] Ibid., 163.
[7] Ibid., 56, and MS A 3, 147v.   [8] MS A 23, 65v.   [9] *Analecta*, 124.
[10] MS A 23, 72v. Aubrey quoted Gadbury on this point.   [11] MS A 1, 145.
[12] MS A 2, 169: see above, p. 124.   [13] *Miscellanies*, 144.

the sun enters Aries'.[1] It is therefore hardly surprising that when it came to 'rational' explanations Aubrey was often inconsistent, as in his uncertainty whether 'vitriolish' soil encouraged or diminished longevity.[2]

Aubrey's ideas were muddled and vague, and he rarely pressed one explanation so rigorously as to exclude another. When considering 'markes of minerals', at different points in his scientific manuscripts he noted that yew was associated with thunderstones,[3] with lead,[4] with grey marl[5] and with freestone,[6] that hazel also seemed to be found near lead[7] and freestone[8] as well as on chalky soils,[9] but that the indicators of freestone also included betony and oak:[10] all of which might have made him wonder whether there could be any significant correlation of this kind at all. But Aubrey was too busy hurrying on to record the next piece of information that he had encountered to spend time arranging his material in a way that would prove certain possibilities and exclude others. So haphazard were his scientific collections that even after accumulating all this information about the minerals associated with yew, he still noted of yew trees in another place in his *Naturall Historie of Wiltshire*: 'What they doe indicate, let the Mineralists consider',[11] and he hardly ever got round to testing any theory that he espoused. 'It is matter of fact: and therefore easily to be prov'd', he might write,[12] but he rarely managed to do so.

The result was that for Aubrey almost anything was possible, almost any hypothesis worth considering. 'For ought I know (saith Mr Aubrey) our dreams come to us in our Braines, as the Idea does into the Cristall'.[13] He was intrigued to learn that the corpses of plague victims rotted immediately and that the smell of those bitten by rattlesnakes was unendurable.[14] He was fascinated by the story of a gravedigger at Woking in Surrey about a kind of plant that sprouted from the putrefaction of corpses, 'about the bignesse of the middle of a Tobacco-pipe, which came neer the surface of the

---

[1] *Analecta*, 169.

[2] Ibid., 124, has Herefordshire people long-lived perhaps because of drinking vitriolate waters; but MS A 1, 60, attributes this to the freedom of their ground from salt.

[3] MS A 1, 9.    [4] Ibid., 11.    [5] *Analecta*, 163.    [6] MS A 4, 209.
[7] MS A 1, 11.    [8] Ibid., 10.    [9] Cf. MS A 4, 82.    [10] Ibid., 209.
[11] MS A 1, 122. Cf. *Analecta*, 174x.    [12] MS A 1, 119.

[13] Ashmole's notes from Aubrey's 'Collection of dreames, phantasmes, Instincts &c:', British Library MS Sloane 3846, 114v.

[14] *Analecta*, 267. Both pieces of information came from H. Dennys, Apothecary.

earth but *never appeered above it*. It is very tough and about a yard
long, the rind of it is almost black, and tender so that when you pluck
it it slippes-off; and underneath it is red, it hath a small button on
the top not much unlike the top of an Asparagus . . . he is sure it is
not a Ferne roote'.[1] He gladly believed 'that the Air doth encrease
the Gold. quod N B',[2] or that when someone was sleeping on the
ground at harvest time 'a toade crept into his codpiece & suckt his
penis, whereof he dyed: it rotted'.[3] And his *Miscellanies* was full of
succinct narrations of supernatural visitations, like the one cited
as a model ghost story by Jonathan Oldbuck in Scott's *Antiquary*:
'*Anno*. 1670, not far from *Cirencester*, was an Apparition: Being
demanded, whether a good Spirit or a bad? Returned no answer, but
disappeared with a curious Perfume and most melodious Twang.
Mr. *W. Lilly* believes it was a Fairie'.[4]

## Aubrey and the Science of his Age

To some extent this was due to the nature of Aubrey's scientific
activity, for his collections were haphazard and unsystematic. Even
his *Naturall Historie of Wiltshire*, as he explained in his preface,
consisted chiefly of 'the Observations of my frequent Road between
South and North Wilts; that is, between Broad-Chalke and Eston-
Piers. If I had had then leisure, I would willingly have searched the
Naturals of the whole County'.[5] Moreover Aubrey's classification
was never rigorous enough to give him more than convenient
chapter headings, and his obsession with utility, including his
interest in the environment as it affected man rather than in its own
right, blinded him to more 'luciferous' considerations. It is indica-
tive that Martin Lister, for whom Aubrey wrote out his 'Chorographia', was interested in geology for its own sake, aspiring only
through studying rocks and soils to be 'better able to judge of the
make of the *Earth* and of many *Phænomena* belonging thereto'.[6]

For Aubrey stands in contrast to contemporary scientists like
Lister, John Ray, Edward Lhwyd or Robert Morison, whose exhaustive collecting and systematic classification of groups of pheno-

---

[1] MS A 4, 163. This Aubrey learnt by talking to the man himself, though he also
had an account of the phenomenon from Plot (cf. above, p. 77).
[2] MS A 26, 10. He was told this by John Huniades.      [3] *Analecta*, 165.
[4] *Miscellanies*, 80. Cf. W. Scott, *The Antiquary* (Edinburgh, 1816), I, 200-1.
[5] MS A 1, 7.      [6] *Philosophical Transactions* XIV (1684), 739.

mena broke new ground in the study of nature. A description of
Morison's botanical method in a letter from Thomas Pigott to
Aubrey is sufficient to show how different his work was from Aubrey's
piecemeal collections. Morison aimed to achieve a classification
along natural lines, intending in every chapter 'to put down some
plants of a like nature, a Generall description, a Scheme of differences
&c, an Explication thereof, with paragraphs of Usus, locus, tempus
& nomina'.[1] Ray's careful catalogues were equally systematic and
accurate,[2] and careful method was crucial to most of the achievements of Restoration science, in the physical and medical sciences
as well as the botanical. It is revealing to contrast the experiments
of Aubrey's friends Wren and Hooke with his scrappy work, and
to observe how even Hooke's outline of the desiderata of natural
history was far more methodical than anything in Aubrey's scientific writings.[3] The result was that Aubrey always remained an
amateur. He sadly noted how he would 'have been a Botanist,
had I had leisure, which is a Jewell I could be never Master of'.[4]
Instead, he had constantly to apply for information to experts who
had made studies of this kind. 'Quaere the Learned of this', he
noted in connection with different phenomena,[5] and John Ray, in
particular, advised him about classification[6] and answered his
questions about plants,[7] providing expert notes and corrections to
the manuscript of the *Naturall Historie of Wiltshire*.

Ray's attitude towards Aubrey appears in his remarks on this
work. 'I think, (if you can give me leave to be free with you),' he
wrote, 'that you are a little too inclinable to credit strange relations.
I have found men that are not skilfull in the History of Nature, very
credulous, & apt to impose upon themselves & others; & therefore
dare not give a firm assent to any thing they report, upon their own
Authority; but are ever suspicious that they may either be deceived
themselves, or delight to teratologize, (pardon the word) & to make

[1] Pigott-Aubrey, 15 April 1678, MS A 13, 113. Morison's *Plantarum Historiae
Universitatis Oxoniensis Pars Secunda* appeared in 1680.

[2] Cf. I. P. Stevenson, 'John Ray and his contributions to plant and animal classification', *Journal of the History of Medicine* II (1947), 250 f.

[3] Hooke, *Works*, 1 f., 'A *General Scheme, or Idea* of the Present State of Natural
Philosophy, and how its Defects may be remedied'. On Wren, see Sprat, *History*, 311 f.,
and H. W. Jones, art. cit. (above, p. 23, n. 4).

[4] MS A 1, 106.     [5] Ibid., 106v.     [6] Ray-Aubrey, (n.d.), MS A 13, 181.

[7] Aubrey sent Ray plants for his advice: cf. Ray-Aubrey, 15 Feb. 1682/3, MS A 13,
172. Ray answered Aubrey's queries, etc., in letters of 17 Aug. 1691, 20 Dec. 1692;
ibid., 173, 177.

shew of knowing strange things.'[1] 'The story concerning the drawing out the nail driven crosse the Woodpeckers hole,' he assured
Aubrey, referring to a somewhat unlikely tale that he had told, 'is
without doubt a fable',[2] and elsewhere he marked beside a place in
the text where Aubrey accepted a country divination of the weather,
'I reject as superstitious all Prognosticks from the weather on particular days'.[3] He 'did distrust' a story that strawberries eaten by
someone with a wound in the head were fatal,[4] and what the little
yellow insect was that Aubrey said was always found in grounds
abounding in saltpeter, which 'never fails the salt peter men', 'I
cannot conjecture'.[5]

Ray was not alone in his scepticism of Aubrey and his ideas and
concerns. White Kennett said that he was known as 'the Coruption
Carrier to the Royal Society',[6] and on at least two occasions Aubrey
was tacitly condemned at its meetings. In 1683, 'Mr. Aubrey related
from an eminent embalmer, that he found a sort of insects in dead
bodies, which he concluded to be bred in the brain; but,' continues
the minute book disapprovingly, 'of this there was no proof
offered',[7] and when in 1662/3 Morison was consulted on a similar
question raised by Aubrey, he 'knew of no such thing'.[8] Aubrey's
interests were also not universally approved. Hooke thought
'Astrology vaine'[9] and Walter Charleton, another scientist friend
of Aubrey, thought the 'very fundaments' of judicial astrology
'seem to be precarious & fraudulent'.[10] Thomas Sprat in his *History
of the Royal Society* assailed both this and the study of omens and
prophecies,[11] while Thomas Smith, an erudite divine to whom
Aubrey showed his *Miscellanies* before publication, 'disliked ⟨it⟩
extremely, and would have had him left out several chapters, and

[1] Ray-Aubrey, 27 Oct. 1691, MS A 1, 13.
[2] Loc. cit. The reference is to ibid., 141.    [3] Ibid., 11v.
[4] Ray-Aubrey, 17 Aug. 1691, MS A 13, 173. This story is told in MS A 1, 106v;
Aubrey reported it to Ray in a letter of 5 Aug. 1691 (Ray, *Letters*, 251).
[5] Ray-Aubrey, 20 Dec. 1692, MS A 13, 177. Cf. MS A 1, 146; reported by Aubrey to
Ray in a letter of 15 Dec. 1692 (Ray, *Letters*, 269).
[6] British Library MS Lansdowne 937, 63 (an entry in Kennett's Memorandum Book
for Tuesday, 20 Jan. 1684/5).
[7] Birch, *History*, IV, 209.
[8] Ibid., I, 212-13 (this time it concerned insects bred from the putrefaction of vegetables). The background to these observations lay in Aubrey's interest in equivocal
generation: see above, p. 124.
[9] Hooke, *Diary*, 386 (25 Nov. 1678). This follows the note 'Sir J. Hoskins and Aubery
at Jonathans' (the coffee house they often patronised).
[10] Charleton-Aubrey, 4 Feb. 1671/2, MS A 12, 66.    [11] Sprat, *History*, 97, 364-5.

mended several places in the rest'.[1] 'You Vertuosi are very curious
and inquisitive, and where you haue found out all the secretts in
this world you would faine haue some newes from the other,' wrote
Thomas Mariet, High Sheriff of Warwickshire and a friend since
undergraduate days, when replying to Aubrey's enquiries in 1686.[2]
He also criticized Aubrey and his like for being 'too apt to take
every thing upon trust: which fills their naturall historyes as full of
Lyes as Pliny'.[3]

Yet interests and attitudes like Aubrey's were widespread even
among officers of the Royal Society, as they were among his friends.
John Evelyn, for a while Secretary of the Society, was curious
about such subjects as apparitions,[4] magical recipes[5] and subterranean people in England and Malta,[6] as Aubrey's works and
Evelyn's notes to them reveal. Sir John Hoskyns, President and
Secretary, showed in his letters to Aubrey his interest in subjects
ranging from astrology to sympathetic powders, which he called 'a
piece of naturall science' and recommended for Hooke when he was
ill.[7] Robert Plot, at one time Secretary and editor of the *Philosophical
Transactions*, included accounts of occult phenomena in his writings
on natural history,[8] and he devoted much time to the study of
alchemy, even hoping that a college might be established in England
where adepti could prepare the elixir of life.[9] Sir James Long's
letters to Aubrey mention astrology,[10] witchcraft[11] and natural
magic;[12] he hoped to combine an account of these with conjectures
concerning unicorns and a natural history of animals in a demonstration of God's wisdom in the creation.[13] Edmund Wyld, with
whom Aubrey lived, studied spontaneous generation,[14] portents[15]
and occult manuscripts, one of which he bought from Elias Ashmole,[16] with whom Aubrey shared his interest in magic and astrology.

[1] Smith-Hearne, 23 July 1709: Hearne, *Collections*, II (Oxford, 1886), 225–6.
[2] Mariet-Aubrey, 9 Aug. 1686, MS A 12, 330.   [3] Id., 4 April 1687, ibid., 328.
[4] *Miscellanies*, 87.   [5] *Gentilisme*, 248 (Evelyn's note to Aubrey's MS).
[6] MS A 1, 88v (Evelyn's note).
[7] Hoskyns-Aubrey, 27 May 1672, MS A 12, 201. See also below, p. 141.
[8] Plot, *Oxfordshire*, 204 f., *The Natural History of Stafford-shire* (Oxford, 1686), 329–
330, and Plot in *Analecta*, e.g. 31, 71, 73, 139.
[9] Cf. *Early Science in Oxford*, XII, 411–13, taken from British Library MS Sloane
3646, a volume containing Plot's alchemical papers: see F. Sherwood Taylor, 'Alchemical
Papers of Dr. Robert Plot', *Ambix* IV (1949), 67 f., who suggests that Plot felt he ought
to keep his alchemy secret (p. 76); Sprat attacked alchemists in his *History*, 37–8.
[10] Long-Aubrey, 18 June 1681, MS A 12, 285v.
[11] Id., 5 March 1682/3, and n.d., ibid, 280, 290v.   [12] Id., n.d., ibid., 290v.
[13] Loc. cit.   [14] MS A 1, 67.   [15] E.g. *Analecta*, 205x.   [16] *Miscellanies*, 170.

Ashmole was a keen supporter of the Royal Society; he thought its experiments would prove the validity of astrology and alchemy, and he saw its foundation heralded by a conjunction of Saturn and Jupiter.[1]

Among minor supporters of the Society, an ability to believe in such phenomena and a wish to study them, like Aubrey's, seem to have been the norm. The Society's papers, like Aubrey's letters, reveal them taking an interest in a miscellaneous range of subjects, from natural phenomena like earth tremors and prodigies to magic and prognostic dreams.[2] Among Henry Oldenburg's country correspondents were many like Peter Nelson, who wrote 'I could heartily wish (if this were not out of their way) to see something from the Royall Society about Spirits & Witches', requesting information on recent 'Bookes, that treat sollidly and particularly of Motion, of Gravity, of Magnetisme, of a Meridian at Sea and of Spirits',[3] while Joshua Childrey expressed surprise that Hooke's account of the weather in Sprat's *History* omitted all reference to the astrological circumstances of its changes.[4] Oldenburg held corpuscularian views like Boyle and other prominent scientists of the Society and he deliberately tried to discourage such interests: when Childrey offered him an account of sorcery Oldenburg pointedly noted of his reply 'said nothing of MS. of Sorcery'.[5] But there is no doubt that among scientific enthusiasts of the Restoration there were more whose interests were of this heterogeneous and uncritical kind than there were rigorous mechanists like Oldenburg or Ray.

Indeed, such activities must have seemed as characteristic of the early Royal Society to contemporaries as the achievements of its members in anatomy, chemistry and physics that seem remarkable today. When Thomas Deare, a country lawyer and family friend of Aubrey, wanted astrological advice from him and his friends, he addressed his letter to him as 'one of the Noble Assacyates of the Royale Seacyety att Gresham Colledge',[6] and it is hardly

---

[1] C. H. Josten, *Elias Ashmole*, I, 136.

[2] Cf., for example, P. Chester-Aubrey, 22 May 1678, MS A 12, 67; Wyld Clarke-Aubrey, 24 Nov. 1681(?), MS A 12, 78 (there are other letters from Wyld Clarke to Aubrey in MS A 12, and he may have been acting on behalf of the Royal Society in requesting such information). For similar letters, cf. A. R. Hall and M. B. Hall *eds.*, *The Correspondence of Henry Oldenburg* (Madison, 1965 et seq.), passim.

[3] P. Nelson-Oldenburg, 22 Aug. 1668, Oldenburg, *Correspondence*, v, 25.

[4] Childrey-Oldenburg, 12 July 1669, ibid., VI, 110.

[5] Oldenburg-Childrey, 23 April 1669, noted in ibid., v, 497.

[6] Deare-Aubrey, 9 March 1675/6, MS A 23, 7.

surprising that those who satirised the new science, like Samuel Butler in *Hudibras*, confused the mystical and more 'modern' strains.[1] It was, in fact, only to be expected that such activities would flourish among members of the Society, for opponents of the old pedantic Aristotelianism still championed by some in the Universities were glad of allies wherever they could find them. 'They must shut a roome very close that will have no species admitted but thorough their owne glasse,' thought Sir John Hoskyns,[2] and Ray explained to Aubrey: 'I would not willingly give offence to any man; but permitt every one to enjoy his own sence concerning subjects that are not of any ill influence or consequence . . . In such things as are clear, if any man be contentious, I would permitt him to enjoy his opinion, Nec ullum ultra verbum aut operam sumere inanem', 'and not waste any pointless word or pains'.[3]

For Aubrey and others like him were all good Baconians. Aubrey could claim Baconian precedents not only for his accumulation of scientific materials, but also for his interest in the power of the imagination,[4] the recurrence of plagues at regular intervals[5] and other non-mechanical reactions and events, concerning which he often cited Bacon's authority: 'My Lord Chancellor Bacon sayes that wee oftentimes mistake Sympathy for Antipathy & e contra'.[6] Indeed, scientists like Aubrey were Baconian, in preoccupations as well as in programme, in a way that the more advanced thinkers of their age were not,[7] and Bacon's *Sylva Sylvarum* is reminiscent of later natural histories like Aubrey's in its omnivorous curiosity, its non-mechanist theories and its ambivalence of belief and scepticism. It is therefore revealing that although Sprat criticised it in his *History* because 'in many places, he seems rather to take all that comes, then to choose; and to heap, rather, then to register', he

[1] Cf. J. T. Curtiss, 'Butler's *Sidrophel*', *Publications of the Modern Language Association of America* XLIV (1929), 1066 f., who is wrong in assuming that Sidrophel, at once astrologer and scientist, must be a composite figure because 'the two sides of his character are incompatible' (1075), though his identification of Butler's possible sources is unaffected by this. Shadwell's *The Virtuoso* also associates occult interests with the new scientists: cf. C. Lloyd, 'Shadwell and the Virtuosi', *P.M.L.A.* XLIV (1929), 489-90.

[2] Hoskyns-Aubrey, 22 Nov. 1673, MS A 12, 213. He was referring to the Society's attitude to Hobbes, 'that stout old blade that defyes limits of enquiry', though it is equally applicable to Aubrey and others.

[3] Ray-Aubrey, n.d., MS A 13, 182.     [4] Cf. above, p. 125.     [5] MS A 1, 171.

[6] *Analecta*, 224, and Bacon, *Works*, II, 493-4.

[7] Compare, for instance, the frequency with which Bacon's views are cited in John Evelyn's *Philosophical Discourse of Earth* (1676).

continued 'I hope this accusation of mine can be no great injury to his Memory'.[1]

With Aubrey's collections, as with Bacon's, it was easy for other scientists to value the information without accepting it all as true. For the '*Relations* of the effects of *Nature*, and *Art*'[2] provided by him and other 'plain, diligent, and laborious observers'[3] were worth considering, even 'though many of them have not a sufficient confirmation, to raise *Theories*, or *Histories* on their *Infallibility*'.[4] The Society was glad to take two or three days' entertainment in having Aubrey's scientific papers read in 1675–6, 'which they were pleased to like',[5] and these were quite at home when transcribed and placed among the classified papers of the Society. For the list of '*Relations*' that the Society recorded, published in Sprat's *History*, shows the close similarity between many of the Society's concerns and the subjects of Aubrey's *Naturall Historie of Wiltshire*, including winds and storms, mines and medicinal springs, agriculture and inventions, monsters and sympathetic cures.[6]

There was also common ground in the theories which mystical and mechanist thinkers might put forward, and scientists like Boyle deliberately eschewed interpretation of their observations so that virtuosi could interpret them 'according to the differing *Hypotheses* and Inquisitions, to which men are inclined'.[7] 'Fermentation', for instance, could be understood in a variety of ways, from van Helmont's mysticism to the purely mechanist corpuscularianism pioneered by the Oxford scientists of the Interregnum.[8] Equally revealing are the Helmontians' views of the experiments in blood transfusion conducted in London and Paris in the 1660s, for they conceived their potentialities in occult terms, hoping that the 'specifick proprieties' of different animals might 'have curative virtues peculiar to several Diseases',[9] whereas corpuscularian scientists saw them as purely physical. In the same way, within Aubrey's own writings, his observation of overlapping rainbows in

---

[1] Sprat, *History*, 36. Cf. Bacon, *Works*, II, 331 f.     [2] Sprat, *History*, 195.
[3] Ibid., 72.     [4] Ibid., 195.
[5] A-W, Twelfeday 1675/6, B. 14, 116, and see above, p. 95.
[6] Sprat, *History*, 195 f. Cf. his list of '*Observations*', 241–2.
[7] *Philosophical Transactions* II (1667), 592.
[8] Cf. R. G. Frank, 'Oxford and the Harveian Tradition in the Seventeenth Century', unpublished Harvard D.Phil. dissertation (1971).
[9] Geo. Acton, *Physical Reflections upon a Letter written by J. Denis ... Concerning a New Way of Curing sundry Diseases by Transfusion of Blood* (London, 1668), 10.

1647 appears in one place as a purely natural phenomenon[1] and in another as a portent significant because of 'the next remarkable Thing that followed'.[2]

There is also some evidence that mystical views like Aubrey's were discussed at Gresham College: among his papers are some notes which show that either at a meeting of the Royal Society or in reflecting on it afterwards, Aubrey evidently considered how fauns, dryads and naiades generated and died, comparing the way that fishes did, and citing the sixteenth-century occultist Cornelius Agrippa on the subject.[3] What is more, his notes reveal that several prominent scientists were at least curious about several of his more questionable concerns. He quoted William Harvey that the biting of an enraged man was poisonous[4] and that three drops of cat's blood in a spoonful of sherry-sack would prevent a new-born child from having fits.[5] It was Christopher Wren who informed him that strawberries, though normally harmless, were fatal to someone with a wound in the head (the story which Ray 'did distrust').[6] Robert Boyle told Aubrey 'that he alwayes weares a peice of gold about his neck: as Magnetique to mercuriall humours that are in the body & he very well sayes that there are no doubt many other occult quali-tyes not yet discovered'.[7] He also noted of his sympathetic cure involving an egg boiled in the victim's urine wasting in an ants' hill, 'Mr R. Boyle hath it'.[8] It was with Robert Hooke that Aubrey discussed an abortive Rosicrucian club in 1676;[9] and John Locke

[1] R.S. MS 92, 38.    [2] *Miscellanies*, 36.

[3] MS A 21, 54v (the passage, hastily written on a crumpled piece of paper, is difficult to read). Dryads and naiades were thought by the Paracelsians and others to have been produced by the cohabitation of fauns with maids before the flood. For Aubrey's views on fauns, see *Gentilisme*, 204.

[4] MS A 1, 160.

[5] *Analecta*, 257. This information came from Harvey's niece, Lady Dering. On Harvey's somewhat mixed ideas, cf. Walter Pagel, *William Harvey's Biological Ideas* (Basel, 1967).

[6] MS A 1, 106v. For the background to such views, cf. H. W. Jones, art. cit. (above p. 23, n. 4.), esp. 21.

[7] *Analecta*, 216x.

[8] Ashmole 1567 (Aubrey's copy of Wase's *Grati Falisci Cynegeticon*, London, 1654), front fly-leaf. Cf. MS A 1, 147. For Boyle's views on such phenomena, see his *Works*, e.g. I, lxxxiii-iv, II, 167-8, III, 317-18: he explained their effects in terms of 'subtile effluvia' (II, 167). Aubrey's quotation from him echoes the concluding remark of his *Continuation of New Experiments* (1668) (*Works*, III, 287). Note also Boyle's interest in a turquoise ring of Aubrey's that clouded over in a peculiar way (Aubrey-Boyle, 15 March 1665, and 6 Sept. 1672; *Works*, VI, 544, 546. Cf. MS A 1, 85v).

[9] Hooke, *Diary*, 242 (14 July 1676): 'At Honiwood view with Mr Aubery to whom I spoke of Rosicrusian club. He named tongue' (i.e. Ezerel Tonge; cf. *B.L.* II, 261-2).

was glad to transcribe letters about second sight that Aubrey had received from one of his informants, Dr James Garden, Professor of Divinity at Aberdeen.[1] It is symptomatic, on the other hand, that it was for proposing Francis Potter's work on blood transfusion to the Royal Society that Aubrey was 'putt to the Blush, it being generally answered that it was absurd, and impossible, wherefore it would be a blemish to the honour of the Society to experiment it'.[2]

For views on such subjects were by no means as clear as they seem in retrospect. Many possibilities remained open, and people applied their scepticism at different points for sometimes arbitrary reasons. Even Edmond Halley was uncertain about the validity of astrology: 'As to the advice you give me, to study Astrology,' he told Aubrey, 'I profess it seems a very ill time for it, when the Arch-conjurer Gadbury is in some prospect of being hanged for it. however I went to the library and lookt out the booke you recommended to me which I find to be published in anno 1557, so that I doubt not but the more moderne Astrologers having more experience of things may have added to him considerably, however upon your recommendations I will read it over'.[3]

The difficulties that lesser men encountered are illustrated by the

---

Cf. how when John Archer saw the list of contents of Aubrey's *Miscellanies* he told Tanner 'You see what a Volume of Rosicrusian: philosophy we may expect' (Archer-Tanner, 22 April 1695, Tanner 24, 29v). But he was speaking in a generalised or metaphorical way, for Aubrey was certainly not closely associated with the Rosicrucian tradition. When carrying out biographical researches for Wood in 1681, Aubrey claimed to have 'asked all the Chymists, & lovers of the Rosie-crosse, that I know for the name of Eirenaus Philalethes' (A-W, 15 July 1681, B. 14, 133), and when in 1694 Dr James Garden of Aberdeen wrote to him 'Its like your book of hermetick philosophie (which I conceive wilbe very diverting to the reader) may contain some account of the Rosicrucians; if not, pray, let me know if there be anie persons in England that goe under that name & what may be beleeved concerning them' (Garden-Aubrey, 4 May 1694, MS A 12, 133v; cf. id., 25 March 1694/5, ibid., 134v, where he gently reminds Aubrey that he still had not had such an account), Aubrey evidently had to apply to William Holder to find out about the origins and nature of the Rosicrucians (cf. Holder-Aubrey, 2 July 1695, ibid., 173). On Hooke's interest in alchemy, cf. p. 141, n. 9.

[1] Locke's copy is in Bodleian MS Locke c. 31, 111 f. Cf. John Buchanan-Brown's note in *T.P.W.*, 395.

[2] *T.P.W.*, 359.

[3] Halley-Aubrey, 16 Nov. 1679, MS A 12, 148 (printed in E. F. MacPike *ed.*, *Correspondence and Papers of Edmond Halley* (Oxford 1932), 47–8). The book in question was C. Leovitius' *De Conjunctionibus Magnis* (Aubrey's copy is now Worcester College CC 8 29; he recommended this and Leovitius' *Introductio* in MS A 10, 103). Gadbury had been taken into custody on suspicion on 2 November 1679 in connection with the Meal Tub Plot.

differing beliefs of Aubrey's friends. Sir John Hoskyns accepted astrology, quoting Hobbes that 'All things have causes',[1] and Henry Coley dedicated his almanac to him in 1677. Hoskyns also told stories of premonitory dreams and other occult phenomena and he thought phantoms not unlikely.[2] But he querulously noted 'o my conscience there are great temptations to superstition for us small witted folke',[3] and he was anxious to have astrological predictions 'covertly' tried,[4] suspecting William Lilly of charlatanry.[5] He was sceptical about witchcraft and second sight,[6] and he noted how Cornelius Agrippa 'the most famous author of nat⟨ural⟩ mag⟨ic⟩ writing de vanitate scientiarum scoffs at it to some purpose'.[7]

Andrew Paschall, on the other hand, had no time for astrology: 'I remember Melancthon owns it as his constant recreation. They say there is something in it, but I cannot learne that it proceeds on good grounds'.[8] But he was fascinated by alchemy,[9] and he contributed material for Aubrey's *Miscellanies* on 'Transportation by an Invisible Power'.[10] Thomas Mariet showed the same mixture of scepticism and belief. He criticised Aubrey in phrases already quoted for his credulity in claiming in his 'Chorographia' that particular lands would 'turne Cattle of a blewish Collour', which he called a 'ridiculous story'.[11] Yet he was glad to recommend as 'brave worke' for the Royal Society the testing of a house with mysterious lights,[12] and he provided Aubrey with information about apparitions and 'voices'.[13]

Many gladly tempered their scepticism by considering the possibility of the occult phenomena that fascinated Aubrey, if only so as to combat the atheistic threat of the rigorously mechanistic system of explanation postulated by authors like Hobbes. This argument underlay Joseph Glanvill's attempt to prove the existence

---

[1] Hoskyns-Aubrey, 27 May 1672, MS A 12 201. Cf. id., 7 Dec. 1672, ibid., 206.

[2] Id., 27 Feb. 1672/3, ibid., 209. Cf. id., 4 Sept. 1672, ibid., 205.

[3] Id., n.d., ibid., 225.     [4] Id., 27 July 1672, ibid., 202.

[5] Id., 4 Sept. 1672, ibid., 205.     [6] Id., 7 Dec. 1672, ibid., 206.

[7] Id., 4 Sept. 1672, ibid., 205.

[8] Paschall-Aubrey, 8 Nov. ⟨1681⟩ (damaged), MS A 13, 48.

[9] Cf. Paschall-Lodwick, 30 Sept. 1681, Royal Society Early Letters P 58; Paschall-Hooke, 21 Oct. 1681, ibid., P 59; Paschall-Lodwick, 9 Aug. 1682, ibid., P 60. These letters also show Hooke's interest in the subject.

[10] *Miscellanies*, 149 f.     [11] Mariet-Aubrey, 4 April 1687, MS A 12, 328.

[12] Loc. cit.

[13] *Miscellanies*, 81 (cf. Mariet-Aubrey, 9 Aug. 1686, MS A 12, 330) and 112–13.

of witches in his *Saducismus Triumphatus*, in which he was encouraged by Robert Boyle and Henry More, the Cambridge
Platonist, who valued evidence of supernatural interference as 'an
undeniable Argument, that there be such things as *Spirits* or
*Incorporeal Substances* in the world'.[1] But if religious scruples
explain why people accepted some of the phenomena that interested
Aubrey, they also explain why they refused to dabble in others.
Joshua Childrey, though as interested as Aubrey in the influence of
the planets on mundane affairs,[2] condemned the use of incantations
over divining rods as 'partly Sottish, partly impious',[3] and cabbalis-
tic magic like Aubrey's was widely disapproved of for reasons that
echoed the anti-magical views of the sixteenth-century adversaries
of Ficino and Paracelsus.[4]

In an old copy of Pliny's *Natural History* that he acquired,
Aubrey can hardly have avoided seeing these words written in an
unidentified seventeenth-century hand beside a paragraph about a
cure effected by repeating a magical charm: 'Which thinge no understanding man will attempt But follow the course ordayned by god:
how should we know that these words, Perteyne to this cure, or
what vertues can ther Be in words to Perswad or coniure an insen-
sible thinge for tho the diseased have sense; the disease hath none
of words—It may be some wicked munke or other Person hath
maid some couenant with the divell the father of all deceit; that
upon recytall of this sorcerous charme, he should Bestir himselfe;
& he worketh (in my opynion) these Dangerous cures, And the
Partie cured is much more dangerously insnared, as he groweth
well in his Body, sick in his soule. no holy man hath, euer attempted
these cures. Job or Ezekiah &c.'[5] Similarly, judicial astrology was
widely attacked for its deterministic threat to Christianity, for its
claims left 'indeed no Religion exempted from the vertue and
power whether good or bad of the Stars',[6] and Henry More was

[1] Quoted in M. E. Prior, 'Joseph Glanvill, witchcraft, and seventeenth-century
science', *Modern Philology* xxx (1932–3), 180, from More's *Immortality of the Human
Soul.*

[2] *Britannia Baconica*, B5–6.    [3] Ibid., 45.

[4] Cf. D. P. Walker, *Spiritual and Demonic Magic*, esp. 145 f.

[5] Ashmole G 17, Aubrey's copy of Holland's translation of Pliny's *Natural History*
(London, 1601). I am indebted to John Buchanan-Brown for bringing my attention to
this note, which is on page 289 of vol. II of the work (the two volumes are bound together). Aubrey at one time lent this book to Ray, as a note inside the front cover shows,
but I do not think that the note is in his hand.

[6] Henry More, *Tetractys Anti-Astrologica* (London, 1681), vi.

at pains to illustrate 'the great Affinity of *Astrology* with *Dæmono-latry*, and of the secret Agency of *Dæmons* in bringing about Predictions'.[1]

Aubrey's views differed entirely, for there is no evidence that he saw any of his occult interests as impious, and he cited orthodox testimony in their defence. Did not the Book of Job, after all, provide evidence of chiromancy,[2] just as *Tobit* gave biblical testimony of fatality?[3] He cited the Collect for Michaelmas and *The Certainty of the Worlds of Spirits* (1691) by the famous Presbyterian divine Richard Baxter concerning the existence of angels;[4] indeed, he emphasised how Dr. Richard Napier's 'Knees were Horny with frequent Praying' as the background to his converse with angels in the *Miscellanies*, 'which whom only Men of great Piety, Humility and Charity, could be acquainted'.[5] He quoted Archbishop Laud that the power of prayer could even overcome the malignity of a conjunction or opposition of Saturn or Mars,[6] and it is easy to see how his belief in the one led to his concern with the other, to his effort to investigate 'the Oeconomy of the Invisible World, which . . . sometimes is so kind as to afford us a glimpse of its Præscience'.[7]

Moreover Aubrey's interest in different aspects of the supernatural were all linked to one another. Mr Marsh of Dunstable claimed to be an astrologer as a countenance for his converse with spirits, he believed,[8] and 'They have the truest Dreams whose IXth House is well dignified' in their horoscope.[9] The planetary sigils that interested him in his magical manuscript combined the virtues of magic and astrology,[10] just as he believed that the use of gold to cure the King's evil depended on its being 'stamped according to some Rule Astrological'.[11] His views can only have been confirmed by supernatural incidents that he investigated: one of the cases of witchcraft in his *Naturall Historie of Wiltshire* concerned a girl the coverlid of whose bed showed the lines of a blank horoscope,[12] while the evidence against another suspected witch included the accusation that she showed visions in a glass.[13] Aubrey made no attempt to separate different areas of the occult. There is no dividing line between his interest in religious and

[1] Ibid., 130.  [2] *Gentilisme*, 209.  [3] *Miscellanies*, 31.  [4] Ibid., 173–5.
[5] Ibid., 171–2.  [6] Ibid., 174.  [7] Ibid., A6v ('*Dedication*').  [8] Ibid., 171.
[9] Ibid., 65–6.  [10] MS A 24, 86, 100.
[11] *Gentilisme*, 238. He also noted that 'the old Gold was very pure: and printed with St. Mich⟨ael⟩ the Arch-Angel'.
[12] R.S. MS 92, 364.  [13] Ibid., 363.

psychic phenomena and his curiosity about black magic of a kind
of which even modern practitioners are shy, fearful that 'the evil will
recoil' on the agent.[1]

Aubrey did try to draw a line between the natural and the supernatural, as is shown in the very conception of his *Miscellanies*,
devoted to 'Things præternatural'.[2] But, in view of the way that he
thought natural things functioned, it is not surprising that he was
inconsistent about it. Even when he tried to separate 'rational'
and magical recipes in a copy of Pliny's *Natural History* that he
owned, his categories overlapped, and recipes such as one to prevent
a cock crowing by putting vine-twigs round its neck were marked as
'rational'.[3] Moreover he was convinced that '*Hermetick Philosophy*'
was 'worthy of serious Consideration', just as natural philosophy
was,[4] and he and his friends despised those who ignored the supernatural, particularly the study of astrology. 'The D⟨ean⟩ of W⟨ells⟩
⟨i.e. Ralph Bathurst⟩ would laugh at this, but Kepler & Tycho Brahe
would not', he told Wood;[5] Thomas Flatman was disdainful of the
Royal Society, 'whose curiosity was either too little, or their capa-
cities not comprehensive enough of so accurate a piece of learning';[6]
while Henry Vaughan, the poet, a relation of Aubrey's, complained
how most physicians 'have not only an unkindnes for, butt are
persecutors of Astrologie', for, 'having once enterd upon the practice, they were loath to leave off, and learn to be acquainted with
another world'.[7]

Perhaps most striking is the view of John Gadbury, for the preface to his 1671 almanac, admired by Aubrey, contained much more
than mere rules for classifying genitures. When Gadbury 'consider'd the great *Differences* among the *Learned* of the World, in
reducing the many stupendious *effects* of Nature to their proper
*Causes*,' 'the great reason of this miscarriage seems to me most

[1] S. L. McG. Mathers, *The Key of Solomon the King*, viii.

[2] The list of contents in MS A 1, 25v has a chapter (separate from 'Accidents &c') devoted to 'Things præternatural e.g. Witchcraft, Phantômes &c:'; it is not thus separate
in the text, but this shows that the idea of separating this material out from the rest
of 'Accidents &c' occurred to him before he decided to develop it into a separate book.

[3] On the back fly-leaf of the third volume of his Latin copy of Pliny, Ashmole D 21,
magical recipes (e.g. 'Bitony. a defensative to Houses') are marked $\mu$, while rational ones
(e.g. 'against a stinking breath') are marked $\text{R}$. The cock-crowing recipe appears in the
text of this volume at page 273.

[4] *Miscellanies*, 1.

[5] A-W, 17 Nov. 1670, F 39, 128v.

[6] Flatman-Aubrey, 6 Sept. 1670, MS A 12, 116.

[7] Vaughan-Aubrey, 28 June 1680, MS A 13, 238.

apparent in our *partial* choice of things'. 'If men would understand the *true reason* of things in Nature, they must not explode the *Noblest* of Natures Studies, with a *Nullam esse Astrologiam*', 'there is no such thing as astrology'. Gassendi's atoms, Helmont's gas, Descartes' *materia subtilis* and Plato's ideas, he thought, were merely useful hypotheses: 'if *time* and *motion* be the *Parents* of all things sublunar, the onely way to bring the *Obelisk* to a *point*, is (I humbly conceive) to get a *Divorce* from *particular* Opinion for a time, and court the Divine URANIA; and to be well acquainted with the *Celestial* Clock-work which *distinguisheth* both of *causes* and *effects* most truly.' The virtuosi should study astrology, 'which impartially done, I dare aver, will far contribute to the quieting the *quarrels* that are so stoutly maintained in the Philosophique world'. 'I do not hereby designe to *destroy*, or to render of *mean* use, the Speculation of *propinquate causes*; but to compare *effects* with them and their *remote causes* together . . . *Original* and *propinquate* causes both *club* to the producing an *effect* . . . should we exclude *superior* causes, and rely onely on the *inferiour*, we might render our advantage of *Speculation* not much beyond that of *Brutes*'—like a dog that looks on a stone as his injurer rather than the hand that threw it. And Gadbury proposed that careful studies should be made of the relations between the movements of the planets and the weather, health, plenty and scarcity and so on. 'This *Method* observed, and encouraged, would be a means to bring Astrologie to that *degree* of *perfection*, that scarcely any Art at present can boast of; and *possibly* teach us a *surer* way to the discovery of the *Truths* of Nature, than hath been hitherto practised by the greatest *Philosophers* in the world'.[1]

But astrology was more vulnerable than any of Aubrey's studies to lack of rigour and inconsistency. Even the horoscopical predictions of Aubrey and his friends show the constant qualifications with which their astrological deductions were bound up, and these saved them both from questioning their basic beliefs and from checking their conclusions. Only too often Coley's horoscopic predictions for Aubrey revealed a struggle of good and bad influences, some making for a long life, some abating, 'Yet doubtless the Native may live to a Considerable Age'.[2] 'The Naturall portents of the stars' could in any case always 'in a great measure be Regulated

---

[1] 'Εφημερίς: or, A Diary . . . For . . . 1671, A3–A6.  [2] MS A 23, 105v.

10

or rather Mitigated by Industry and prudence';[1] indeed, without 'an Active Industry' 'the Cœlestiall effects' could not be put forward at all.[2] It was even admitted that 'a bad revolutionall figure or transit may cause the tymes not to agree exactly',[3] and Coley and Aubrey could actually disagree over what somebody's ascendant was[4] without ever questioning that there were, somewhere, 'the genuine Rules of Astrologie',[5] on which bad practitioners would bring scandal by thwarting them and forcing 'the starrs ⟨to⟩ speak any thing'.[6]

For it was not that second sight, magic and Aubrey's other interests were necessarily fallacious: their validity remains an open question. The difficulty was that Aubrey and others like him, haphazard, inconsistent and credulous, were never likely to prove or disprove them. They did not make the scientific revolution: that was the work of rigorous mechanists like Ray, who set their sights low enough to produce definitive analyses of particular fields, proving certain hypotheses and eliminating others, and avoiding speculation on matters about which they were dubious, sceptical or ignorant. Even when such scientists studied 'effluvia' they tended to think in terms of quantifying them in 'mechanical wayes',[7] a concept entirely alien to Aubrey's occultism. Aubrey and others like him could only contribute by accumulating information and possibilities, noting correlations that seemed significant in terms of the wide range of natural and supernatural interactions that they considered likely. But their views on these subjects were old, accepted and untested, many of them inherited from classical times and the sixteenth century, as Aubrey's citations show. He quoted Ovid and Pliny to support astrology,[8] Cicero as evidence of the value of portents and divine dreams,[9] and he cited sixteenth-century authors like Cardan and Agrippa with as much enthusiasm as Descartes, Hobbes and his colleagues in the Royal Society.[10]

The scientific revolution was a questioning of such accepted wisdom, and this Aubrey never began, despite his advocacy of Cartesian clarity in his educational writings. As far as his scientific

---

[1] Ibid., 114. Coley's loquacious style might well have suggested that he was mountebanking. Cf. above, p. 129.
[2] Ibid., 110.  [3] Snell-Aubrey, 12 Aug. 1676, ibid., 116.  [4] Ibid., 58v.
[5] Snell-Aubrey, 15 March 1678/9, ibid., 34.  [6] Coley in ibid., 86.
[7] Hooke, *Micrographia* (London, 1665), b3.  [8] *Gentilisme*, 270.
[9] *Miscellanies*, 36, 47 f. (also on voices, 110, impulses, 117, and prophecies, 124).
[10] Cf. above, pp. 97-8, 123.

work was concerned, he had learnt from Bacon the need to 'seek out and gather together such store and variety of things as may suffice for the formation of true axioms',[1] but his collecting overwhelmed any effort at synthesis. 'Grand practicers have not the leisure to be analytics,' he assured John Locke,[2] noting how Hobbes' *Dialogue of the Common Laws* had revealed the paralogisms of the Lawyers, 'building on old fashiond maximes (some right some wrong)'.[3] This aptly describes Aubrey's writings on natural history, in which collecting was not a means to induction but a substitute for it, supporting accepted views instead of testing them. The range and interconnections of his interests are significant and revealing: but he cannot be said to have made a major contribution to the advancement of learning.

[1] Bacon, *Parasceve*, 2, in *Works*, IV, 254.
[2] Aubrey-Locke, Shrove Tuesday 1672/3, in M. Cranston, *John Locke*, 152.
[3] A-W., 3 Feb. 1672/3, F 39, 196v.

CHAPTER THREE

# The Study of Antiquities

The seventeenth century was a great age of English antiquarian scholarship. A short-lived Society of Antiquaries had been established in the late Elizabethan period, and the preoccupations of this group were reflected in a number of illuminating studies of medieval English rights and institutions made in the early seventeenth century, notably by John Selden and Sir Henry Spelman. To Spelman has been attributed the discovery of English feudalism, and Aubrey much admired his 'great monuments of antiquarian knowledge'.[1] Later in the century the work of these pioneers was consolidated into a great tradition of antiquarianism, celebrated by David Douglas in his *English Scholars, 1660–1730*. A school of 'Saxonists' extended from William Somner and Abraham Wheloc in the Interregnum to George Hickes and Humfrey Wanley in the early eighteenth century; several scholars devoted years to editing texts and documents, including Henry Wharton, Thomas Rymer, Thomas Madox and the irascible Thomas Hearne; while others, notably Robert Brady, used records to reconstruct the institutions of medieval England. All these scholars were fascinated by the origins of rights and privileges and by the history of the English constitution and the English church. Many of them were prominent lawyers, politicians or churchmen, and their historical interests were moulded by their contemporary concerns. But, in an age when some even preferred rolls and records to Virgil and Cicero,[2] their scholarly achievement transcended their polemical preconceptions, and they made a contribution to the study of medieval England that still has to be reckoned with.

Several of these scholars were acquaintances of Aubrey. He frequently sought the advice of Fabian Philipps, an elderly antiquary who developed Spelman's study of feudal institutions. He showed his own antiquarian works to Thomas Gale, High Master of St

---

[1] *B.L.* II, 231. On seventeenth-century historical scholarship, see J. G. A. Pococke, *The Ancient Constitution and the Feudal Law*, F. S. Fussner, *The Historical Revolution*, and Levi Fox *ed., English Historical Scholarship in the Sixteenth and Seventeenth Centuries* (London, 1956).

[2] D. C. Douglas, *English Scholars*, 15, citing *The Spectator*.

Paul's School, later Dean of York, and editor of several important historical texts, whose learned opinions Aubrey much valued, and to White Kennett, another wide-ranging historical scholar who was later to be Bishop of Peterborough.[1] We have already seen how his collections were employed by Edmund Gibson, Saxonist, editor of Camden's *Britannia* and later Bishop of London, and how in his later years Aubrey made provision for his study of the antiquities of Wiltshire to be completed by Thomas Tanner, another prominent member of these antiquarian circles who ultimately became Bishop of St Asaph.[2] But most important was Aubrey's association with Sir William Dugdale, perhaps the greatest of this whole tradition of antiquaries. Dugdale was 'in a sense, to set the pace to those who followed after'[3] by the great collection of charters that he produced in collaboration with Roger Dodsworth, the *Monasticon Anglicanum*, the first volume of which appeared in 1655, and by his *Antiquities of Warwickshire* (1656), which set new standards of method and accuracy in the documentary study of local history.[4] Aubrey was a friend and admirer of Dugdale: he ran errands for him,[5] gratefully accepted his advice on various antiquarian topics,[6] and in 1661 was proud to supply as an illustration to the second volume of the *Monasticon* one of the pictures of the ruins of Osney Abbey which he had commissioned while an undergraduate at Oxford.[7]

Anthony Wood spoke for many contemporaries in considering Dugdale's *Antiquities of Warwickshire* 'the best book of its kind that hitherto was made extant'.[8] It served as a model for local histories from the moment it appeared, and it is not surprising that Aubrey was party to a scheme to imitate it in Wiltshire. At a meeting of gentlemen at Devizes in 1659, 'it was wish't by some, that this County (wherein are many observeable Antiquities) were surveyed

---

[1] See above, pp. 88, 90.    [2] See above, pp. 84–5.    [3] Douglas, *English Scholars*, 17.
[4] For the tradition of county topography before Dugdale, see above, p. 69.
[5] MS A 21, 102, is a written question of Dugdale's for Wood to look up, evidently transmitted by Aubrey. Cf. Dugdale-Aubrey, 1 June 1678, MS A 12, 98, and A-W, 6 June 1678, F 39, 307.
[6] Of his 'Chronologia Aspidologia', Aubrey wrote, 'This I did with the advice of Sir William Dugdale' (T.G.c.25, 182); Dugdale encouraged him to print 'Templa Druidum' (A-W, 8 Sept. 1680, F 39, 348; cf. 5 Feb. 1686/7, B. 14, 141); and Aubrey quoted Dugdale's opinion on various points (e.g. MS A 2, 73; MS A 3, 11av, 85; T.G.c.25, 167).
[7] Plate 10; cf. above, p. 68.
[8] Wood, *Life and Times*, I, 209.

in Imitation of Mr Dugdales Illustration of Warwickshire', and Aubrey undertook the north division of the county while others promised to assist with the rest.[1] The collaborative project 'vanish't in Fumo sc: Tabaci ⟨in tobacco smoke⟩, & was never thought on since',[2] but Aubrey worked at his *Essay towards the Description of the North Division of Wiltshire* for many years, particularly before he left his Wiltshire home in 1671,[3] collecting material from memorial inscriptions and heraldic bearings in local churches, from old charters and from the ledger-books of monastic and secular land-owners, including Glastonbury Abbey.[4] The work, as he left it in manuscript, was closely modelled on Dugdale's. Its chosen area was divided into hundreds and treated parish by parish; its text illu-strated the history of local families and the descent of lands from documentary and monumental sources, with an admixture of descriptive and miscellaneous matter characteristic of the topography of the time.[5]

Aubrey would have liked to add antiquarian material of this docu-mentary kind to the topographical description of Surrey that he wrote for John Ogilby in 1673. He told Wood that he had 'gott the favour of a great Antiq⟨uary⟩ of Surrey' to have extracts made of the records in the Tower of London relating to the county, and 'Mr Dugdale & Mr Ashmole both say, unless J.O. make use of them his booke will be a bable'; he was also keen to include visitation records.[6] In the 1680s he told Andrew Paschall, who was planning a history of Somerset, 'Mr Fab⟨ian⟩ Philips sayes, you must search Domes-day-booke & the records ⟨of⟩ the Tower',[7] and Aubrey spent a great deal of time collecting such antiquarian material. His *Wiltshire Antiquities* devote many pages to transcriptions of old deeds,[8] and he made a list of 'ʰΛη Antiquaria', 'antiquarian materials', ranging from Domesday Book to the fourteenth-century ledger book of Edmund Mortimer, third earl of March, and full of entries like: 'Col-

---

[1] MS A 3, 10.      [2] Loc. cit.

[3] Aubrey refers to his near completion of the project in letters to Wood of Easter Tuesday 1670, T. 456a, 9, 17 Nov. 1670 and 27 Oct. 1671, F 39, 128, 141. But he continued to add to MS A 3 all his life.

[4] E.g. MS A 3, 68 f., 143 f.

[5] These remarks apply only to Liber A of the *Wiltshire Antiquities* (MS A 3). On the lost Liber B, see 'Aubrey's Lost Works'.

[6] A-W, Morrow after St Matthew's Day 1673, F 39, 229.

[7] Aubrey's note on Paschall's scheme for a history of Somerset, appended to Paschall-Aubrey, 5 Oct. 1683, MS A 13, 64.

[8] MS A 3, 55 f.: 'Extract of my old Deedes.'

⟨onel⟩ W⟨illia⟩m Eyres of Neston in Cosham parish hath the Legier-booke of the Family of Tropnel of Neston. it is an excellent booke; in parchment well writt and retrives the ancient & extinct families of this North division'.[1] Numerous copies of coats of arms in the text of the *Antiquities* bear witness to Aubrey's concern with heraldry. He spent hours copying out inscriptions and devices in the church of Lydiard Tregoze, which contained 'but little that savours of venerable antiquitie: but for modern monuments, and ornaments not unworthy the observation of a Student in Heraldie, it exceeds all the Churches in this Countie'.[2] In the 1670s he was involved in a scheme for having a French synopsis of heraldry translated and engraved by his friend, the Bohemian artist Wenceslaus Hollar.[3] And his topographical descriptions of both Wiltshire and Surrey sometimes degenerate into gazetteers of memorial inscriptions, the space devoted to each church depending largely on its richness in such remains.

Although Aubrey knew that local history should be 'illustrated; From Records, Leiger-Books, Manuscripts, Charters, Evidences, Tombes, and Armes',[4] however, and despite his 'Love of Antiquities', he frequently baulked at research of the kind undertaken by scholars like Dugdale, which he tried to share. 'The Records will keepe cold,' he said, preferring his Wiltshire fieldwork to archival research,[5] and he found that 'this searching after Antiquities is a wearisome Taske', that 'of all studies I take the least delight in this'.[6] When he did get around to making transcriptions from Domesday Book, a favourite source of antiquaries like Dugdale, full of information about land tenure, he copied out some entries, but marked the result 'NB I have left-out, through hast, and *lazinesse*, halfe as many more Towneships',[7] and his comment in another context is revealing—'they are very delightfull: but I am tyred with transcribing, this hott weather'.[8] As Canon J. E. Jackson, the nineteenth-century editor of Aubrey's *Wiltshire Antiquities*,

---

[1] Ibid., 1av.    [2] Ibid., 162.

[3] A-W, 22 Oct. 1672, F 39, 190. He sent it to Thomas Gore for more professional emendation, but it was apparently not published.

[4] Dugdale, *The Antiquities of Warwickshire* (London, 1656), title-page.

[5] A-W, 27 Oct. 1671, F 39, 141v.    [6] MS A 3, 11v.

[7] MS A 4, 162v. These notes from Domesday Book, etc., were copied from 'an old manuscript in the hands of the parish-clarke at Woking'.

[8] MS A 11, 15v: this concerned a section in Charleton's *Chorea Gigantum* about the monuments of the ancient world; in fact, Aubrey subsequently copied it out and inserted it (f. 17).

put it, 'the truth is, that upon the more serious labours of Parochial History—the long investigation of evidences, the thoughtful comparison of them, and the drawing of correct conclusions from them—Aubrey was either unable or unwilling to enter'.[1]

It is also revealing that Aubrey is hardly mentioned in Douglas' *English Scholars*, for he lacked the preoccupations of that group. Aubrey shows none of their concern for political history, for constitutional issues, and for tracing the origins and development of laws and institutions; it is interesting that in his educational scheme he considered History 'a large Field: and too long a worke for this cursus, and too sowre for their sweet Relish'.[2] In this he was independent and somewhat unusual, as in his interests in the present. For, in an age preoccupied by political debate, Aubrey's involvement in political and constitutional matters was almost non-existent, despite his attendance at Harrington's Rota. 'A Pox on Parties', he exclaimed,[3] and he owned few books on this subject, just as he owned unusually few works of religious polemic.[4] He hardly wrote about it at all: the section on politics in the *Idea of Education* is scarcely more than a short reading list, though he wished to 'Let 'em understand the severall Methods [wayes] of Setling Goverment after Conquests': 'Me thinkes, the Gothick method is the best of all'.[5]

Aubrey was interested in people. He quoted a saying of John Lambert, the Parliamentary general, that 'the best of men are but men at the best' as a motto for his *Brief Lives*,[6] and they show his fascination with personality, often at the expense of more abstract considerations. The *Lives* are full of examples and wise sayings, from which the reader could learn a sort of common-sense morality of a strikingly unidealised kind. This is also reflected in the section 'Mundane Prudence' in the *Idea of Education*, which is made up of advice on how to deal with the world and all its guile, stressing the value of friendship, generosity and humility.[7] He pointed out how 'a slight, or a disdainfull aspect is like a small scratch of a venemous

[1] J. E. Jackson, *Wiltshire. The Topographical Collections of John Aubrey*, viii.
[2] MS A 10, 97.
[3] A-W, 13 Jan. 1680/1, F 39, 351. He cites it as 'honest G. Ents saying'.
[4] For qualifications to this remark, see 'Aubrey's Library'.
[5] MS A 10, 78. This section grew out of the chapter on law (cf. ibid., 70). Aubrey's recommendations include Petty's unpublished *Political Arithmetic*. Aubrey's interest in 'the Gothick method' doubtless owed something to Harrington's study of it: cf. S. B. Liljegren *ed.*, *Oceana* (Lund, 1923), 42 f.
[6] A-W, 15 June 1680, *B.L.* I, 11–12.     [7] MS A 10, 81 f.

10. Osney Abbey, engraved by Wenceslaus Hollar for Dodsworth's and Dugdale's *Monasticon Anglicanum* from a drawing provided by Aubrey

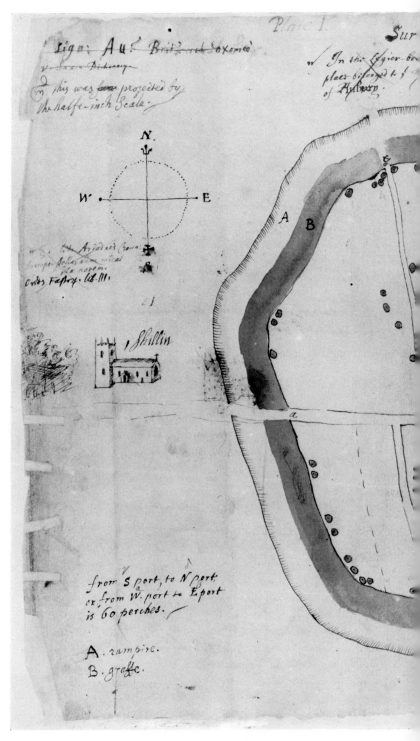

11. Aubrey's plan of Avebury, from his *Monumenta Britannica*

AVEBURY.

φ is the plant of 𐰀

way to Marlborough

Profil of rampire & grasse.

a. fower perches
b. fewer perches

12. Old Sarum 'by Imagination', from Aubrey's *Monumenta Britannica*

13. A page of Aubrey's 'Chronologia Graphica', showing his facsimiles of the old scripts that he studied

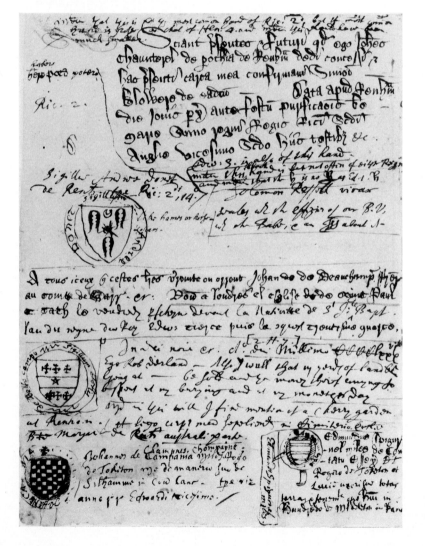

Creature, which rancles, and burnes: it is longer remembred than a hundred Obligations',[1] and that 'Carters & Draymen may use *wild Justice* in Righting of Wrongs; but Gentlemen having to doe with Carters & Clownes must resort to Civil Justice. for a Countrey-fellow strikes a blow twice as smart at a Gentleman, as he does to one of his ranke'.[2] Elsewhere he gave as 'A certaine Rule, that Desolation will ever tread on the heeles of Abomination',[3] and he noted that a vindictive man who died in bed had 'too easy a death for such a thirster after blood'.[4] In 'Mundane Prudence' Aubrey also advocated attention to prudential tracts like the *Distichs* of the elder Cato and Francis Osborne's *Advice to a Son*,[5] and in some ways this section can be seen as the climax of the *Idea*. For throughout his educational scheme he showed that he was primarily interested in turning out competent and well-balanced individual members of the ruling class, 'than which there is not any thing of greater moment in a Nation. For it is the root, & source of their good Administration of Justice'.[6]

When he went beyond individuals, Aubrey's political views meant taking the *status quo* for granted—he had no sympathy for the Levellers, 'which were like to have turned the world upside-downe'.[7] He was interested in how people lived: his chapter on politics in the *Idea* moved quickly to a section on the 'Œconomicks' of family life,[8] and in the past he was concerned, apart from biography, with changes in the life-style of men. It is revealing that almost the only references to political works in Aubrey's writings illustrate points of this kind: he cited Machiavelli's *Prince* on the advantage to gentlemen of knowing how to guide themselves in a rout,[9] and Harrington's *Oceana* on the retinues of noblemen in feudal times.[10] Similarly, when he made notes on Polybius' *History* his concern was not with the political theory of balance but with morality—

[1] Ibid., 84.  [2] Ibid., 82.  [3] MS A 21, 22v (a note for *The Countrey Revell*).
[4] *Analecta*, 125.
[5] MS A 10, 81 cites these and other similar works. He also quoted Osborne elsewhere in the *Idea* (ibid., 35a, 93, 114); his copy of Sir Richard Baker's *Cato Variegatus* (London, 1636) (Ashmole 1621(5) ) has some marginal markings.
[6] MS A 10, 7.
[7] MS A 4, 60v. Though Aubrey says 'Levellers', he was in fact referring to the settlement of True Levellers, or Diggers, at St George's Hill.
[8] MS A 10, 78.
[9] MS A 21, 10v (notes for *The Countrey Revell*). Cf. MS A 10, 116, where he quotes Machiavelli's *Prince* on a similar point.
[10] MS A 21, 10v (notes for *The Countrey Revell*).

whether equity or friendship was preferable, for instance[1]—with parallels between ancient and modern figures like Publius Scipio and Cromwell,[2] and with how people fought and how they lived in classical times.[3]

The effect of this upon Aubrey's historical writing is seen clearly in the historical sections of his *Naturall Historie of Wiltshire*, and it is not coincidental that, as shown in Chapter II,[4] these have something in common with the rather old-fashioned tradition of historical writing that preceded the more sophisticated antiquarian movement which reached its climax with Dugdale, exemplified by the *Description of England* by William Harrison prefixed to Holinshed's *Chronicle* (1577). Aubrey devoted much space to Wiltshire personalities of past times—apart from making lengthy extracts from the Wiltshire section of Fuller's *Worthies*, he added sections on the Earls of Pembroke and their house at Wilton, on the learned men to whom they gave pensions, and on the eminent clothiers of the county. Otherwise the bulk of the historical material described changes in how people had lived. He considered disafforestation in relation to its effect on the way of life of the common people, whose 'lamentable' cry he quoted,[5] and when he wrote about 'Falling of Rents' and the prices of wool, he was interested in servants' wages too, and how the two compared.[6] Much of the remainder of his second part dealt with hawking, 'The Race', the shepherds, fairs and markets, and the history of hunting. Equally symptomatic, his chapter 'Of the Number of Attornies in this Countie now and heretofore' showed how they increasingly spoiled people's lives; he quoted statistics from Somerset to demonstrate how they 'swarme there like Locusts' whereas formerly they had been rare, breeding contention just as 'The more Spannells the more Game'.[7]

---

[1] Ibid., 62.    [2] Loc. cit.

[3] MS A 21, 60 f., comprises notes made on Polybius and other classical authors in the 1680s. Apart from the subjects mentioned in the text, Aubrey also noted natural historical information. The material on military affairs was for the *Monumenta*. There are several quotations from Polybius in 'Mundane Prudence' in the *Idea* (MS A 10, 81 f.). There are further notes from classical authors, some concerning the 'Gaules manner of Living' and their language, in MS A 5, 88 f.

[4] See above, pp. 101–2.    [5] MS A 1, 128.

[6] MS A 2, 123. Cf. his interest in wages in the context of the price of corn and such other necessities of life as shoes in T.G.c.25, 215.

[7] MS A 2, 164. The Somerset information came from Dr Thomas Guidott. The abuses of attornies had been a common complaint for a century and a half: cf. G. R. Elton, *Reform and Renewal* (Cambridge, 1973), 149; C. Hill, *Intellectual Origins of the English Revolution* (Oxford, 1965), 227 f.

He made no mention of the institutions of local government, and, unlike Fuller, did not even give lists of sheriffs.[1]

The same is true of the most famous of Aubrey's historical writings, the preface that he wrote for his *Wiltshire Antiquities* in 1670, when he had evidently almost completed the book. Here too slander actions appear merely as evidence of the morality of an age;[2] land-tenures are mentioned primarily as evidence of monastic benevolence;[3] and the feudal system is described more as a way of life than as an institutional entity.[4] The preface is almost entirely devoted to social history, to the 'manners and customs' of past ages.

In this, Aubrey was unusual among antiquaries of his day and in many ways rather old fashioned. He was equally exceptional in his stress on tangible, visual and hearsay evidence collected in the field, even in his attempt at topographical writing in the style of Dugdale, but in this regard he was highly original. In his perambulation of Wiltshire, he took an unusual interest in customs and traditions, notably 'Revells',[5] and in buildings, and his interest in this kind of evidence was so great that at either end of his *Wiltshire Antiquities* he collected together notes on such subjects to the exclusion of the miscellaneous matter topographically arranged that filled the text. At the end he made a collection of 'Fabulæ Aniles ⟨old wives' tales⟩ whence the measure of those daies', which gave a series of country traditions about St Aldhelm, the learned Saxon abbot of Malmesbury, and various customs and superstitions 'verily beleeved' by local people.[6] He placed before the beginning of the text brief notes showing the development in shape of medieval escutcheons[7] and also, much more important, a collection of drawings of architectural details chronologically arranged, the first work of its kind.[8] These collections, which can thus be seen as excrescences growing from his more normal antiquarian investigations, are

---

[1] These appear under each county in *The History of the Worthies of England* (London, 1662).

[2] MS A 3, 11a.

[3] Loc. cit.

[4] Ibid., 10v and 9a (the leaves are misbound: f. 10 should precede f. 9).

[5] For references showing his interest in these, ibid., 20c, 21v, 80v, 81v, 98, 140. Cf. A-W, Whitsun Eve 1671, F 39 133: 'I would be satisfied of the certain origen of Revells.'

[6] MS A 3, 185v. One of the additions is dated 1671, so the bulk of the matter on this leaf may be earlier than that.

[7] Ibid., 7v.

[8] Ibid., 2af. F. 4 has 'now 1672'; f. 4v 'now [1670]'. See further below.

immensely important, for they, together with brief hints elsewhere in the *Wiltshire Antiquities*, contain the germ of Aubrey's strikingly original writings on antiquarian subjects.

The 'Fabulæ Aniles', together with similar traditions that Aubrey had collected since his boyhood[1] and continued to accumulate throughout his life, he used to compile the first English work devoted to folk-lore, the *Remaines of Gentilisme and Judaisme*, written between 1686 and 1689, in which he assembled an unprecedented quantity of a type of historical evidence that had previously been almost entirely ignored, the rituals and superstitions of the country people of his time.[2] At the same time he developed a hint attached to the preface of the *Wiltshire Antiquities*[3] into *An Interpretation of Villare Anglicanum*,[4] the first book entirely devoted to the elucidation of English place-names.[5]

He also compiled a book called 'Στρώματα sive Miscellanea', into which he inserted out of the *Wiltshire Antiquities* the 'Chronologia Architectonica', as his collection of architectural details was called,[6] and his 'Chronologia Aspidologica', or of shields. It also contained a 'Chronologia Graphica', a study of different handwritings of successive medieval centuries which he began in 1672, being 'led

---

[1] E.g. *Gentilisme*, 212, 229, 237. Some of the material on MS A 3, 185v was collected 'An⟨no⟩ Dom⟨ini⟩ 1645 from old Ambrose Browne'.

[2] The only precedent is Camden's 'The Maners of the Irishry, both of old and of later times', *Britain* (London, 1610), (second pagination) 140 f. Cf. R. M. Dorson, *The British Folklorists, A History* (London, 1968). The *Remaines of Gentilisme* is linked to Aubrey's interest in social history by his inclusion among materials about country life that he intended for his *Countrey Revell* instances of 'Countrey Magique', such as girls divining who would be their husbands by observing how branches of orpin leant (MS A 21, 11b, 24v); at ibid., 23v, he noted 'v⟨ide⟩ what Horace saies of Gentility'.

[3] MS A 3, 10: 'q⟨uaere⟩ for a Biscayan Dictionary; if any British words are to be found there.' On the way in which the more general *Interpretation* developed from this, see below, p. 169.

[4] Cf. above, p. 83.

[5] William Lambarde's *Dictionarium Angliae Topographicum & Historicum* listed the place-names of the country in alphabetical order and tried to interpret a number of them, like Aubrey, but the bulk of the work comprises miscellaneous historical matter; it was in any case not published until 1730, and Aubrey certainly did not know it. He did know, and cited, Richard Verstegan's *Restitution of Decayed Intelligence* (Antwerp, 1605), which (278 f.), like Camden's *Remaines of a Greater Worke, Concerning Britaine* (London, 1605, 98 f.), devoted space to the interpretation of place-name elements in connection with English proper names. Most earlier topographical works had speculated about the etymology of certain names (e.g. H. Lhwyd's *Breviary of Britayn* (1573), which Aubrey quoted: see below, p. 190, n. 2).

[6] In fact, he made a fresh copy, which differs slightly from the original in MS A 3, mainly in being better arranged.

on to the thought' by his 'Chronologia Architectonica',[1] and a
'Chronologia Vestiaria', a study of changes of costume in different
centuries, partly based on drawings of stained glass and funeral
monuments in Wiltshire churches, in which he had expressed
interest in his *Antiquities* 'for the habitt's sake'.[2] He also included
information about changes in prices and related topics, on which he
had also made notes from old deeds in his more orthodox antiquarian collections.[3]

Early in the 1690s[4] Aubrey added the 'Στρώματα' to his most
important and original antiquarian work, *Monumenta Britannica*,
which had evolved separately, although his cross-references to it in
his *Wiltshire Antiquities* show that it too was not unrelated to that
work,[5] and some of its materials were also scattered in the Wiltshire
text.[6] Aubrey apparently began to write his 'Templa Druidum'
and 'Chorographia Antiquaria', which made up Books I to III
of the *Monumenta*, in 1663, but he had collected some materials
earlier. He had discovered the prehistoric monument at Avebury on
a hunting party in January 1649, when 'I was wonderfully surprized
at the sight of those vast stones: of which I had never heard before:
as also at the mighty Bank & graffe about it', which he found 'a more

---

[1] T.G.c.25, 185. Cf. a note attached to the 'Chronologia Architectonica' in MS A 3,
3v, pointing out that ' 'Twere an easy matter to make a Scriptura Chronologica'. The
heart of the work is a pair of leaves of notes made from the deeds of the Earl of Thanet
in 1672 (T.G.c.25, 189–90), though the date on the title-page in T.G.c.25, 185, is 1689.
It was originally entitled 'Chronologia Scriptoria', but later renamed 'Chronologia
Graphica'.

[2] MS A 3, 98v. Cf. the Wiltshire illustrations in the 'Chronologia Vestiaria' (e.g.
T.G.c.25, 202). This was a pioneering study. Aubrey's interest in tombs as illustrating
the history of costume is entirely lacking in Weever's *Ancient Funerall Monuments*
(1631), which concentrates entirely on their inscriptions, though it includes pictures of
a few. Notes on the history of 'Apparell' will, however, be found in Camden's *Remaines*
(second edition, London, 1614, 230 f.).

[3] T.G.c.25, 215 f. He noted 'See my collections of prices of corne out of old Deedes,
in lib⟨er⟩ A, or B' (ibid., 215), and in a letter to Wood of 7 April 1673 (F 39, 200), he
mentions notes on such subjects that he had made from the deeds of the Earl of Thanet
at Hothfield, which, since they are not in 'Στρώματα', were presumably in the lost
Liber B.

[4] In 1692 Aubrey still conceived of the 'Στρώματα' as a volume of miscellanies
separate from the three volumes of *Monumenta Britannica* (cf. the list of hi.s works in
MS A 5, 123v), and the title-page of 'Στρώματα' (T.G.c.25, 150) calls it 'An Appendix
the Antiquities of Wiltshire' (erased). But he had decided to add it to the *Monumenta*
by 1692/3 (A–L, 4 Feb. 1692/3, A. 1814, 102). In the contents list in T.G.c.24, 22,
the details of 'Στρώματα' are literally stuck on at the bottom of those of Books I to
III of the *Monumenta*.

[5] MS A 3, 10, 99v, 130.　　[6] E.g., ibid., 82, 96, 98, 104v, 107v, 149, 153.

delightfull indaegation' than the hounds.[1] His perusal of Inigo Jones'
*Stone-Heng Restored*, published in 1655 after the great architect's
death, 'which I read with great delight . . . gave me an edge to make
more researches';[2] and on other hunting parties and in his travels
to his estates in Wales in the 1650s Aubrey found further opportunities to observe prehistoric antiquities such as megaliths, barrows
and hill-forts[3] and Roman ones like the mosaics and inscriptions of
Bath and Caerleon.[4] He had seen some earlier still: he had known
Salisbury Plain and Stonehenge since he was eight, for 'I was inclin'd by my *Genius*, from my Childhood to the Love of Antiquities:
and my Fate dropt me in a Countrey most suitable for such Enquiries'.[5]

The most important stimulus to the composition of the *Monumenta*, however, came after the Restoration. In 1663, Charles II
was 'discoursing one morning' about Stonehenge with William,
Viscount Brounker, President of the Royal Society and Chancellor
to the Queen, and Walter Charleton, another scientist with court
connections, perhaps discussing Charleton's views on the antiquity,
which he had published in 1663 in a work entitled *Chorea Gigantum*. They told the King that they had heard Aubrey say that Avebury 'did as much excell *Stoneheng*, as a Cathedral does a Parish
church', and the King, intrigued, sent for Aubrey, who brought a
draught of Avebury 'donne by memorie only'.[6] Later he showed the
King 'that stupendious Antiquity' itself, 'with the view whereof,
He and his Royal Highnesse the Duke of *Yorke* were very well
pleased. His Majesty then commanded me to write a Description
of it, and present it to him: and the Duke of Yorke commanded me

---

[1] T.G.c.24, 23–23v. Aubrey was the first to notice the megaliths at Avebury, but not
the earthwork, which is described as a camp in the 1610 edition of Camden's *Britain*,
255; Aubrey was therefore at pains to show that the ditch was not defensive—T.G.c.24,
31.

[2] Ibid., 23v–4.

[3] Cf. T.G.c.25, 17 (1649), 55 (1655), 60 (1659), 65 (1656).

[4] Bath: T.G.c.24, 222, T.G.c.25, 104; Caerleon: T.G.c.24, 219, T.G.c.25, 103.
Other Roman finds: T.G.c.25, 112, 123.

[5] T.G.c.24, 23.

[6] T.G.c.24, 24. It was also in 1663 that Charleton presented a plan of Avebury to the
Royal Society and Aubrey and Sir James Long 'were desired to make farther inquiry'
concerning the site (Birch, *History*, I, 272). There is a pencil plan of Avebury in Royal
Society MS 131, 67, inscribed 'By Mr Awbrey july 8. 1663'. This was the date of the
meeting mentioned by Birch, so this must have been the plan that Charleton presented.
Is it even conceivable (since it is somewhat schematic) that this is the plan 'donne by
memorie only' mentioned in the text?

to give an account of the old Camps, and Barrows on the Plaines'.[1]

This Aubrey did, and, having started from these field antiquities in Wiltshire, he continued to seek more examples elsewhere for the sake of completeness and lucidity. He turned his review of Avebury and Stonehenge into a complete 'Templa Druidum', in which he tried to prove his almost unprecedented hypothesis that such megalithic monuments were not built by the Romans or anyone since, but had been erected by the Druids, 'being the most eminent Priests [or Order of Priests] among the Britaines'.[2] He also extended his 'Chorographia Antiquaria', including Roman remains as well as prehistoric, and by 1670 he could claim 'I have a quire of Chorographia Antiquaria: in a map and discourses upon it: viz. the Rom-⟨an⟩ & British & danish Camps—highways & traced Offas dyke from Severne to Dee, and Wednesdyke, and rectified Mr Camden in some places';[3] he also made a novel attempt to date hill-forts by their shape.[4] The King in 1663 commanded him to print these treatises,[5] and various friends later encouraged him to do so;[6] but he never succeeded in this, and he continued to add material to them to the end of his life.

All these antiquarian works are remarkable for the way in which Aubrey brought together observations of relics of the past that had previously almost always been dismissed as insignificant or noted merely as peripheral appendages to narratives on other subjects. Just as he collected folk traditions in the *Remaines of Gentilisme*, so he amassed stone circles in the 'Templa Druidum' and hill-forts, castles, Roman towns, pits, horns, barrows, urns, sepulchres, ditches, old highways, Roman pavements and coins in his 'Chorographia Antiquaria', each in its separate category, and his *Monumenta Britannica* is the first English book that can be called 'archaeological' in the modern sense.

For modern archaeology differs from other historical disciplines

---

[1] T.G.c.24, 24v.

[2] Ibid., 26. On the context of Aubrey's association of the megaliths with the Druids, see S. Piggott, *The Druids* (London, 1968), ch. IV, and A. L. Owen, *The Famous Druids* (Oxford, 1962), 101 f. Aubrey's hypothesis was unprecedented except that Inigo Jones had mentioned it to refute it in his *Stone-Heng Restored* (London, 1655), 2 f.

[3] A-W, 17 Nov. 1670, F 39, 128v.

[4] See below, pp. 188–9. Earlier writers like Camden, who had sometimes noted hill-forts, had never tried to date them by such means.

[5] T.G.c.24, 25.

[6] Cf. above, pp. 76–7, and p. 149, n. 4, and, on Aubrey's abortive attempts to publish the *Monumenta*, p. 89.

in its use of non-literary, material relics like pot-sherds and earth-works to reconstruct the human past, in contrast to the written records valued by the historian, and the origins and growth of archaeology depended on the realisation that such uninscribed antiquities, if collected and compared, could lead to conclusions not available from historical sources. Though earlier antiquaries had occasionally made notes of such relics, Aubrey's *Monumenta* is the first English book entirely devoted to them, and in this it marks a real change of emphasis in antiquarian study, a shift away from the almost exclusive emphasis on written sources of Dugdale and his like.[1]

Aubrey justified his work by 'the novelty of it', as well as 'the faithfulness of the delivery', which 'may make some amends for the un-correctness of the Stile'.[2] 'Nothing is in it yet (except some eminent wayes) that hath been donne already', he claimed,[3] just as he was aware, of his hypothesis about the Druids, that he had 'gonne farther in this Essay than any one before me'.[4] In his enthusiasm for these almost unstudied kinds of antiquities he recorded much accurate information that had previously been ignored, noting antiquarian finds made by others which would be unknown but for him. Thus he discovered from a local resident that George Villiers, Duke of Buckingham, Charles I's favourite, had engaged in barrow-digging on Salisbury Plain out of curiosity, but nothing had been recorded because nothing was found except a silver-tipped bugle-horn which 'his Grace kept in his Closet as a great Relique'.[5] Although uncovered mosaic pavements commonly 'drew many Spectators',[6] while the discovery of ancient coins made the inhabitants 'give £2 per acre more than elswhere, for the hope of finding more',[7] Aubrey was almost alone in recording such finds.

---

[1] On the rare examples of an 'archaeological' approach before Aubrey, cf. M. C. W. Hunter, 'The Royal Society and the origins of British archaeology', *Antiquity* LXV (1971), 118 f., and on its general absence, 114. Old coins occupy an intermediate position between historical and archaeological sources as defined in the text: some antiquaries had collected and studied these before (cf. R. H. M. Dolley, 'The Cotton Collection of Anglo-Saxon coins', *British Museum Quarterly* XIX (1954), 75 f.)—they fitted more naturally than most antiquities found in the field into a 'historical' framework—but Aubrey was a pioneer in advocating complete and systematic recording of finds (cf. above, p. 69, and the section on coins in T.G.c.25, 111 f.).

[2] T.G.c.24, 26.

[3] A-W, 17 Nov. 1670, F 39, 128v.

[4] T.G.c.24, 26.

[5] Ibid., 93. He had the information from Mrs Trotman, wife of the farmer who owned the land.

[6] T.G.c.25, 110 (quoted from a letter from Paschall).     [7] Ibid., 111v.

Their normal fate is apparent from his notes: a Roman sword was used as a cheese-toaster and lost;[1] children played with Roman coins;[2] and 'the rude people' 'utterly spoyled' mosaics.[3] Even when antiquities had been noted before, Aubrey recorded detail more carefully than anyone previously. He was aware that he had traced the course of Wansdyke more exactly than Camden, thus revealing its irregularities,[4] and although Stonehenge had long been admired, Aubrey was the first to note the series of depressions just inside the bank encircling it, which have been called the 'Aubrey Holes' after him.[5] He very often noted of antiquities that 'I cannot find any Account of them',[6] 'I wonder it is so little taken notice of'[7] or 'no body hath taken notice of it before, though obvious enough'.[8]

Aubrey's interest in archaeological antiquities and the equally novel preoccupation with folk-lore shown in his *Remaines of Gentilisme* had a further importance, for it inspired greater concern in others. John Evelyn, White Kennett and B. G. Cramer, a German scholar who was at one time clerk to the Royal Society, all annotated the manuscript of the *Remaines* with profuse details of folk customs in England and abroad,[9] and Evelyn's annotations to 'Στρώματα' also record information that he never bothered to write down elsewhere.[10] Without Aubrey, we should lack the information on Highland customs, beliefs and antiquities in the letters he received from Professor James Garden of Aberdeen in reply to his enquiries.[11] Similarly, though it was Dugdale who perceptively noticed that churches dedicated to St Michael the Archangel usually stood on a high hill or had an unusually tall steeple, it was Aubrey, not Dugdale, who recorded this,[12] for the information fitted into his concerns,

---

[1] Ibid., 119.  [2] Ibid., 111v.  [3] T.G.c.24, 219.  [4] T.G.c.25, 88.
[5] T.G.c.24, 64v.  [6] T.G.c.25, 93.  [7] Ibid., 153v.  [8] T.G.c.24, 181.
[9] These annotations are clearly indicated as such by John Buchanan-Brown in his edition of *Gentilisme* (in Britten's edition (Folk-lore Society, 1881) it is not always clear what is Aubrey's work and what is not). However, I disagree with Mr Buchanan-Brown's view that the third principal annotator, with Evelyn and Kennett, is John Ray: in fact there is no evidence that Ray saw *Gentilisme*, and the third annotator was undoubtedly B. G. Cramer—the hand in which the notes are written is identical with that of R.S. MS 92 (cf. p. 89, n. 1).
[10] On one occasion, Aubrey actually asked Evelyn for information (T.G.c.25, 200v).
[11] MS A 12, 122 f. and one further letter which is now in Britton's grangerised copy of his *Memoir of John Aubrey* in the library of the Wiltshire Archaeological and Natural History Society at Devizes. All are printed in C. A. Gordon *ed.*, 'Professor James Garden's Letters to John Aubrey 1692–1695', *The Miscellany of the Third Spalding Club* III (Aberdeen, 1960), 1 f.
[12] T.G.c.25, 155v. Cf. *Gentilisme*, 150.

just as it is fortunate that Aubrey ignored Dugdale's advice that 'by no meanes I must not putt in writing *Hear-sayes*'.[1]

## The Sense of Change and the Reconstruction of the Past

Merely as a catalogue of information on an unusual range of subjects, Aubrey's antiquarian writings have a certain value. But, though some of them are no more than this, others show an insight into history that goes beyond mere recording. He was particularly fascinated by change, especially technological change, and this was the theme of his 'Στρώματα', which he subtitled 'Containing Discourses Chronological'.[2] The most highly developed of these was the 'Chronologia Architectonica', which traced the history of English architecture from the Dark Ages up to his own time, mainly by illustrating details like mouldings and window tracery from buildings in Oxford, Wiltshire and elsewhere which he could date from historical documents.[3] 'Memorandum that the Fashions of Building doe last about 100 yeare or less,' he noted; 'the windows the most remarkeable thing. Hence one may give a guesse about what time, the building was'.[4] He traced the development from Romanesque to Gothic, the sequence of Gothic styles, with tracery 'at the highest pitch in King Richard the second's time',[5] and the progress of the revival of 'the old Roman Architecture' from the sixteenth century,[6] till in his own day 'the old Roman fashion is become the common Mode'.[7]

He applied the same treatment to the development of handwriting. 'As the Roman Architecture did degenerate into Gothick in like manner did the Roman Character,' he explained.[8] 'As they deviated from the Roman character, so they grew wanton in their manner of writing, and run into the hand now called Court hand: and their Capital letters were very flourishing and phantastick'.[9] With the same eye for significant detail seen in his study of architectural development, he categorised the script of a charter of

---

[1] A-W, Vigil St. Pet⟨ri⟩ & Pauli 1681, F 39, 397. This was of a Dorset tradition about Cardinal Morton that Aubrey had heard when a schoolboy there.

[2] Quoted from the *Proposals for Printing Monumenta Britannica* (cf. above, p. 89, n. 7).

[3] See plate 14, and cf. H. M. Colvin, 'Aubrey's *Chronologia Architectonica*', in J. Summerson *ed.*, *Concerning Architecture: Essays on Architectural Writers and Writing presented to Nikolaus Pevsner* (London, 1968), 1 f.

[4] MS A 3, 3v (this passage was not copied into the *Monumenta* draft of the 'Chronologia').

[5] T.G.c.25, 171.     [6] Ibid., 168.     [7] Ibid., 169.     [8] Ibid., 186.     [9] Ibid., 185v.

Edgar as 'neer Roman',[1] that of the time of Edward I as 'a black hand and difficult for the crinkum crankum',[2] or that of Edward III's time as 'a fine small legible kind of court hand'.[3] In the time of Henry IV and V 'they writt more like Soldiers then Clarkes',[4] while 'In Hen⟨ry⟩ sixth, an ugly scraggeling hand like a blocke-headed schooleboy' prevailed,[5] and he continued his treatment right up to the seventeenth century.[6]

In his 'Chronologia Aspidologica' he traced five successive shapes of shields used on tombs of different periods,[7] and his 'Chronologia Vestiaria' illustrated changes of fashions in clothes from sources ranging from tombs and stained glass in churches to pictures in books, anecdotes, old sayings and survivals: 'Cappes, sc. Bonnets, were the generall Fashion, till about the middle of Queen Elizabeths raigne. King Edward the sixth, and his Father are alwaies drawn with Cappes [like those worne by the Doctors of Lawe] and so all the Aldermen of London, downe pretty late in Queen Elizabeth's time. I have heard my honoured & learned friend Dr Edw⟨ard⟩ Davenant S.Th.D. say, that his father [a London Merchant eldest brother of J. Davenant B⟨isho⟩p of Salisbury] was the first Citizen of London that wore a Hatt; and brought them into use among the Citizens; as also coloured Clothes: before the Citizens wore Tawny, or puke-coloured Cloathes, and short Rockets'.[8] He discussed the development of crowns since Roman times,[9] of gowns,[10] the use of girdles,[11] and of head-dresses, illustrating those of women of the reign of Edward III, for example, from funerary monuments.[12] He even noted 'a very troublesome and ridiculous fashion' in shoes of about 1647–8,[13] and he described survivals of older customs like the 'Party-coloured Coates' of beadles and water-men.[14]

This subject overlapped with the next section of 'Στρώματα,' 'Nouvelles', a study of the introduction of fashions, techniques and commodities into England. Its content ranges from the first apothe-cary, who arrived in the reign of Edward III[15] to an old lady 'who

---

[1] Ibid., 190v.   [2] Ibid., 189.   [3] Loc. cit.   [4] Ibid., 190.   [5] Ibid., 189.
[6] Ibid., 190. See plate 13.
[7] Ibid., 182. In the text of his *Wiltshire Antiquities* Aubrey noted that a coat of arms seemed very ancient 'according to Mr Ant⟨hony⟩ Woods rule' (MS A 3, 135v), so this section may owe something to Wood. Cf. also above p. 149, n. 4. Aubrey also instructed himself to see Spelman's *Aspilogia* (1654) (T.G.c.25, 183): but though this section of 'Στρώματα' is very rudimentary compared with Spelman's technical treatise, Spel-man did not try to date shields by shape like Aubrey.
[8] T.G.c.25, 199.   [9] Ibid., 198a, 198v, 201.   [10] Ibid., 205.   [11] Ibid., 198b.
[12] Ibid., 199v.   [13] Ibid., 203.   [14] Ibid., 199.   [15] Ibid., 207.

remembred when all the Cabbages were brought out of Holland',[1] through cane chairs,[2] coffee,[3] gunpowder,[4] tobacco[5] and sedans.[6] 'Catts', runs a typical entry: 'W. Laud A⟨rch⟩ B⟨ishop⟩ ⟨of⟩ Cant⟨erbury⟩ was a great lover of Catts; He was presented with some Cyprus-catts i.e. our Tabby-catts, which were sold at first for £5 a piece: this was about 1637, or 1638. I doe well remember, that the common English Catt, was white with some blewish piednesse: sc: a gallipot-blew: the race or breed of them are now almost lost'.[7] Others involve events more recent still, as 'Flax & Linnen. About the 2d yeare of King William & Queen Mary, Queen Mary encouraged the Establishing of the Flax & linnen Manufacture in the Salisbury-exchange in the Strand'.[8]

The remainder of the notes in 'Στρώματα' indicate an interest in change almost for its own sake. He noted 'the Diversity of Standarts, or the value of Moneys'[9] and the differences of prices of corn and other commodities in the Middle Ages and his own time,[10] and he copied information about the variety of 'Measures & Weights' out of a fifteenth-century manuscript, the 'Red Book of Bath', and other sources.[11] This theme of change recurs throughout the *Monumenta*: he drew diagrams to illustrate the transformation of methods of fortification caused by the introduction of gunpowder,[12] and he was fascinated by stratigraphy, by changes in the street level of London and the level of the Thames,[13] and by finds made forty feet deep during the reclamation of the Fens.[14] When he studied etymology he was alive to the implications of linguistic development, suggesting by parallel with Slavonic how different the Greek used by the Druids was likely to be from that familiar to modern scholars,[15] and in his *Interpretation of Villare Anglicanum* he claimed that 'Graines of allowance are ⟨to⟩ be given to these Etymologies',

[1] Ibid., 209.  [2] Ibid., 208v.  [3] Ibid., 208.  [4] Loc. cit.  [5] Loc. cit.  [6] Ibid., 208v.  [7] Loc. cit.

[8] Ibid., 209. This section was compiled in its present form *c.* 1688–90, and the contents list in T.G.c.24, 22 (into which it was inserted after being originally omitted), suggests that it was added last to 'Στρώματα'. But he had already been collecting information that was used in 'Vestiaria' and 'Nouvelles' in 1670 (MS A 21, 95v), and one observation dated from 1656 (T.G.c.25, 207v).

[9] T.G.c.25, 210v.  [10] Ibid., 215 f.

[11] Ibid., 221v f. Other sources include Fabian Philipps' *Antiquity, Legality, Reason, Duty and Necessity of Prae-emption and Pourveyance, for the King: or Compositions for his Pourveyance* (1663) and Edmund Wingate's *Arithmetique Made Easie* (1630).

[12] T.G.c.24, 211v.  [13] Ibid., 243, 243v (where he quotes Hooke), 244.

[14] T.G.c.25, 97, 106.  [15] T.G.c.24, 88v. Cf. MS A 11, 5v.

because a thousand years were bound to alter pronunciation, to disguise words and to mix languages.[1]

Aubrey shared this heightened sense of change, this acute awareness of the difference between past and present and between different past periods, with many contemporaries.[2] Indeed, though he evidently stumbled upon his rudimentary conclusions about linguistic change on his own, ignorant of earlier studies of the same subject, in fact French and English scholars had long been aware of the development of language and the implications of this for the study of the past, and had come to technical conclusions about it that Aubrey never emulated.[3] So with his palaeographical studies, for, independently of Aubrey, the great Benedictine scholar Jean Mabillon had spent years preparing his great *De Re Diplomatica*, published in 1681,[4] and both he and the younger Englishman Humfrey Wanley, who aspired to write a similar work on English palaeography,[5] made a technical and erudite study of ancient texts that Aubrey hardly began.

Aubrey was unique only in applying concepts of change to the tangible antiquities that he was a pioneer in studying, particularly architecture, for the slightest interest in architectural history was

[1] MS A 5, 17. He also drew attention to local differences of dialect. Cf. his interest in early forms of place-names (e.g. ibid., 44v, 48v, 86b), though he makes little allowance for such considerations in his etymologies (see below, pp. 189–90).

[2] For a useful anthology of contemporary opinion, see L. Stone, *Social Change and Revolution in England 1540–1640* (London, 1965), 115 f. Cf. the heightened awareness of change reflected, for example, in P. Delany, *British Autobiography in the Seventeenth Century* (London, 1969), esp. 8–11. Also interesting is M. Aston, 'English ruins and English history: the Dissolution and the sense of the past', *Journal of the Warburg and Courtauld Institutes* XXXVI (1973), 231 f., though her particular theme tends to disguise a more general sense of mutability and change common in the period, and Aubrey's prominence in her article is slightly artificial since he wrote relatively little about monasteries and monastic ruins.

[3] Cf. above, p. 25. Aubrey was familiar with the English protagonists of this tradition, and he also knew and quoted (cf. below, p. 171) Meric Casaubon's *Treatise of Use and Custome* (1638), an interesting expression of historicist ideas, with references to French antiquaries of the sixteenth century as well as to Spelman and others. But Aubrey evidently knew little of the technicalities of their erudition.

[4] Aubrey refers to Mabillon (whose work he heard about after making his original notes on the subject) in T.G.c.25, 185. He also refers there to a table of scripts made by Edward Bernard and published in 1689, of which he inserted a copy into the *Monumenta* (ibid., 194). He was certainly ignorant of the only earlier English palaeographical treatise, Spelman's *Archaismus Graphicus* (1606), which is still unpublished (British Library MS Stowe 1059): it is in any case almost exclusively concerned with diplomatic.

[5] Cf. K. Sisam, 'Humfrey Wanley', in *Studies in the History of Old English Literature* (Oxford, 1953), 263.

very rare indeed at this time,[1] and Aubrey's attempt at a chronology
remained unsurpassed until the work of Thomas Rickman a century
and a half later.[2] But there is a unity to Aubrey's sense of change
which links those areas in which he was original with those in
which he merely reiterated commonplaces. His study of palaeography, though paralleled in other scholars, was suggested to him
by his work on architecture[3]—indeed Aubrey evidently came his
own way to the sense of anachronism that earlier scholars had
derived from linguistic and documentary evidence—and his fascination with change percolates all his antiquarian interests, linguistic, textual, sartorial or archaeological.

Aubrey's obsession with change was accompanied by an eagerness to seek out and interpret the surviving relics of earlier periods
the vestiges of which had otherwise totally perished, for, like many
contemporaries, he had first-hand knowledge of how easily antiquities were destroyed. He saw earthworks 'yearly eaten-out by the
Plough'—some of those made in the New Parks at Oxford in 1642
were hardly traceable by 1688[4]—and, seeing one site almost dug
away for sarsen stones, he noted 'so nothing is permenant'.[5] 'Mors
etiam saxis, Nominibusque venit', he wrote, 'death comes even to
stones and names',[6] and he was particularly conscious of the
destruction wrought by the Civil War. He frequently bewailed the
damage done by 'the Barbarous soldiers',[7] 'these Puritanicall
zealotts',[8] 'in the warre-time',[9] recording old trees cut down,[10] old
glass broken,[11] ancient buildings burnt down[12] and customs dis-
used[13] owing to 'the fanatique rage of the late times'.[14]

His view of the Dark Ages was comparable, and he deliberately
paralleled his own time with them in remarking of the destruction
of Gorhambury, Bacon's mansion, 'one would have thought the
most barbarous nation had made a conquest here'.[15] He quoted the

---

[1] Even books profusely illustrated with pictures of buildings, like Dugdale's *Monasticon*, show no interest in architectural history, and I know of only two contemporaries
who made even a rudimentary study of this kind—William Somner in his *Antiquities
of Canterbury* (London, 1640), 164 f., confirmed the date of the architecture of parts of
the cathedral that he had established from historical sources 'by comparing it with other
pieces of that age', while Thomas Staveley in his *History of Churches in England* (posthu-
mously published, London, 1712; Staveley died in 1684) suggested that buildings
could be dated 'from the Observation and View of the *Fabrick* it self' (152–3).

[2] See below, p. 206.      [3] Cf. above, pp. 156–7.      [4] T.G.c.24, 140.      [5] Ibid., 179.
[6] MS A 3, 190.      [7] Ibid., 148.      [8] Ibid., 151.      [9] T.G.c.25, 89.      [10] Loc. cit.
[11] E.g. MS A 3, 81v, 159.      [12] Ibid., 11v, 24v.      [13] E.g. MS A 5, 67v.
[14] MS A 3, 81v.      [15] *B.L.* I, 393.

'Cholerique Rhetorication' of the early seventeenth-century French essayist Balzac that 'the Northern people who seemed to come to hasten time and precipitate the end of the world, declared so particular a war to written things, that it was not wanting in them but that even the Alphabet had been abolished'.[1] 'In that deluge of Historie',[2] prehistoric and Roman antiquities were destroyed and even the knowledge of them and their builders lost, just as he noted of the Egyptian pyramids, despite their 'stupendous greatness', 'history reaches not to their Antiquity'.[3]

'The Saxon Conquerors [being no searchers into matters of Antiquity] ascribed Works great, and strange to the Devil, or some Giant, e.g. the Devils ditch: the Devills Arrows: Gogmagog-hills &c.; and handed downe to us only Fables'.[4] He quoted William of Malmesbury's account of how, when he came to write his history of Dark Age England in the early twelfth century, 'he was faine to pick up matter out of old Ballads and Songs',[5] noting how 'before William the Conquerors time, the Chronicles were handed down only by Tradition, from father to son: by which meanes are utterly lost many notable Roman remarques: and noble Trueths dwindled away into old Wives fables'.[6] Aubrey wrote about such stories with contempt—'Thus the height of Antiquity ends in Fable: and the depth of Ignorance discends to Credulity'[7]—and he was indignant about the hold they had on country women, 'so powerfull a thing is custome, joynd with ignorance'.[8] 'Fabula Anilis', he heads them,[9] or 'an old S⟨omerse⟩t Cant-story',[10] and as he told them he interspersed his narrative with 'forsooth'[11] or 'the vulgar doe fancy'[12] and often denied them: 'It sounds more like an old Romance, than true Historie';[13] 'credat Judeus apella, non ego', 'let the Jew Apella believe, I will not'.[14]

But Aubrey did not entirely despise these traditions. 'I know that some will nauseate these old Fables: but I doe profess, to regard them as the most considerable pieces of Antiquity, I collect: and that they are to be registred for posterity, to let them understand the Encroachment of Ignorance on Mankind: and to learne, what strange Absurdities Man can by Custome & education be brought

---

[1] T.G.c.24, 29–30.　　[2] Loc. cit.　　[3] T.G.c.25, 8.　　[4] T.G.c.24, 29.
[5] Ibid., 51v.　　[6] T.G.c.25, 133.　　[7] MS A 1, 132v.　　[8] MS A 4, 140.
[9] T.G.c.24, 153. Cf. MS A 3, 185v.
[10] *Gentilisme*, 154.　　[11] MS A 2, 70v.　　[12] MS A 4, 75.　　[13] Ibid., 10.
[14] Ibid., 133. This is a quotation from Horace, *Satires*, I, v, 100, alluding to the proverbial superstitiousness of the Jews.

to believe'.[1] Ancient customs and old wives' tales 'ought not to be quite rejected',[2] because 'perhaps, one might elicit some trueth out of their fabulous Traditions'.[3] He quoted, under the heading 'Fabula', the tradition of Surrey peasants that the Devil built Stane Street, a Roman road in the Weald, but was surprised and dropped the stones he was using 'which made a Hill at one of the Causewayes'. 'Quære,' Aubrey continued, 'where about this Hill is: for I presume it will be found to be a Tumulus, or Barrow of the Romans'.[4] Similarly, of a tradition that Salisbury Cathedral was 'built upon Wooll-packs', 'doubtlesse there is something in it, which is now forgot' and 'I shall endeavour to retrive and unriddle it by comparison'. He explained that a tower at Rouen was called the Butter Tower because it was built from the proceeds of a toll on butter, 'as now there is a ⟨Tax⟩ layd upon every Chaldron of Coales towards the building of Saint Paul's church London: so hereafter they may say, that that Church was built upon New-castle-coales. In like manner it might be, that heretofore when Salisbury church was building (which was long before Wooll was manufactured in England: the Merchants of the Staple sent it then in Wooll-packs, beyond sea to Flanders &c:) that an imposition might be putt on the Wiltshire Wooll-packs towards the carrying-on of this magnificent Structure. The County of Wilts hath the most Sheep of any County in England: There is a saying also, That London-bridge was built upon Wooll-packs: upon the same account'.[5]

He was also aware that country traditions could preserve survivals of ancient beliefs and practices. He remarked on an account of seeing nuns spinning given by 'old Jaquez' of the Wiltshire village of Kington St Michael because he said they used 'Rocks', which were utterly unknown in Wiltshire as in most counties but common in Staffordshire, and Aubrey considered that 'they are certainly of the elder house to the spinning-Wheele'.[6] Realising that the 'Fabulae Aniles' that he had collected in Wiltshire might prove

---

[1] T.G.c.24, 52.

[2] *Gentilisme*, 132 (but 'not' is unfortunately omitted in this edition: cf. 'A Note on Manuscript and Printed Texts of Aubrey's Works').

[3] MS A 4, 88v.

[4] Ibid., 123v, Cf. T.G.c.25, 97v.

[5] MS A 2, 72. Cf. *Gentilisme*, 153, presumably the source of this passage, since the parallel with London Bridge is added to the MS in Kennett's hand.

[6] T.G.c.25, 207.

of value, he erased 'vaine' from his original phrase to describe them, 'old men's vaine Traditions'.[1] So with the 'old Customes' he recorded, the invocation of 'St Sythe' by making the sign of a cross in raked ashes,[2] the propitiation of the fairies whom the old women 'veryly beleeved' could steal away young children,[3] or the prayers to St Catherine of an old man who kept oxen in a parish whose church was dedicated to her.[4] Such practices, he saw, even if now done 'only for custome-sake',[5] were in fact relics of ancient belief which could be understood by comparing them with the Bible and with Ovid, Virgil, Homer and Pliny.[6] This was the theme of his *Remaines of Gentilisme and Judaisme*: he traced the church-ales of old England to the 'ἀγαπαι' of the New Testament;[7] the 'Originall of Faires' on the hills of Wessex was due to 'bringing the Christian Customes as neer as might be, to the British';[8] and a variety of country customs, from curtseying to the moon[9] to the rain charms of children,[10] he recorded because 'I have a Conceit, that this childish Custome is of great antiquity: & that it is derived from the Gentiles'.[11]

Aubrey's *Interpretation of Villare Anglicanum* was a similar attempt to understand survivals of the past. For, though this developed into a study of the meaning of all the place-names of England, its original and more modest aim was 'only to pick-out the small Remnant of British words, that have escaped the Deluge of the Saxon Conquest'[12] (for 'as the Saying is, 'Tis a hard victory where none of the vanquish't escape').[13] This was part of Aubrey's wish to show 'for the honor of Wales'[14] how the British language was formerly spoken from the Orkneys to the Apennines and the Pyre-

---

[1] MS A 3, 185v.    [2] Loc. cit. Cf. *Gentilisme*, 163: i.e., St Osythe.
[3] Loc. cit. Cf. *Gentilisme*, 203–4.    [4] Loc. cit. Cf. *Gentilisme*, 162.
[5] *Gentilisme*, 143.
[6] The relevance of the Old Testament and of the addition 'and Judaisme' to the title, 'Remaines of Gentilisme', stems from the belief, common in Aubrey's period, that all races were diffused from Noah after the flood.
[7] *Gentilisme*, 149–50.    [8] Ibid., 142.    [9] Ibid., 241.    [10] Ibid., 256.
[11] Loc. cit. The idea of 'relic⟨s⟩ of Gentilism' is found in chapter XLV of Hobbes' *Leviathan* (*Works*, III, 637 f.), which Aubrey cites about images in *Gentilisme* (cf. Britten's edition, 6; in John Buchanan-Brown's edition, 155, the note 'See his Leviathan pag⟨inam⟩_____' is unfortunately omitted), and his views on the Christians adapting pagan rites in *Gentilisme*, 133, 155, are very similar to Hobbes' in this chapter. The citations in *Gentilisme* from other contemporary authors like Selden, Sanderson, Browne and Tombes show how common such ideas were, though nobody else made a collection of country customs to illustrate them.
[12] MS A 5, 17.    [13] Ibid., 8v.    [14] T.G.c.24, 252v. Cf. MS A 3, 10.

nees,[1] if not to Asia Minor.[2] He hoped to illustrate the same theme
by studying the French language and discovering British words in
it; it might, he thought, 'be donne at the house of Office with more
ease by much then Cardinal Bellarmin wrot his Hebrew Grammar'.[3]
A related project that he completed and inserted in his 'Στρώματα'
was a table of 'the Proportion of the several Languages, Ingredients
of our English';[4] and in his *Interpretation of Villare Anglicanum*
there is a list of words used by the Jacobean translator Philemon
Holland but since antiquated,[5] which shows how Aubrey's interest
in survivals was related to his concern with the process of change,
just as he used dialect words and words used by authors like Chaucer
to help him interpret place-names.[6] He even recorded that Archbishop Laud had used the words '*I trow*', now out of fashion except
among old people in North Wiltshire,[7] and that John Dryden had
told him that thirty or forty French words had been absorbed into
English since the Restoration.[8]

Aubrey used old words and names to illuminate the past in
various ways. He was glad to use his supposed etymologies to suggest
how the Romans pronounced Latin.[9] Place-names often sent him
looking for antiquities like camps and barrows now almost obliterated by the ravages of time,[10] and they sometimes made him link

---

[1] MS A 5, 17v.      [2] Ibid., 21.

[3] T.G.c.24, 252v. This passage has been crossed out, but I have not found it recopied anywhere else. The allusion to Bellarmine is not quite clear: his speed in teaching Hebrew was proverbial, but his grammar was vast. Aubrey claimed to have
suggested this project to Sir Leoline Jenkins, but there is no evidence that it was ever
carried out. At the time of his compilation of the *Interpretation*, he hoped for collaboration in studying Celtic languages from the Earl of Castlemaine in Ireland, Sir Robert
Gordon in Scotland, Bishop Baptist Levinz in the Isle of Man (MS A 5, 19v) and a Mr
Kegwin in Cornwall (A-L, 20 Feb. 1691/2, A. 1814, 96). But the only result of this was
that, on Aubrey's 'overture', the Earl of Castlemaine 'recommended to an ingeniose
Irishman' the task of making an Irish Dictionary (A-W, 23 Oct. 1688, T. 456a, 35).

[4] T.G.c.25, 238 f. It is dated 1692/3. The project is referred to in MS A 5, 8v and in
letters from Aubrey to Lhwyd of 31 December 1691 (A. 1814, 98, which suggests
that the project had been recommended to Aubrey by William Holder, and he now
suggests it to Lhwyd, 20 Feb. 1691/2. (A. 1814, 96, which seems to imply that it was
Lhwyd's idea) and 10 May 1694 (A. 1814, 112, by which time Aubrey had done it himself). This provides an interesting context, associated with the Royal Society, for this
pioneering attempt to quantify the component parts of English. Earlier attempts to
identify Germanic and foreign words in English include Edward Phillips' *New World
of English Words* (London, 1658) and Stephen Skinner's *Etymologicon Linguae Angli-
canae* (London, 1671).

[5] MS A 5, 91 f. It is referred to at T.G.c.25, 238v.      [6] MS A 5, 22 f.

[7] Ibid., 91.      [8] T.G.c.25, 238v.      [9] MS A 5, 21v, 82, 82v.

[10] E.g. Ibid., 39, 43v, 76v; T.G.c.24, 192v.

them with historical personages such as Boadicea:[1] 'Memorandum there is a pretty Hillock, (I believe artificiall) towards Ashford in Kent, enquire the Name of it: perhaps it may retain the name of some Kentish King, or Regulus'.[2] On a related theme, he wondered why, when the Saxons made so absolute a conquest, we should still retain Roman measures, 'more neer the Roman Acre, foot, ounce &c. than any other Nation in Europe',[3] and he also sought to prove that the husbandry and utensils used in England had been taught the Britons by the Romans,[4] that harvest-homes were derived from the Roman *Cerealia* and May-day games from the *Florialia*.[5] Looking further back, he thought it probable that the Ancient Britons baked their cakes mixed with poppy seed on hearthstones, as the poor people in Wales did still,[6] and he corroborated the evidence from literary sources that the Druids esteemed the woodpecker for divination by the fact that country people still used it to divine rain.[7]

This idea that relics surviving in the present could be used to reconstruct the past, though less explicit, recurs in Aubrey's collection of archaeological antiquities. As a motto to Book III of his *Monumenta Britannica*, 'haec Collectanea', as he called it in his dedication,[8] he quoted Meric Casaubon's *Treatise of Use and Custome* (1638) 'That Antiquaries are so taken with the sight of old things, not as doting upon the bare forme or matter (though both oftentimes be very notable in old things) but because these visible superviving evidences of Antiquity represent unto their minds former times, with as strong an impression, as if they were actually present, and in sight, as it were'.[9] At the very least Aubrey felt that he was leaving materials for others to reconstruct ancient times: 'I deemed it worth the little labour to prick downe in a Mappe these Remaines of Antiquity, which I beheld with so much delight; and peradventure by this meanes some that have more learning and leisure than my selfe, may retrieve the places of many of those

---

[1] This is the implication of his interest in 'Badwood' in T.G.c.24, 254. Cf. ibid., 164, where he notes in connection with 'Oister-hill' that Ostorius Scapula was in those parts.

[2] Ibid., 266. This passage has been crossed out, but I have not found it recopied elsewhere.

[3] T.G.c.25, 221v. He cited Willibrord Snellius' *Tiphys Batavus* as his authority for this: cf. *Gentilisme*, 132, where he cites his *Eratosthenes Batavus*.

[4] T.G.c.25, 221v, and MS A 2, 117.    [5] MS A 2, 117.    [6] T.G.c.24, 212v.

[7] Ibid., 100. He also quoted Aldrovandus and Gessner in this connection.

[8] T.G.c.25, 6.    [9] Ibid., 5v.

memorable Battailes mentioned by Tacitus and other Historians'.[1]

Aubrey had shown the same modest attitude concerning the relics of the geological history of the world that he had observed in his *Naturall Historie of Wiltshire*. 'I have heard Sir Will⟨iam⟩ Davenant say, That Witt did seem to be the easiest thing in the world: for when it is delivered, it appeares so naturall, that everyone thinkes he could have sayd the same: this of his, may also be applied to Inventions, and Discoveries: so after the discovery of America by Columbus, then every Navigator could have donne as much. So, now (me thinkes) I could be angry with my selfe for my Stupidity, that have so often trod upon, and rid over these Remaines of the old world, without makeing a due Reflexion, which deserves so much a greater admiration and research, than the Ruines of the August Buildings of the Greeks & Romans: as this Globe excells in magnitude those ancient monuments'.[2] It was only after Robert Hooke pointed it out to him, he declared, that he had realised that the present landscape comprised the vestiges of the primitive world ravaged by earthquakes.[3]

Aubrey hardly needed to be so modest, however, for he had no lack of the 'wit' required to make such reconstructions, even if he had originally needed Hooke to alert him to the implications of the evidence. His view that the rocky mountains of Scotland and Wales 'have (me thinkes) a resemblance of the Ribbes of Arches in Architecture';[4] his belief that 'the Ragges, oker-coloured sand, Cindres &c: give evidence that Vulcanos have been in these parts';[5] his passing references to vestiges of earthquakes like the large stones scattered over the Downs and the faults they left;[6] and his quotation of parallel accounts of modern earthquakes;[7] all these show how vividly he imagined the processes by which the world had evolved. Similarly, it was of course commonplace in the Renaissance and in Aubrey's century to argue that 'seeds and sparkes' of earlier ages could be traced in contemporary language, customs and traditions, and that such survivals could be used to postulate former states of society and technology.[8] But Aubrey's vivid imagination made it

---

[1] T.G.c.24, 149v. (He subsequently erased this draft for the preface to the section of the *Monumenta* on camps, and did not insert this passage in the final version, ibid., 138 f.).

[2] MS A 1, 88.  [3] Ibid., 88–9. Cf. above, p. 58.  [4] Ibid., 11v.  [5] MS A 4, 128v.
[6] MS A 1, 17v, 18.  [7] Ibid., 89v.

[8] Quoted in M. T. Hodgen, *Early Anthropology in the 16th and 17th Centuries* (Philadelphia, 1964), 442, from H. Estienne, *A World of Wonders*. Cf. in general Hod-

unusually easy for him to reconstruct the past from the antiquities that he observed.

As he rode on the Downs, he meditated how 'the greatnesse, and numerousness of the Barrowes (the Beds of Honour where now so many Heroes lie buried in Oblivion) doe speak plainly to us, that Death & Slaughter once rag'd here, and that here were the Scenes, where terrible Battles were fought: wherein fell so many thousands, mentioned by the Historians. By the burying places it might be presumed whereabout the Engagement began, and which way the Victor made his pursuit: and by the vestigia of the Imperial Camps (whereon now sheep feed, and the Plough goes) one may trace-out the way the victorious Roman Eagle tooke her Course'.[1] Elsewhere he actually reconstructed the strategy of a battle: 'One might make bold to give a ghesse, that the Engagement began west from the River, where the Enemy of the British Campe stood to receive their shoc on the Brow of the Hill, where the great Barrows be: the flight was Westward';[2] and the importance of strategic considerations in his interpretation of field antiquities appears in his constant interest in the nearness of water to sites,[3] in their freedom from damp,[4] or in the relation of banks to their associated ditches.[5] It was equally characteristic that when he saw a depiction in a church window of a mail-clad knight with a lady lying at his feet, he reflected, 'There was (no doubt) some story of Knight-errantry did belong to this Picture'.[6]

This vividness was enhanced by Aubrey's use of modern parallels and ancient authorities to illuminate his finds. He quoted Homer and Virgil concerning the ancient practice of barrow-burial,[7] and he inserted pages from a printed edition of Polybius into his *Monumenta* to illustrate how the Romans built and used their camps.[8] He was fascinated to learn of the use of cairns to commemorate those killed in battle in contemporary Carolina and Jamaica.[9] He paralleled

---

gen's chapter XI, 'From hierarchy to history'; and chapter VIII, 'Similarities and their documentary properties', which illustrates how common it was to use parallels between contemporary savages and earlier stages of European society. Cf. T. D. Kendrick, *British Antiquity*, 122 f.

[1] T.G.c.24, 139.  [2] Ibid., 188.
[3] E.g. MS A 4, 212; T.G.c.24, 154, 159, 181.
[4] E.g. T.G.c.25, 47, 49 (quoting Sir Thomas Browne), or 18 (presenting it as his own opinion).
[5] E.g. T.G.c.24, 31; T.G.c.25, 87.  [6] MS A 3, 98v.  [7] T.G.c.25, 15v, 16.
[8] T.G.c.24, 141 f.  [9] T.G.c.25, 15, 67.

a decisive defeat of the Britons with Naseby,[1] and he cited a recent descent by the Indians on the settlements of New England to show why the Romans needed to fortify their towns.[2] He illustrated the strategic value of Mersea island in Saxon times by citing Cromwell's policy towards it,[3] and he quoted Sir Jonas Moore that the current cost of building Silbury Hill, 'according to the Rate of worke for Labourers in the Tower', would be 'threescore or rather (I thinke) fourscore thousand pounds'.[4] The great ditches on Salisbury Plain 'putt me in mind of Sir Walter Raleigh's advice to cutt Barricados',[5] and he quoted Giraldus Cambrensis, the thirteenth-century topographer, 'that the Druides were Composers of Differences between Princes: and they did sett-out the Bounds between them',[6] observing that the dykes 'I ghesse to have been old Divisions of Dukedoms, or Despoties'.[7] He similarly argued that the Ancient Britons were likely to have had ceremonies at their burials as the Christians had masses;[8] he quoted a wide range of ancient and modern authors to illustrate the 'Religion & Manners' of the Druids;[9] and, in 'An apparatus of The Bards', he copied out the letters of James Garden and others about survivals of Gaelic superstitions and customs.[10]

Thus Aubrey tried literally to re-create the past. He drew a small sketch of Old Sarum, to show 'by Imagination',[11] the 'most stately and delectable Prospect' it must have presented when complete.[12] He put together a map of ancient Wessex, marking on it hill-forts, barrows, roads and dykes, and even attempting to fill in ancient place-names, so that he effectively reconstructed the total ancient environment.[13] His notes on the back of it show how he thought it illustrated ancient strategy and he gave cross-references to it when describing ditches elsewhere in the *Monumenta*,[14] just as his 'quaere whither they tend?' of 'Old High-wayes'[15] reveals his concern for their combination as a network. The theme of reconstruction is also implicit in his 'Templa Druidum': 'some of their Temples I

---

[1] T.G.c.24, 165.   [2] Ibid., 213v.   [3] Ibid., 176 (cf. 208).   [4] T.G.c.25, 11.
[5] Ibid., 92.
[6] Ibid., 90. He also quoted Ponticus Virunnius, the Italian humanist and historian of Britain, on this point.
[7] Loc. cit.   [8] T.G.c.24, 91v.
[9] 'Mantissa. De Religione & Moribus Druidum', ibid., 94 f.   [10] Ibid., 105 f.
[11] Ibid., 201.   [12] Ibid., 199. See plate 12.   [13] Plate 15, from ibid., 250v–251.
[14] E.g. T.G.c.25, 85v, 93.
[15] Ibid., 96. Cf. his interest in 'Old wayes now lost but some vestigia left' in Wiltshire, MS A 3, 59.

pretend to have restored: as Auebury, Stoneheng &c.', he claimed,[1] and Anthony Wood suggested as an alternative title for the book 'Druidum Templa Rediviva', 'The Temples of the Druids Restored to Life'.[2]

In the most vivid of all Aubrey's writings about the past, the preface to his *Wiltshire Antiquities*, he similarly tried to reconstruct the life of past times from relics and traditions that he had collected while travelling in the countryside. He cited the coracles 'which the poore people in Wales use to this day' to show how the Ancient Britons voyaged on the Avon;[3] he postulated Roman colonies from finds of 'foundations of howses, hearthes, coles and a great deale of Rom⟨an⟩ coine silver & brasse';[4] and though few relics of the architecture of Roman Britain had survived 'time and Northerne incursions', he used a fragment of a Corinthian frieze in a wall at Bath to postulate that there had formerly been more 'of that richest Order'.[5] His reconstruction of the social life of the feudal period owes just as much to tangible vestiges, such as the 'great Gothique Halls'[6] that still survived 'almost entirely the same as they were in the time of the old English Barons'.[7] He illustrated seignorial jurisdiction by a set of gallows at Combe 'standing within these 50 yeares',[8] and by a private dungeon that he had seen in Gloucestershire, complete with 'iron rings fastned in the wall, which was (probably) to tye offending Villaines'.[9] Church ales were recalled by the church houses and utensils employed for them that still survived,[10] while texts painted on the walls of halls and parlours,[11] and sedilia,[12] lychnoscopes[13] and niches 'to sett images in &c:'[14] in churches recalled the 'great Devotion' of the Middle Ages.[15]

Such relics were illuminated by parallels and by memories surviving into the present. The Ancient Britons 'were 2 or 3 degrees I suppose lesse salvage then the Americans'.[16] All of Wiltshire before the enclosures was, according to Aubrey's grandfather, Isaac Lyte, 'a lovely Campania, as that about Sherston and Cotes-wold',

---

[1] MS A 3, 10.

[2] MS Aubrey 9, 55v (a title-page of 'Templa Druidum' reused for part of 'The Life of Mr Thomas Hobbes'): in the margin is the note 'or if Druidum Templa Rediviva', in a hand that is almost certainly Wood's.

[3] MS A 3, 10.   [4] Ibid., 10v.   [5] T.G.c.25, 168.   [6] MS A 3, 9a.

[7] Ibid., 174.   [8] Ibid., 9a.   [9] Ibid., 11v.   [10] Ibid., 9av. Cf. MS A 4, 140.

[11] MS A 3, 11a.   [12] Loc. cit.

[13] Ibid., 40v: 'I suppose was for Confession'. Cf. his citation of Sandys' *Europae Speculum* about the functions of confession, ibid., 11a.

[14] Ibid., 134v.   [15] Loc. cit.   [16] Ibid., 10v.

while Aubrey himself could add that 'in my remembrance much
hath been enclosed, and every yeare more & more is taken', and thus
another vestige of the past lost.[1] He remembered 'old Sir Walter
Long', grandfather of his friend Sir James Long, who 'kept
a Trumpeter: rode with xxx servants and retainers to Marleborough
⟨Assize⟩ & so for others of his ranke in his time',[2] and 'old John
Wastfield of Langley, ⟨who⟩ was Peter-man at St. Peters chapell
there. at which time is yet one of the greatest Revells in these parts.
but the chappell converted into a dwelling-howse'.[3]

These were his materials when he began 'Let us imagine then
what kind of Countrie this was in the time of the ancient Britons',
with 'the inhabitants almost as salvage as the beasts whose skins
were their only rayment'.[4] His narrative ran through the Romans,
and the Saxons, who 'lived sluttishly in poor howses where they
ate a great deale of beefe & mutton, and dranke good Ale in a
browne mazard: and their very Kings were but a sort of Farmers',[5]
to the feudal period. 'It was then too common amongst their Masters
to have Feuds with one another & their servants at Market or where
they mett (in that slashing age) did commonly bang one anothers
bucklers . . . the poor boyes did turne the spitts, & lick't the drip-
ping-pan, & grew to be huge lusty knaves . . . The Halls of Justices of
the Peace were dreadfull to behold; the Skreenes were garnished
with corsletts, and helmetts gaping with open mouth; with coates of
mail, Lances, pikes, halberts, browne-bills, batterdashes, bucklers
and the moderne colivers and petronells, (in King Charles I. time)
tur⟨ned⟩ into Musketts, & pistolls[6] . . . The solemnities of Proces-
sions in and about the Churches, & the Perambulations in the Fields
besides their convenience were fine pleasing diversions[7] . . . Lent
was a dismal time: strictly observed by fasting, prayer and Confes-
sing against Easter: during the 40 dayes, the Friars preached every
day. This Countrey was very full of Religious howses: a man
could not have travelled but he must have mett Monkes, Fryars,
Bonhommes &c: in their severall habits black, white, gray &c:
and the tingle-tangle of their Convent-bells I fancie made very
pretty musique, like the College bells at Oxon'.[8]

The picture is striking, vivid, even dramatic, communicating a
sense of the past far more immediate than could most historians of
his time. It is significant that Aubrey began to write a play about

[1] Ibid., 9a. Cf 25, 55.    [2] Ibid., 10v.    [3] Ibid., 9av.    [4] Ibid., 10.
[5] Ibid., 10v.    [6] Ibid., 9a.    [7] Ibid., 9av.    [8] Ibid., 11a.

country life, a comedy entitled *The Countrey Revell*,[1] for the surviving fragments of this show the same skill in creating scenes from
unusual and striking observations; indeed, he actually incorporated
some of the memories that he noted down for the play in the preface
to the *Wiltshire Antiquities*.[2] *The Countrey Revell* has the same acuteness, vivid imagery and concise style as Aubrey's portraits of contemporaries in *Brief Lives*, and it was on such observations that the
characters of the play were based. He noted that Sir Thomas Ivy's
*Alimony Arraign'd* and his wife's answer contained 'as much baudy,
beastlinesse & buggery, as can be imagined',[3] and intended to incorporate such detail into the *Revell*. Its characters range from the
country girls who 'whisper & squeak like mares in the spring'[4] to
'Sir Surly, so precise, he cannot endure a fiddle nor dance. keepes
his wife severely, pinches her . . . passionately in love with Dælia
the dayry mayd, with great black browes, hard brawny armes &
thighes'.[5] 'No woeman pleases Sir Libid⟨inous⟩ that smells not
*strong* of the Kitchen', Aubrey wrote, remarking on the 'strange
smells that some love'; 'Sir Surly; of the Cheese clowts, some
Ladies are fascinated with the smell of the Groome, some the foot
boy & sweaty feete, as some love Parmezan'.[6] And he described
at a country dance 'How a Fiddle makes the sp⟨irits⟩ daunce in the
veines of a young brisque sanguine wench! & her eies dance a
cadance with joy; & marke with what impatience shee stands,
whilst the first straine is playeing, & at the 2nd, away shee springs
like a Doe'.[7]

The immediacy of such descriptions is characteristic of Aubrey,
whether he wrote about the present or the past, and even in his
theoretical writings he tended to use precise particulars to illuminate general points: so in his *Idea of Education* he even named real
people to illustrate the general type of person he wanted as 'Infor-

[1] This incomplete play, with Aubrey's notes for it, is to be found written on the back
of an old legal document of several leaves in MS A 21. It was written at Easton Pierce
*c*. 1670 (cf. 'Aubrey's Lost Works'). Clark prints two of the complete scenes in *B.L.* II,
Appendix II, but the play is so imperfect that it is scarcely possible to evaluate it in the
dramatic tradition of its time.

[2] Some of the views of old Thomas Tyndale recorded in MS A 21, 10v, on the retinues
of great men in former times, the robustness of the gentry and their degeneracy since,
and on revels, are paraphrased in MS A 3, 10v–9av.

[3] MS A 21, 6v. Sir Thomas' book was published in 1654; I have not found his wife's
reply, which is also mentioned by Aubrey in a letter to Wood of 26 June 1679 (F 39, 328),
where he claims Lady Ivy as his 'most intimate shee-friend'.

[4] Ibid., 19.    [5] Ibid., 6v. Aubrey notes 'like Sir Oliver Cockwood'.
[6] Ibid., 6v.    [7] Ibid., 15v.

mators' in his projected school.[1] His *Brief Lives* constantly manifest his fascination with details when describing people, and through them he tried to illustrate personality. When writing about character, he often entirely eschewed generalisation, flying immediately to the particular, and his attempt through collecting small and fragmentary memories of the sayings, habits, views and actions of the eminent to give a view of the whole man is not dissimilar to the fusion of field antiquities and popular traditions in his imagination to produce the vivid reconstruction of ancient times characteristic of his best historical writing. It is therefore interesting that Aubrey used the same phrase to describe both the antiquities and the minute biographical particulars that he accumulated: in the preface to his *Wiltshire Antiquities* he explained how 'these Remaynes are tanquam Tabulata Naufragii', 'like planks of a shipwreck',[2] and he repeated this phrase as a motto for his *Brief Lives*.[3]

## Aubrey's Antiquarian Method

Aubrey's style was natural; his method of writing biography, beyond his obsession with miscellaneous preservation, was largely unconscious, implicit in his fascination with the particular and his strength of 'fancy' since childhood. But in the preface to his *Wiltshire Antiquities* he tried to justify his reconstruction of the past from fragmentary relics and piecemeal memories, and his conception of his historical method shows great acuteness. He compared himself with the Greek philosopher Pythagoras: 'as Pythagoras did guesse at the vastnesse of Hercules stature by the length of his foote (by which were meted the Olympick⟨stadia⟩), so among these ruines, are Remaynes enough left for a man to give a guesse what noble Buildings &c: were made by the piety, charity, & magnanimity of our forefathers'[4]—an allusion he repeated elsewhere when justifying his attempt to reconstruct the grandeur of Roman Britain from the fragments that survived.[5] 'The eie & mind is no lesse affected with these stately ruines, than they would have been when standing & entire', he wrote, after quoting a poem by Sir John Suckling about how those prospects

---

[1] MS A 10, 10v, 12.    [2] MS A 3, 10.    [3] *B.L.* 1, 9. Cf. ibid., 1, 18.
[4] MS A 3, 10. Aubrey left a gap after 'Olympick'.
[5] T.G.c.25, 168. The story of Pythagoras and Hercules' foot is told by Aulus Gellius in *Noctes Atticae*, I, 1.

were most pleasing that left 'roome to guesse': 'They breed in generous mindes a kind of pittie: and sett the thoughts aworke to make out their magnifice, as they were when in perfection'.[1] He then compared the ruins with fragments of a shipwreck, 'that after the revolution of so many yeares and goverments, have escaped the teeth of time, and (which is more dangerous) the hands of mistaken Zeale. So, that the retriving of these forgotten things from Oblivion in some sort resembles the Art of a Conjurer, who makes those walke & appeare that have layen in their graves many hundreds of yeares: and to represent as it were to the eie the places, Customes and Fashions, that were of old Time'.[2]

Aubrey thus showed how conscious he was of the importance of 'fancy' to his antiquarianism, and in many ways the essence of his achievement as an antiquary was his imaginative approach to fragmentary relics that would otherwise have seemed of little value, an approach that owed most to his personal gifts as an author rather than to any external factors. If an attempt is made to link his antiquarian method with the intellectual traditions of the period that he admired and espoused, it is disappointing to find that, although his phrase 'tanquam Tabulata Naufragii' echoes Bacon's definition of antiquities in his *Advancement of Learning*, those 'Remnants of History' which 'industrious persons' used to 'save and recover somewhat from the deluge of time',[3] there is no evidence that Aubrey was aware of this,[4] and to see his attempts to reconstruct the past as Baconian would certainly be mistaken, for the idea that past periods could be reconstructed from surviving vestiges had been common for a century and a half. But it is worth considering the possible influence on Aubrey's antiquarianism of his admiration for the clarity of the thought of the scientific movement, although, as we have seen, this is hardly in evidence in his studies of natural phenomena. For it is interesting to find that parts of the preface to his 'Templa Druidum' comprise a veritable essay in the inductive method.

He attacked Inigo Jones' *Stone-Heng Restored* because though 'there is a great deale of Learning in it', he had compared Jones' scheme with the antiquity itself and 'found he had not dealt fairly: but had made a Lesbians rule, which is conformed

[1] MS A 3, 10.    [2] Loc. cit.    [3] Bacon, *Works*, III, 333-4.
[4] When he used the phrase (with 'tabulam' instead of 'tabulata') in *B.L.* I, 18, he wrote beside it in the margin 'Vide Erasmi *Adagia* and quaere Dr. ⟨Richard⟩ Bl⟨ackbourne⟩', which suggests that he was not familiar with Bacon's use of it.

to the stone: that is, he framed the monument to his own Hypothesis, which is much differing from the Thing it self. This gave me an edge to make more researches', he wrote,[1] not only on Stonehenge but on other megalithic circles too, for he distrusted accounts in books (such as there were), 'for that I had scarcely seen hitherto any Antiquitie, which did not either fall-short of Fame, or exceeded it, I was for relying on my owne Eiesight'.[2] He stressed that, 'being but an ill Orator my selfe,' he wished 'to make the Stones give Evidence for themselves',[3] with a Baconian faith that the accumulation of information was the key to induction, and he filled the 'Templa Druidum' and the 'Chorographia Antiquaria' with accurately paced measurements and drawings of numerous examples of the antiquities that interested him.

Having accumulated all this information, he attempted to arrange and interpret it by the comparative method. 'I have arranged these Monuments together, for the neer resemblance they have to one another,' he explained at one point,[4] and elsewhere he juxtaposed the comparative measurements of the city walls of London, Bristol and Yarmouth.[5] Moreover he interpreted the megaliths 'by comparative Arguments',[6] attempting 'to work-out and restore after a kind of Algebraical method, by comparing them that I have seen, one with another; and reducing them to a kind of Æquation'.[7] 'I shall proceed gradually, à notioribus ad minus nota ⟨from those better known to those less known⟩: that is to say, from the Remaines of Antiquity less imperfect to those more imperfect, and ruinated':[8] and he applied this approach in discovering the remains of the avenue at Stonehenge by comparison with Avebury and other sites.[9] Elsewhere he always looked for ditches and straggling stones while studying stone circles,[10] and, in his section on 'Sepulchres', he considered that the lack of stones on the long barrow of Hubbaslow in contrast to Lugbury suggested that it was incomplete.[11]

---

[1] T.G.c.24, 23v–24. On the Lesbian rule, cf. Aristotle, *Ethics*, v, 10. Jones' hypothesis was that the design of Stonehenge was Vitruvian: cf. Graham Parry's introduction to the Scolar Press reprint of *Stone-Heng Restored* (1972).

[2] T.G.c.24, 25.

[3] Ibid., 30. Aubrey inserted 'give Evidence' in preference to 'speake', but then had second thoughts about it; I have preferred 'give Evidence'.

[4] T.G.c.25, 56, where he inserted French examples of megalithic tombs after English ones.

[5] T.G.c.24, 210. He also noted those of Colchester (210v) and Tangier (211).

[6] Ibid., 25v.　　　[7] Ibid., 30.　　　[8] Loc. cit.　　　[9] Ibid., 59.　　　[10] Ibid., 69, 75.

[11] T.G.c.25, 58.

His approach in his 'Chronologia Architectonica' and 'Chronologia Graphica' was related, of comparing specimens of architecture or calligraphy and thus building a definitive chronological scheme. Having constructed his sequence of dated examples, he dated others by analogy, sometimes noting slight differences which allowed him to refine his sequence—as with the 'world of mouldings' that differentiated some early Gothic buildings from others[1]—and he postulated a school of architecture in thirteenth-century Wiltshire by parallels with Salisbury.[2] His palaeographical deductions were similar, like the one he made when examining the antiquarian collections of his friend Thomas Guidott, a Bath doctor: 'As soon as I cast my eie on that delicate MS of Bathe which Dr. Guydot shewd me, I told him 'twas writt in the reigne of King Henry the sixth: why so it was sayd he, and presently turnd to the Date. So I know that the Legier-book of the Priory St Maries iuxta Kington St Michael in Wilts, is of the same time. à pari'.[3] He frequently applied his comparative deductions to date undated specimens of architecture and handwriting, as in Surrey in 1673,[4] and in general he hoped that his palaeography might 'also be usefull for detection of Forgeries'.[5]

Aubrey may even have been feeling his way towards an objective science of antiquities distinct from traditional history. It was admittedly because 'these Antiquities are so exceeding old, that no Bookes doe reach them: so that there is no way to retrive them but by comparative antiquitie, which I have writt upon the *spott* from the Monuments themselves'[6] that he applied this technique to megaliths. But it is significant that he deliberately separated such evidence about Stonehenge from traditional sources: 'In the first part of this Discourse I have sett-downe only the Schemes of this Antiquity; because I would not perplex and confound it with Story. But having gonne thorough that part, [which is comparative] I now come to the Historical, and Traditional part'.[7] Elsewhere he considered, perhaps less wisely, that the name of the Picts' Wall 'sufficiently declares who made it: without turning of Histories'.[8] He also agreed with several 'learned Gentlemen of Wales' that a collection of 'the Greeke words yet remaining in the welsh ... would afford good Evidence (without being beholding to Historie) that

---

[1] Ibid., 153v.    [2] Ibid., 155v.    [3] Ibid., 186v.
[4] MS A 4, 117v, 134, 141 (architecture), 132 (handwriting). Cf. 107 (an escutcheon).
[5] T.G.c.25, 185.    [6] T.G.c.24, 26.    [7] Ibid., 82.    [8] T.G.c.25, 90v.

there was a time, when the Greekes had Colonies here'.[1] Such
scattered remarks are important, for they show the germ of the
notion of prehistory that was to flower in the nineteenth century:
in Aubrey's period, as long afterwards, the general view was that
'all that is really known of the ancient state of Britain is contained
in a few pages. We can know no more than what old writers have
told us.'[2]

Equally striking is the care with which Aubrey distinguished
certainty and probability in his deduction about the stone circles.
He humbly admitted that 'this Inquiry I must confess is a grope-
ing in the Dark: but although I have not brought it into a cleer
light; yet I can affirm, that I have brought it from an utter darkness,
to a thin Mist'.[3] But he made it plain that it was 'by comparative
Arguments' that he gave 'a clear evidence that these monuments
were Pagan-Temples: which was not made out before', whereas it
was only a '*probability*, that they were *Temples* of the *Druids*',[4] a
distinction that modern archaeologists can only admire. He was sure
that they must be prehistoric because they were found in areas,
including Ireland, Scotland and Wales as well as England, which
had no common denominator in the Roman period or the Dark
Ages, whereas 'all these Monuments are of the same fashion, and
antique rudenesse',[5] but he was aware that their actual association
with the Druids was not certain. Just as 'when a Traveller rides
along by the Ruines of a Monastery, he knowes by the manner of
building, sc. Chapell, Cloysters &c: that it was a Convent, but of
what Order [sc. Benedictine, Dominican &c] it was, he cannot tell
by the bare View. So it is cleer, that all the Monuments, which I
have here recounted, were Temples; Now my presumption is, That
the *Druids* being the most eminent Priests [or Order of Priests]
among the Britaines: 'tis odds, but that these ancient Monuments
[sc. *Aubury, Stonehenge*, Kerrig y Druidd⟨on⟩ &c.] were Temples
of the Priests of the most eminent Order, viz, *Druids*'.[6] He was
anxious, however, for confirmation of this, and he therefore particularly valued the observations of Edward Lhwyd in Wales[7] and his

[1] MS A 5, 19. These included Sir Leoline Jenkins and Meredith Lloyd.
[2] G. E. Daniel, *A Hundred Years of Archaeology* (London, 1950), 25, quoting
Dr Johnson. Cf. G. E. Daniel, *The Idea of Prehistory* (London, 1962).
[3] T.G.c.24, 26.    [4] Ibid., 25v.    [5] Ibid., 80.    [6] Ibid., 25v–26.
[7] Cf. ibid., 25 and 76–7 (a copy of Lhwyd's additions to Pembrokeshire in Gibson's
Camden's *Britannia*).

letters from James Garden of Aberdeen,[1] which cited evidence from the nomenclature actually linking stone circles with the Druids, for such evidence he saw as 'the Hinge of this Discourse'.[2]

This laborious collection of evidence, its interpretation by the comparative method, and this careful separation of certain from merely probable deductions, are impressive and reminiscent of the most advanced thought of the new philosophy. It is therefore particularly interesting that Aubrey considered that his approach to the antiquities was 'after a kind of Algebraical method . . . reducing them to a kind of Æquation'.[3] For this suggests a parallel between such rigorous antiquarian method and the stress on mathematically-based clear and logical thought in his *Idea of Education*, which might imply an important link between the scientific movement and changes in historical method. But, before such a view is espoused too readily, it should be pointed out that Aubrey saw the techniques that he employed as no prerogative of the new philosophy, elsewhere using other metaphors to justify exactly the same approach: 'as the Divines doe interpret Scripture by Scripture: so shall I explaine these antiquated Antiquities one by another', he wrote,[4] and on another occasion he claimed that his archaeological deductions 'would be evidence to a Jury'.[5] If the new science offered anything to Aubrey's methods as an antiquary, it was only an intensified stress on habits of thought that were no novelty. Moreover Aubrey was far from consistent in applying the rigorous techniques that he advocated. As we have already seen, he had shown no such attention to careful method in his scientific writings, his studies of natural phenomena, and he was far from consistent in applying it in his antiquarianism.

For in general he was content to accept received ideas for the interpretation of antiquities rather than to examine these ideas sceptically on the basis of conclusions derived from the study of the relics in isolation from them. Despite the stress laid on 'comparative Arguments' in the 'Templa Druidum', it is difficult

---

[1] Cf. ibid., 25v. Ibid., 114 f. comprises Aubrey's copies of the letters.

[2] Ibid., 25 (this was of Cerrig y Drudion, which he had read of in Camden and would have liked to have seen).

[3] Ibid., 30.

[4] Ibid., 39 (but this passage, which is part of an earlier draft of the preface to 'Templa Druidum', is erased).

[5] A-W, 17 Nov. 1670, F 39, 128v: 'I have surveyd the camps: found out the places of the battles by the barrowes, & pretend to tell you where Bunducas battle was, which I think would be evidence to a Jury'.

to believe that it is coincidental that the principal subject to which
Aubrey applied them was stone circles, concerning which he had to
decide between the conflicting recent theories of Jones' *Stone-Heng
Restored*, which claimed Stonehenge as Roman, and Charleton's
*Chorea Gigantum*, which sought to prove it Danish.[1] It may be
significant that the other two subjects of which he made a comparative study were architecture and palaeography, which had hardly
been studied before, though too much stress should not be laid on
this, for in his theories on other antiquities which he was equally
original in studying, such as hill-forts, he failed to be so inductively
critical. Elsewhere he frequently followed earlier views, often
without questioning them at all, a trait that was encouraged by his
imaginative approach to the past, which made him hurry on to reconstruct antiquity without always considering the reliability of the
materials that he was using.

He often took the view that the Romans had brought excellence
in almost all things to Britain, which degenerated under the on-
slaught of barbarity in the Dark Ages, an *a priori* argument not
dissimilar to those which persuaded Inigo Jones that Stonehenge
was Roman. Even in the introduction to his 'Chronologia Architectonica' Aubrey echoed the commonplace that 'this excellent
Architecture degenerated into what we call Gothick, by the inundation of the Goths',[2] silently ignoring the conflict between this
traditional connection of the Goths with the pointed arch and his
own observation that the 'ox-eie' arch (which he considered to have
first been formed by the intersection of two round-headed ones) 'came
not in fashion till about Henry third: a little enclining in King
John'.[3] He claimed that the Goths had a similar effect on 'Habits: as
also in the Sadlers, & Upholsterers Trades',[4] whereas he believed
that the Roman methods of husbandry had remained in use until
they were 'lost and discontinued in the Barons-warres: and that of
Yorke and Lancastre',[5] and he often used such assumptions as a
substitute for analysis rather than as a means to it, dating antiquities
by them when their period was unclear to him.

---

[1] MS A 11 is Aubrey's transcript of parts of Charleton's book. (The contents list in
T.G.c.24, 13, suggests that this was intended to be bound in as part of the *Monumenta*
but in that at f. 20 it is erased.)

[2] T.G.c.25, 168.    [3] Ibid., 156.    [4] Ibid., 197.

[5] MS A 2, 85v. He cited Smith of Nibley concerning the date when marling was discontinued (cf. *The Berkeley Manuscripts* (Gloucester, 1883–5), III, 40 f.: but Smith did
not mention the Romans as Aubrey did).

The old west Windowes of St Paules church London as were of the fashion in the margent.

All the windowes of the Abbey at Reding built by King Henry the first, were of the same fashion.

Item the arch, called the Ox-eie, came not in fashion till about Henry third: a little enclining in King John, as in the margent. the Ox-eie-arch, &c is made by the intersection of two circles described from the extremities of the distance of the pillars, or &c.

Dowr-abbey in Herefordshire [a stately monastery] was built by King John; he reigned 17 years & 9 months: died 1216. Sr Jo: Hoskins Kt at Bar-sayth it was founded about 1050, et since.

The abbey of Reding-windowes are like those of Dowr-abbey; but I thinke, are not so perplext with mouldings. K. Henry the first was founder, & lies interred there. obijt 1135. Decoral.

The Windowes of the Church at Dowr-abbey are as in the margent, single with various mouldings. at the east end of the Choire are three of these windowes, as at Wimborne-minster in the east end of the Choire there. the Pillars are big and round, with an ill-favoured capitall. the capitalls of the small pillars are like those of the Temple cloysters.

Woodstock-Mannour-house was built (as the old building) by King Henry the second. In the north east of this house is an old windowe remayning with many old fashion-mouldings, as in the margent. &c.

The Chapelle-windowes here (expressed by D) resemble the south windowes of Westminster abbey; but that they have no pillar and capitall. The capitall of this pillar is like the capitalls of the small pillers in the Temple cloysters. In the Hall at Woodstock were two rowes of pillars, as in a church. The painting in water-colours [ for oyle-painting was not then known) red, and blew, is not yet

1672

15. Aubrey's map of Ancient Wessex, from his *Monumenta Britannica*

16. The east front of the Old Ashmolean Museum, Oxford, engraved by Michael Burghers, 1685

LIBRI IMPRESSI ET MANUSCRIPTI E DONIS CLARISS.
VIRORUM D. ELIÆ ASHMOLE ET MARTINI LISTER.
QUIBUS NON PAUCOS ADDIDIT VIR INDUSTRIUS
NEC INFIME DE RE ANTIQUARIA PROMERITUS
D. JOANNES AUBREY DE EASTON PEIRCE
APUD WILTONIENSES ARM. ET SOC. REG. SOCIUS.

17. The inscription in the Old Ashmolean commemorating Aubrey's and other bequests

He thought Chepstow and other castles belonged to the Roman period because he accepted the notion popularised by John Stow and others that the Saxons 'were so far from knowing Arts, that they could not build wall with stone',[1] whereas the Romans were the 'greatest masters of Architecture'.[2] It was thus that he pronounced Caerphilly the 'oldest & most entire piece of Roman Architecture that I know in this Island: I wonder it is so little taken notice of'.[3] He applied similar arguments in the *Remaines of Gentilisme*, claiming that the Britons imbibed their beliefs from the Romans and that 'the Inundation of the Goths, drove it out together with the Language',[4] although the survival of similar customs in purely English areas and in Germany might have suggested to him a wider interpretation.[5] A similar untested assumption is implicit in his claim in the *Interpretation of Villare Anglicanum* that any words common to Welsh and English must have originated in Welsh.[6]

The combination of such assumptions with Aubrey's rather unusual approach to the past often had unfortunate consequences. He believed that 'when the Romans were setteled here, they made great Improvements by Embanking and Dreyning; which though I doe not remember expressly mentioned in any Historian of any particular place: we must conclude that these great Dreyns were donne by them: who were skilfull in all Arts: and the Saxons were barbarous & ignorant'.[7] The bulk of the chapter 'Of Embanking, Dreyning & Currents' in his *Monumenta* comprised a section 'Of St Vincents Rocks, and Bristow',[8] in which Aubrey attempted, using local traditions ('perhaps some sparke of Trueth might be pick't out in this Mist')[9] and other evidence, to prove that the Romans had hoped to clear the Avon and thus drain the surrounding countryside. In fact, however, there was no real evidence for artificial draining at all, and in the second part of the chapter Aubrey turned instead to discussing the possibility that the original fault at St Vincent's Rocks was due to an ancient earthquake.[10] His

---

[1] MS A 3, 10v (he also quoted Spelman that the church at Glastonbury was thatched). On Stow's view, cf. M. Hunter, 'The Study of Saxon Architecture since 1770', *Proceedings of the Cambridge Antiquarian Society* LXVI (1975), forthcoming.

[2] T.G.c.24, 205.     [3] T.G.c.25, 153v.     [4] *Gentilisme*, 132.

[5] He admitted that some customs had been brought by the Trojans (ibid., 367, 368) and others came from Scandinavia (288, 300).

[6] MS A 5, 82.     [7] T.G.c.25, 132.     [8] Ibid., 133f.     [9] Ibid., 134.

[10] The chapter contains other miscellaneous material, including a mention of his hopes to clear the 'Lids' at St Vincent's Rocks and thus open the passage to Bristol: cf. above p. 110, n. 13.

reasoning was similar when, with no evidence except the names and the fact that clothiers still used the water there, he interpreted the name of the river Windrush, and that of Witney, where it ran, as 'white-water' and added, 'The Romans brought in the Art of Cloathing and Dyeing: and in probality, by reason of the goodnesse of the water so fitt for that Trade, manufactured Cloath here'— though he erased his further speculation 'and why may we not without vanity, suppose that here have been died Senatorian purple?'[1]

Aubrey also had a tendency to oversimplify the past, fusing almost all history together in a single 'old time', which lasted from the period of the practices described in classical authors to the way of life that left survivals almost into his own day. Though the doctrine of survivals underlying the *Remaines of Gentilisme* was in many ways very sophisticated, it occasionally led Aubrey to connections that seem almost naive, as when he quoted a line written by Propertius in the early Empire on weapons hung in houses and said 'Before the Civill Warres, a Justice-of-peace's hall was so furnisht & lookt dreadfull'.[2] For him, the whole of the Middle Ages fused together in a confused but chronologically static picture of chivalry and piety, crusades and good living, a 'good old days' not unlike that of the Commonwealthsmen of the sixteenth century.[3] He traced its decline to the Tudor Age, when by the destroying of petty manors and the sale of church lands 'is the Ballance of the Goverment quite altered and putt into the handes of the common people'[4] —thus echoing the somewhat simplistic opinion of his friend Harrington.[5] He also attributed a cataclysmic significance to the Civil War, to which he sometimes attributed events which, when he had originally recorded them, he had thought to be unrelated.[6]

With this went a somewhat uncritical attitude towards historical sources. Though in his *Idea of Education* Aubrey quoted the 'Advice

---

[1] MS A 5, 77.    [2] *Gentilisme*, 304.    [3] Esp. MS A 3, 9a f.    [4] Ibid., 9a.

[5] Cf. J. G. A. Pococke, *The Ancient Constitution*, 140–1. Pococke's opinion (135) that Harrington's ideas were heavily indebted to Selden is borne out by Aubrey's view that 'Mr J. Seldens Titles of Honour is a Scale to measure the old Balance of Goverment' (MS A 3, 11v). Aubrey also cited Raleigh's *History* (ibid., 9a, 9b) and More's *Utopia* (ibid., 9a) on the enclosures and related events in the sixteenth century.

[6] For example, in his 'Chronologia Vestiaria' (T.G.c.25, 200b) he described the 'High-shoes' which 'were the common wearing for Husbandmen in Wiltshire &c: in 1633, and after: and it was a very usefull fashion', claiming that 'in 1642 the warres brake-out and then both Citizens and ploughmen wore bootes altogether; which was very un-commodious & ridiculous'. But in MS A 3, 9av he has the people wearing such boots 'till about 1631' (cf. *B.L.* ii, 324: 'till 1633'); in his account of the same change in T.G.c.25, 203, he compromised with 'just before the Scotts warres'.

to me for the reading of our English Historie' of William Prynne, the Puritan lawyer and pamphleteer—'to read the Authors, that wrote of their owne Times. quod N B'[1]—this was a principle which only too often he ignored. On Roman Britain he sought evidence from the late and unreliable Chronicles of Caxton, Holinshed and Sir Richard Baker,[2] and in his *Monumenta Britannica* he cited works of such small historical value as Edward Leigh's entirely derivative *England Described* (1659)[3] and Aylett Sammes' fantastic *Britannia Antiqua Illustrata* (1676).[4] Aubrey was also often too hasty in correlating antiquities with historical events and personalities. He accepted that an oak in Worcestershire was the very spot where Bede said the Welsh and English bishops met to decide the date of Easter;[5] that a camp was Danish 'as appeares by the Chronicle';[6] and that 'Gaer Cradock' was the very place where the British leader Caractacus was defeated by the Romans in A.D. 50.[7]

Such traits are to be found even in his study of Stonehenge, for he quoted a number of late and untrustworthy sources which associated the site with Ambrosius Aurelianus, the fifth-century British leader, and the events of his time, to prove that 'Ergo Stone-heng not a Worke of the Danes: nor yet of the Saxons, quod N B'.[8] His study of stone circles showed other shortcomings. In arguing against Charleton's theory about the megaliths, some of his factual information was actually wrong: 'Quaere the Doctor's authority for the Danes over-running Wales? I have only his owne Word for it'.[9] Moreover, having dismissed the Vitruvian six-fold structure for Stonehenge postulated by Inigo Jones, claiming that 'the Ruines of it doe cleerly enough shew, (without farther demonstration) that it could neither be a Hexagon, or heptagon',[10] he contradicted himself in another place by suggesting that it was a heptagon, adding: 'Why might not then, the seaven-sided figure in the foregoing scheme be made in relation to the seaven Planets, & seaven daies of the Weeke?'[11]

---

[1] MS A 10, 97.    [2] MS A 5, 3, 80-1.    [3] T.G.c.25, 87v.    [4] T.G.c.24, 102.
[5] T.G.c.24, 227.    [6] MS A 4, 35.    [7] T.G.c.24, 166.
[8] MS A 11, 4v. This followed a list of dates of burials of 'Aurelius Ambrosius' and others, from 'Mr J. Gibbon's [Blewmantle] marginal Notes'. Aubrey subsequently added references to Matthew of Westminster, Simeon of Durham and Henry Huntingdon. In ibid., 14v, he cited the latter three and also Geoffrey of Monmouth and 'an old manuscript Roll of the time of Henry VI' owned by John Conyers, arguing similarly that Stonehenge was pre-Danish. Cf. T.G.c.24, 92.
[9] MS A 11, 14v.    [10] T.G.c.24, 58.    [11] Ibid., 65.

'I can not determine: I only suggest,' he wrote of this theory,[1] and in general his restraint in extrapolating from literary sources back to his antiquities saved him from the fancifulness of eighteenth-century antiquaries like William Stukeley, who saw Avebury as a 'Dracontium' or serpent temple and the Druids as patriarchal Christians.[2] But this was largely due to Aubrey's life-long difficulty in consolidating his notes into connected narratives. His hypo-thesis that the mortices of the mortice and tenon joints at Stone-henge were the nesting-places of the 'aves Druidum', the holy birds of the Druids,[3] shows that the restraint was not wholly deliberate, and he was possibly more fanciful in conversation than on paper. When he was shown a strigil from the Roman site at Reculver in the collection of John Batteley, a Canterbury divine and keen antiquary, 'he immediately exclaimed, "Behold the golden sickle with which the Druids used to cut mistletoe!" This writer,' Batteley continued, 'in other respects a man of learning, was apt superstitiously and idly to wrest almost everything to the religion and worship of the Druids'.[4]

Besides, though Aubrey's comparative dating of megaliths was exemplary, there were other classes of antiquities, such as the hill-forts of the British Iron Age, which he dated with complete con-fidence although he had no 'analytic' evidence at all. Here his inconsistent theories were based on questionable assumptions and ideas derived by hearsay from informants like 'Mr . . . Gethyng of the Mid⟨dle⟩ Temple (an Irish gentleman)', who assured Aubrey 'that in Ireland are a great number of Danish Camps, which are all round, and with double or treble workes'.[5] He decided that 'the Roman Campes are allwayes Square, or at least squarish; and a single worke' (though in fact most of his examples are 'squarish' and not Roman at all), but camps that were 'Round, or roundish, and double or treble Workes'[6] he found more difficult to date, sometimes claiming them as British and sometimes Danish

---

[1] Loc. cit.

[2] Cf. S. Piggott, *William Stukeley* (Oxford, 1950), 126–7, 177; *Celts, Saxons and the Early Antiquaries* (Edinburgh, 1967), 20.

[3] T.G.c.24, 89, 100.

[4] John Batteley, *The Antiquities of Richborough and Reculver* (English translation, London, 1774), 116. Aubrey was also mistaken in thinking it gold rather than gilt. A strigil was an implement used for scraping the skin in bath-houses.

[5] T.G.c.24, 152v.     [6] Ibid., 250v.

('me thinks they are too artish for the old Britaines').[1] Yet he
boldly dated specimens, even changing 'seemes to be' to 'is' on
one occasion,[2] fiercely criticising Camden for his 'grosse mistake'
in failing to distinguish camps of different periods that were
in fact wholly illusory,[3] and denying local traditions on similar
grounds.[4]

Inconsistency is indeed common in Aubrey's antiquarian writings,
owing something to the haphazard quality of his notes, in which he
frequently contradicted himself, and even something to his vivid
approach to the past. Having used barrows as graphic evidence of
military manoeuvres on the downs—'so great a signe of Slaughter
I never found'[5]—he was naturally loath to abandon this, even when
he equally imaginatively suggested the rival theory that they were
really peacetime burial grounds, for soldiers 'flagrante bello', 'in
the heat of battle', would not have had time and leisure enough to
collect so many thousand loads of earth.[6] 'My conceit is that the
Seaven-Barrowes &c: (where are severall together) were not
tumulii or barrowes erected upon the account of any great person
slain there in Battle: but in those times they chose to lye drye
upon such hilly ground: and those of the same familie would desire
to lie neer one another; as the Kings at Westminster abbey, or at
St Dionyse in France'.[7] Similarly, though he usually assumed
that all ancient masonry must be Roman, on one occasion he
said of some, 'I beleive brittish, for the Saxons were dunces'.[8]
He was not sure whether Salisbury Plain was disafforested by the
Romans (in the same manner as the Virginian natives cleared their
land),[9] or whether it was part of the smooth original world.[10] He
was also uncertain whether the Uffington White Horse was 'made
by Hengist'[11] or was pre-Roman, for he perceptively noted its
similarity to a horse on a Belgic coin from Colchester.[12]

In his studies of place-names Aubrey was equally inconsistent,
frequently recording different possible derivations of words between which he never attempted to decide. Was 'Ampt-' a place of
justice, or was it connected with 'ant', an emmet;[13] and did 'lite' mean

---

[1] Ibid., 152v. He also compared them with examples that he thought were 'certainly'
Danish. Aubrey seems to have held both theories in 1668: the passage just quoted is in
close proximity to a note concerning 'this summer [1668]', and the map in ibid., 250v–
251, where the 'British' theory appears, is dated 1668.
[2] Ibid., 155v.   [3] Ibid., 159.   [4] Ibid., 175.   [5] Ibid., 254.   [6] Ibid., 92–3.
[7] T.G.c.25, 18.   [8] *Analecta*, 162.   [9] MS A 1, 18v–19.   [10] Ibid., 87.
[11] T.G.c.24, 179.   [12] T.G.c.25, 122v.   [13] MS A 5, 23.

little, or was it derived from 'liten', a garden, or from the dialect
word 'lit', to die?[1] Though his interest in Celtic and old English gave
him correct insights into the etymology of many names, his less
happy etymologies ranged from the received,[2] to the descriptive,[3]
the fanciful[4] and the plain wrong.[5] He was also vague about the
linguistic origins of many roots,[6] and some of his most interesting
insights went unrealised—like his observation that place-names
ending in '-holt' and '-hurst' were found only in the south-east of
England while those ending in '-by' and '-beck' recurred solely in
the north, which brought him to the brink of realising how place-
names could be correlated with the areas of Danish settlement in
late Saxon times.[7]

His *Interpretation of Villare Anglicanum*, though full of interesting observations, is one of his least satisfactory works, for he was
an amateur, who had never made the careful study of old language
and linguistic usage and change necessary for accurate and systematic interpretation. 'I understand but little Welsh,' he admitted;[8]
he hoped that 'this designe of mine, which I have here begun,
should be embraced by some learned men to putt their helping
hands to compleat the Interpretations',[9] and he often quoted the
views of Edward Lhwyd[10] and also occasionally of Thomas Gale,[11]
William Baxter, a schoolmaster and 'a great critique in the British

---

[1] Ibid., 46. The first meaning was supposed to be Dutch, and was quoted from Ray.
[2] He quoted etymologies suggested by Humphrey Lhwyd, Richard Verstegan and
others in MS A 5, passim (there are also some pages of notes from Lhwyd's *Breviary of
Britayne* in ibid., 9 f.).
[3] E.g. he noted of Brinkworth (which he explained as Brin-meadow and worth-way),
'This great rich Parish is all mowing & feeding-ground' (ibid., 30v); he connected
Minety with wild mints growing locally (ibid., 48v); and at Alresford he suggested, by
parallel with Arles, that the name meant 'a way upon or over a Marish: which is the
perfect description of this Place' (T.G.c.25, 96).
[4] E.g. of 'Lurgershall', he noted the proverb 'a long lazie Lurges; and to lye lurgeing'
and continued 'it's probable they were huge great men, and had not spiritt in proportion to their bulke' (MS A 3, 158); of Patenham, 'Pate is the abbreviation of Pater
n⟨oste⟩r' (MS A 5, 51v); and of Thanet, he observed that 'Tane' is the British for fire,
adding 'the waves beating against the Rocks of this Island doe give a light in the night
like Fire to the saylers; from whence, it has its Denomination' (ibid., 65).
[5] E.g. Worth – way (ibid., 22) and Vorða – good way ('da is good') (ibid., 41v).
[6] For example, several are marked 'SB', i.e. Saxon and British (ibid., 50v, 62, 78;
cf. 'BS', 74v, 77; etc).
[7] Ibid., 19av. Cf. his interest in tautologous place-names, ibid., 29, 52, 68v, 78v.
[8] T.G.c.25, 238v.        [9] MS A 5, 21.
[10] Cf. MS A 4, 5av; MS A 5, unpaginated insertion between fols. 34–5, etc.
[11] Cf. MS A 4, 5av; MS A 5, 45v.

language',[1] and others.[2] His letters to Lhwyd contain numerous requests for expert advice on etymological matters,[3] and he hoped that Lhwyd would finish the *Interpretation*, for 'there is no body that I know, that is so fitt to goe through with that Designe as your selfe'.[4]

This difference between the dilettante Aubrey and the professional Lhwyd parallels the contrast between their scientific work, in which Lhwyd's collecting and classification was as methodical as Ray's. Indeed, it is symptomatic that the careful Ray declined Aubrey's invitation to help him with the *Interpretation of Villare Anglicanum* since he did not know Saxon and Welsh well enough.[5] With the paradoxical exception of the 'Templa Druidum' and the 'Chronologias', Aubrey's antiquarian work, like his scientific, was a collection of piecemeal facts and untested and inconsistent hypotheses, with no evidence of inductive reasoning at all. It is significant that when he quoted a motto from Bacon at the beginning of Book II of *Monumenta Britannica* (the 'Chorographia Antiquaria'), it was the sentence from the *Instauratio Magna* that he had remembered through Ralph Austen, about the value of an active man writing books.[6] He thus invoked the collecting Bacon of *Sylva Sylvarum*, who recorded almost any possibility in his insatiable appetite for information—like Aubrey and other 'Baconian' scientists of the Restoration, who had no time to consider the material and test it analytically, and who represented, as we have already seen, a somewhat backward-looking and unconstructive tradition in the science of the time.

## Natural History and Antiquities

It is possible to demonstrate an important and influential link between Aubrey's studies of natural phenomena and his antiquarian activity, but this was connected not with the quality of his

---

[1] A-L, 27 March 1694, A. 1814, 109. Aubrey quotes him in MS A 4, 5av, and tells himself to 'q⟨uaere⟩' him in T.G.c.24, 215v.

[2] Including Mr Evans of the Bridge House at London (MS A 5, 17), Thomas Henshawe (ibid., 44v), Meredith Lloyd (ibid., 53, etc.).

[3] A-L, 21 April 1691, ibid., 2, 29 March 1692, A. 1814, 99; cf. Lhwyd-Aubrey, 3 April 1693, 24 May 1693, 13 Oct. 1693, MS A 12, 243, 247, 248.

[4] A-L, 21 April 1691, MS A 5, 2.

[5] Ray-Aubrey, 15 Feb. 1687/8, MS A 13, 172.

[6] T.G.c.24, 138. Cf. above, p. 95.

deductions but with the kind of material that he collected. The most strikingly original feature of Aubrey's antiquarianism was its unusual emphasis on relics and traditions collected in the field: as we have seen, his works include the first English books entirely devoted to archaeology, place-names and folk-lore. What is more, his activity in collecting such material can be directly associated with the new kind of scholarly fieldwork in which he was engaged. There had been fieldwork before Aubrey, in the form of the century-and-a-half-old tradition of miscellaneous topography stretching from Leland to his own time, and archaeological, traditional and etymological evidence had occasionally been gathered up with historical and descriptive material. Indeed, Aubrey's *Perambulation of Surrey* shows a curiosity about almost all phenomena, old and new, of this traditional kind, and even parts of the *Naturall Historie of Wiltshire* have something in common with it.[1] But, despite such similarity to earlier writings, Aubrey's topography had an element of great originality. For his *Naturall Historie of Wiltshire*, which he claimed that he began in 1656, like Plot's natural histories of Oxfordshire and Staffordshire, represented an approach very different from that of earlier county surveys, contrasting with them in the greater detail with which the natural and artificial phenomena of counties were described and arranged in chapters according to type, air, stones, beasts and so on.

Aubrey's novel antiquarianism was directly comparable. Not only were his observations of field antiquities as detailed as the notes of flora and fauna that he made at the same time—the way in which material is sometimes misplaced shows how in his original notes he mixed the two together.[2] His arrangement of the antiquities in *Monumenta Britannica* (particularly the 'Chorographia Antiquaria') is just like his classification of natural phenomena in the *Naturall Historie of Wiltshire*; he divided them into categories such as camps, barrows, urns and roads arranged in chapters under rubricated titles just as if they were medicinal springs, plants or fishes. If Aubrey's antiquarian originality consisted largely of collecting antiquities and studying them in their own right, it is clear that both the activity itself and the way he went about it were directly inspired by his natural history. Indeed,

[1] Cf. above, pp. 69–70, 101–2.
[2] Natural historical material appears, e.g., in T.G.c.24, 182, 186v.

he felt that the two were closely connected: when he was considering the fate of his *Naturall Historie of Wiltshire*, he noted that his 'Templa Druidum' and 'Chorographia Antiquaria' 'doe belong to this Historie & to be printed with it'.[1]

It is thus no coincidence that the title 'Chorographia Antiquaria' parallels that of Aubrey's 'Chorographia super- et subterranea naturalis', and there is also some overlap between his preoccupations in his natural history and his antiquarianism. An interest in geographical diversity plays a small part in his study of antiquities: churches as well as cheese, he thought, were better in the West of England than in the East,[2] and he was puzzled to find that those of Somerset were best of all and, 'which is stranger', particularly the moorland ones.[3] Observations of the natural environment occasionally helped him to evaluate relics of the past—his study of geology enabled him to observe with interest that the pebbles used on Roman roads were often not local, and had sometimes been brought from the sea-shore miles away,[4] and he added observations of crop marks made by John Wilkins and Seth Ward as a 'Philosophicall Corollary' to his description of the antiquities of Silchester.[5] His interest in place-names was perhaps most closely related to his studies of natural history, for in interpreting them he frequently tried to make their original meanings descriptive of the natural surroundings of places—marshes, woods or hills, hazels, chalk or wild mints—and he cited such evidence in his 'Chorographia super- et subterranea naturalis'.[6]

More significant is Aubrey's use of evidence from the past to extend backward in time the interest in diversity that is so prominent in his scientific writings, and his fascination with change was certainly linked to this. His statistics on weights and measures, prices of corn and wages in the past seem to have been connected with, if not inspired by, a curiosity about how prices and

---

[1] John Britton, *Memoir of John Aubrey*, 61. This is quoted from a draft of a will relating mainly to the *Naturall Historie of Wiltshire*, apparently dating from the late 1680s, which Britton had in his possession (it was evidently a leaf of the work, signed and sealed in the presence of witnesses). Britton gives 'Chronologia', not 'Chorographia', but since it speaks of the 'Chronologia Architectonica' separately, I suspect that 'Chronologia' is here a mistake. I do not know of the present whereabouts of the original. Cf. above, p.102, on the significance of Aubrey's view.

[2] T.G.c.25, 153 and MS A 2, 74. On cheese, cf. above, pp. 116–17    [3] MSA 2, 73v.

[4] T.G.c.25, 92v, 97, 97v. He intended to ask Wren the reason for this (92v).

[5] T.G.c.24, 215.    [6] MS A 1, 9 f.

measures varied in different places;[1] though he inserted them in the *Monumenta* he had originally intended them for the *Naturall Historie of Wiltshire*.[2] He was interested not only in contemporary fairs and markets in Wiltshire, but in their rise and the decay of old ones,[3] and he quoted Sir Christopher Wren about differences in climate not only in different places but at different times.[4] He noted that 'Winchelsea haven now a great green meadow',[5] and he was fascinated by the fact that the Fens were 'the garden of England' in the thirteenth century,[6] and by the possibility that their draining in his own time had caused greater feverishness in Northamptonshire than hitherto.[7] In his *Naturall Historie of Wiltshire* he also discussed the extinction of animals like beavers, reindeer and wolves,[8] and he was curious about fossils with no modern counterpart, 'the species whereof Mr R. Hooke sayes is now lost'.[9]

Above all, it is possible to observe how Aubrey's enthusiasm for technological progress in the present and future was reflected in his study of the past. We have already seen how, in his scientific manuscripts, his concern to disseminate useful information overlapped with an interest in the history of improvements, with the result that his chapters on agriculture and inventions are a curious hybrid between collections of recipes and eulogies of improvers. It is therefore revealing that the section in 'Στρώματα' called 'Nouvelles' has the sub-title 'Naturall & Artificiall things by whom & when brought into England'[10]—which echoes the subject-matter of Aubrey's natural history—and that some of its material had also appeared in the chapter on 'Agriculture' in the *Naturall Historie of Wiltshire*, which includes a section on topics like the introduc-

---

[1] T.G.c.25, 215, 221v f. Cf. MS A 4, in which he cites the different prices of corn in various places in Sussex and Surrey (135, 143v) and also quotes old documents on corn prices in the past (231).

[2] Cf. the list of contents in MS A 1, 25v. In MS A 2, 122–3, he expresses an interest in changes of prices and wages, but hardly cites any evidence. He hoped to see a collection of corn prices over the last century made by Thomas Axe, a Somerset attorney with scientific interests (he also mentions this in T.G.c.25, 215), and to obtain help from others, notably Petty and Robert Good.

[3] Cf. contents list in MS A 1, 25v, 'Faires & markets, their Rise & decay', and MS A 2, 149, 151. For similar material in his *Surrey*, cf. MS A 4, 54v, 120, 155.

[4] R.S. MS 92, 31.   [5] MS A 1, 17v.   [6] Loc. cit.   [7] Ibid., 15v.   [8] Ibid., 128 f.

[9] Ibid., 17. In ibid., 84, he noted the lack of counterpart. For the context of Hooke's remark in terms of the palaeontological debate of the time, see M. J. S. Rudwick, *The Meaning of Fossils*, ch. 11, esp. 65.

[10] T.G.c.25, 208.

tion of carrots, cabbages, turnips and pearmains into England, headed by the identical title 'Nouvelles'.[1] This chapter also has information about technological changes like the replacement of wagons by carts and the introduction of wheel-ploughs,[2] and it is easy to see how the concern with technological change that dominates the whole of 'Στρώματα' was related to this. Material on 'Nouvelles' also appears in the manuscripts of *Brief Lives*,[3] thus linking with the adulation of projectors seen there and elsewhere; and, having recorded in 'Στρώματα' that Charles Howard, one of his colleagues on the Georgical committee of the Royal Society, had first brought to England 'scores of Plants, now common', Aubrey noted with evident surprise 'but he values it not'.[4]

Aubrey even hoped that antiquities might reveal useful recipes. He presented 'Several Examples of MORTARS of old Castles and *Roman* Buildings' to the Royal Society 'for comparing them with those now in use',[5] just as he thought that an excellent mortar at Mortlake, made from Thames sand and lime, might prove 'a good hint for the retreiving of the old way'.[6] He sought recipes for brick-making from Roman examples,[7] and for gilding letters and making ink from old manuscripts;[8] he noted the manufacture of enamelled bricks for old floors and thought ' 'tis pitty it is not revived and improved';[9] and he described an 'ancient Gothick workt chimney' at Wells because it operated on the same principle as an engine to cap smoking chimneys devised by Wren.[10] He even wanted to retrieve the course of Stane Street through the Weald '& gett it setled by the Parliament, or K⟨ing⟩'s prerogative: ... it runnes through the unpassable dirty part of Sussex, and would be of extraordinary use to the Travellers, who are faine to hire Oxen to drawe their coaches out of this miry tract of land'.[11]

To some extent this hope to find out useful information lay behind Aubrey's interest in country traditions, his curiosity about the observations of folk wisdom, 'some whereof I do not disdain

---

[1] MS A 2 ,88. Cf. MS A 1, 14v, which has more information about the introduction of plants.

[2] MS A 2, 89.

[3] The information is mainly collected together on MS Aubrey 6, 11, and MS Aubrey 8, 28v, which has the title 'Nouvelles': printed in *B.L.* 11, 317 f.

[4] T.G.c.25, 209.      [5] N. Grew, *Musæum Regalis Societatis*, 380.

[6] *Analecta*, 172. Cf. MS A 4, 204a.      [7] *Analecta*, 180.

[8] MS A 3, 189, mentions these in the authority of Christopher Wase: cf. *Analecta*, 136.

[9] MS A 3, 174. Cf. MS A 2, 79.      [10] *Analecta*, 156.      [11] T.G.c.24, 153.

to learn from ignorant old women'.[1] 'For Proverbs are drawn
from the experience and Observations of many Ages: and are
the ancient Natural Philosophy of the Vulgar, preserved in old
English; in bad Rhythms handed downe to us; and which I set
here as Instantiae Crucis, for our curious moderne Philosophers to
examine, and give διοτι to their ὅτις' (i.e. justification to their
statements).[2] 'It would doe well', he thought, 'if the signes of raine
or wet weather in the shepherds booke of knowledge were carefully examined',[3] and he quoted many 'Prognostiques'[4] concerning the weather, as 'If the Downe [sc. of Dandelion, Thistles,
Coltsfoot] flieth off, when there is no wind, is a sign of Raine.
quod N B'.[5] His informants ranged from Thames boatmen to
Spanish shepherds,[6] and he was anxious that 'the rules, whereby
they know this, be enquired'.[7] He was equally keen to test the waters
of holy wells, for they might prove to have medicinal virtues:
'medicinall waters were anciently (before Christs time and since)
dedicated to some Deity or Saint, to whome they imputed the
Vertue: being ignorant of the Minerall that impregnated it.'[8]

In the same way he was interested in country recipes, explaining
that 'doubtlesse there have been in all ages good witts in the world.
And though 5 or 600 years of the Saxons were a darke time, we are
not to beleive they had no glimpse of light: St Dunstan was a
Chymist, & no question many fryars (whose names & many of
theire inventions are buryed in oblivion) found out many good
medicines, which they did communicate to theire friends & Peni-
tents (especially the good women) whose Daughters have handed
downe many to this age, that doe admirable cures; for which I have
known eminent Phisitians offer great rates & could not obtaine
them. Platerus was so ingenious as to confesse that many of his rare
recipes he had from old women.'[9]

It was while he was collecting medical and other recipes from
such sources—like an excellent recipe for metheglin from Mrs
Hatchwell[10] or a preparation for eye-drops from goodwife Holly,
'a poore woman of Chalke'[11]—that Aubrey encountered country

---

[1] Aubrey-Boyle, 15 March 1665, Boyle, *Works* VI, 544.     [2] MS A I, 7–8.
[3] *Analecta*, 210.     [4] R.S. MS 92, 33.     [5] Ibid., 34.     [6] Ibid., 32.
[7] *T.P.W.*, 337.     [8] MS A 3, 84v.
[9] *Analecta*, 215–16x. Platerus was presumably the sixteenth-century Basle doctor
referred to in *Miscellanies*, 33, and MS A I, 170, though it could be the twelfth-century
Salerno doctor of that name, who made a collection of recipes.
[10] MS A I, 148.     [11] Ibid., 162.

customs. Some of the traditions he quoted he saw only as misunderstood survivals, just as he sometimes recorded country remedies, like one prescribing drinking leeches in sack, because 'I believe
'tis but a piece of wantonnesse: but this is an ancient custome'.[1]
But as recipes often proved useful, so might old traditions. Thus at
first he considered the custom of moulding the cockle-bread 'meer
Wantonnesse of Youth';[2] but a reference in the Decretals of Bur-
chardus, an eleventh-century Archbishop of Worms, showed him
that it was in fact 'a relique of Naturall Magick',[3] and he went on:
'The Lord Chancellor Bacon sayes—thus the fables of the Poets
are the Mysteries of the Philosophers: and I allude here, that (out
of fulsome Ribaldrie) I have picked-out the profoundest natural
Magick, that ever I met with in all my Life'.[4] Aubrey's interpretation of this custom can still be admired by modern folklorists,[5]
and it is interesting that it was his hope of finding magical overtones
in country customs that led him to this insight.

Some of the contents of Aubrey's *Remaines of Gentilisme* can
actually be identified as material that he collected for magical pur-
poses[6]—he even intended to include a mystical pentangle from his
copy of the *Clavicula Salamonis*[7]—and the sceptical, interpretative
attitude of some of his remarks did not exclude accepting belief
in others.[8] Here, as in his magical collection, he told how to
please and how to exorcise spirits,[9] how to work charms[10] or to
make yourself invisible,[11] and how Edward VI 'was killed by

---

[1] Ibid., 139.  [2] *Gentilisme*, 254.

[3] Loc. cit. Cf. John Buchanan-Brown's note in *T.P.W.*, 439, and Migne, *Patrologia
Latina* CXL (Paris, 1853), 537 f.

[4] *Gentilisme*, 255. Cf. Bacon, *Of the Wisdom of the Ancients, Works*, VI, esp. 695f.

[5] Cf. R. M. Dorson, *The British Folklorists*, 10, and Britten's edition of *Gentilisme*,
225.

[6] Ashmole's notes from 'Mr. Aubry's Collection of dreames, phantasmes, Instincts
&c:' in British Library MS Sloane 3846, 114v–115v show that in 1673, for instance,
Aubrey was collecting material some of which went into *Gentilisme* (e.g. 231–2, 261),
while some went into the *Miscellanies* (e.g. 145–6, 148). Aubrey also evidently removed
material from *Gentilisme* to insert in *Miscellanies* (or its precursor, 'Dreames'): cf.
*T.P.W.*, 369.

[7] MS A 24, 56a–7 is a leaf that Aubrey intended to insert in *Gentilisme*, but he never
managed it; *Gentilisme*, 245, refers to it.

[8] It is interesting that on the leaf referred to above (MS A 24, 56a–7), he copied out
the virtues of the pentangle as well as giving an account of its history as a symbol.

[9] *Gentilisme*, 158, 201.

[10] Ibid., ch. xv, 'Magick' (i.e., as organised by John Buchanan-Brown), passim; a
recipe on page 231, for instance, has '*ut probat*', as in Aubrey's magical collection.

[11] Ibid., 253.

Witch-craft'.[1] Here, too, his piecemeal scepticism only reinforced his general belief. Indeed, the way in which interpretation was superimposed on credulity is shown by this entry: 'A Spell to cure the Biting of a mad Dog. Rebus Rubus Epitepscum. Write these words in paper, and give it to the party, or beast bitten, to eate in bread, or &c.: Mr. Dennys of Poole in Dorsetshire sayeth, this Receipt never failes.' Such a recipe could have appeared in Aubrey's magical notes, but here he continued: 'Perhaps this spell may be the anagramme of some sence, or Recipe: as Dr. Bathurst hath discovered in Abracadabra, which I thought had been nonsense.'[2] Moreover the fact that Bathurst had identified 'Abracadabra' as corrupt Hebrew did not reduce Aubrey's faith in it as a magical charm, and as such he inserted it into his *Miscellanies*, noting 'With this Spell, one of *Wells* hath cured above an Hundred of the Ague'.[3]

Such a combination of rationalisation and belief is hardly surprising, for any other interpretation of Aubrey's approach would presuppose a split in his intellectual attitudes for which there is no evidence. Even when, in his other antiquarian writings, he was interested in country traditions in order to extract evidence from them that was not immediately obvious, he had a tendency to try to take them literally, sometimes with occult implications. 'Why! was not Lot's wife turn'd into a pillar of salt?' he asked, having noted a similar tradition at Stanton Drew,[4] and he cited Curtius' *History* on the building of Alexandria in seventeen days after recording a local tradition that Silbury Hill 'was raysed whilst a posnet of Milke was seething'.[5] It was doubtless in a similar frame of mind that he took evidence combining the old and the occult, from Roman *mentulae* worn 'for fertilitys sake'[6] to apparitions associated with archaeological finds,[7] and he also considered the possibility that the Druids 'did converse with Eagles, and could understand their Language'.[8] What is more, the treatise 'Στρώματα' was at one time to have contained not only the 'Chronologias' that were Aubrey's contribution to the study of anachronism but also

---

[1] Ibid., 228.    [2] Ibid., 260–1.    [3] *Miscellanies*, 141.

[4] T.G.c.24, 52. He subsequently erased this sentence.    [5] T.G.c.25, 9v.

[6] T.G.c.24, 243. Cf. *Gentilisme*, 232.

[7] T.G.c.24, 163v; T.G.c.25, 67, and the broadsheet *A Strange and Wonderful Discovery Newly made of Houses Under Ground, At Colton's-Field in Gloucester-shire* (London, 1685) which Aubrey inserted in ibid., 107. Cf. *Miscellanies*, 112.

[8] T.G.c.24, 100, and T.G.c.25, 90. He quoted Ponticus Virunnius about this, and intended to 'q⟨uaere⟩ E⟨dmund⟩ W⟨yld⟩ Esq. + de hiis'.

the tracts on 'Day-fatality', 'Omens' and 'Divine Dreames' which were subsequently published in the *Miscellanies*.[1]

Aubrey's antiquarian interests were, then, intimately connected with his studies of natural and supernatural phenomena, and considerably influenced by them. The importance of this influence can be proved by considering other scholars with similar scientific interests who developed comparable antiquarian ones. This is certainly true of Robert Plot, whose scientific studies were perhaps closest to Aubrey's.[2] Like Aubrey, Plot was aware that the proper concerns of the antiquary were inscriptions, ancient texts and similar sources, and in his prospectuses for his natural histories, his *Plinius Anglicus* and his letter to Dr Fell, he expressed the hope of listing manuscripts[3] and of extending Weever's *Ancient Funerall Monuments* to other dioceses.[4] But he also outlined a programme of archaeological antiquarianism like Aubrey's, hoping to study barrows, hill-forts and Roman roads,[5] and when he got into the field studying 'things natural and artificial',[6] this part of his project overwhelmed the more traditional part. He showed a combination of interests like Aubrey's, from technology and improvement in the present to change in the past, studying tangible antiquities like barrows, pavements, coins and roads as if they were plants, mines or fossils.[7]

Moreover, though, like Aubrey, he made some efforts towards antiquarianism of a more historical kind,[8] in the chapters 'Of

[1] These are listed on the title-page of 'Στρώματα' in T. G.c.25, 150.

[2] Though Aubrey claimed that Plot's dating of hill-forts by their shape owed something to him (see below, p. 206), the development of his antiquarian interests was evidently independent of Aubrey's. When Plot wrote to Aubrey in February 1675/6 saying that Aubrey's 'Chorographia Antiquaria' sounded from his description of it 'an acceptable thing', he explained that his *Oxfordshire*, which was shortly going to press, included an account of such subjects, while its map, which was already done, had camps and highways delineated on it (MS A 13, 137).

[3] Plot, *Plinius*, 13, and R. T. Gunther *ed., Early Science in Oxford*, XII, 336–7.

[4] Ibid., 344 (Weever only covered London and Canterbury). Cf. the interest in rebuses and ancient inscriptions in Plot, *Plinius*, 12.

[5] Plot, *Plinius*, 12–13, and *Early Science in Oxford*, XII, 341–2. In both prospectuses (ibid., 343, and Plot, *Plinius*, 13) Plot also expressed the hope of supplementing Spelman's *Villare Anglicum* with the British, Roman and Saxon names of places, an interesting parallel to Aubrey's *Interpretation*; but there is no evidence that he carried this out. He also recorded a few old customs: *Oxfordshire*, 200 f.

[6] Plot, *Plinius*, 13.    [7] Cf. Plot in *Analecta*, passim.

[8] Cf. the 'Directions for the Search of Records, and making Use of them, in order to an Historicall Discourse of the Antiquities of Staffordshire' that Sir William Dugdale evidently prepared for Plot's use (*Select Papers chiefly relating to English Antiquities: published from the Originals, in the possession of John Ives* (London, 1773), 34 f.).

Antiquities' in his *Natural Histories* of Oxfordshire and Stafford-
shire, he deliberately wrote about '*things*' to the exclusion of '*persons*
and *actions*'. As he explained in his *Stafford-shire*, 'For Satisfaction
of the *Reader*, upon what terms I add this *Chapter* of *Antiquities* to
my *Natural History*, it seeming to some altogether forraigne to
the purpose: I take leave to acquaint him, before I advance any
further, that I intend not to meddle with *pedigrees* or *descents* either
of *families* or *lands* . . . ; nor of the *antiquities* or *foundations* of
*Religious houses*, or any other pious or Civil performances: it being
indeed my designe in this *Chapter*, to omit, as much as may be, both
*persons* and *actions*, and cheifly apply my self to *things*; and amongst
these too, only of such as are very remote from the present *Age*,
whether found under ground, or whereof there yet remain any foot-
steps above it; such as ancient *Medalls, Ways, Lows, Pavements,
Urns, Monuments* of *Stone, Fortifications, &c.* whether of the ancient
*Britans, Romans, Saxons, Danes,* or *Normans.* Which being all made
and fashioned out of *Natural* things, may as well be brought under a
*Natural History* as any thing of *Art*: so that *this* seems little else
but a continuation of the former *Chapter* ⟨i.e. 'Of Arts'⟩; the subject of *that*, being the *Novel Arts* exercised here in this present
age; and of *this*, the *ancient ones*'.[1]

Among Aubrey's other scientist colleagues who investigated
natural phenomena in the field, several developed antiquarian
interests with a bias towards material relics and oral traditions.
Martin Lister wrote papers on archaeological antiquities that
Aubrey considered 'excellent',[2] as might posterity;[3] he, too, claimed
to study them 'only in the relation they may have to the advancement of Natural Philosophy and Arts'.[4] Others with antiquarian
concerns of this archaeological kind included the Scottish natural
philosopher, Sir Robert Sibbald,[5] John Conyers, a London apothe-
cary, William Musgrave, at one time Secretary to the Royal Society,
and Sir Christopher Wren, whose views on archaeological topics
Aubrey often quoted.[6] Sir John Hoskyns, characteristically enthu-

[1] Plot, *The Natural History of Stafford-shire*, 392. Plot explained that the descents
of families and land were to be dealt with by Walter Chetwynd.

[2] T.G.c.24, 273.

[3] Cf. M. C. W. Hunter, 'The Royal Society and the origins of British archaeology',
*Antiquity* LXV (1971), 114.

[4] *Philosophical Collections* IV (1681/2), 87.

[5] Cf. S. Piggott, 'Antiquarian thought in the sixteenth and seventeenth centuries' in
Levi Fox *ed., English Historical Scholarship*, 112.

[6] On these and other archaeologists who were members of the Royal Society, see

siastic but inactive, told Aubrey in 1670 that his 'Chorographia Antiquaria' was the best thing he had done,[1] and he also echoed Aubrey's interests in advising him not to ignore 'the traditions of the Indigenae, which may give ground to rare conjectures'.[2] Edward Lhwyd (encouraged by Aubrey's friend Edmund Wyld)[3] combined his botany and palaeontology with a study of megalithic remains and the dialect vocabulary of the Celtic languages collected in the field, the materials for his great *Archaeologia Britannica* (1707).[4] Similarly, if less specifically antiquarian, John Ray extended his activities from collecting natural phenomena to include important compilations of proverbs (which he hoped to rationalise and thus extract useful information)[5] and dialect. This, he hoped, would be useful to travellers as well as diverting to the curious[6] and it is symptomatic that he devoted the second half of the book to '*Catalogues* of *English Birds* and *Fishes*: And an Account of the preparing and refining such Metals and Minerals as are gotten in *England*'.[7] Moving further afield, it is interesting that a study of field antiquities was combined with natural history by the only foreign scholar for whom Aubrey showed much concern in his archaeological work, the Danish scholar Olaf Worm—on whose *Danicorum Monumentorum Libri Sex* (1643) he deliberately modelled the title of his *Monumenta Britannica*.[8]

---

Hunter, art. cit. Aubrey quotes Wren in, e.g., MS A 3, 9a; T.G.c.25, 9, 90, 92v, 95v, 96v, 100v, 103, 119, 132, and he recorded some of Wren's London finds in T.G.c.24, 241 f. There is no evidence that Aubrey was seen by the Royal Society as an antiquarian specialist: he spoke at few of the discussions of antiquities recorded in Birch's *History*.

[1] A-W, 17 Nov. 1670, F 39, 128v. Dr William Ball, another scientist friend, had also told Aubrey this.

[2] Hoskyns-Aubrey, 21 Aug. 1672, MS A 12, 204v.

[3] Cf. Lhwyd-Aubrey, 16 Nov. 1693, ibid., 250.

[4] Cf. G. E. Daniel, 'Edward Lhwyd: antiquary and archaeologist', *Welsh History Review* III (1967), 345 f. and F. Emery, *Edward Lhuyd, 1660–1709* (Cardiff, 1971).

[5] *A Collection of English Proverbs* (Cambridge, 1670), e.g. 32 f.: 'Proverbs and Proverbial Observations belonging to Health, Diet and Physick'.

[6] *A Collection of English Words* (London, 1674), A6.

[7] Ibid., title-page. For Aubrey's interest in dialect, cf. MS A 4, 180v, a half-page list of 'Certaine Words used by the Vulgar in Surrey'. Paschall-Aubrey, 2 June 1672, MS A 13, 2, shows that Aubrey suggested to Paschall that he should collect local words not in Skinner's *Etymologicon*; Paschall also offered proverbs for Ray.

[8] At first Aubrey gave this title to 'Templa Druidum': cf. A-W, 22 May 1680, F 39, 340, 'Upon better advisement I have alterd my Title of Monumenta Drydum to Monumenta Britannica'; but by the 1690s he had decided to apply the title to the whole work of

Of course, different scientists had different antiquarian interests, and they applied varying degrees of scepticism and systematic argument to the antiquities they collected, depending on their personal predilections. Ray explained in his *Collection of English Proverbs* that 'all superstitious and groundless Observations of Augury, days, hours and the like I have purposely omitted, because I wish that they were quite erased out of peoples memories, and should be loath to be any way instrumental in transmitting them to posterity'.[1] Lhwyd was as systematic in classifying his linguistic and antiquarian collections as his scientific ones, by contrast with Aubrey, and here, as in his palaeontology, he was less willing to theorise than to observe. He was hesitant even in accepting Aubrey's connection between the stone circles and the Druids,[2] and he criticised the hasty assumptions in some of Plot's antiquarian arguments.[3] For Plot tended to interpret antiquities piecemeal by received ideas as Aubrey often did,[4] and certain other natural historians were still more uncritical, like Charles Leigh, who wrote a *Natural History of Lancashire, Cheshire and the Peak in Derbyshire* (1700).[5] What these scientist antiquaries had in common was not rigour of method—for the quality of their antiquarian deductions varied just as Aubrey's did—but the kind of material that they collected, and the field-work of all of them was undoubtedly influential in forming their antiquarian interests.

## The Shaping of English Antiquarianism

Studies of such subjects did not begin with these authors, but the influence of natural history in the late seventeenth century gave a new emphasis to the collection and interpretation of field antiquities, and in the next century and a half they increased more and

---

which 'Templa Druidum' was the first book. His section on 'Hornes' in the *Monumenta* was greatly indebted to Worm's 'much curious learning' (T.G.c.24, 271v) and he also quotes him in T.G.c.25, 62 and 75 f. ('Sepulchres'). On Worm's influence on English antiquarianism, see Hunter, art. cit., 117; his *Museum Wormianum seu Historia Rerum Rariorum* (1655) was also a popular work in England.

[1] *A Collection of English Proverbs*, A3–A3v.

[2] Cf. F. Emery, *Edward Lhuyd*, 61.

[3] In a marginal note to p. 164 of the Ashmolean copy of Plot's *Oxfordshire* (Ashmole 1722), he denies Plot's assumption that all pots must be Roman, not British.

[4] Hunter, art. cit., 188–9. Similar examples may be found in Plot's notes in *Analecta*.

[5] Hunter, art. cit., 190.

more. Archaeological treatises like Aubrey's, previously almost non-existent, became common in works like William Stukeley's *Itinerarium Curiosum* (1724 and 1776) and his *Stonehenge* (1740) and *Abury* (1743); in articles in the early volumes of *Archaeologia*, published by the Society of Antiquaries from 1770; and in such books as James Douglas' *Nenia Britannica* (1793), Samuel Lysons' excavation reports on Roman sites,[1] and Sir Richard Colt Hoare's *History of Ancient Wiltshire* (1812 and 1819). By the time of Richard Gough's edition of Camden's *Britannia* of 1789, his additions to the book had transformed it into a veritable gazetteer of field antiquities, and Gough stressed how 'the face of the country, and the monuments remaining on it' were as important to the antiquary as written evidence.[2] He also urged attention to popular traditions,[3] and these were collected by a succession of antiquaries from Henry Bourne and John Brand in the eighteenth century to W. J. Thoms, who coined the word 'folk-lore' in the 1840s and who looked forward to the later Victorian enthusiasm for the subject.[4] Such old customs were used with tangible and visual survivals of the past to reconstruct the 'Manners and Customs' of former ages in the popular writings of Joseph Strutt and others, notably his *Complete View of the Dress and Habits* (1796–9) and *The Sports and Pastimes of the People of England* (1801).

At the same time, an increasing concern with architectural history is reflected by the development from collections of engravings of ruins like Francis Grose's *Antiquities of England and Wales* (1773–1789), through the works of authors like Andrew Ducarel,[5] John Carter[6] and Edward King,[7] to the carefully descriptive *Architectural Antiquities* (1807–26) and *Cathedral Antiquities* (1814–37) of John Britton. Just as Strutt's interest in illuminated manuscripts as evidence on such topics as medieval buildings, clothing and armour is wholly unparalleled in earlier scholars like George

---

[1] Lysons published accounts of Woodchester, Bath, Bignor and other Romano-British sites between 1797 and 1820.

[2] *British Topography* (London, 1780), I, xxii.

[3] Ibid., I, xxxvii.

[4] Cf. R. M. Dorson, *The British Folklorists.*

[5] Notably his *Anglo-Norman Antiquities Considered* (1767).

[6] *Specimens of the Ancient Sculpture and Painting now remaining in this Kingdom* (1780–1794); *Views of Ancient Buildings in England* (1786–93); *The Ancient Architecture of England* (1795–1814); *Specimens of Gothic Architecture* (1824); etc.

[7] Notably *Munimenta Antiqua; or Observations on Ancient Castles* (1799–1805).

Hickes,[1] so Britton never ceased to be amazed that former antiquaries could write pages on the manorial history of a parish while
ignoring the best architectural detail of its church.[2] His architectural descriptions of the English cathedrals stand in complete
contrast to a series similarly entitled, published a century before.[3]
For the antiquaries who wrote the earlier works devoted almost all
their space to transcriptions of records and lists of memorials and
dignitaries; their interest in architectural history was so small that
their descriptions of the fabric merely comprised measurements,
lists of furnishings and desultory comments like 'the Body of the
Church consists of a Nave, and two Side-Isles; it is all cover'd
with Lead, and in good Repair'.[4]

There were various stimuli to this growth of archaeological
antiquarianism, which reached its climax with the foundation of a
succession of national and county antiquarian societies in the 1830s
and 1840s,[5] just as the interests and abilities of its practitioners
were as varied as those of the late seventeenth century. The study
of natural history, encouraged by Plot's *Natural History of Oxfordshire* in the seventeenth century and by the steadily growing popularity of the new science in the localities in the eighteenth, was
certainly influential. John Morton included an excellent chapter
on antiquities in his *Natural History of Northamptonshire* (1712),
and William Borlase, who published his important *Antiquities of
Cornwall* in 1754, was meanwhile working towards his *Natural
History of Cornwall*, which appeared in 1758. But here, as in other
fields, ideas developed by scientists in the seventeenth century
became an unconscious part of the intellectual equipment of all,[6]
and numerous other and independent philosophical, sentimental

---

[1] For instance, Hickes' interest in the Bodleian drawing of Dunstan at the feet of
Christ (Auct. F.4.32) was purely palaeographical (*Linguarum Vett. Septrionalium
Thesaurus Grammatico-Criticus et Archaeologicus*, Oxford, 1705, I, 144).

[2] Cf. *Architectural Antiquities*, I (London, 1807), Bb I.

[3] Browne Willis wrote *A Survey of the Cathedrals* (1727–30); he had earlier written
*Surveys* of St. Davids (1717), Landaff (1719), St. Asaph (1720), Bangor (1721). Richard
Rawlinson wrote similar works on Hereford (1717) and on Salisbury Cathedral and Bath
Abbey (1719). Samuel Gale published in 1715 a *History of the Cathedral Church of
Winchester*, supposed to have been begun by Henry Hyde, Earl of Clarendon.

[4] Browne Willis, *A Survey of the Cathedral Church of St. David's* (London, 1717), 2.

[5] Cf. S. Piggott, 'The origins of the English county archaeological societies', *Transactions of the Birmingham Archaeological Society* LXXXVI (1974), 1f. I am indebted to
Professor Piggott for showing me a copy of this article before it was published.

[6] Cf. the case concerning aesthetic ideas argued by M. H. Nicolson in *Mountain Gloom
and Mountain Glory* (Cornell, 1959).

and practical stimuli contributed to shape the enthusiasm.[1] The personal influence of figures like Stukeley and Britton was also considerable,[2] and even that of Aubrey was not entirely unimportant.

For though most of Aubrey's works were unpublished and hardly known in the eighteenth century,[3] and his *Naturall Historie of Wiltshire*, unlike Plot's books, had no following at all, his *Monumenta Britannica*, paradoxically his only major work that is still almost entirely unpublished, was not wholly uninfluential. Aubrey's views on stone circles were widely popularised through the citations of his 'Templa Druidum' in Gibson's edition of Camden's *Britannia*:[4] Lhwyd made it clear in his section that Aubrey, 'for what I can learn, was the first that suspected these Circles for *Temples of the Druids*',[5] and the theory was frequently cited as Aubrey's throughout the eighteenth century.[6] Indeed, in many ways this was Aubrey's most significant contribution to the study of English prehistory, for the effect on English antiquarianism of the association of Druids and megaliths, which he originated, was immense and not entirely salutary.[7] The theory that earthworks could be dated by their shape, which he had pioneered, was likewise common,[8] and Aubrey was also remembered in this connection: in the first volume of *Archaeologia*, Aubrey was identified as the scholar 'who first brought us acquainted with the earliest monuments

---

[1] Cf. K. Clark, *The Gothic Revival* (third edition, London, 1962), S. Piggott, 'Prehistory and the Romantic Movement', *Antiquity* XI (1937), 31 f. and 'The ancestors of Jonathan Oldbuck', ibid., XXIX (1955), 150 f.

[2] See S. Piggott, *William Stukeley*, and J. M. Crook, 'John Britton and the genesis of the Gothic Revival' in J. Summerson *ed.*, *Concerning Architecture*, 98 f.

[3] See 'A Note on Manuscript and Printed Texts of Aubrey's Works'. This includes the *Remaines of Gentilisme*, which apparently had no influence on the development of the study of folk-lore.

[4] E. Gibson *ed.*, *Camden's Britannia* (London, 1695), 81, 108–9, 618, 637.

[5] Ibid., 637.

[6] Toland in 'A Specimen of the Critical History of the Celtic Religion and Learning: containing an Account of the Druids' in his *Miscellaneous Works* (London, 1747), I, 112, claimed that Aubrey was 'the only person I ever then met' when he was at Oxford who realised that stone circles were Druid Temples. The commonness of the knowledge that the theory was Aubrey's is illustrated, for instance, by an eighteenth-century annotation to page 145 (3rd pagination; sig. Ttt) of a copy of Fuller's *History of the Worthies of England* in the Bodleian, Rawlinson Q.c.3 (presumably by Dr John Baron, Master of Balliol, from whose library Hearne bought it): where Fuller quotes Inigo Jones' views on Stonehenge, he notes 'Disalloed by the continu⟨ato⟩r of Camd⟨en's⟩ Britt⟨annia⟩. Mr. Aubrey'. Most eighteenth-century accounts of Aubrey single out the 'Templa Druidum' for mention.

[7] Cf. S. Piggott, *The Druids*; A. L. Owen, *The Famous Druids*.

[8] Cf., for example, Hunter, art. cit., 191.

on the face of the country, the remains of Druidism, and of Roman, Saxon, and Danish fortifications'.[1] Plot, who popularised similar views about hill-forts, may also have owed something to Aubrey's theories.[2]

What is more, his *Monumenta Britannica* was read by many of the most important antiquaries of the century: Stukeley made lengthy notes from a copy of the manuscript owned by Thomas Gale, and indeed it may have been this that first drew his attention to the great monument at Avebury;[3] Gough transcribed the substantial extracts from it made by John Hutchins, the Dorset historian;[4] Britton made a copy of Gough's notes; and Colt Hoare used that and subsequently had access to the original manuscript, which he employed for his *History of Ancient Wiltshire*.[5] One part of the *Monumenta* was even published, the 'Chronologia Architectonica', which was engraved under the auspices of Andrew Ducarel in 1761–2.[6] But although Gough drew attention to it in his *British Topography*,[7] it was not widely known and it had no perceptible influence, for the first work of equal sophistication, Thomas Rickman's *Attempt to Discriminate the Styles of English Architecture* (1817), owed nothing to it.[8] Another of Aubrey's most characteristic

---

[1] *Archaeologia* I (1770), xxiii. It is paraphrased in J. Batteley, *The Antiquities of Richborough and Reculver*, 116n. Gibson's *Camden's Britannia*, 180, cites *Monumenta Britannica* on the likely Danish date of the Trundle owing to its circular form.

[2] In his copy of Plot's *Oxfordshire* (Ashmole 1722), Aubrey noted beside Plot's statement on page 336 that Danish forts were round 'This note the Dr had from J. Aubrey', though of Plot's view that Saxon ones were square he noted ' 'Tis false'; cf.T. G.c.24, 158. But Plot cited other sources in *Oxfordshire*, 334.

[3] Cf. S. Piggott, *William Stukeley*, 44–5.

[4] Bodleian MS Gough Gen. Top. 14, dated 1769. Hutchins' extracts from the *Monumenta* are apparently now preserved as Christ Church Evelyn Collection MS 140, which lacks a title-page. That Gough's transcript was made from this MS is suggested by the fact that Gough has in ink some entries that this has in pencil.

[5] Cf. Britton, *Memoir of John Aubrey*, 88–9. T.G.c.24 is introduced by a life of Aubrey in Colt Hoare's hand and he also made occasional notes. He quotes it at length in *The Ancient History of North Wiltshire* (London, 1819), 57 f. Colt Hoare's notes are now in the library of the Wiltshire Archaeological and Natural History Society at Devizes, as are Britton's (I am indebted to Mr Richard Sandell, the librarian, for this information).

[6] On this edition, for which the engravings were made from a copy of Hutchins' epitome by Francis Perry, see John Nichols, *Literary Anecdotes of the Eighteenth Century* (London, 1812), V, 512–4n, VI, 385; *Literary Illustrations* (London, 1817), I, 821, IV, 631–2. A copy of it is preserved in Cambridge University Library, LE.28.95, with an MS title-page dated 1765. It is said to have been issued as an appendix to Perry's *Series of English Medals* (London, 1762) (Britton, *Architectural Antiquities*, V (London, 1826), 43).

[7] *British Topography*, I, xxv.

[8] The eighteenth-century transcript of the 'Chronologia Architectonica' now preserved

antiquarian writings had already been substantially published, the preface to his *Wiltshire Antiquities*, which appeared in a volume of *Miscellanies* edited by Richard Rawlinson, the topographer and non-juring bishop, in 1714;[1] parts of it were subsequently printed in *The Antiquarian Repertory*, a popularising antiquarian compilation published from 1775 onwards and reprinted in 1807-9.[2]

Except for specific theories like those of megaliths and hill-forts, it is difficult to estimate the importance of all this, and to separate Aubrey's personal influence from the independent development of antiquarian interests like his due to similar stimuli. But, even so, this interweaving of Aubrey's posthumous affairs with the most characteristic products of eighteenth-century antiquarianism has a symbolic significance. It is above all interesting that John Britton, who stands at the climax of the tradition that Aubrey had pioneered, published an excellent life of Aubrey in which he summed him up as a scholar and acclaimed him as the first English archaeologist: 'He may be regarded as essentially an *Archaeologist*, and the first person in this country who fairly deserves the name. Historians, chroniclers, and topographers there had been before his time; but he was the first who devoted his studies and abilities to archaeology, in its various ramifications of architecture, genealogy, palæography, numismatics, heraldry, &c'.[3] He also highly praised Aubrey's 'Chronologia Architectonica' as the earliest attempt of its kind and stressed his originality in studying Avebury and attributing stone circles to the Druids.[4]

It was appropriate that Aubrey should be thus acclaimed, just when the archaeological antiquarianism that he and other scientists of his time had pioneered was being consolidated by the county

---

as MS Aubrey 16 is presumably the one made by Huddesford, referred to in a letter from him to Gough in 1769 in Nichols, *Illustrations*, IV, 478. It is copied from the version in MS A 3, not T.G.c.25.

[1] Rawlinson *ed.*, *Miscellanies on Several Curious Subjects* (London, 1714), 22 f.

[2] *The Antiquarian Repertory* III (London, 1780), 43 f.; second edition, I (London, 1807), 69 f. It was 'taken from the MS Collections'; it is less complete than the version published by Rawlinson, but it has some parts that he had omitted.

[3] Britton, *Memoir of John Aubrey*, 3-4.

[4] Loc. cit. It is perhaps worth noting that when he wrote this Britton did not know of the whereabouts of the original of the *Monumenta* and had only seen Hutchins' epitome (ibid., ix and 89). In fact, it had been bought for the Bodleian in 1836. Britton's interest in Aubrey owed something to the coincidence that both were born in the parish of Kington St Michael; they are commemorated together in a stained-glass window in the church there.

archaeological societies. Britton's peroration greatly impressed reviewers of his *Memoir of John Aubrey*, many of whom echoed it,[1] and to a large extent it can be echoed still. For, though Britton's definition of 'archaeologist' attributed to Aubrey an originality in subjects like genealogy and heraldry that he did not deserve, he was right to see Aubrey as presiding over a refashioning of antiquarianism. Aubrey and the other scientist antiquaries of his time have a real importance in the development of English historiography, because of the new concern with field antiquities that they added to the traditional textual sources of the antiquary. In these terms, it is not too much to attribute the origins of archaeology to the influence of the scientific movement on the study of the past.

[1] Reviews from *The Gloucester Journal*, 3 Jan. 1846, *The Builder*, 23 Aug 1845, and *The Illustrated London News*, 7 Sept. 1845, all making this point, are inserted, among others, in Britton's grangerised copy of his *Memoir* in the library of the Wiltshire Archaeological and Natural History Society at Devizes.

# CHAPTER FOUR

## *The Past and the Future*

Of Ralph Kettell, President of Trinity College, Oxford, in his under-graduate days, Aubrey quoted one of the Fellows that his 'braine was like a *hasty-pudding, where there was memorie, judgement, and phancy all stirred together*. He had all these faculties in great measure, but they were all just so jumbled together. If you had to doe with him, taking him for a foole, you would have found in him great subtilty and reach; *è contra*, if you treated with him as a wise man, you would have mistaken him for a foole'.[1]

It is tempting to apply this dictum to Aubrey himself, who often seems bafflingly inconsistent as an intellectual figure. The most obvious contrast is between the rationalist ideas on education, mathematics and related subjects that he shared with friends like Hobbes, Petty and Locke and his credulous belief in black magic and many other supernatural phenomena. The modern reader is tempted to echo Aubrey's expostulation 'yet they were crafty, subtile merchants', after giving a true account that he had received from his friend Wyld Clarke, a London merchant, of a magical ceremony that he had seen some Jews perform in London; for Clarke assured him 'that they did believe it'.[2]

Equally strange is the contrast between the logical clarity of argument which Aubrey advocated and attained in the best of his antiquarian writings, and his general tendency to accept received and even inconsistent ideas. In Aubrey, paradox follows paradox. He was at once a pioneer of a sense of anachronism and a firm believer in the value of ancient prophecies.[3] His life-long absorp-tion in useful knowledge on practical subjects like agriculture contrasts with the entire unreality of the business affairs of his own life, and even the utilitarian information with which he filled his scientific manuscripts has a faint air of impracticality and remained largely unapplied and therefore of little value. His view that 'Nulla res efficacius multitudinem regit quam superstitio', 'nothing rules the

[1] *B.L.* II, 19.  [2] *Gentilisme*, 237.
[3] Cf. *Miscellanies*, 124 f. On the way in which the growing sense of anachronism worked against such beliefs, cf. K. Thomas, *Religion and the Decline of Magic*, 428–9.

14

mob more efficiently than superstition',[1] and his functionalist, interpreting attitude towards some beliefs contrasts with his own uncritical acceptance of others.

It might have been hoped that the chronology of his works might solve some of these problems, that a 'best' period would precede an 'uncritical' one, or vice versa. This was certainly the view of the eighteenth-century antiquary Thomas Hearne, who praised Aubrey's 'no *inconsiderable Skill*' in antiquities, citing his *Wiltshire Antiquities*, 'which Work tho' *imperfect* and *unfinish'd*, yet evidently shews that he could write well enough upon a Subject to the Study of which he was led by a *Natural Inclination*; and the *World* might have justly expected other *curious* and *useful Notices* of Things from him, both with respect to the *Antiquities* of OXFORD as well as those in his own and other *Counties*, had not he by his *intimate Aquaintance* with Mr. *Ashmole* in his latter Years too much indulg'd his *Fancy*, and wholly addicted himself to the *Whimseys* and *Conceits* of *Astrologers, Sooth-Sayers*, and such like *ignorant* and *superstitious Writers*, which have no *Foundation* in *Nature, Philosophy* or *Reason*'.[2]

There is an element of truth in Hearne's judgement, for Aubrey certainly seems to have taken more interest in astrology and magic in the 1670s than he had before, perhaps due to his uncertain status in the years after his absconding. But there is no evidence that his association with Ashmole was particularly influential on him,[3] and his studies of occult phenomena, with which his astrology and magic naturally fitted, went back at least to 1650.[4] Besides, if there is no evidence of these interests before about 1670, it must also be admitted that there is relatively little evidence for Aubrey's biographical

[1] A-W, 17 Nov. 1670, F 39, 128v. This was a quotation from Curtius: cf. *Analecta*, 216x (in *Gentilisme*, 133, Aubrey identifies it as a saying of Numa Pompilius.).

[2] T. Hearne ed., *The Itinerary of John Leland* (Oxford, 1711), II, 70. Though Hearne presents this opinion as his own, it is in fact based on a letter to him from Thomas Smith of 23 July 1709 (Hearne, *Collections*, II, 226n.): however, Smith does not make the causal connection between Aubrey's occult studies and his association with Ashmole that Hearne does, which further discredits Hearne's opinion.

[3] Cf. above, pp. 22–3.

[4] One of his letters to John Lydall had evidently requested information about apparitions that appeared to the commission for selling Woodstock: cf. Lydall-Aubrey, 11 March 1649/50, MS A 12, 306, and *Miscellanies*, 83–4. The mention in the same letter of the cutting of an oak might conceivably have been connected with the Hamadryades' revenge: cf. above, p. 129. Frank, art. cit. (above, p. 42, n. 4), does not print this, and thus gives a misleading impression of Aubrey's scientific interests at this time.

collecting before Wood enlisted his help in 1667.[1] Yet Aubrey without his characteristic *Brief Lives* is inconceivable, and the attitudes towards collecting and moralising in the *Lives* were as implicit in Aubrey's intellectual development since his childhood as his concern for the supernatural was integral to his system of scientific explanation.

With Aubrey's antiquarianism, there might be thought to be a 'best' period in the 1660s and early 1670s. The impressive inductive reasoning of the 'Templa Druidum' evidently dates from about 1665;[2] he was at work on the 'Chronologia Architectonica' in 1669;[3] the preface to his *Wiltshire Antiquities* is dated 28 April 1670;[4] and he was making the notes that formed the 'Chronologia Graphica' in 1672.[5] Yet in part this was merely because in those years—particularly the years before 1671, when he was working in the field in Wiltshire and then frantically completing his collections, expecting to leave his patrimony—he did more antiquarian work at once than he ever did later. For some of his least sound antiquarian efforts, his inconsistent theories of camps and the section 'Of St Vincents Rocks, and Bristow', date from the same period as well;[6] his misleading notions about 'true Roman Architecture' are apparently earlier still.[7]

Nor is there any evidence that a relatively 'sceptical' attitude to local traditions preceded or followed a more 'credulous' one. Sometimes he erased his first comment accepting a local tradition, replacing it by another more sceptical, but on other occasions he was critical at first and then came to take the information more seriously.[8] So with his science: the surviving evidence will sustain no claim

[1] Cf. above, p. 73.

[2] The date '1665' appears on T.G.c.24, 80, just after Aubrey's excellent 'comparative' dating of the megaliths to the prehistoric period. The prefatory sections ff. 23-6 and 29-30 are undated; the former certainly dates in its present form from the 1690s, as is shown by its citation of Lhwyd's contribution to Gibson's edition of Camden's *Britannia* and Garden's letters to Aubrey, but it incorporates earlier material, some of which can be traced as palimpsests elsewhere in the MS (e.g. f. 39).

[3] Cf. A-W, 7 Aug. 1669, F 39, 123.

[4] MS A 3, 11av.   [5] Cf. above, p. 157, n. 1.

[6] Cf. above, p. 189, n. 1. The section on St Vincent's Rocks incorporates the date 'now [1668]' (T.G.c.24, 138), though other parts of the chapter 'Of Embanking, Drayning & Currents' date from 1675 (ibid., 132).

[7] Caerphilly Castle is described thus in T.G.c.24, 203; this passage is quickly followed by an entry incorporating the date 1656 and it was evidently written then, though recopied later. Cf. above, p. 185.

[8] Cf. above, pp. 168-9, 198 and n. 4.

of significant variations in his approach to supernatural and non-mechanist phenomena, and in general his scientific concerns show a remarkable continuity. He was interested in occult phenomena in 1650,[1] and he was still having mathematical instruments made at the time when he was assembling the contents of the *Miscellanies*.[2] Nor did he ever separate his mystical from his more rational concerns, and concepts like antipathy and the potentialities of physiognomy and astrology are quite seriously treated in his *Idea of Education*.[3]

Aubrey has a unity as an intellectual figure in spite of, or perhaps partly because of, all his superficial inconsistency. There is a unity, above all, in his enthusiasm for almost every kind of learning. 'A professed virtuoso, and always replete with new discoveries' was Roger North's description of Aubrey in his *Lives of the Norths*,[4] and John Evelyn summed him up by noting how his 'Inquisitive Genius' led him to make widespread investigations '& being very Curious to set downe whatsoever he found Remarkable & Extraordinary'.[5] His eagerness amounted almost to eccentricity: Ralph Sheldon, an antiquary friend, was referring to more than Aubrey's stutter when he remarked that Aubrey's 'head is so full that it will not give his tongue leave to utter one word after another',[6] if he was not 'a little crazed'.[7] In the same vein, Anthony Wood found Aubrey 'roving and magotie-headed' and 'exceedingly credulous',[8] though John Toland's view was more generous and more grateful: Aubrey, he considered, 'tho he was extremely superstitious, or seem'd to be so: yet he was a very honest man, and most accurate in his accounts of matters of fact'.[9]

Aubrey's credulity was linked to his omnivorousness as a collector. Just as he was glad to collect information on all sorts of topics, so he was glad to consider all kinds of possibilities. If megaliths, architectural details and biographical anecdotes were worth collect-

---

[1] Cf. the letter from Lydall cited above, p. 210, n. 4.

[2] Cf. above, p. 50, n. 6, and p. 103, n. 5.     [3] Cf. above, pp. 105, 118, 126–7.

[4] A. Jessopp *ed.*, Roger North, *The Lives of the Norths* (London, 1890), I, 374.

[5] Evelyn-Churchill, the Bookseller, 23 Aug. 1693; Evelyn's copy, preserved in his letter-book, Christ Church Evelyn Collection MS 39, no. 685. Evelyn echoed this in his *Numismata* (London, 1697), 208, where he refers to 'Mr. *Aubrie*'s Inquisitive and Laudable Perambulations'.

[6] Sheldon-Wood, 27 May 1679, Wood F 44, 11.

[7] Id., 28 April 1681, ibid., 131. Admittedly he said this after twice meeting Aubrey in the street 'talking to himselfe and passing forward without regarding any body'.

[8] Wood, *Life and Times*, II, 117.     [9] Toland, *Miscellaneous Works*, I, 112.

ing, and could sometimes be used to draw illuminating conclusions that more strait-laced commentators would miss, why might there not also be something in old wives' tales, in sympathetic remedies, in astrological predictions, even in magical incantations? It was typical of Aubrey's intellectual humility, the humility that made him so excellent a research assistant, that he refused to doubt any phenomenon on doctrinaire grounds. Indeed, in this he merely manifested in an extreme form that distrust of the 'Vanity of Dogmatizing' which he shared with many scientist contemporaries.[1] Even his willingness to note down complementary or conflicting explanations of the same phenomenon shows a certain consistency in intellectual attitude, despite some superficial confusion.

Moreover his strength as a gatherer had something to do with his weakness as a writer. 'Had his memorie been greater his judgement had been lesse,' he noted of Robert Sanderson, Bishop of Lincoln, in *Brief Lives*: 'they are like two well-bucketts'.[2] Aubrey was so indefatigable in accumulating that he rarely had leisure to synthesise his collections. The untidiness of many of his writings is remarkable—though few authors would care to be judged, like him, almost exclusively from working papers, which reflect not only his second thoughts but also accidents like the displacement of leaves 'through hast upon my removall from my chamber for the small-pox'.[3] 'I have not time to polish: but I thinke the matter will commend it selfe', he explained even of his *Monumenta Britannica*, which he thought was suitable for publication,[4] and Edmund Gibson was horrified by the manuscript when he saw it in 1694: 'the accounts of things are soe broken and short, the parts soe much disorder'd, and the whole such a mere Rhapsody, that I cannot but wonder how that poor man could entertain any thoughts of a present Impression'.[5] No wonder that Aubrey felt the need for an 'Aristarchus' for this even when it was almost in the press,[6] and his hope that others could help to 'methodize' his notes did not mean that he denied their scholarly value in their own right.

There were certainly weaknesses in Aubrey's intellectual method. In some ways he was happier accumulating information for others to use than in consolidating it himself, and when he wrote he worked

---

[1] Cf. Sprat's view that the Royal Society would vindicate the truth of unlikely phenomena: *History*, 194, 214. See also M. E. Prior, art. cit. (above, p. 142, n. 1).
[2] *B.L.* II, 212.     [3] T.G.c.25, 18v.     [4] A-T, 6 April 1693, T. 25, 30.
[5] Gibson-Tanner, 12 April 1694, T. 25, 134.
[6] Cf. A-W, 5 July 1690 and 29 April 1691, F 39, 405v, 426.

more by suggestion than by definition. He was glad to record, but he tended to be unsystematic; he was fascinated by hypotheses, but he lacked enthusiasm for eliminating some and proving the truth of others. It is revealing to compare his notes on palaeontology and etymology with Lhwyd's, for it would be difficult to find a greater contrast between Lhwyd's combination of careful and systematic collection with hesitant and careful hypotheses[1] and Aubrey's superficial observations leading to hasty, varied and inconsistent conclusions. Equally suggestive is the difference between Aubrey's scientific studies and those of Ray and others like him, and even the contrast between Aubrey's brilliant excursion into palaeography and the methodical studies of Mabillon and Wanley says much about his characteristics as a scholar, his love of imaginatively indicating subjects rather than systematically exploring them.

He was not incapable of occasional more sustained work, as the 'Templa Druidum' and the 'Chronologia Architectonica' show. His respect for the conclusions of scholars like Ray, based on studies like these in fields where Aubrey never began them, proves that he realised that such conclusions based on careful induction were the proper end of all his investigations. It was, however, characteristic of Aubrey that though he occasionally showed that he could attain the logical clarity that he preached when he thought about the techniques proper to scholarship, he only rarely managed to do so. Even when studying megaliths and architecture he did not entirely abandon the conclusions of his predecessors, which he might have eliminated by his novel induction, and elsewhere he hurried on to record fresh possibilities and facts, glad to espouse the theories of others to interpret finds that he did not have time to think about rigorously himself.

But Aubrey was more than a mere collector, a noter of the curious in the manner of eighteenth-century antiquaries. It is true that he collected much miscellaneous information, but this was not the limit of his activity. For his fascination with hypotheses made him constantly collect facts to illustrate particular themes, marshalling his information into chapters and separate treatises which, even when he did not make his aim explicit, show by the limits of their content and by the comments he made in passing what kind of conclusions he hoped to draw. He was interested not only in recording information about the past, but in understanding how it had

[1] Cf. F. Emery, *Edward Lhuyd*.

become the present, and in reconstructing it in all its strangeness. He wished not only to describe natural and supernatural phenomena but to understand how the universe worked, and he went about this by trying to draw up determinist rules about the effect of such phenomena on each other and on man.

There were, on the other hand, many subjects in which he had little interest. He despised the useless learning of the Aristotelian schoolmen; he distrusted religious controversy; he had little time for politics. 'I never medled with Controversy in my Life, nor ever shall,' he told Anthony Wood.[1] What mattered to him was the life-style of man, and as in the present he wanted education to turn out useful and well-balanced citizens, so in biography he sought useful lessons in morality, and in the past he was bored by polemics about institutions and stressed the changes in the way that people lived. This was what mattered, this was 'real' knowledge, and we have seen how even his interest in the past sometimes partook of his anxiety to find out information that could be used in the present. So too, his obsession with the practical application of his scientific studies led him to record endless remedies, spells and inventions and to a boundless faith in man's ingenuity to improve his condition in the present and future.

This faith in the present and the future might seem to conflict with Aubrey's esteem for the past. Sometimes, it is true, the 'veneration' that the 'great Antiquity' of relics 'claimed' in him[2] was neutral: 'me thought the venerableness of them did require a stop and respect,' he wrote of the hill-forts on the Wiltshire downs; 'the prodigious graffes and rampires of the old Encampings seemed justly to claime Admiration in the beholder'.[3] But often, his respect had moralising overtones. He thought that 'the stately remaines of the Abbey of Malmesbury cannot but affect with sadnes, the mind of any ingeniose & good man',[4] and he was always citing evidence about the Middle Ages 'which argues the goodness of that age'.[5]

[1] A-W, 2 April 1681, F 39, 358.
[2] This is paraphrased from Aubrey's description of stag-headed oaks at Woodstock Park that had had no leaves for a century, on the back fly-leaves of his copy of Plot's *Oxfordshire*, Ashmole 1722.
[3] T.G.c.24, 138–9.
[4] A-W, 17 Aug. 1678, F 39, 311.
[5] MS A 10, 110. This was of moral sentences on painted hangings in old houses.

His view of ancient Wiltshire in the preface to his *Wiltshire Anti-quities*[1] gave an idealised view of an old 'Merrie England', with revels and voluntary support of the poor and monasteries—indeed he 'wished monastrys had not been putt downe, that the reformers would have been more moderate as to that point . . . What a pleasure 'twould have been to have travelled from monastery to monastery'.[2]

The enclosures had been for private, not the public good, he considered;[3] he quoted Sir Walter Raleigh on how the bond-servants had become rogues[4] and, noting that the dismemberment of signories had not been allowed in France, thought that 'They better considerd it, then Wee'.[5] In the Middle Ages 'charity did more abound then of later dayes',[6] and he compared the number of law-suits at that time with the increase since to the detriment of the present: 'Attorneys doe encrease, as the Actions doe encrease, and Actions grow more numerous, as men grow worse and worse'.[7] He considered the decent educational facilities provided by monas-teries and nunneries, and, citing Plato 'that the foundation of Gover-ment is the Education of Youth', thought 'by this meanes it is most probable that then was a Golden-age'.[8] Looking back to the good old days when 'they then thought not the noise of the Threshold ill musique',[9] he contrasted the virile gentry with their heirs: 'now the Gentrey of ⟨the⟩ Nation is so effeminated by Coaches, they are so farre from manageing great-horses, that they know not how to ride hunting horses'.[10] 'The pious and publique minded of those dayes'[11] frequently aroused his admiration—like the fourteenth-century poet John Gower, for 'questionlesse he was a pious good Man: as appears by his Writings, wherein is ⟨a⟩ great deale of Morality'[12]—and he thanked Anthony Wood for his 'kindnes stilo veteri, and more *antiquo*', 'in old style and ancient manner'.[13]

By such standards he criticised the morality and piety of his own day. His comedy *The Countrey Revell* was conceived at least partly as an exercise in social criticism, for he thought 'surlinesse & inurbanitie too common in England: Chastise these very severely'.[14]

---

[1] MS A 3, 9 af.    [2] *B.L.* 1, 41.    [3] MS A 3, 9av.    [4] Ibid., 9bv.    [5] Ibid., 9b.
[6] MS A 2, 167. This was partly, he thought, because men's consciences were kept clean by confession.
[7] Ibid., 165.    [8] MS A 3, 11a.    [9] MS A 2, 80.
[10] MS A 3, 9a. This was paraphrased from Thomas Tyndale, Aubrey's old neighbour: cf. above, p. 177, n. 2.
[11] A-W, St Paul's Day 1669, B. 14, 86.    [12] MS A 4, 16.
[13] A-W, 8 Sept. 1680, F 39, 347.
[14] MS A 21, 11v. It should, however, be pointed out that most of the attacks on modern

Through various characters he wished to attack the drunkenness, rudeness and lack of politeness of the county society of his day, which he considered to be 'dregs of the Civill warre'.[1] *The Countrey Revell* is full of the immorality of his contemporaries: he sadly noted how common it was for a young man to have 'his braines & understanding suckt out at his codpiece',[2] whereas in the Middle Ages, 'all things were civill, & without scandall'.[3] 'The piety of those dayes, more then now' seemed to him equally evident:[4] he criticised the excessive anti-Catholic controversy of William Chillingworth and other Caroline divines,[5] the fanaticism of the Puritans, and the low quality of the clergy in his own time.[6] This may well have been one of the themes of his lost work *Hypothesis Ethicorum & Scala Religionis*, which had the alternative title *Religio Naturalis, or a Scale of the decay of the Christian Religion, with a prospect or foresight where it will settle.*[7]

Yet this belief in the moral decline of man since the good old days was paralleled, even in Aubrey's writings on antiquarian topics, by a constant enthusiasm for improvement, which he believed was going on in his own century. Despite the stress in his writings on the effect of the Civil War in destroying antiquities and traditional modes of behaviour, he thought that 'the Civil-wars did mightily refine our Language, Husbandry & Agriculture'.[8] Having noted exotic garden plants available in the sixteenth century he noted 'How far doe wee exceed this now';[9] he knew that 'in our gr⟨and⟩-fathers or gr⟨eat⟩-gr⟨andfathers'⟩ dayes few gent⟨lemen⟩ could write a letter';[10] and concerning the study of philology, he compared 'this searching age' with the previous century, to the advantage of his own.[11] Aesthetically also his sympathy was with his contem-

---

effeminacy were to be made by Sir Eubule Nestor, the old courtier: and, on the other hand, that not all the moderns were degenerate—he was hoping to contrast the 'smooth & generous humour of the brisque & obligeing Cavalier Sir Eglamour' with the individual whom he cited to illustrate the failings he was referring to in the passage quoted in the text, Gwin, the Earl of Oxford's secretary, whose 'sower faces . . . would turne the milke in a faire Ladies breast' (loc. cit.).

[1] Ibid., 13    [2] Ibid., 16v.    [3] MS A 3, 9av.    [4] Ibid., 11a.    [5] MS A 3, 18v.
[6] See above, p. 56.
[7] T.G.c.24, 13v. Cf. Aubrey's view in *Gentilisme*, 133, that if superstition were taken away, 'Atheisme, and (consequently) Libertinisme will certainly come into its sted'.
[8] MS A 2, 83.    [9] Ibid., 51.    [10] MS A 21, 13v.
[11] MS A 11, 5v: concerning an inscription found at Stonehenge in the early sixteenth century which no one could then read, he wrote, ' 'Tis pity, that Mr Lilly nor Sir Th⟨omas⟩ Eliot did not copie-out that illegible Inscription, for Posterity. perhaps in this searching age it might have been understood.'

poraries. ' 'Tis pleasant to see how poetry is since that age advanced,'
he commented on the early Tudor poet John Skelton;[1] Sir Philip
Sidney was 'the reviver of poetry in those darke times, which was
then at a very low ebbe',[2] just as Edmund Waller was 'one of the
first refiners of our English language and poetry'.[3] He could see
little merit in medieval verse: 'As to this Gothique way of Romans,
and attempting to write above Nature, we see what fulsome stuffe
they give us; like Grotesco, with Dogs, and Fishes terminating in
Flowers ... Memorandum Sir John Denham told me, that King
Arthur would be as good a Subject, for a Romance as can be. 'Tis
great pity, that so great and famous a Worthie, should have ever
been abused, either by Monkish verses, or vile painting in an
Ale-house'.[4]

His architectural views were comparable. Gothic was 'the
Barbarous fashion',[5] and he wrote with relief about the classical
revival which had produced Inigo Jones' Banqueting House at
Whitehall, 'so exquisite a piece, that if all the Books of Architecture
were lost, the true art of building might be retrived thence'.[6]
Indeed Aubrey was quite expert on modern architecture and its
rules, making well-informed remarks on recent buildings like
Bishop Morley's additions to Farnham Castle in Surrey, which he
criticised because the windows were not placed exactly above one
another, 'which is not only weake: but offends the eie'.[7] He also
devised a broadsheet expounding *Elements of Architecture*, which he
hoped that young men might 'relish & like, & so fall to the study',[8]
though in fact he never completed or published it. This shows his
familiarity with the standard texts of the classical revival, including
the works of Palladio, Scamozzi and Serlio and Evelyn's translation
of Fréart's *Parallel*,[9] and it illustrates the background to his criticism
of Camden for 'not being acquainted with Architecture'.[10]

---

[1] MS A 4, 48v.   [2] *B.L.* II, 248.   [3] *B.L.* II, 275.

[4] T.G.c.24, 257v. Aubrey's attitude towards romance and his usage of the word are
typical of his period: cf. A. Johnstone, *Enchanted Ground* (London, 1964), ch. VIII.

[5] T.G.c.25, 168.   [6] Ibid., 169.   [7] MS A 4, 148.

[8] A-L, 1 Dec. 1692, A. 1814, 101.

[9] This is now preserved in Ashmole 1819, item 43; it is endorsed 'Let Rob⟨ert⟩
Wiseman goe for the Author of it' (i.e. Aubrey's servant, cf. Powell, *John Aubrey and his
Friends*, 112). It is very incomplete, but it is divided as a chart, with a column for each
of the classical orders; various details are illustrated, as well as plans for rooms, etc., with,
at the bottom, 'Generall Rules', both aesthetic and practical, and a reading list on mathematics and architecture.

[10] T.G.c.25, 168.

Nor was he merely fashionably interested in the achievements of his day. He also aspired to reform. His studies of linguistic survivals never shook his conviction that 'languages are valueable, so much, as the usefulness of good Bookes come to, written in them'.[1] This was the criterion by which he sought to prove that the British language was as significant as any, and it was in his *Interpretation of Villare Anglicanum* that he pointed out that 'to those that are Masters of the Reall Character [& universall Language] all other Languages appeare full of Defects, and æquivocations: for they were made by chance: and we make Rules from the Language; whereas a Language should be made from Rules: e.g. the Universall Language by J⟨ohn⟩ W⟨ilkins⟩ B⟨isho⟩p of Chester'.[2] Aubrey's interest in the diversity of measures in the past, as in the present, arose from his hope to reform them, as he showed in the section 'Measures & Weights' in his *Monumenta Britannica*.[3] He had no nostalgia about the associations of the old measures, quoting a letter of Sir William Petty's bewailing their diversity,[4] and urging uniformity, perhaps using universal measures based on a standard established by the use of a pendulum at the Royal Society.[5] Thus Aubrey hoped to help the poor, although 'what the reason is I cannot tell; but the poor (who are ignorant) are against it'.[6] It is symptomatic that he intended to tack on to the 'Στρώματα', in which his notes on the variety of measures, prices and wages appear, Henry Milbourne's mercantilist discourse on setting the poor to work and a similar paper of Thomas Firmin's,[7] just as in the chapter on 'Falling of Rents' in his *Naturall Historie of Wiltshire* his interest in what had happened in the past joined with schemes for potential remedy in the future.[8]

There is a certain rationale to this view of the relation between present and past, in Aubrey's fusion of artistic and technological aspiration with a backward-looking morality. But, needless to say, Aubrey was not fully consistent in it. Despite his fashionable architectural principles, he sometimes praised Gothic buildings.[9]

---

[1] MS A 5, 21.   [2] Loc. cit.   [3] T.G.c.25, 221vf.

[4] This letter (of 22 Aug. 1685) survives in MS A 13, 103–4.

[5] Cf. Sprat, *History*, 247, 254, 314 and Cope and Jones' references on pages 43 and 45 of their *Notes*.

[6] T.G.c.25, 222.   [7] Cf. T.G.c.24, 13 and T.G.c.25, 151.

[8] MS A 2, 123 f.

[9] For example, the royal palace at Richmond, built by Henry VII was 'after the most exquisite way of architecture of that age; scilicet as Henry the 7th chapell at West-

Though in general he saw the Elizabethan and Jacobean periods as a 'darke time' for science as for other forms of learning,[1] he once wrote of the Elizabethans, 'the old men in those dayes were not so ignorant in philosophy, as the virtuosi forsooth, doe thinke they were'.[2] Moreover he sometimes wrote about the Middle Ages without idealising them, noting that they were 'so infested with robbers & howsebreakers' and admitting that 'those evils' were due to the 'idle lazie life' of noblemen's retainers.[3]

He also sometimes criticised as superstitious the legacy of the Middle Ages. 'When I was a Child (& so before the Civill warres) the fashion was for old woman & maydes to tell fabulous stories nightimes and of Sprights, and walking of Ghosts &c: this was derived downe from mother to Daughter &c: from the Monkish Ballance, which upheld Holy church: for the Divines say, deny spirits, you are an Atheist. When the Warres came & with them Liberty of Conscience, & liberty of Inquisition—the phantômes vanished. Now children feare no such things, having heard not of them, and are not checked with such feares'.[4] In France, he noted, it was the Jesuits, 'clearer sighted than the other Orders', who omitted 'much of the fulsome Superstition and Ceremonies ... as being ridiculous and giving scandall'.[5] As we have seen in Chapter I, there is evidence that Aubrey, for all his respect for medieval piety, had taken his rationalism far enough to distrust traditional forms of religion altogether. His enthusiasm for the '*New* (Cartesian or &c.) *Philosophy*' had evidently led him on to an enthusiasm for the 'new divinity' which his friend Edward Davenant had predicted 'would shortly follow' Cartesianism,[6] and his *Religio Naturalis* was probably, as its title suggests, mainly *avant garde* and rationalist rather than backward-looking.[7]

---

minster' (MS A 4, 203). He also admired King's College Chapel at Cambridge, 'the best Gothick architecture that I doe heare of in the world' (T.G.c.25, 153). His admiration seems to have been confined to the grandest buildings of the Perpendicular style.

[1] Cf. *B.L.* I, 27, II, 141, 162 and MS A 3, 18v, 30
[2] MS A 21, 13. This followed the passage: 'Summer-Watch. V⟨ide⟩ Sir Th⟨omas⟩ Smyth Commonwealth de hoc, cause is, that the blood is then high. keepe downe the Juvenilis impetus'.
[3] MS A 3, 95v.
[4] Ibid., 30. For more statements, of a neutral kind, on the decline of belief in such subjects, cf. *Gentilisme*, 207 and 290.
[5] *Gentilisme*, 130.   [6] *B.L.* I, 201.
[7] Cf. above, pp. 56–8. A clue to its subject-matter is possibly contained in the 'private opinion' of Sir William Davenant quoted by Aubrey in *B.L.* I, 209, 'that Religion

Despite such complications, it is interesting to see how Aubrey combined an admiration for the advancement of learning among his contemporaries with a respect for older times, and it is not surprising that his view of the ancients was equally ambivalent. There were occasions when he was glad to dismiss the ancients as irrelevant to the moderns: he thought the subject of G. P. Maffei's *History of the Indies*, an account of the voyages of discovery, 'much more delightfull than that of any old Classic author',[1] and 'the armada of the Argonautes was but a trifle' to the huge fleet of shipping that George Clifford, Earl of Cumberland, assembled in the 1580s and 1590s.[2] Elsewhere, however, he showed an almost Renaissance respect for classical authors, whose works, like most contemporaries, he read profusely. In his *Designatio de Easton-Piers*,[3] which he compiled in 1669 in the expectation of leaving his birthplace, he used quotations from the Latin poets as more than mere literary conceits, expressing the deep feelings he had in leaving 'this beloved place, where I first drew breathe'.[4] On many occasions contemporary phenomena 'did putt me in mind of' analogues in classical literature,[5] and his *Remaines of Gentilisme*, which he described as 'being observations on Ovid's *Fastorum*',[6] owed something to this attitude, for he would note of a folk-custom that he recorded that it 'seemes to answer' to rituals mentioned in ancient texts.[7]

In the case of Ovid, his respect went further. Not only did he record that his friend Francis Potter had taken the hint of the transfusion of blood from Ovid's story of Medea and Jason[8] in as matter of fact a way as he noted John Evelyn's view that out of such Roman authors on agriculture as Varro, Cato and Columella 'are to be extracted all good Rules of Husbandry'.[9] He also used Ovid as an authority on subjects like the early history of the world. In 'An Hypothesis of the Terraquious Globe' in his *Naturall Historie of Wiltshire*, he attempted, by fitting evidence to Ovid's

---

at last,—e.g. a hundred yeares hence,—would come to settlement, and that in a kind of ingeniose Quakerisme'. It should also be pointed out that there is an eirenic implication in the parallel between Christian and non-Christian rites in his *Remaines of Gentilisme* (cf. Agrippa's views: D. P. Walker, *Spiritual and Demonic Magic*, 94 f.); but Aubrey does not make it explicit.

[1] MS A 10, 23.    [2] *B.L.* I, 176.    [3] MS A 17.
[4] A-W, Easter Tuesday 1670, T. 456a, 9.    [5] MS A 4, 163v. Cf. e.g. ibid., 84v.
[6] Cf. *B.L.* I, 44.    [7] *Gentilisme*, 144.    [8] *B.L.* II, 166.    [9] MS A 2, 85v.

narrative in the *Metamorphoses*, to demonstrate that what he said had actually happened.[1] This was presumably because, like Robert Hooke, on whose ideas it was based,[2] he saw Ovid as the heir through Pythagoras of the most ancient and venerable wisdom of Egyptian and Greek philosophy,[3] though Aubrey never explicitly states this. He also claimed that 'Ovid prophecieth' the manner in which the world would end,[4] and, concerning a light that appeared in the sky at night in 1576, he observed that 'This Phaenomenon must undoubtedly proceed from an Irruption of fire at Mount Hecla so Ovid sayes

> Vidimus Ætnæa Coelum splendescere flammâ
> Suppositus monti quam vomit ore Gigas'

'We have seen the sky glow bright with flame from Ætna, which the giant placed beneath the mountain belches from his mouth', an observation that he considered suitable for the chapter on 'Air' in his *Naturall Historie of Wiltshire*.[5]

This dual attitude towards older ideas, sometimes doubting, sometimes accepting, is typical of Aubrey, and it is found throughout his writings, scientific, antiquarian and educational. A section like that on 'Ethics' in Aubrey's *Idea of Education*[6] is characteristic not only in its blending of the analytic, the imaginative and the practical (he would even have had his boys read plays to learn the 'Mores Hominum', 'the manners of men'), but in its combination of old and new ideas. His recommendations ranged from Aristotle and the ethical textbooks he had had while an undergraduate at Oxford to authors like Hobbes and Pierre Charron, the sixteenth-century French sceptic, and he was typically inconsistent in sometimes quoting Hobbes that 'were it not for the Lawes, that many Men would not make so much a scruple to kill a man, as I or &c: would doe to kill a little Bird'[7] and sometimes accepting traditional criteria of natural justice as 'derived from the Starres' and vouchsafed to those 'who have sweet, even, and Harmonicall soules given them from GOD',[8] referring to 'the Seeds and sparks of

---

[1] MS A 1, 87f.  [2] Cf. above, p. 58, and below, p. 223.  [3] Cf. Hooke, *Works*, 377f.
[4] MS A 1, 101.
[5] R.S. MS 92, 38 (cf. MS A 1, 28v). Cf. T.G.c.25, 131, where he quotes lines from Ovid as a motto for 'Of Embanking, Drayning & Currents' and annotates them with modern instances.
[6] MS A 10, 45 f.  [7] Ibid., 70.  [8] Ibid., 45.

virtue, that lie buried in our Soules'.[1] His blend of the old and the new was not always entirely satisfactory.

Its unsatisfactoriness had something to do with Aubrey's independence as a thinker, the way in which, with an empiricism characteristic of his age, he built his own synthesis in ethics as in other subjects rather than taking anyone else's for granted, combining all sorts of ideas in his own eclectic mixture. Even when Aubrey's ideas were clearly unoriginal, it is not always obvious from exactly what sources they were derived—he often attributes them vaguely to 'the Mineralists', 'the Astrologers' or 'the Historians', and it is doubtful if he could have been more precise himself[2]—and it is not even clear that, in his combination of the original and the unoriginal, he was invariably sure which was which. Yet the acknowledgment of sources was a subject on which he had pronounced views. 'I will owne nothing that is not my owne', he told Wood,[3] and he felt so strongly that his 'Hypothesis of the Terraquious Globe' was based on Hooke's theories that he sometimes referred to it as his—'This Hypothesis is Mr Hookes: I say so: and 'tis the best thing in the Book'.[4] But even this contains material that Aubrey had collected for himself and views on geological topics that he had certainly worked out on his own.[5]

Aubrey was always particularly anxious that justice should be done to the genius of his friend Hooke. 'Mr Wood!', he wrote of Hooke's 'theorie of explaining the coelestial motions mechanically' in his *Attempt to Prove the Motion of the Earth* (1674), which he believed that Newton had plagiarised; 'this is the greatest discovery in nature that ever was since the world's creation. It never was so much as hinted by any man before', and he was eager

---

[1] Ibid., 91. He notes in the margin 'H.C.' (Henry Coley?).

[2] See above, pp. 122, 173.     [3] A-W, 3 Nov. 1680, F 39, 350.

[4] Aubrey's note on a letter to him from Ray of 22 Sept. 1691, MS A 13, 174. Cf. A-W, 13 Feb. 1691/2, F 39, 438.

[5] The 'Hypothesis' represents a somewhat superficial presentation of ideas that Hooke had put forward in lectures to the Royal Society, which were subsequently published as 'Lectures and Discourses of Earthquakes and Subterranean Eruptions' in his *Works*, 277 f. Though Aubrey's ideas on the subject were undoubtedly dominated by Hooke's, he added references to the work of Halley (MS A 1, 88v), Kircher (89), Jorden (97–8), L'Emery (98–9) and Burnet (101); that he had found these out for himself is suggested by his instruction to himself to ask Hooke of Kircher's views 'if this is not a proper Hint for the origination of (most) Springs' (89) (though this somewhat superficial comment does not suggest deep acquaintance with Kircher's encyclopaedic *Mundus Subterraneus* (1678)). His conclusion about the age of the world (see above, p. 59) was certainly his own.

that Wood should 'doe him right' for this and other discoveries.[1] But such anxiety was typical of Aubrey, for he put a high value on originality. When he inserted the theory about winds of Thomas Axe, a Somerset attorney and amateur scientist, into his *Naturall Historie of Wiltshire*, he noted 'Quaere Mr. . . . if this be new? if so, it may stand here',[2] and he harshly criticised John Wallis, the mathematician, for stealing other men's inventions.[3] He was conscious that he could be original himself too. He often made observations 'which, though obvious enough, I doe not remember to have seen in any Booke',[4] recording phenomena 'of which there hath not been any notice taken: but I doe guesse it to be materiall'.[5] We have already seen how he prided himself on the novelty of his archaeological and biographical collections—of *Brief Lives* he knew that '50 yeares hence, it will be a rarity worth it's weight in Gold'[6]— and he was aware that his *Naturall Historie of Wiltshire* was the first work of its kind '(for ought I know) in the Nation'.[7]

But with this awareness of originality went a diffidence about it and about his intellectual activity in general. Though usually he showed no regret about his unconventional education, he occasionally felt sorry for the lack of opportunity that had resulted in his being 'bred ignorant at Eston' and his consequent lack of learning.[8] His instruction to himself to 'quaere the Learned of this'[9] showed more than a mere desire to have particular points of fact elucidated, and throughout his work he reassured himself by quoting the opinions of colleagues even on subjects about which he had perfectly clear ideas himself. His hypotheses, he claimed, were made only 'with humble submission to better judgements',[10] and his faith in his theory that the Druids built stone circles was easily shattered when someone told him that so erudite a scholar as Sir Robert Sibbald backed the Danes,[11] apart from the more anonymous

---

[1] A-W, 15 Sept. 1689, *B.L.* I, 415. Cf. above, p. 83.

[2] R.S. MS 92, 27. Aubrey left blank the name of the person whom he was hoping to consult.

[3] *B.L.* II, 281–2. He did, however, admit that he published some things that would otherwise have been lost.

[4] R.S. MS 92, 40.　　[5] T.G.c.24, 59.　　[6] A-W, 6 Sept. 1680, F 39, 347.

[7] MS A I, 6.　　[8] *B.L.* I, 49 (n.2).　　[9] MS A I, 106v.

[10] T.G.c.24, 25v.

[11] Cf. Garden-Aubrey, 4 May 1694, MS A 12, 133v: a gentleman had told Aubrey at a meeting of the Royal Society that Sibbald claimed that circular monuments in the Orkneys were built by the Danes, and Aubrey had evidently reported this in alarm to Garden; but Garden had turned a good part of Sibbald's *Scotia Illustrata* without

'spightfull' critics who made him anxious for James Garden's help
in bolstering his view in the 1690s.[1]

His diffidence as an author is reflected by the frequency with
which his letters to Wood cite other scholars on the value of his
works—like Locke's, Dugdale's and Hoskyns' admiration of
*Monumenta Britannica*[2]—and we have already seen how he often
discovered his potentialities as a writer only through projects which
he originally undertook as an assistant to others, and how important a catalyst the life that he started as a posthumous duty to
Hobbes proved to his authorship in the 1680s. Even for this 'Life of
Mr Thomas Hobbes of Malmesbury' Aubrey consulted his friends
about what to put in and leave out, and he might well have been less
sure of himself when complaining about Blackbourne's censorship of
his notes if he had not been advised 'to let *all* stand'.[3] Indeed, such
was his lack of confidence that to justify his novel minuteness he
not only cited the opinion of his friends, but added: 'besides I
have precedents of reverend writers to plead, who have in some
lives recited things as triviall', giving John Fell's *Life of Hammond*
(1661) as an example.[4] Similarly, he found solace in precedents in
respectable old authors even for his original antiquarian projects: his
*Interpretation of Villare Anglicanum*, he told Wood, 'some persons
looke upon as a Whimwham: but if it be so, the learned Verstegan
was also liable to that severe censure'.[5]

There is also some evidence that his ambition to be intellectually
respectable tended to detract from the originality of his 'pure
naturall witt, delightfull and easie'.[6] When he considered how a
biography ought to be written he tried to be orthodox, recalling
how 'the writers of the lives of the ancient philosophers used to, in
the first place, to speake of their lineage . . . Why should now that
method be omitted in this *Historiola* of our Malmesbury philosopher?'[7]

---

finding it (there is, indeed, no such claim in the book), and he added 'supposing he had
said so that were not enough to overturn your opinion concerning these monuments'
as if Aubrey had thought it was, and repeated some of the evidence.
  [1] Garden-Aubrey, 6 March 1692/3, MS A 12, 127. Who these were is not clear. A
letter from William Rogers to Aubrey of 19 April 1693 (MS A 13, 183) criticises the
theory.
  [2] Cf. above, pp. 76, 149, n. 4, 200–1.    [3] Cf. above, p. 78.    [4] *B.L.* I, 19.
  [5] A-W, 23 Oct. 1688, T. 456a, 35. Verstegan had argued the value of a knowledge of
old English in understanding nomenclature: cf. above, p. 156, n. 5.
  [6] *B.L.* I, 187: this was Aubrey's description of Corbet's poems.
  [7] *B.L.* I, 322. Cf. his concern about whether details were suitable for publication:
ibid., I, 324, 340.

In the same way, though self-consciously not a 'wit',[1] he occasionally tried to make his works more like theirs by inserting somewhat artificial conceits,[2] or by copying into them passages from eloquent authors like Sir Thomas Browne.[3] In his *Monumenta Britannica* he observed how St Vincent's Rocks at Bristol were 'a subject fit for a Philosopher, Poet or Painter',[4] and, as if to make up for his own limitations as a writer, he inserted an 'ingeniose and florid Poëmation' about the place by his friend William Holder, Dean of Windsor.[5] Moreover his changes in style in revising his texts—for example, from 'Rhetorical Choler' to 'Cholerique Rhetorication'[6]—do not suggest that he was particularly conscious of the literary merits of his concise and effective prose, though his alterations show that he was conscious of its limitations.[7]

Even in his later years Aubrey remained uncertain about presenting his works to the public. He explained in the preface to the *Naturall Historie of Wiltshire* how 'though I have not had leisure to make any considerable proficiency in it; yet I was carried on with a strong Impulse to undertake this Taske, I know not why: unles for my owne particular pleasure ... but I could not rest quiet till I had obey'd this secret Call'.[8] And though he was proud that scientists to whom he showed the work in the 1690s thought highly of it, he still wondered if it would not be better to 'let these memoires lye conceal'd as a Sacred Arcanum'.[9] Although he encouraged admirers to read and copy the *Idea of Education*, he called it on its title-page 'a private Essay only'[10] and was resigned to see it 'coffin'd-up' for posterity.[11] He even told Thomas Tanner that the 'Collectanea of Hermetique Philosophie' which was published in 1696 as

---

[1] Cf. above, p. 79.

[2] For example, the passage in his autobiography under the year 1642 about how 'Bellona thundered ...' (*B.L.* I, 37). These are not, however, very common.

[3] Notably the extracts from *Hydriotaphia* in T.G.c.25, 26 f. The quotations from Browne in ibid., 12 f. and MS A 2, 155 f., however, seem to be valued more for their factual content, and Aubrey's annotations to his copies of Browne's *Hydriotaphia* and *The Garden of Cyrus* (Ashmole D 12) and his *Certain Miscellany Tracts* (Ashmole C 23) suggest that he was mainly interested in information for his own works.

[4] T.G.c.25, 141.     [5] Ibid., 138v. The poem is ff. 139-40.     [6] T.G.c.24, 29.

[7] On this, see the exhaustive discussion in N. P. Barker, 'John Aubrey's *Brief Lives*' (Minnesota Ph.D., 1966), ch. IV. Concerning Aubrey's vocabulary, it is interesting that John Ray remarked on new-coined words he used (Ray-Aubrey, 22 Sept. 1691, MS A 13, 174), and wondered if the wits would allow them (id., 27 Oct. 1691, MS A 1, 13v).

[8] MS A 1, 6. Aubrey replaced 'strong' with 'secret', but I have preferred to retain 'strong'.

[9] Ibid., 21. This was partly due to the offensive nature of some of its information.

[10] MS A 10, 5.     [11] Aubrey-Henley, 27 Feb. 1693/4, ibid., 2.

*Miscellanies* was 'for my owne private divertisement only'.[1] 'We must not be too bold in this censorious age,' he assured Edward Lhwyd, when considering the possibility of publishing the *Adversaria Physica*.[2]

But Aubrey was not only humble about his own merits in comparison with those of his more erudite contemporaries: he was concerned with such questions in general terms. He applied the attention to intellectual ancestry seen in his concern for the achievements of friends like Hooke more generally when he observed with interest that a 'Spanish History' that he had read showed that making salt-water fresh (a subject on which he owned several projecting pamphlets) was not new,[3] or observed that Denshiring, the principal agricultural improvement that he noted in his scientific manuscripts, was merely 'a piece of the old Roman Agriculture revived'.[4] Aubrey mingled an element of doubt in his hopes for the advancement of learning. There were times when he even wondered whether astrology was as hopeful as he had thought: 'It would be of great use if it were only an Allurement to make 'em in love with Mathematiques: as some too severely say Stulta Filia aluit matrem sapientiorem', 'a stupid daughter has nourished a wiser mother', he wrote in his *Idea of Education*. But he reassured himself that 'surely there is good use to be made of it; & it is capable of much improvement'.[5]

So with human learning in general: Lancelot Morehouse, a priest who lived near Aubrey's Wiltshire home, 'a very learned man, and a solid and profound mathematician . . . writt in 4to de Quadratura Circuli; wherein is a great deale of witt and learning; but at last Dr. Davenant (his neighbour) evinced him of his paralogisme. I,' continued Aubrey, 'would have it printed (for it is learnedly donne) to show where and how great witts may erre and be deceived'.[6] At a more humble level, he was fascinated by local traditions partly because ' 'tis a pleasure to consider the Errours that enveloped former ages: as also the present',[7] and he quoted the story of the serpent painted on the wall of the church of Mordiford in Herefordshire, which had four pairs of wings, one of them 'added since my remembrance', 'to shew how apt the World is to be imposd upon, even in things against Nature, and against the Staticks'.[8] He also

---

[1] A-T, 6 Feb. 1693/4, T. 25, 118.　　[2] A-L, 4 Feb. 1692/3, A. 1814, 102.
[3] MS A 1, 89v. On his pamphlets, see above, p. 111, n. 6.　　[4] MS A 2, 82v.
[5] MS A 10, 29c.　　[6] *B.L.* 11, 86.　　[7] *Gentilisme*, 132.　　[8] MS A 1, 132v.

quoted Hobbes' view that when Homer wrote in the tenth book of the *Odyssey* of a town sited at the very spot where night joined day, he knew that it was nonsense 'but had a mind to tell the Learned, how much the Un-learned can believe'.[1]

Yet we have already seen how much of value Aubrey believed that the scholar could learn from old wives' tales and remedies. The humility that he considered proper in intellectual pursuits is seen from the view of William Harvey that he put into the mouth of the character Sowgelder in his play *The Countrey Revell*: 'Why! had he been stiffe proud starcht & retired as other formall Doctors are he had known no more than they. From the meanest person in some way or other, the learnedst may learn something. Pride has been one of the greatest retarders of the Advancement of Learning.'[2] Sowgelder again reflects Aubrey in: 'oh Sir I ride up & downe the Country, and observe things: I have made it my businesse to study mankind these . . . yeares—they that doe not doe soe, their reading will profitt them little. the foundation of lawe & Policy is to be taken from the puris naturalibus ⟨pure natural things⟩ which I dayly converse with.'[3]

'I did not thinke to have found so much knowledge in that Sowgelder,' commented one of the other characters in the play,[4] and the reader may have been surprised to find so much philosophy in Aubrey. For Aubrey, despite his limitations as a scholar, illuminates the modes of thought of his age, proud of the present yet respectful of the past, *avant garde* yet credulous, disdainful of traditional learning yet uncertain in rejecting it. It is, after all, perhaps unfair to criticise Aubrey's ethical views as inconsistent when Hobbes' were too,[5] and mixed ideas like Aubrey's can be found to a greater or lesser extent in almost every thinker of his age.

Equally characteristic was the way in which Aubrey was a pioneer in some fields and a reactionary in others, and this aspect of his period is illustrated by his greatest single contribution to its understanding, *Brief Lives*, many of the subjects of which mixed some interests that looked forward with others that looked back. Francis Potter, Aubrey's close friend, was remarkable not only for his pioneering experiments in blood transfusion, but also for his discovery of the Number of the Beast—at 10 o'clock on 10 December 1625, as he was going upstairs to his chamber, as Aubrey carefully

---

[1] T.G.c.24, 52.　　[2] MS A 21, 15v.　　[3] Loc. cit. The omission is Aubrey's.
[4] Loc. cit.　　[5] See above, p. 19.

noted. And while his experiments were hardly known, his *Interpretation of the Number 666* (1642) was 'twice translated into Latin, into French, and other languages'.[1] William Oughtred, an original mathematician who numbered among his pupils Wallis, Ward, Moore and Wren, was also an astrologer and 'a great lover of chymistry', who thought he had come near to discovering the Philosopher's Stone at the time of his death.[2] Ezerel Tonge, who appears both in Aubrey's *Idea of Education* and in *Brief Lives* as an enlightened educationalist, also left 'two tomes in folio of alchymie' at his death, and, according to Aubrey, 'his excellency lay *there*'.[3] Such men were as characteristic as Aubrey of his Janus-headed age.

But it is not coincidental that the most striking of such cases were older men than Aubrey, and few of the younger scientists in the *Lives* were so confused. Though Aubrey's own mixture of mystical science with more modern views on other subjects still seemed normal enough in his time, in the eighteenth century, as science became a more single-minded and rational discipline, mixed cosmologies like his seemed increasingly strange. To the inscription on the title-page of the copy of his *Miscellanies* that he presented to the Ashmolean, 'ex dono clarissimi Authoris', the word 'superstitiosi' has been added in some anonymous early-eighteenth-century hand,[4] and people were increasingly inclined to put Aubrey down as 'somewhat credulous, and strongly tinctured with superstition',[5] perhaps not least because only the *Miscellanies* and the miscellaneous *Perambulation of Surrey* had been published. Aubrey, it was said, was 'very easy to be imposed upon. . . . he adopted every thing for truth which was in the least tinctured with the marvellous',[6] just as Richard Gough, though admiring Robert Plot's industry as a natural historian, felt that 'the frequent appearances of want of judgement must be ascribed in great measure to the credulous temper of the age he lived in'.[7]

Indeed, there was a tendency to see Aubrey as no more than an ignorant and gullible collector of curious phenomena, who 'thought

---

[1] *B.L.* II, 164.    [2] *B.L.* II, 109.    [3] *B.L.* II, 261.    [4] Ashmole E 11.

[5] *Biographia Britannica* (London, 1747), I, 277. This was an influential work, and this opinion of Aubrey was widely quoted. For a list of earlier biographical writings, see John Britton, *Memoir of John Aubrey*, vii–viii.

[6] John Hutchins, *The History and Antiquities of the County of Dorset* (second edition, *ed.* R. Gough and J. B. Nichols, London, 1803), II, 150n. This remark does not appear in the first edition (London, 1774; I, 453).

[7] Gough, *British Topography*, I, xix.

little, believed much, and confused every thing',[1] an impression which, for some at least, was only confirmed by the partial publication in the early nineteenth century of the *Remaines of Gentilisme, Brief Lives* and the *Naturall Historie of Wiltshire*,[2] which could be seen as mere compendiums of curious information quaintly told. Such evaluations at least had a certain consistency, but they raised problems for scholars in the late eighteenth and early nineteenth centuries who admired the novelty of Aubrey's archaeological work and the accuracy and detail of his biographical collections, for these felt bound to erect a dichotomy in Aubrey's intellectual attitudes. Edmund Malone, the great Shakespeare scholar, who thought highly of *Brief Lives* and hoped to publish them,[3] felt that 'however fantastical Aubrey may have been on the subject of chemistry and ghosts, his character for veracity has never been impeached',[4] and John Britton's view is even more revealing. For when Britton looked back to Aubrey from his 'present times of political, literary, and scientific high-pressure power', he was able to admire him almost as an equal, 'for he evidently possessed that element of sympathy for art and nature which is the germ of greatness', separating this from Aubrey's participation in the 'appalling and degrading fanaticism, with the frivolous superstition' of his age.[5]

Yet the arbitrariness of such distinctions is revealed by Britton's contemporary, the popular author Charles Knight, for he separated some aspects of *Brief Lives* from others; though he valued some of what Aubrey recorded, 'the Boswell of the first coffee-houses', there were parts he refused to accept, for 'I will not believe Aubrey when he deprecates those whom history loves'.[6] Appropriately, it was Lytton Strachey, that irreverent enthusiast for the intimate style of biography that Aubrey had pioneered, who, a century later, wrote the best short appreciation of Aubrey in his wholeness. 'It would be

---

[1] W. Gifford *ed.*, *The Works of Ben Jonson* (London, 1816), I, xxn. Cf. also I, clxxxiiin.

[2] See 'A Note on Manuscript and Printed Texts of Aubrey's Works'.

[3] Cf. M. Hunter, 'The bibliography of John Aubrey's *Brief Lives*', *Antiquarian Book Monthly Review*, I (February 1974), 7.

[4] Malone *ed.*, *The Plays and Poems of William Shakespeare* (London, 1790), I part 2, 168. Opinions on the value of the lives have ranged between Malone's acceptance and Gifford's rejection ever since: there are still those who are prepared to dismiss them as 'second-hand gossip' (T. G. Barnes, *Somerset 1625–1640* (Oxford, 1961), 341).

[5] *Memoir of John Aubrey*, 124. These sentiments are echoed in the preface and notes to Britton's edition of the *Naturall Historie of Wiltshire* (1847).

[6] C. Knight, 'John Aubrey, and his Eminent Men' in *Once upon a Time* (London, 1854), I, 311–12.

an error to dismiss Aubrey as a mere superstitious trifler,' he wrote; 'he was something more interesting than that': for Aubrey's ability both to admire Newton and to practise astrology was itself an important symptom of 'a curious twilight period—a period of gestation and preparation, confused, and only dimly conscious of the end towards which it was moving'.[1]

The appeal of Aubrey is not only that of the biographer who shows that 'the best of men are but men at the best':[2] as an intellectual of his age his role is equally revealing. For he illustrates a moment in intellectual history when old certainties were no longer certain and new ones not yet formed, when novelty was at a premium yet the past was a solace against the doubt and dissension of the present. Aubrey made his own perplexed combination of scepticism and credulity, of hope and fear, of debts to the past and bequests to the future. But, not least in the brave empiricism with which he went about it, he illustrates perhaps better than anyone the contradictions, aspirations and failings of his 'searching age'.[3]

---

[1] 'John Aubrey' in *Portraits in Miniature* (London, 1931), 23–4, 19. Cf. also G. M. Young's delightful essay 'The Man Who Noticed' in *Last Essays* (London, 1950), 248 f.
[2] Cf. above, p. 152.    [3] Cf. above, p. 217.

# A NOTE ON MANUSCRIPT AND PRINTED TEXTS
# OF AUBREY'S WORKS

The history of the publication, non-publication and inadequate publication of Aubrey's writings is rather complicated. Though only a few still remain entirely unpublished, there are reliable editions of even fewer, and I have used the original manuscripts of several works of which printed editions exist. I have only used printed texts when satisfied that they omit only the most trivial matter from the manuscripts on which they are based. Whenever it was necessary to consult the manuscript to ensure that none of Aubrey's text was ignored or misunderstood, I have preferred, for the sake of consistency, to use the manuscript throughout rather than to give references to the printed edition for those parts of the work that were reproduced adequately and to the manuscript only for those parts that were not. What I shall do here, therefore, is to go through Aubrey's writings in the order in which they were first made generally available to the reading public, explaining which editions I have used and which I have ignored, and why.

The *Miscellanies* was published in 1696. A second edition came out in 1721, incorporating the author's additions and corrections,[1] and I have used this; the manuscript of this work does not survive.[2]

*A Perambulation of Surrey* was rearranged, enlarged and published in 1718 by Richard Rawlinson as *The Natural History and Antiquities of the County of Surrey*.[3] Since Rawlinson omitted some of Aubrey's text and since it is often difficult to disentangle Aubrey's original from Rawlinson's additions, I have preferred to use the original manuscript of this work, Bodleian MS Aubrey 4.

Aubrey's *Brief Lives* were first substantially published in 1813 in a compilation entitled *Letters written by Eminent Persons in the Seventeenth and Eighteenth Centuries* . . . .[4] They were subsequently edited

---

[1] Cf. *T.P.W.*, 371–2.  [2] Cf. above, p. 91, n. 2.

[3] See B. J. Enright, 'Richard Rawlinson and the publication of Aubrey's "Natural History and Antiquities of Surrey",' *Surrey Archaeological Collections* LIV (1956), 124 f.

[4] An earlier edition by James Caulfield, *The Oxford Cabinet* (1797), was terminated when he was forbidden access to the Aubrey manuscripts in the Ashmolean at the behest of Edmund Malone: cf. M. Hunter, 'The bibliography of John Aubrey's *Brief Lives*', *Antiquarian Book Monthly Review* I (February, 1974), 6 f.

by Andrew Clark in an excellent edition, published by the Clarendon Press in 1898, and I have used this here for the contents of Bodleian MSS Aubrey 6, 7, 8 and 9, the manuscripts of the *Lives*.[1] Clark rearranged the material to some extent, and he altered punctuation and capitalisation, but neither is a serious difficulty. More important is his omission of a few passages which he considered indecent, but I have not had occasion to use any of these in this book.[2] Though Clark included extracts from Aubrey's *Countrey Revell* and other papers in Bodleian MS Aubrey 21, from his *Collectio Geniturarum* (Bodleian MS Aubrey 23) and from his *Faber Fortunæ* (Bodleian MS Aubrey 26), his use of these was partial, and in each case I have always referred to the original manuscript. Clark also used material from Aubrey's letters to Wood, but again he was selective, and therefore I have given all my citations to the originals in the Ballard, Tanner and Wood collections in the Bodleian.

John Britton published an edition of *The Naturall Historie of Wiltshire* in 1847, which has recently been reprinted. But Britton was highly selective, for he was mainly interested in curious facts about old Wiltshire, dismissing many of Aubrey's ideas as 'comparatively obsolete',[3] and much of the text remains unprinted. For most of the work, I have therefore used Bodleian MSS Aubrey 1 and 2, Aubrey's holograph manuscript, which incorporates his latest additions and which was annotated by his friends. However, as I explained above,[4] at the end of his life Aubrey removed parts from this, including most of the chapter on 'Air', and for these sections I have used the copy of the work made for the Royal Society in 1690-1 by B. G. Cramer, which is now Royal Society MS 92.

The *Wiltshire Antiquities* were edited by Canon J. E. Jackson in 1862 as *Wiltshire. The Topographical Collections of John Aubrey*.[5] Though Jackson's edition is generally reliable, it has some important

---

[1] I have also used Clark as my source for a few leaves in Aubrey's hand among the Rawlinson manuscripts in the Bodleian. The popular editions of John Collier, Oliver Lawson Dick and Anthony Powell add nothing to Clark, except for the salacious stories which he bowdlerised.

[2] Clark generally indicates when he has made such omissions; there are very few omissions which he does not indicate (for an example, cf. above p. 175, n. 2).

[3] John Britton *ed.*, *The Natural History of Wiltshire* (London, 1847, reprinted Newton Abbot, 1969), iii. Sir Thomas Phillipps' proposed edition of the work got no further than a twelve-page specimen. The preface had already been printed in Rawlinson's edition of Aubrey's *Surrey*, v, 403 f.

[4] See pp. 102, n. 5, 103.

[5] Sir Thomas Phillipps had earlier published two sections of the work, in 1828 and 1838, but he never completed it.

omissions, including the 'Chronologia Architectonica', the 'Fabulæ Aniles' and parts of the preface.[1] I have therefore used the manuscript of this work, Bodleian MS Aubrey 3.

The *Remaines of Gentilisme and Judaisme* was first properly published by James Britten for the Folk-lore Society in 1881.[2] Britten presented the work exactly as it appears in British Library MS Lansdowne 231, whereas John Buchanan-Brown, who has recently re-edited it in his edition of *Three Prose Works* of Aubrey (1972), has rearranged the material in a more systematic form. He has also distinguished the work of Aubrey from the annotations of early readers of the manuscript more clearly than Britten did, and I have therefore used his edition.[3] Though it regrettably has a number of typographical errors, Mr Buchanan-Brown has very kindly eliminated these from my quotations in this book by collating my typescript with the original manuscript.

*An Idea of Education of Young Gentlemen* remained unpublished until 1972, when it was printed by J. E. Stephens. Unfortunately, however, this edition is extremely unsatisfactory,[4] and I have therefore not used it here, giving all my references to Bodleian MS Aubrey 10.[5]

Henry Oldenburg's copies of the scientific papers by Aubrey that were read at the Royal Society, preserved among the Society's Classified Papers, were published by John Buchanan-Brown as *Observations* in his edition of *Three Prose Works* (1972), and for them I have used this edition.

The rest of Aubrey's works are almost entirely unpublished, including his *Monumenta Britannica*,[6] though I understand that Professor Richard Atkinson of Cardiff University has a critical edition in hand; the manuscript of this work is Bodleian Top.Gen.c.

---

[1] This had already been substantially published. See above, p. 207.

[2] Extracts had already been published in H. Ellis *ed.*, J. Brand, *Observations on Popular Antiquities* (1813), in *Time's Telescope for 1826* and in W. J. Thoms *ed.*, *Anecdotes and Traditions* (Camden Society, 1839), 80 f.

[3] There are a few very trivial omissions. Cf. above, p. 169, n. 11, for an example.

[4] See my review in *Journal of Educational Administration and History* VI (1974), 61.

[5] I have also used the text in MS A 10 of Aubrey's earlier educational work, *Idea Filioli seu Educatio Pueri*.

[6] Apart from short extracts relating to particular antiquities, the following sections have been published: the 'Chronologia Architectonica', published in 1761–2 (see above, p. 206), and the preface to 'Templa Druidum' with the description of Avebury, partly printed by Colt Hoare (see p. 206, n. 5), and more fully in *Wiltshire Archaeological and Natural History Magazine* IV (1858), 311 f. and VII (1862), 224 f. and in Jackson's edition of the *Wiltshire Antiquities*, 314 f.

24–5. *An Interpretation of Villare Anglicanum* is Bodleian MS Aubrey 5; the *Designatio de Easton-Piers* is Bodleian MS Aubrey 17; Aubrey's transcription of the *Clavicula Salomonis*, with his additional magical notes, is Bodleian MS Aubrey 24; his *Elements of Architecture* is item 43 of Bodleian MS Ashmole 1819. I should also point out here that I have used throughout the original manuscript of the collection of letters to Aubrey now preserved as Bodleian MSS Aubrey 12–13, though some have been published.[1] These and Aubrey's other manuscripts in the Bodleian are described in the *Summary Catalogue of Western Manuscripts in the Bodleian Library at Oxford*.[2] Aubrey's mathematical manuscripts at Worcester College, Oxford, are described above.[3] Other manuscript sources, including Aubrey's letters to his friends surviving in collections in the Bodleian, the British Library and elsewhere, have been referred to piecemeal in the notes.

[1] Notably the letters from Ray printed in R. W. T. Gunther *ed., Further Correspondence of John Ray* (Ray Society, 1928), 156 f., and the letters from Garden printed in C. A. Gordon, *ed. cit.* (p. 161, n. 11).

[2] Cf. vols II part 2 (Oxford, 1937), 1093, 1138 (but this entry is unfortunately inaccurate concerning the contents of this copy and the authorship and whereabouts of the Royal Society's), 1151, 1157; and v (Oxford, 1905), 103 f., 449–50.

[3] See above, p. 49, n. 1.

# A NOTE ON *ANALECTA*

Aubrey's *Adversaria Physica* is lost, but two recent discoveries have made possible its partial reconstruction. In 1972 John Buchanan-Brown published, among the material transcribed by Henry Oldenburg from Aubrey's scientific papers, some notes to which he gave the title 'Adversaria Physica', which are clearly derived from the lost book.[1] Meanwhile, I had discovered in the Bodleian another source which provides further evidence of the content of this lost work, and since the importance of this text for the study of Aubrey has not hitherto been recognised, I shall give a full account of it here. The item in question is Bodleian MS Hearne's Diaries 158–9, a transcript made by Thomas Hearne in the late 1720s of a manuscript volume of notes on natural history by Robert Plot, entitled *Analecta Ro⟨berti⟩ Plot*, which is now lost. Hearne even notes misspellings and changes in handwriting, and his copy may therefore be presumed to be extremely reliable.[2]

Pages 198 f. comprise a long series of notes entitled 'Extracts out of Mr Aubrey's booke', which Hearne indicates (by underlining) are in a different hand from Plot's normal one. Earlier in the manuscript, a number of other notes (arranged by county with other material) are also underlined, and these were also clearly copied from notes by Aubrey. At first Hearne thought that this different hand was Aubrey's,[3] but he later realised that the only part actually in Aubrey's hand was a letter from him to Plot that Plot had inserted into the manuscript:[4] instead one can only suppose that Plot used a special facsimile hand for his extracts from Aubrey, or that he employed an amanuensis—the first half page of the sustained 'Extracts' are not underlined, and these were perhaps copied by Plot himself before handing the task over to an assistant.

[1] Cf. *T.P.W.*, 336 f. and 454 f.
[2] The two volumes are paginated consecutively, but there are two errors of pagination: 202–21 are repeated and the second series has an 'X' added in the MS; 171–80 are also repeated, and, although the error is not corrected in the text, I have added an 'X' to denote the second series (the error in fact originated at page 140, but Hearne corrected it up to the end of the first volume (the first page 180), and I have used his second pagination for those leaves).
[3] *Analecta*, 48.    [4] Ibid., 180x–181.

237

There can be no doubt that the 'Extracts out of Mr Aubrey's booke' are from Aubrey's lost *Adversaria Physica*. They were probably all copied in 1675/6, when Plot borrowed Aubrey's 'booke',[1] since none of the dated references is later than that. There is considerable overlap with the notes by Oldenburg printed by John Buchanan-Brown as 'Adversaria Physica' in *Three Prose Works*, but the material here is in a different order and it is fuller. Where they overlap, I have preferred to use Plot's fuller transcript rather than Oldenburg's. Both Oldenburg's and Plot's transcripts may have been quite selective, since in a letter to Lhwyd of 4 Feb. 1692/3 Aubrey told him that the *Adversaria* was by then 'fol⟨io⟩ an inch thick',[2] but nothing now survives of the *Adversaria* except these transcripts, unless pages from an earlier manuscript inserted into the *Naturall Historie of Wiltshire*, which are less specifically devoted to Wiltshire,[3] derive from it.

The underlined material arranged topographically among Plot's notes before page 198 is probably partly copied from the *Adversaria Physica* and partly from the notes that Aubrey wrote out for Plot in 1675 on Wiltshire, Surrey and other counties, 'Ten sheetes closely written and shall send him more':[4] at times, Aubrey actually addresses the recipient of the notes in phrases like 'as in the paper presented to you'.[5] Plot evidently copied this material into his notes (or had it copied) under its respective counties: in his manuscript, a certain amount of space was probably allocated to each county which he filled up as material came along.[6] That these notes are consciously separate from the 'Extracts' is suggested by such cross-references as 'vide the extracts out of Mr Aubrey's booke',[7] or 'vid⟨e⟩ Somerset & the Extracts',[8] or (in the 'Extracts') 'vide Com⟨itatum⟩ Wilts'.[9]

All quotations from *Analecta* are from the sections copied from Aubrey's writings, unless otherwise stated.

---

[1] Cf. Plot-Aubrey, Feb. 1675/6, MS A 13, 137.　　[2] A. 1814, 102.
[3] E.g. MS A 1, 158.　　[4] A-W, Twelfeday 1675/6, B. 14, 116.
[5] *Analecta*, 178.　　[6] E.g. at page 174 he refers to events in 1695.　　[7] Ibid., 180.
[8] Ibid., 95.　　[9] Ibid., 256.

# AUBREY'S LOST WORKS

Aubrey drew up a list of his works at the request of Edward Lhwyd in 1692,[1] and this mentions a number which no longer survive. One is the *Adversaria Physica*, but this can fortunately be partly reconstructed.[2] Another is the *Hypothesis Ethicorum & Scala Religionis*, on the likely theme and content of which I have speculated in the text.[3] Also included in the list is *A Collection of Approved Receipts*, which Patricia Owen assumed to be Bodleian MS Aubrey 19, a seventeenth-century recipe book with no apparent connection with Aubrey.[4] But in his *Naturall Historie of Wiltshire* Aubrey notes at one point 'see in my Booke of Receipts. pag ⟨inam⟩ 98. [now with Mr Ant⟨hony⟩ Wood.]',[5] and since MS Aubrey 19 has only thirty-eight leaves, this cannot refer to that and presumably concerns some lost manuscript. There is, however, no evidence as to its likely content.

Another work included in the list that is now lost is Aubrey's *Villa. or a Description of the Prospects from Easton-Piers*, which he coupled with 'Easton-Piers-delineated' (ie., *Designatio de Easton-Piers* now Bodleian MS Aubrey 17) as 'nugae', 'trifles'.[6] In a letter to Wood of 15 August 1682 Aubrey describes it as 'a *trifle of mine* writt 1671 in my solitude at Sir R Henleys in Hants & among the Beeches, being a Description (13 or 14 sh⟨eets⟩) in verse & prose 30 miles round Easton viz: within the Prospect'.[7] It was evidently a literary companion to the *Designatio de Easton-Piers* (though it is confusing that that, too, is entitled 'Villa' on f.2). Aubrey also mentions in a letter to Wood of 8 November 1692 his 'verses of the Robin-red-breast'; 'I should be very sorry to have it lost,' he wrote, and he wanted it to be pinned into his *Villa*.[8] Since, despite Aubrey's anxiety, these verses do not survive, they were presumably attached to the description in verse and prose rather than to the *Designatio*.

---

[1] MS A 5, 123v.  [2] See 'A Note on *Analecta*'.  [3] Especially pp. 56–8, 217, 220.
[4] P. Owen, 'A Revaluation of the Writings of John Aubrey' (Oxford B. Litt., 1954), 75.
[5] MS A 1, 117. He subsequently erased the bracketed phrase.
[6] MS A 5, 123v.  [7] F 39, 369v.  [8] F 39, 437.

The only clue to the possible content of this lost literary work is provided by some notes on an old document used for mathematical calculations in Worcester College MS 5.4,[1] which are evidently related to some literary composition associated with the Wiltshire countryside. They are hastily written, and have subsequently been scored through. Apart from the reference to Bacon through Ralph Austen, quoted on page 95 (which, since he intended it for his 'Chorographia Antiquaria', also has local associations), the content of the page is as follows. In one corner is this passage:

'In such fine solitude as these shades the Muses wont[2] in vision to appeare to their *worshippers*, of good mind, & free from worldly cares & sometimes with a . . .[3] divine, to impart to their Bards some glimpse of Prophecy: to build in the mans phancy, magnif⟨icent⟩[4] castles, palaces, gardins &c: describe stories (?) &c: make things past to be present, & present past: raise up the old Hero's long since dead & gon, & (but for them) forgott had been. Bring their absent Mistrisses to them, & with quaint metaphors curle once again their curld hair again.[5] dresse them in antique habits, with antique crownes ⟨illegible⟩ of Sun beames. and with such curiositie as a watch-maker takes a watch to pieces, so they there Loves, —— & describe 'em. with ⟨sun⟩ and ⟨stars⟩ &c:'[6]

This is slightly reminiscent of the passage in the chapter on 'The Downes' in Aubrey's *Naturall Historie of Wiltshire* about how ''Twas about these purlieu's that the Muses were wont to appeare to Sir Philip Sydney'.[7] Opposite this is the following:

'Monkes at Bradstock abbey skilld in Astrology Geomancy & Arsmetrie contained in old MSS & had old astrolabes & Instruments, of old confuted projection. with old fashion Arabique characters / Alchymists.'

Further down the page, after the quotation 'mine enemy sharpeneth his eyes upon me' from *Job* 16.9, is this:[8]

---

[1] Unpaginated; it is the third leaf after the title-page 'Algebra Literalis'.

[2] Substituted for 'ought'.     [3] Aubrey's gap.     [4] Duplicated with 'stately'.

[5] I have left this phrase as it is, although there is a lacuna in the sense due to Aubrey's originally writing 'curle once again their curld hair', then realising he had repeated 'curle' and therefore rewriting the latter part of the passage as '... their curld hair again' without changing the earlier part, except for erasing the first 'again'.

[6] Here (and below) Aubrey uses the symbol ⊙ for the 'sun' and ✳ for 'stars'.

[7] MS A 2, 112.

[8] Above the quotation from Job is a word beginning with Φ which I have not been able to read.

'The Larke like the Jacks of the clock howse at Wells, as soon as ever the ⟨sun⟩ comes to such a degree—gives warning.

'⟨Sun⟩rise—then the pretty flowers begin to lift up ther heads & to open their eies. his leaves he displaies she casts abroad her (?) rais (?).'

And in the very corner of the page is the following couplet, confirming the suspicion that at least some of these notes are connected with some lost verses; it might be part of a stanza about sunset related to the sentences about sunrise just quoted:

'downe he sinkes
the marigold she winkes'.

Such hints are the only evidence concerning this lost work on Wiltshire, and equally frustrating is a single reference to a play that Aubrey wrote which has also not survived. In a letter to Wood of 26 October 1671,[1] Aubrey wrote 'I am writing of a Comedy for Th⟨omas⟩ Shadwell. which I have now almost finished since I came here, et quorum pars magna fuis⟨ti⟩ ⟨and in which you played a great part⟩. & I shall fitt him with another the Countrey Revell: both humours untoucht, which I in my tumbling up & downe have collected', and, referring to *The Countrey Revell*, he added between the lines 'but of this Mum. for tis very satyricall again some of my mischievous enemies'. This brief mention is all that is known of the lost play.

Lastly, in some ways the most regrettable loss of all is that of Liber B of the *Wiltshire Antiquities*. Some idea of its content can be gained from Aubrey's references to it in other places. He sometimes refers to it, with Liber A, as 'my two volumnes of Antiquities of Wilts A & B',[2] and it was presumably because it contained much antiquarian information on Wiltshire that William Aubrey borrowed it from the Ashmolean in 1703.[3] It is slightly puzzling, however, that the references in Liber A and Aubrey's letters to information that it contained do not suggest that the two volumes were geographically complementary. It was possibly a more miscellaneous volume: among its contents were the pastorals by George Ferraby that Aubrey used in his *Naturall Historie of Wiltshire*[4] and 'a Table of Blazon 10 severall wayes in halfe a sheet of paper'

---

[1] F 39, 141v.  [2] A-W, 17 Aug. 1685, F 39, 375.  [3] Cf. above, p. 91.
[4] A-W, 9 Aug. 1671, F 39, 136. cf. MS A 2, 119 f.

by Thomas Gore;[1] it may also have contained notes on old corn prices.[2] It was clearly more wide-ranging geographically than Liber A: some notes in *Monumenta Britannica* show that it included material on Corfe Castle, Woodstock, St Albans and other places;[3] it also had Gore's notes on coats of arms in a house at Fairford[4] and information on Christ Church, Oxford.[5]

Most interestingly of all, it seems to have contained biographical material. In it were the notes on Gorhambury that Aubrey made in 1656,[6] descriptions of funerary monuments in Montgomeryshire,[7] details of the interment of Selden[8] and 'the Epitaph &c: of Dr. W. Harveys life'.[9] It also had a note on the supposed burial of Sir John Mandeville at St Albans,[10] and in a letter to Wood of 29 November 1673[11] Aubrey refers to verses under a picture of Richard Martin[12] 'which Tho⟨mas⟩ Gore lost out of my booke of Wilts'. It seems likely that it was the repository of such biographical notes as Aubrey kept before he began *Brief Lives*.

[1] A-W, 21 June 1681, F 39 354v.      [2] Cf. above, p. 157, n. 3.      [3] T.G.c.25, IV.
[4] Wood, *Life and Times*, II, 407.
[5] Wood, *Antiquities of the City of Oxford*, II (Oxford, 1890), 177; cf. MS A 3, 133.
[6] *B.L.* I, 393–4.      [7] *B.L.* I, 307, 313.      [8] A-W, 7 April 1673, F 39, 199.
[9] A-W, 2 July 1674, B. 14, 103.
[10] *B.L.* II, 42–3, which almost implies that it contained notes on the burial places of the famous.
[11] F 39, 237v.      [12] Cf. *B.L.* II, 47 f.

As has already been mentioned, Aubrey gave many books to public libraries during his life-time. His gifts to the Royal Society from 1670 onwards have been exhaustively studied by John Buchanan-Brown in 'The books presented to the Royal Society by John Aubrey, F.R.S.', *Notes and Records of the Royal Society*, XXVIII, (1974), 167 f.

Aubrey presented a few books to the 'public library' at Oxford. In a letter to Aubrey of 6 March 1674/5, George Ent mentioned the reception into the Bodleian of two volumes of Aubrey's, his copy of *Mercurius Pragmaticus* and 'your Italian book'[1] (i.e. *Li Tre Trattati di Messer Mattia Giegher Bavaro di Mosburc* (Padua, 1639) bound with *La Scherma di Francesco Fer° Alfieri* (Padua, 1640)): these are now class-marked 4° v 1 Art and 4° v 2 Art respectively.[2] Aubrey frequently mentioned these books and his intention to present them to some library in his letters to Wood in the early 1670s. Ent also presented other books to the Bodleian on Aubrey's behalf, but these were not Aubrey's own, and Ent listed them for him in a letter of 20 April 1675.[3] Later in 1675 Aubrey presented to the Bodleian, through Wood, a fourteenth-century manuscript of the *Flores Historiarum* from his collection.[4]

Aubrey's largest bequest of books was to the Ashmolean, and these are listed (with a few omissions) by R. T. Gunther in 'The Library of John Aubrey, F.R.S.', *Bodleian Quarterly Record*, VI (1931), 230 f., reprinted in Appendix B of Anthony Powell's *John Aubrey and his Friends*. These are now in the Bodleian, as are a few books that Aubrey gave to Anthony Wood, which are in the Wood Collection.[5]

A smaller bequest of Aubrey's later years was to New Inn Hall,

---

[1] MS A 12, 105.
[2] This means that the Italian fencing book cannot ever have reached the Royal Society, a possibility discussed by John Buchanan-Brown, art. cit., 170, 179–81.
[3] MS A 12, 109.
[4] Now Bodleian MS e. Mus. 149.
[5] These are referred to in the notes to Andrew Clark's edition of Wood's *Life and Times* I, 14, 144, 229–30; II, 116–17, 237.

Oxford. In a letter to Aubrey of 8 February 1690/1, Thomas Bayley, the Principal, thanked Aubrey for his gift of 'St. Hieromes Bible, & the Venerable Beads works', the first benefaction to their new library.[1] Aubrey was related to a former Principal, which perhaps explains why he made this donation. In a letter to Wood of 4 February 1690/1,[2] Aubrey mentioned his intention of giving his copies of Hobbes' *Leviathan* and Plot's *Natural History of Oxford-shire* to the Hall. The latter was apparently the author's presentation copy to the Ashmolean, which was exchanged for Aubrey's because of the manuscript notes that he had added to his (now Bodleian Ashmole 1722). He gave it to the Hall in 1692; it was later in the possession of R. T. Gunther,[3] and is now in the Museum of the History of Science at Oxford. This and the other books given by Aubrey to the Hall were evidently all sold off at some stage, and there are no books presented by Aubrey among the residue of the library of the Hall now surviving at Balliol College, Oxford.[4]

Aubrey's largest bequest, apart from the books he gave the Ashmolean, was to Gloucester Hall (now Worcester College), Oxford. The books he gave to the Hall (mainly mathematical) are listed in *The Times Literary Supplement*, 13 and 20 January 1950, and in Appendix B of the 1963 edition of Powell's *John Aubrey and his Friends*, with shelf-marks added. The gift of two of the volumes (*Philosophical Transactions*, vol. 1, and Heydon's *Astrological Discourse*) is recorded in the Hall's benefactors' book under the year 1695.[5] Aubrey probably presented this rather specialised set of books to the Hall at the request of its Principal, Benjamin Woodroffe, whom he knew.[6] Woodroffe planned a college at Oxford for Greek Orthodox students,[7] but his original scheme, promulgated in 1692, was unsuccessful, not least because there was little incentive for Greeks to come to Oxford. In a revised version of 1694, therefore, Woodroffe tried to attract them by making the course more 'useful' and including the study of mathematics and medicine,[8] and, doubtless knowing that Aubrey was anxious to find a home for

[1] MS A 12, 31.    [2] F 39, 414.    [3] *Bodleian Quarterly Record* VI (1931), 165–6.
[4] I am indebted to the librarian of Balliol, Mr E. V. Quinn, for help in this connection.
[5] Worcester College, Oxford, MS 4.4., 16.    [6] See above, pp. 84, 88.
[7] Cf. E. D. Tappe, 'The Greek College at Oxford, 1699–1705', *Oxoniensia* XIX (1954), 92 f.
[8] Ibid., 96–7, 108.

his books, Woodroffe must have approached him with a request for a mathematical library.[1]

Thus quite a large number of books from Aubrey's library survive. It is clear, however, that many are none the less lost, for his letters and writings often mention volumes that were once in his possession but which are not in any of these bequests.[2] Some may possibly have gone to collections, like that of New Inn Hall, that have since been dispersed, but others were probably sold by Aubrey himself. For, however public-spirited he was, he was also poor, and he apparently sold books both to friends like Hooke[3] and to book-sellers.[4]

The result is that Aubrey's library is a somewhat frustrating tool, and I have made relatively little use of it in this book, except for individual volumes, particularly those with annotations by him. Though it might have been hoped that the general physiognomy of the library would be a useful source of evidence on the areas of Aubrey's interests, in fact these are almost always better illustrated by evidence from his writings and letters. The surviving books from the library reflect the concerns which one would have predicted from such sources, with a relatively large number of books on science, technology, education, mathematics and the occult, and relatively few works of political and religious polemic (except for gifts from friends like James Harrington and Edward Bagshawe).

But a note of caution is needed concerning such negative conclusions, for one of the most striking features of the surviving volumes is the relative lack of 'antiquary's' books. There could, however, be various reasons for this. Aubrey's donation of mathematical books to Gloucester Hall shows how he deliberately removed whole classes of books from his library in his later years, and it is possible that he presented the bulk of his volumes on antiquities to some other source not yet located. Alternatively, since Aubrey lived a vagrant life from 1671 onwards (though he did keep some books

---

[1] I do not think that Aubrey's over-hopeful aspiration to the Principalship of the Hall in 1675 explains his donation, as suggested in *T.L.S.*, 13 January 1950.

[2] For example, the books referred to in his will of the early 1650s (MS A 21, 75), or the books he bought from Cartwright's library while at Oxford (cf. *Gentilisme*, 156), or the copy of Highmore referred to above, p. 124, n. 4.

[3] Cf. John Buchanan-Brown, art. cit., 181.

[4] Cf. MS A 23, 103v, where he refers to such a sale in 1677.

at the family farm at Broad Chalke until quite late),[1] it is possible that he tended to discard the heaviest books first; since many antiquarian books, including Camden's *Britannia*, Weever's *Ancient Funerall Monuments*, Guillim's *Display of Heraldry* and Dugdale's *Warwickshire*, were heavy folios, he may have disposed of them early, keeping lighter octavos (of which almost all the surviving bequests consist) longer.[2] Such considerations make general conclusions about the content of the library extremely hazardous.

[1] Cf. A-W, 24 April 1690, F 39, 402, and A-L, 27 Feb. 1693/4, A. 1814, 94, which lists some books that were still there, including four folios.

[2] For another suggestion concerning these antiquarian books, cf. J. Buchanan-Brown, art. cit., 191 n.35.

# INDEX